Toddler Taming
— & —
Beyond
Toddlerdom

Toddler Taming
— & —
Beyond Toddlerdom

**All you need to know about your child
from one to twelve**

DR CHRISTOPHER GREEN

DOUBLEDAY
SYDNEY • AUCKLAND • TORONTO • NEW YORK • LONDON

TODDLER TAMING AND BEYOND TODDLERDOM
A DOUBLEDAY BOOK

This omnibus edition first published in Australia and New Zealand in 2003 by Doubleday

National Library of Australia
Cataloguing-in-Publication Entry

Green, Christopher, 1943 Feb. 23– .
Toddler taming; and, Beyond toddlerdom: all you need to know about your child from
one to twelve.

Includes indexes.
ISBN 1 86471 080 2.

1. Children – Health and hygiene. 2. Child rearing. 3. Child care. 4. Parenting.
5. Discipline of children. I. Green, Christopher, 1943 Feb. 23– Beyond toddlerdom.
II. Title.

649.1

Transworld Publishers,
a division of Random House Australia Pty Ltd
20 Alfred Street, Milsons Point, NSW 2061
http://www.randomhouse.com.au

Random House New Zealand Limited
18 Poland Road, Glenfield, Auckland

Transworld Publishers,
a division of The Random House Group Ltd
61-63 Uxbridge Road, Ealing, London W5 5SA

Random House Inc
1540 Broadway, New York, New York 10036

Cover design by Darian Causby/Highway 51
Cover illustration by Roger Roberts
Author photograph by Louise Lister
Text designed and typeset in 10.3/14 Stone Serif by Midland Typesetters,
Maryborough, Victoria
Printed and bound by Griffin Press, South Australia

10 9 8 7 6 5 4 3

Toddler Taming

To the caring and compassionate staff who make the Children's Hospital, Westmead one of the great children's hospitals

Toddler Taming

The guide to your child from one to four

Dr Christopher Green

with illustrations by Roger Roberts

DOUBLEDAY

Sydney • Auckland • New York • Toronto • London

Contents

Acknowledgements

Thanks to:

My wife Dr Hilary Green, for her clever ideas which made this book work.

James and Tim, without whose help this book would have been completed much earlier but would have contained less practical wisdom.

Dr John Coveney, Department of Public Health, Flinders University, South Australia, for his advice on tucker without tantrums in every edition of this book.

Dr Natalie Silove, paediatrician at the Child Development Unit, the Children's Hospital, Westmead. A mother and fellow toddler-tamer.

Professor Kim Oates, Dr Peter Procopis and Dr John Yu, my bosses at the Children's Hospital for their belief in my work which gave me the freedom to talk to parents all over Australia and around the world.

Jayne Hyde RN, someone who understands what makes children tick. Bronwyn Harman, a mother from the Playgroup Association of Western Australia. Lorraine Partington, who brought order to my chaos for more than twelve years.

Jon Attenborough, who heard me speak, liked my ideas and asked me to write a book. A publisher whose vision and encouragement produced *Toddler Taming*.

Finally, Michael Morton-Evans, for his editorial abilities and for giving me the confidence to write in my own style.

Introduction

I used to think I was a real expert on child care, but that was before I had children of my own. When my boisterous boys arrived, I discovered how little I knew, and how out of touch and impractical was the vast majority of child care information available.

That was 25 years ago, and from there I set out to find some more appropriate ways of managing and enjoying our young. I started by bouncing my own amateur ideas off the parents I saw each day in my practice. Some returned a week later, amazed with the success of my suggestions, while others told me I was crazy.

As the months and years went by, the ineffective techniques were dumped, while the good ones were built on, refined and tested by the hundreds of parents I saw. After eight years, I realised that I had been given an unique education thanks to the thousands of parents who showed me the realities of child care. Thus *Toddler Taming* was born.

The *Toddler Taming* message in the new 2001 edition is still the same. The important things in child care will always remain: love, consistency, example, tension-free homes and above all sensible expectations.

It's all too easy to believe that child care is a complex science, when in fact it is very natural. Parents have been doing it well for years without authors like me interfering. Time with our children passes all too quickly. Life is not a video, you can't press the rewind button to view it again.

Children are fun – enjoy them now!

Christopher Green
Sydney 2001

ONE

The Toddler

The toddler is an interesting little person, aged between 1 and 4 years. Some people call this stage the 'terrible twos', but it's not terrible – it's really a time of sweet innocence, dependence and a magic mind. Toddlers are built to a design that is perfect in every detail, but for one small defect – they have all the activity of an international airport, but the control tower doesn't work.

Toddlerhood starts at around the first birthday. You are in no doubt of its arrival when one day you put the dinner down and instead of the usual appreciation, your littlie takes one look and says 'Yuk!' You take this badly, jump up and down and in fact have a tantrum of your own. Toddler looks up, likes it and thinks 'Wow! Me do this again'. Now you have a problem.

Don't let me depress you. I know that as you look back some years down the track, you will see this as one of the most enjoyable stages of childhood. Toddlers are so alive, so full of fun and what's more they seem to see life with innocent eyes and the most vivid of vivid imaginations. To enjoy toddlerhood, you need to know what to expect, then tuck some toddler taming techniques up your sleeve and go for it. First let's see what makes toddlers tick.

Behavioural development – the overview

In simple terms, we can expect our children to go through four very different stages of psychological development between birth and 8 years of age. The first stage is from birth up to 1 year – the baby. Stage 2 goes from 1 to $2^{1}/_{2}$ years – the younger toddler. Stage 3 is the preschool toddler – $2^{1}/_{2}$ to 4 years. And finally stage 4 moves on up to about the age of 8 years – the early school-age child. Within this framework, as our children grow in size and cleverness, their behaviour will alter, but not necessarily for the better.

The baby: birth to 1 year

The baby from birth to 1 year is a cuddly little article who spends most of the time getting to know mum and dad, while they get to know him. This is the important process of bonding. The aim of the first year is to develop a secure and trusting child who has a secure and trusting relationship with his parents. The views of child care change regularly, but the current belief is that babies cannot be spoilt in the first year of life. When hungry, they should be fed; when frightened they should be comforted; when crying they should be cuddled, and when just being a nuisance, they should be given the benefit of the doubt anyway.

Babies do not need discipline – they need to be taught regular routines and then enjoyed. There are times when it is not so easy and this is when parents must drop the theory and change the ground rules.

The younger toddler: 1 to 2¹/₂ years

At this age, little ones discover that they have the muscle to manipulate and challenge and are not backward about flexing it. This stage starts gradually after the first birthday with senseless and unthinking acts predominant up to the age of 1¹/₂ years, when more considered forms of manipulation take over. Toddlerhood hits a peak at about 2 years and then gradually eases. I say it eases but the behaviour challenges do not disappear, they just take on a more artistic form.

The brain is a wonderful gadget where self-monitoring and sense are housed up top, in the frontal lobes. These are the bits that check behaviour before it happens and, below the age of 3, frontal function is limited.

Some parents expect adult attitudes from their 2-year-olds, but at this age the 'sense centres' aren't yet on line. Parents who are unaware of this conduct deep and meaningful debates with their toddler. The child looks interested, but this is about as useful as discussing the good qualities of postmen with a Rottweiler. When Fido sees a blue trouser leg, he'll forget philosophy and think with his teeth. The same is true of your spontaneous tot.

At playgroup, parents are embarrassed when their 2-year-old is rough with other children, grabs, bites and won't share things. There's no waiting at this stage. They interrupt, won't take turns and when they need a wee it has to be in 'this flowerpot'. The toddler has no malice or aggression, his problem is simply caused by an under-developed control system. There's not a bad bone in these little bodies. It's easy for me to call these behaviours normal, but it's not so easy when parents are struggling at the battlefront. The anti-social toddler is criticised by experts who have never had children, or who've been fortunate enough to score an angel. Don't let others send you on a guilt trip – believe me, the most unsharing, shoving two-year-old will turn into a polite, loving, grown-up. There would be fewer stressed parents if it were universally understood that these innocent little people are not capable of adult logic. During the toddler years, the aim is to steer them from trouble, savour the magic that they bring to new experiences and introduce adult attitudes when the child's brain is good and ready.

The pre-school toddler: 2½ to 4 years

Somewhere between 2½ to 3 years children start to control their impulsive toddler behaviour. At pre-school they start to play together instead of side-by-side as the younger child does. They learn to wait – though not for very long, they can control their tantrums, and they can separate from their mum and be left with friends.

At 3½ years children have a lot of words but not much logic, and they debate and argue.

I remember one 3-year-old I was treating for a sleep problem – she woke every night for no apparent reason.

'Why do you wake up every night?' I asked her, pen poised to write down her answer.

'I wake at night because of the thunder.' She replied. (She was a very verbal little girl!)

'But there isn't any thunder,' the clever Dr Green pointed out.

'I wake at night because the ships keep going up and down the harbour blowing their horns,' she said next.

'But you live a long way from the sea,' I objected, scribbling notes.

Then she said with an air of finality, 'And anyway, I can't sleep because the horses keep galloping up and down outside my window.'

That stumped me! I wrote busily away, thinking to myself, *this is great, I'll put it in my next book*, and just then the little monkey looked up at me and said, 'Are you getting this down OK?'

The early school-age child: 4 to 8 years

A kindergarten teacher told me that she once went on holidays to Bali and brought back a carving of a native woman with large breasts. She showed it to her class and one little boy said: 'My mum used to have breasts like that, but the baby ate them off!'

Somewhere around the fourth birthday the child gradually slips out of toddlerhood to become an early school-age child. There is no firm developmental age for this. With some it may be as early as 3 years, and others 4½. This fourth behavioural stage is once again

4

quite different from all that has gone before. We now have a child who thinks of the repercussions of his actions, exhibits quite a bit of sense, is interested in rules and, what is more, will often obey them. It is thought that at this stage, some of our best bureaucrats are born.

Many 5-year-olds at school will sit at their desk, not only obeying the class rules themselves but seeing that the laws are applied equally to all. They take on the role of the class policeman, reporting the slightest transgression to their teacher. This is the age when it is fashionable to 'dob on your mates', an activity which becomes unpopular after the age of 8 years.

Parents can cash in on this obsession with rules, now at last being able to lay down 'laws of the house' that have a fair chance of being obeyed. At this stage of psychological development, the child can be treated more like a little adult, with more trust, democracy and reason.

For more information about the early school-age child, read my book *Beyond Toddlerdom: Keeping five to twelve year olds on the rails.*

The toddler – his goals

As children move from being babies to being toddlers, they are amazed at the unbelievable acceleration of freedoms that appear. Suddenly they can stand, walk, climb and run. They have the ability to manipulate objects, touch, take things apart and fiddle. They are amazed and overawed at their behavioural power. It is almost as if someone had left open the door of a mighty arsenal of behavioural weapons, but unfortunately they don't know how to use them wisely.

This is an exciting time for toddlers, but not without its fair share of confusion and frustration. They find that by using their new-found behavioural weapons they may get lots of attention, but this often backfires as the angry reaction they may provoke can rob them of the closeness and love they enjoyed as babies. They are frustrated as their little brains run hot with good ideas, which the immaturity of their bodily co-ordination prevents them from seeing through.

For the parents, toddlerhood is a time of introducing controls, guiding gently, setting limits, avoiding confrontation and being 100 per cent firm when needed. For the children, toddlerhood is all about control – learning to control their bodies and behaviours.

- *Control of bodily functions* Becoming toilet trained.

- *Control of impulses* Learning that their demands cannot be met immediately.

- *Controlling the frustration of failure* Knowing they want to feed themselves but accepting that they can't do it successfully.

- *Control of behaviour* Learning that tantrums are not an appropriate way to influence people.

- *Control of separation anxiety* Moving from the close clinginess usual at 1 year to be able to separate for pre-school and later for school.

- *Control over selfishness* Sharing attention, sharing belongings, not interrupting and realising that others also have rights.

The toddler will learn these controls and even take on board a smattering of commonsense and something that vaguely resembles a conscience.

What makes toddlers tick?

Whether you think of your bundle of joy as 'a little treasure', 'an ankle biter', 'a midget mafiosa', or 'the terrible 2-year-old', all toddlers have one thing in common and that is an interesting collection of behavioural traits that are their trademark.

Plenty of power

Small toddlers can exert an amazing amount of power over adults. If they don't get what they want, such is their protest that parents often buckle under the onslaught. Toddlerhood may be an age when children show little self-control but it doesn't stop them trying to control those around them.

It is not the power that causes the problem but rather how it is used. Toddlers are negative, show little sense and totally lack appreciation of the rights of others. With such a strong hand, all they have to do is to dig in their heels and shout, and adults jump.

Power without sense is a combination that characterises many of our politicians.

Little sense

I'm going to be a bore and repeat this many times because knowing about sense is so important. If you were to list the attributes of the toddler, it is unlikely that sense would immediately spring to mind. It is my belief that between the ages of 1 and 2 years most toddlers have zero sense. From 2 to $2\frac{1}{2}$ years a delicately calibrated instrument might raise a flicker of a reading, but it is often hard for us parents to see this with the naked eye. Fortunately, from this time on sense starts to grow with a significant amount present by 3 years. By the time they have reached their fourth birthday, most little ones are reasonably reliable.

When people talk of the 'terrible twos' I believe it is really the 'terrible 1½ to 2½-year-olds' that they refer to. This short period is the time of minimum sense with the maximum of mobility and militancy. You don't need to be called Sigmund to know that this combination is going to be psychologically upsetting for someone, and that someone is likely to be you, the parent.

This is the age of unthinking behaviours (e.g. head-banging) and complete disregard for danger, in the interests of the moment.

Young toddlers can argue, fight and get into no-win situations but they don't have the sense to know when to stop. For effective discipline, parents need to know when it is best to back down. Unfortunately some parents find this impossible, as they possess even less sense than their offspring.

One of the saddest aspects of my work is seeing parents who are making very heavy weather of bringing up their children. They misread their toddler's behaviour and feel that the child is deliberately trying to upset them. They start believing their child is malicious – almost the enemy. They forget that having children is supposed to be fun.

Wanting attention 25 hours a day

Toddlers love to be centre stage at all times. They resent it if others steal the limelight, whether it is a friend dropping in for a chat, a lengthy phone call, or when husbands come home from work.

Toddlers want attention 24 hours a day and if you give this, then they will want 25 hours. Attention is important but it does take its toll. After a day of play, answering incessant questions and trying to keep one jump ahead of such inventive and imaginative little people, mothers are exhausted. This is not physical exhaustion but a special sort of tiredness that leaves you numb from the neck upwards. Now dad swans in exclaiming 'Gosh I had a tiring day at work'. He knows nothing of that numbness that leaves you in a state closely resembling brain death.

Self-centredness

Most toddlers have tunnel vision, which focuses only on their own needs and happiness. It never occurs to them that other people may have rights too. When a child is playing and wants a particular toy, it is unlikely that he will ask politely for it when 'smash and grab' is more effective. The idea of taking turns and thinking of another's point of view and sharing is quite foreign. Although young toddlers enjoy being with other children, they tend to play beside them rather than with them. This self-centred behaviour is normal for most toddlers, although it has been known to extend into adulthood! Some of the world's most notable dictators have shown skills that leave the toddler looking an absolute amateur.

Ten-minute time frame

The young toddler lives only for the here and now with an interest in time that extends little past the last ten minutes and the ten to come. At this age praise and rewards must be immediate, while discipline

must happen now or not at all. It is pointless punishing the 2-year-old hours after the event once dad has returned home in the evening. It is equally foolish to expect the toddler to understand that being good today will be rewarded by going to the zoo next week.

Negativity

Children learn to say 'No' long before they learn to say 'Yes' and at the age of 3 this simple little word flows out with the clearest articulation, due mainly to two years of non-stop practice. Some experts say that toddlers only copy their negative parents who say 'No', 'No', 'No' constantly from the child's earliest age. This is an interesting explanation, but I think the trait is inbuilt and can also be seen in the children of the most positive parents.

Conclusion

The toddler is that little person aged between 1 and 4 years who demonstrates some interesting behavioural traits. Young toddlerhood, between the ages of 1 to 21/2 years, is a time of flexing muscles and exhibiting minimal sense, while the pre-school toddler, aged between 21/2 to 4 years, is more verbal, social and focused in their assault on parents.

The trademarks of the toddler are:

■ more power than sense;
■ living for the moment; and
■ demanding centre stage position.

Philosophical, religious and philanthropic ideals are not conspicuous.

Parents should know this is normal, use commonsense and cunning, not blame themselves, then go with the flow.

Confidence is the Key

As I look back on 25 years of my work with children, I often
wonder what, of all the fads and fashions I have seen, was
really important. Certainly it was not the huff and puff over
psychodynamic theories, quality time, hot-housing of infants or
banning the occasional smack.

Most of what has come and gone was just nitpicking, but behind
this there are hidden some solid and vitally important ideas. It is
these which provide the foundation for strong and emotionally
secure children.

I see six ingredients in this important recipe, which were just as
important to past generations as they are today. There is no doubt
that our children thrive best when they:

■ feel loved and wanted;

- live in a happy, tension-free home;

- have parents who are prepared to give their time when the child needs it;

- are given a good adult example;

- receive clear, consistent child care; and

- are brought up by parents who are confident.

This book has not been written for 'head in the clouds' dreamers. It is for parents with feet firmly on the ground who want practical ideas to make their child-rearing both successful and enjoyable. With this aim in mind, where better to start than with the mainstay of successful parenting – confidence.

Confident parenting

Confidence is what makes parents positive, powerful and puts them firmly in charge. When confidence is high the trivial hassles of our day-to-day lives seem like molehills. But as soon as confidence crumbles, we quickly lose all perspective for what's important and those same molehills become as towering as Mount Everest. Confidence has a spin-off in almost everything we do. It promotes effective discipline, which improves children's behaviour and, in the long term, forms much of the basis for the child's own self-confidence.

Some years ago, when addressing a large gathering of good parents, I asked one simple question: 'How confident are you in your own parenting abilities?' Seventy-seven per cent of those who responded to this secret ballot said that they had serious doubts about what they were doing.

It seems strange to me that in these days when there is almost an epidemic of child care gurus, and bookshops are overloaded with how-to-do-it manuals, parental confidence appears to be sinking rather than rising. There are some good reasons for this slide.

Confidence busters

The breakdown of the extended family has left many new parents isolated and uncertain. Many have never experienced a behaviour problem or even held a child before their own. It also seems that the more complicated that child care theory becomes, the less we are prepared to trust our natural instincts. This leaves us very vulnerable to a predictable group of factors that erode our confidence.

Not knowing what's normal

When our first child blasts in on the scene, few of us are prepared for the onslaught that follows. As many of us now live away from our close family, we suffer one of the penalties of this, that we cannot get easy access to advice on the common problems of behaviour and management. Often we feel we are the only ones with troubles when, if only we knew it, everyone else is in the same boat.

With the toddler, some behavioural concerns are so common, they must be seen as a normal part of childhood. Toddlers have fiddly fingers, don't think of the future, have no sense, like constant attention, and often ignore much of what you say. It is said of normal 2-year-olds that 44 per cent attack their younger or older brother or sister, 50 per cent eat too little, 70 per cent resist going to bed, 83 per cent whinge and nag, 94 per cent constantly seek attention, 95 per cent are stubborn and 100 per cent are active and rarely still. Some children show these characteristics to a minor degree while others hold in their hand a full house.

That's life! There are quite enough genuine worries in the world without making ourselves feel inadequate by believing we are to blame for the normal non-problems of our toddlers.

Ground down by competition

We live in a very competitive world and we can't help noticing how other people manage their homes, relationships and children. Soon our lives are lived constantly looking over our shoulder to see that we are performing up to scratch.

This is made worse by the media which presents a strange slant on reality. Many popular magazines overtly promote the everyday endeavour to find perfection. 'The Perfect Marriage', 'Perfect Sex', 'The Perfectly White Business Shirt', 'The Perfectly Balanced Breakfast Cereal', 'The Perfect Child Rearing Method'. Needless to say nothing is perfect and most of what we are striving for are unattainable myth-like goals.

Those who appear regularly on television talk-back or soap operas are just actors, with impressive public faces, who may seem controlled and in charge on the screen but privately get just as confused, tired and unhappy as the rest of us. When one of Australia's trendy women's magazines recently celebrated its tenth anniversary, a cynical reviewer commented . . . 'The typical girl they feature needs – a career, a husband, children, a home, jewels, clothes, excitement and travel.' Faced with this picture it is little wonder that so many women feel they have been cheated. For many of the super mums I look after, the only excitement and travel they get is the train trip down to the hospital to seek help from Christopher Green with their far from perfect child.

In the past, children spent most of their first six years at home, but now we parade them in public from their earliest days and with this comes competition and embarrassment.

As you wait in the baby clinic, you may wonder why all the other children seem bigger, stronger, toothier and more advanced than your meagre scrap. You love playgroup but you think that others watch you and your children. 'Look at that child over there, she's 13 months and not yet walking. I think there is something wrong with her.' 'Look, that one just bit the other, he's a potential juvenile delinquent, and he is barely 1 year old.' At pre-school you may feel the pressure when your little one fails at cutting-out or romps around when the core of children are pasting, painting and listening to stories.

Parents can feel extremely vulnerable when their children do not achieve at school. This is made worse by those painful people who boost their own inadequate egos by boasting about their children's brilliance. As you sit at a parent/teacher night, some opinionated adult makes it clear that 'My boy is 5 and he reads Shakespeare sonnets like Laurence Olivier'. Before you can catch your breath this is trumped by another painful parent who says, 'My girl is 4 years and plays the violin perfectly by the Suzuki method'. All you can think is 'My little one is 5 years old and wets the bed every night'.

Bed wetting is quite common, affecting one in ten of all children at the start of school. In fact there would be three children in your child's class with the same problem, but competitive parents tend to cloud the perspective by boasting about the rare and clever while keeping quiet about those common things that make us feel ashamed.

Overwhelmed by experts

In my more sombre moments I often wonder if all us experts were to be blown from the face of the earth, would parents be any the worse off. As I set out to demystify child care and boost confidence, it seems that a hundred others are out there hell bent on making it all much more difficult. Confidence is fragile enough without being confused by some of the way-out and incorrect ideas I hear, such as:

- Working mothers do great harm to their children. Not true.

- Every mother should want to be a 24-hour-a-day parent. If she does not, she should feel ashamed. Rubbish. Few fathers want to be 24-hour-a-day fathers and some time to ourselves is a help to both parent and child.

- Dummies should never be used. Personally I hate dummies – I think they make children look stupid – but if you have a child who is irritable and you put a dummy in her mouth and it pacifies her, then you can give her two dummies for all I care!

- Babies who fall asleep in their mother's arms will find it very hard to settle themselves down if they wake in the middle of the night. There is all sorts of evidence for this, however, if you love cuddling your baby to sleep and your baby loves being cuddled to sleep, then it's a bit of magic your baby should have.

- Co-sleeping should be discouraged. Don't be brainwashed by what other people say. If your child is sleeping with you every night and you are happy with this situation then as far as I'm concerned they can stay in your bed until they leave to get married, if it feels right and suits you.

- The toddler who wakes often every night must be comforted by its parent. An impractical, out-of-touch theory. This is a sleep problem which should be cured quickly. Sleep deprivation is a form of torture, and parents who chronically lack sleep become a little deranged, which is not good for their children.

- If a baby is not breast-fed it is severely disadvantaged. While the breast is obviously better and strongly recommended, it is never obligatory for the average Australian or New Zealand child.

- The toddlers who play occasionally with their private parts do this as a sign of sexual abuse. Nonsense. Little children do this because it feels pleasant and they are bored.

Books full of impractical, out-of-touch ideas that set unattainably high goals, do nothing but generate fears and create feelings of parental inadequacy. These should be pulped and recycled to save some of the world's trees. Life is tough enough without some smart philosopher producing learned writings that make us feel as though we are second class citizens.

Being unaware of individuality

Every child is born an individual with unique talents and temperament which can be adjusted but not rebuilt by the warmth and skill of the parents. One of the quickest ways to crush confidence is when parents try to force their children to be something they were never designed to be. The child with an active temperament will never sit still long enough to learn to read at the age of 3, any more than the gentle boy with the temperament of St Francis will ever be suitable for the front row of the All Blacks rugby team.

No matter what I say there is still an archaic view, held by many who should know better, that all children are born with an identical clean slate, and every difference, fault and misdemeanour is caused by the actions of their parents.

We all have to learn to accept the child we have been given, and then do our best. Remember that as parents, we too are individuals, with our own temperaments and styles of parenting. We must have the confidence to do our own thing and not be brainwashed by those who do things differently.

Hindrance from the helping professionals

Some of us professionals can make parents feel pretty inadequate. It is easy to shatter a parent's confidence by implying that we know how to bring up our own children perfectly and that behaviour problems only occur in your child. Even worse, some of us are still steeped in the prehistoric ideas of the 1950s and find it impossible to give any practical advice on behaviour without psychoanalysing the parents.

I call this psychodynamic approach 'the Irish weather forecaster technique'. They can tell you every detail of what happened yesterday, the day before and right to the day you were born, but when it comes to helping with today, tomorrow and the future, they turn mute. Choose your professional well. The helping professions should be good at helping, but unfortunately this is not always the case.

Watch for the school of thought that says that unless you bring up your children 'the one and only right way', some form of permanent, psychological damage will ensue. There is no one right way to bring up children. Child care fashions come and go with the regularity of Parisian hemlines. As we chop and change the children look on bemused, showing how well they survive despite our professional interference.

Conclusion

Life is tough for parents today, due to our frantic lifestyles, competition, isolation and unreasonable expectations. There is also an oversupply of unimaginative and impractical information. Most parents are doing an amazingly good job, but many do not realise this. Parents don't need criticism but do need words of encouragement and support.

Parenting is a compromise. We all start out with incredibly high ideals but as tension and tiredness take their toll, we tend to lower our sights to a more middle-of-the-road position, a state of peaceful equilibrium. It is not for others to criticise and compare. What feels right and works for you is as good a way to bring up children as any. If you love them, enjoy them and do what feels right and works for you; no-one can do better.

Remember: slow down and see the magic.

Summary: the foundation for happy, secure children

Love Being wanted and welcome. Love may be a vague term but it is a very important word.

Consistency Children need to know where they stand and that what stands today will still be standing tomorrow.

Tackle tension Tension is probably the most common destructive influence in today's child-rearing. There is no point in bringing up your child by the book, if home feels like a war zone. Friction in adult relationships can never be hidden from children. The most considerate thing we as parents can do for our children is to be kinder to one another.

Good example Children cannot behave better than those whose example they follow.

Reasonable expectations Parents need to know what is normal and what to expect. Unrealistic expectations cause non-problems that undermine parents unnecessarily.

Fun and enjoyment Children should be brought up as apprentices to fun-loving parents who enjoy having them around. Some parents take child-rearing so seriously that it becomes an interesting scientific experiment. You cannot fall in love with some laboratory animal.

Confidence Here is the key to effective parenting. Confident parents are positive and positive parents are very powerful people.

THREE

Behaviour: What is Normal?

The more I work with toddlers, the less surprised I become with the extremes of behaviour that I see. The truth is that there is an immense breadth of behaviour that can be confidently classed as normal. I am less certain of what could be considered average, but when it comes to what is tolerable, I am in no doubt that this decision is in the eye of the beholder.

If you put a busy, noisy toddler in with a busy, noisy family, he will not be noticed, whilst a quiet, violin-playing, well-mannered child would stand out like a vegetarian at a butcher's picnic.

Tolerance depends on the individual make-up of the parents and how the world is treating us. It varies from day to day. When life is going well we can take a lot but on those bad days, a little toddler-hood goes a very long way.

We know that all toddlers have a tendency to be negative and stubborn, to have more power than sense, to live for today and to be short on the humanitarian skills. All toddlers will have a smattering of these. Some will have been dealt a weak hand, others will present with all the trump cards. Over the years there have been a number of studies that have looked at the incidence of toddler behaviour.

The studies – the incidence

If you look at what has been published in overseas literature, it would seem that nine out of ten parents experience some behaviour difficulties with their toddlers while one in four find toddlerhood quite tough. These figures echo our experience in Australia where, in addition, we have found that of parents who attend our education programmes, 77 per cent say they have serious doubts about their parenting abilities, 88 per cent say they will smack their children at some time whilst about 15 per cent find that shopping and toddlers don't mix.

For further figures it is best to look at some old but good studies.

The New York longitudinal study

A study begun in New York in 1966 followed up 133 children from birth to adulthood.[1] During this time researchers were most interested in temperament and behaviour. This study showed children to have individual temperamental traits at birth. When results were analysed, 40 per cent of the group fitted into the 'easy child' category, being a joy to look after as babies and usually during childhood. Parents, teachers and paediatricians all found this group easy. Whether the mother was competent or hopeless and the father a saint or Jack the Ripper, children of this 40 per cent would probably do quite well.

More than half of the 133 children, however, were not so easy to handle. Ten per cent of the study group were little terrors from the word go. They were difficult as babies, often difficult as toddlers with their difficulties frequently accompanying them into school. Parents, paediatricians and teachers all suffered under the strain. These children tended to be particularly negative, extremely loud in both voice and crying, and easily frustrated; they had irregular sleeping and feeding habits and showed great difficulty adjusting to any change. They were hard to handle, disputed decisions and had tantrums like infant McEnroes. Such children quickly knock all confidence out of their parents and if the problems continue through school, a trail of teachers will sign off on sick and recreation leave. Though saint-like parents have less chance of producing and more chance of managing children like these, this group would be extremely difficult in anyone's hands.

A further 15 per cent of the total were described as 'slow to warm up'. They had many of the same characteristics as the last group, but these were not so severe. The difference was that, when handled with care, understanding, persistence and patience, they had a sporting chance of doing well. Parenting this group was a major challenge, where super parents managed and normal parents struggled.

With the 40 per cent angels, 10 per cent terrors and 15 per cent semi-impossibles accounted for, 35 per cent of the total remained in an intermediate group that was neither very easy nor very difficult. Ease of handling this group depends on the parents and on the blend of temperament characteristics inherited by each child. (There is more on temperament in Chapter 4.)

A similar study has just been done in Melbourne.[2]

The Chamberlin study

Another New York study[3] followed up 200 children from age 2 until school age. It demonstrated the main behavioural worries for parents at different ages and set out to stir up specialist paediatricians to give more help. The behaviours commonly seen at ages 2 and 4 were listed and then ranked in the order that causes greatest concern at those two ages. At age 2, many parents said 'He doesn't do a thing I tell him'. These stubborn and wilful characteristics were top of the list. Second place was shared equally between tantrums and 'getting into everything'. Continuing these behavioural Olympics, at age 4, the gold medal was still awarded for stubborn, wilful behaviour, although now verbal abuse and 'back-talk' were also included as problems. The silver medal went to whingeing and nagging and the bronze was taken easily by lack of sharing and frequent fighting.

Also in this study, a number of parents were interviewed and asked to describe their children's behaviour at three different ages (see Table 1). This makes sobering reading: 44 per cent of New York 2-year-olds are said to attack and annoy their younger brother or sister; 50 per cent eat too little; 70 per cent resist going to bed; 83 per cent of these normal little Americans are said to whine and nag mercilessly; 95 per cent were stubborn and 94 per cent had attention-seeking behaviour. These figures may be a bit of an overestimate but it makes you wonder – what is normal?

What about paediatricians' children?

When I wrote the first edition of *Toddler Taming*, I surveyed twenty-eight paediatricians, all specialists at our hospital, about their own children. The questions covered a wide area, with behaviour featuring quite strongly. There were also some general questions which yielded some astonishing answers. For example, four of the experts did not know the date of their children's birth; three were uncertain as to whether their children were fully immunised; nineteen stated that their storage of drugs and medicines at home would be seen as negligent by our hospital's child safety centre.

In the behavioural area, about 40 per cent had endured at least one colicky baby and although experts were at that time disputing the benefit of drugs in helping colic, 75 per cent of them used medication, 50 per cent swearing by it. About 10 per cent of the paediatricians had a child with breath-holding attacks, about 15 per cent had found toilet training a struggle and about 30 per cent had been troubled by feeding difficulties. About 40 per cent of these experts had also experienced at least one child with sleep problems and nearly 50 per cent considered that their discipline was often far from effective.

Table 1: Mothers' behavioural description of their children at ages 2, 3 and 4

	Percentage of age group		
Behaviour	Age 2 %	Age 3 %	Age 4 %
Eats too little	50	26	37
Doesn't eat the right kinds of food	64	43	54
Resists going to bed	70	46	56
Awakens during the night	52	52	56
Has nightmares	17	18	36
Resists sitting on toilet	43	2	2
Has bowel motion in pants	71	17	1
Wets self during day	75	14	7
Wets bed at night	82	49	26
Curious about sex differences	28	45	75
Rubs or plays with sex organs	56	49	51
Modest about dressing	1	7	26
Fights or quarrels	72	75	92
Jealous	54	47	42
Hurts younger sibling	44	51	64
Hits others or takes things	68	52	46
Stubborn	95	92	85
Talks back (behaves cheekily)	42	73	72
Disobedient	82	76	78
Tells fibs	2	26	37
Constantly seeks attention	94	48	42
Clings to mother	79	34	26
Whines and nags	83	65	85
Cries easily	79	53	58
Temper outbursts	83	72	70
Active, hardly ever still	100	48	40

As a last comment, most suspected that at some time their children would have been of interest to our child psychiatry colleagues. All this goes to prove just one thing. Toddler behaviour is a worry to most parents, whether they are psychologists, plumbers, IT experts or paediatricians.

Sensible expectations

It is upsetting that so few parents have any idea what constitutes normal toddler behaviour. We spend much of our lives feeling guilty, inadequate, self-recriminating and believing we are the only ones who cannot control our children. Life is tough enough without immobilising ourselves with such ill-founded guilt.

All toddlers . . .

■ crave attention and hate to be ignored. Some are quite satisfied with their parents' best efforts, others would grumble unless 25 hours a day, 8 days a week were devoted solely to their care.

■ separate poorly from their caretakers. In the first 3 years a toddler prefers to play near his mother and does not like to let her out of his sight for long. For most, an unfamiliar child-minder causes initial problems, while being locked in a room or becoming separated when out shopping constitutes a major trauma.

■ tend to be busy little people. Some are extremely active and hardly ever still; others are just 'active'.

■ have little road sense or in fact little sense of danger. They are impulsive and unpredictable which is a hazard even in the apparently sensible child. All toddlers need close parental protection.

■ show little respect for other people's property. Their fingers are drawn as if by magnetism to everything they pass. Ornaments are broken and cupboards rearranged. Those ten active little digits have an amazing power to spread a sticky, jam-like substance over every surface they meet – rather like a small bee distributing pollen.

■ tend to be stubborn and wilful; some are quite militant but others will bend to reason.

■ tend to be blind to the mountain of mess they generate. The tidy toddler who is neat and even picks up his own toys is the exception rather than the rule.

■ ask endless questions, the same one being repeated again and again, with little interest in the answer. This especially applies to the over-threes.

■ change their minds every minute. One day your toddler says, 'I like Weet-Bix'. When you are at the supermarket, they are on special and you buy a month's supply. 'Don't like Weet-Bix, don't like Weet-Bix,' squawks the mind-bender. What is happening? Are you going mad? No, this is just brainwashing, toddler style.

■ constantly interrupt adults. It is not that they want to be rude, but they believe that what they have got to contribute is much more important than the irrelevant ramblings of their parents. This trick of skilfully interrupting in mid-sentence everything that mum or dad says really jars the nerves.

■ make their mothers feel inferior. Little children have an incredible ability to demoralise their mothers. Many will act as complete angels when in the care of others, reserving their demonic side exclusively for their parents. There is no point telling anyone – who would believe you? Other toddlers are difficult for their mothers and behave perfectly for their fathers. This is because they have long studied mum's vulnerabilities and know how to hit a raw nerve with perfect aim, but are not so sure of dad, as he seems some sort of less known relative.

■ are extremely sensitive to upset, excitement and tension in their environment. Their sound sleep pattern can be upset by illness, holidays or stress. Often quite a minor alteration to the environment can make the child who was fully toilet trained start to leak.

Many toddlers . . .

■ will sit and concentrate briefly to draw, do puzzles or attend to pre-reading tasks. A minority will settle for a long time but most become restless in about five minutes and look for a means of escape. Quite a large proportion of active little children will not sit even for the shortest of periods.

■ are cuddly, affectionate, 'giving' children. There is, however, a minority who resent handling, are distant and seem to give a poor return of love to their parents.

■ are determined and independent. Some become so belligerent that they refuse to be fed or dressed, even though they are far too young to do either task unaided. Other toddlers are passive, dependent and quite happy to be pampered and directed.

■ are compulsive climbers. At an early age they will organise an expedition to the summit of the settee and once this has been scaled, will set out to conquer the benchtops, tables and anything that happens to be there. Other toddlers are more sensible and have a healthy fear of the 'painful stop at the end of the drop'.

- eat well, although many do not consume the quality of food that their parents have read that they should. Some children take food extremely seriously, never lifting their eyes from the plate until the pattern is almost scraped completely off. Others find food an interesting plaything and a bit of a joke, which is a pain to the parent committed to delivering the perfectly balanced diet from the earliest day.

- go off their food around their first birthday, a proper eating pattern not returning for anything up to a year. Some will tolerate a narrow, unimaginative diet; others will eat anything in sight. Some eat main meals; others were born to be snackers.

- continue with a daytime sleep until the age of 3 years. Others discard this at about 18 months and nothing the parents do will bring it back. Most toddlers go to sleep before 8 p.m. each night, but others stay on the rampage until close to midnight. Some are lazy in the morning, finding it hard to get out of bed; others wake at an ungodly hour and disturb the whole household. With busy children who are on the rampage from dawn until after dusk it is often hard to change their pattern with any technique less powerful than a general anaesthetic.

- have fears. Dogs, loud noises, new situations and strange objects and people cause distress in over half of this age group.

- display a multitude of irritating habits. This of course is not only a problem with children.

- have behaviour which fluctuates considerably from day to day and week to week. Some parents tell me that their little children seem almost schizophrenic, with wild alterations in behaviour. Bad days are usually blamed on teething, lack of sleep or 'something they ate'. These all make good scapegoats but it never seems to occur to parents that adults can have good days and bad days and we don't blame this on teething. Even trainers allow racehorses the odd off day.

Conclusion

All caring parents worry about their children, wanting to bring them up as best they can. Many of the behaviours that cause concern would not be problems at all, if only we knew what was normal.

No matter what we do it seems that about nine out of ten toddlers will cause us some behavioural bother with about one in ten ageing us by years. When I look at the figures mentioned in the Chamberlin study I wonder, 'Who are the children with normal behaviour? Are they the docile, compliant, non-whingeing, non-stubborn minority, or the junior Rambos who romp around our homes?'

The Difficult Child: Born or Made?

History

In the nineteenth century, writers were in no doubt that the cause of all deviant behaviour was bad breeding. Some put forward the notion that 'the born criminal and lesser sinners were beyond help due to their abnormal make-up'.

As the twentieth century dawned, this notion gradually changed, and environment was thought to be the major influence on children's behaviour. By the 1950s this notion had become highly refined: all behavioural blame was laid squarely on the shoulders of inadequate mothers. It seemed irrelevant whether the marriage was stable and the parents exceptional. Mothers still collected the blame, regardless of the untold unhappiness, guilt and suffering it caused.

The cause of difficult behaviour: the present view

Behaviour and temperament are now known to have a strong hereditary basis. This hereditary influence gives us the basic material to work with, but the final product depends very much on environmental factors, which is a polite way of saying our standard of parenting.

Toddler temperament has actually been the subject of some serious research and it has been shown that 40 per cent of toddlers are easy going and aren't going to cause you much trouble. Fifteen per cent are pretty hard going, 10 per cent are going to be an all-out challenge and the remaining 35 per cent are somewhere in between easy and difficult.

When it comes to temperament, many children are like their parents. I see busy children who can't sit still with mothers who say, 'How on earth did I ever get a child like this?' Then out of the corner of my eye I see Dad, who's sitting in the corner jingling the car-keys in his pocket and tapping his feet, and it's plain to me where the active genes have come from.

I see some amazing children, and though there is no doubt that environmental characteristics play an enormous part in a child's behaviour, I personally believe that it is the hereditary characteristics that are the most important factor. We can't send our little ones back to their manufacturer for a genetic tune-up, but we can work on improving our parenting skills.

Heredity or environment – a confusion

Because life is never straightforward, the whole heredity–environment debate becomes very muddy in some cases. If an extremely difficult child comes from a home filled with fighting, tension and parental abuse, it seems a black and white case of environmental upset, but this may only be part of the story.

Often adult relationships fall apart because one or both parties have always had a way of behaving that is far from easy to live with. These behaviours have a definite chance of being transmitted through to the genes of the children. The expression, 'like father, like son' is a familiar truth. The parents' behaviour also upsets the home environment and the end product is a complex coalition of heredity and handling.

A stranger in the family

It may seem a strange observation but sometimes a family gets a child that does not suit them. When a peace-loving, polite, quiet, obsessively tidy family is hit by a human tornado, their equilibrium is shattered. To survive this unexpected onslaught, major adjustments must be made. A similar upset occurs when a famous heavyweight football hero spawns a docile, passive boy who prefers picking flowers to jumping on people in the mud.

When a child seems out of place in a family, don't blame the milkman. Nature has a habit of doing this to nice parents, to bring a bit of interest to their lives. Even if our children do not suit us, we have to make the best of what we've got.

A very difficult child
A mother was explaining to me how difficult her child was. She told me that only once had she ever used a babysitter. She and her husband had gone out to dinner. On their return they met the babysitter at the front door, hysterical and clutching her handbag ready to go. 'I don't want any money, I just want to get out of here,' she sobbed.

Children who are too like their parents

Parents would prefer their children to copy all their best points and by-pass their weaknesses. In reality the reverse is more likely to be true, with our children seeking out our worst qualities and displaying them to a similar or greater degree.

Many children who are difficult to live with are often like their parents. For example, totally disorganised children may have totally disorganised parents. Some children who are sent to me because they are unenthusiastic and have little drive to do anything much in life arrive in the company of equally boring parents.

Overactive, impulsive, intolerant fathers frequently produce active children who are chips off the old block, which leads to a major personality clash. Some years ago I was brought 3-year-old twins whose mother complained that they would never sit still and were forever rocking and head banging. In my office I watched them rock, foot to foot, always slightly out of time, like defective windscreen wipers on a car. When dad arrived a little later he burst into my office like a police raid. It was apparent within a minute that he was an overactive, driving athlete, who had never sat still from birth. The more he complained about his children's overactivity, the more I noticed him rocking, swaying, kicking his feet, moving his hands – exhibiting a problem far more severe than his normal children.

Is behaviour worse now?

Fifty years ago, children's behaviour problems appeared to be much less common. Many writers have blamed the current increase on the artificial colourings and other pollutants we give our children. I do not believe this is the main cause; there is, I think, a much simpler explanation. Fifty years ago, if one went to a doctor seeking help for one's child, it would be in the knowledge that all blame for the problem would be laid firmly on the mother, and some long-term psychotherapy for the parents might be suggested. This, in itself, must have been a major deterrent from seeking help, preventing most troubled parents admitting to anyone but their closest family that they could not handle their offspring. Behaviour problems may seem to be more common these days because of the break-up of the extended family and the highly competitive world our children live in. I believe that it's not so much an increase in the problems themselves, as an increase in the awareness of them. Now that they realise that criticism will not be levelled at them, parents are talking more openly about their problems and coming for help earlier. This is a healthy change for the better.

Professionals with prehistoric views

As a doctor who has lived and suffered through the aftermath of the era of psychological abuse of mothers, I am amazed that such an attitude could ever have existed. What is worse, there are still professionals in positions of power who have not yet accepted the influence of heredity on behaviour.

I would have thought that any professional who views life with even partly open eyes, could not help but see the immense variation based on simple heredity in all aspects of human nature. Any parent with more than one child would be aware of their completely different personalities. Such variations cannot possibly be accounted for solely by the different standard of care each child receives, even if it was usual for families to give different care to different children. It is my opinion that some children are born with a difficult temperament, which generates tension and upset in their environment, which then rebounds onto them. It is not a nice thing to say, but some children make themselves harder to love and get on with than others. Happily, the converse is also true.

One place where genetic influence stands out is in the newborn nursery of any hospital. Here we have babies who have hardly been touched by their mothers, already demonstrating their different personalities. In one cot there might be a quiet, loving baby exuding affection, cuddling in tightly and feeding with ease. In the very next cot could be a child in an identical state of health, who is irritable, arches his back, cries most of the time, dislikes being handled and forever spits out his feed. You don't need to be steeped in the psychiatric tradition to know that one would be a joy for any parent, while the other would be a trial for even the most well-intentioned family.

When working at night during my training in maternity hospitals, I would often see a noisy infant banished to a corridor to avoid disturbing the rest of the serious sleepers. Some of the most difficult toddlers I care for started life in this way, their hereditary load bringing problems before they even left hospital.

I am not naive enough to believe that all parents are without fault, but I do resent out-of-date experts blaming parents for temperament and behaviour which is not of their making.

Conclusion

Some children are born to be easy and some are born just plain difficult. We can't send them back but improved handling will make a major difference.

If you are lucky enough to have been sent an angel, give thanks to God for his kindness, but please don't get swollen headed and hold up this child as the perfect reincarnation of a perfect mother. If on the other hand you have a really difficult child, I do sympathise and I hope this book is of help. If you are criticised by some parents on an ego trip with their perfect child, let's jointly hope that next time they get a proper little terror. Then we will know there is some justice in this world.

Remember that behaviour results from both genes and environment. Of these, environment is the one we can change.

FIVE

Understanding Toddler Behaviour

'**O**h why me?' you moan, your head in your hands, as junior puts on yet another Oscar-winning performance for the supermarket crowd. 'I've given him a ton of love and endless attention and still he insists on embarrassing me with these painful performances.'

As your tired brain becomes more tired, it may be easy to believe that your little loved one is in fact the enemy, out to punish you in every way possible for your innumerable faults. But I can assure you it is not like that. In reality he is just an interesting little person with absolutely no sense called a Toddler, engaging in common or garden little person's behaviour.

When I look around at all the children I see, it appears to me that almost all behavioural concerns stem from a handful of triggers. Recognising these triggers can help you deal with the behaviour that follows.

The origin of most toddler behaviour

When we parents are having a bad day, our toddlers' repertoire of behaviour may seem extensive but in fact almost every performance comes from one of seven very predictable origins. Awareness of these brings all behaviours into perspective and allows you to achieve a firm foundation for effective discipline. These behaviours are:

- Attention seeking
- Jealousy and competition
- Frustration
- Fear of separation
- Reaction to illness, tiredness, or emotional upset
- Unreal parental expectations
- Parental dramas

Attention seeking

Toddlers are not unlike pop stars, politicians and other well-known adult exhibitionists. They need to be the centre of attention all the time, a demand which many parents find hard to understand. Why do they need to behave so badly to get attention when they are getting masses of it already? Well, it may not seem very sensible to you, but that's how toddlers are.

About 15 years ago, one of the TV networks in Australia filmed a segment in their '60 Minutes' program called 'The Terrible Twos'. For some weeks before, they advertised for the worst behaved toddler in Sydney and some parents put their children up to be filmed for the show.

The winning segment is a model of attention seeking. A 2½ year old is seen romping around his back yard, while his mother and grandmother are sitting on the back verandah chatting. The boy keeps coming up and wanting to talk to them, but they are having a great conversation and keep ignoring him. Finally the little boy goes to the edge of the yard, picks up a great big broom, and holding it above his head, starts back across the garden as the TV cameras slow down the motion and start playing the theme music from *Jaws*. Then he whacks the old lady across the head with it.

At this point the action stops and the interviewer asks: 'Dr Green, how would you deal with that delinquent behaviour?'

Well, the answer's simple. The child was saying 'Hey, you two, talk to me. I belong in this family too, don't you recognise me?' If you ignore toddlers they will hijack your attention. It's not bad behaviour, it's just how toddlers are.

This kind of scenario needs to be handled a little differently. Take another example. Your friend comes round. Her marriage is breaking down and she wants to talk to you about it. 'Sit down, here's a cup of coffee, tell me all about it,' you say sympathetically. 'Well, I think my husband is about to leave me,' she says.

Within 30 seconds your toddler will be standing between the two of you or trying to get up on your knee, as you launch into counselling mode.

With little children, certainly under the age of 3, I'm afraid it's going to have to be share your attention or have your conversation completely disrupted. So the talk may have to go something like this: 'So, you think your husband's going off with her then? *(Oh well done, that's a good drawing.)* And when do you think he'll leave? *(Yes, he is a lovely teddy, isn't he!)*' and so on. It's either that or don't even attempt to have a sensible adult conversation with a toddler present.

Interpreting behaviour

At one stage in my career, I undertook some formal training in child psychiatry, during which I was taught how to interpret behaviour in psychodynamic terms. We talked of bonding, sibling rivalry, castration anxiety, Oedipal conflict and other high-blown notions. When I say we talked, I mean this was by far our greatest skill. We were able to tell any mother how she had caused the problems in her child. Unfortunately, we were much weaker in giving the practical help, emotional support and management advice that was really needed. Fascinating though these theories are, I have since learnt to interpret toddler behaviour in a much simpler and more practical way.

When a little child performs some particularly antisocial act, stand back and ask yourself why. 'If I was doing what that little terror is doing, what percentage would there be in it for me?' For toddlers, the answer is nearly always the same: 'to gain attention'.

While attention seeking may well be at the root of most behavioural problems, the trouble is that we parents are often too tired and tense to realise what is happening before our very eyes. Our friends can see that we are being utter twits from where they stand, but we are seated too close to the game to see which side is scoring the points. The secret is to stand back a pace and ask, 'What is going on here? What percentage is there in this for junior?' If their antisocial actions are grabbing attention then it is time to look critically at the quality of the attention you are giving.

Grades of attention

Attention is deceptive. It comes in many grades and guises. The aim of every parent should be to give as much high quality attention as possible. This is extremely important to the happiness and emotional well-being of the toddler. But remember, at the end of the day you will feel just as tired if you have given the best, as you would if your home has been a war zone. You might as well resist giving poor quality attention, as there's no percentage in it for you.

If we visualise attention as a spectrum, graded from A to Z, we see two colourful extremes with many shades in between. Grade A (the best) includes all those close parent–child interactions like talking, reading books, playing together and cuddling. At the other end of the scale, Grade Z (the worst) is where children are completely ignored, their presence not even acknowledged.

As we move across the spectrum from A to Z the reward for the child gets progressively less attractive. Our children will usually aim for the best level of attention they can get, and if the best is not on offer they will descend through the grades until they find one that gives them what they want.

Examples through the spectrum

■ If parents have their hands full and Grade A attention is not on offer, toddlers will drop down a grade or two to B, C or D. They will probably start asking endless questions, although they are clearly not in the slightest bit interested in the answers. At least it keeps the lines of communication open and gives them some reasonable attention.

■ If Grades B, C or D don't work, a bit of arguing and debating is often seen as good value. They can argue that black is white, give you a most plausible explanation of why the world is flat and debate with all the skill of an 'egg on face' politician extricating himself from a corruption case. As far as toddlers are concerned, the cause is irrelevant as long as the parents take the bait.

■ Now down in mid-alphabet, toddlers find that saying 'No' to everything will get Mum's undivided attention. If this, by some mischance, doesn't work, they can always climb on top of the baby, turn off the TV halfway through your favourite show, or do unspeakable things to the cat. All these activities are bound to stir up lots of attention.

■ Verbal abuse is another great way of guaranteeing a rise out of mum or dad. 'I hate you Mum. You love Jack more than me.' Such statements will be delivered again and again, just as long as the target audience responds with the necessary attention.

■ By now we are descending into the lower letters of the alphabet of attention. These are the ones which harbour the really big gun stirrers. Tantrums, breath-holding and even vomiting on demand lie in this nether region. Their payoff may be a long way from Grade A but when top quality attention is not on offer it is still worth the effort.

■ The bottom line of attention is of the very poorest quality. Parents shout angrily at their child and may even deliver a few well-aimed smacks. Difficult as it is to understand how such pain and anger can please, bear in mind that even a smack can hurt a child less than being ignored altogether.

Jealousy and competition

At around 2 years, little children are not richly endowed with values of sharing and seeing the other person's point of view. They like to be the star of the show no matter what and when they are dispossessed of this role they can get mighty upset.

Behaviour varies greatly from child to child. A few are pretty laid back and humanitarian in their attitudes but most are downright possessive and resent intruders on their pitch. Jealousy and competition can bring problems for parents and arise from some quite predictable situations.

Nose out of joint with the baby

The arrival of a new baby causes confusion to the toddler. On the one hand it is fun to have this interesting, animated little doll around to play with but the sudden change in attention causes competition and jealousy. Usually toddlers and babies settle in well together but there can be problems if parents are overpossessive and unthinking.

It's quite natural for new mums to be overprotective but it can cause all sorts of difficulties. If a tense mum chucks a wobbly every time the toddler approaches the baby, soon the negative vibration associated with being near the child will damage the developing brother–sister relationship.

Another hazard is the discovery that a quick poke to baby will ensure a fireworks display of Bastille Day proportions. Now all the toddler has to do is poke, prod or pinch to have mum's undivided, if somewhat bad-tempered, attention. It can be a powerful weapon.

Tensions can also arise when friends visit the new arrival and tactlessly by-pass the sitting tenant. There is another potential for problems when tired parents feed, change nappies and give the baby comfort, forgetting that there is another little person who is in need of some attention.

With insight and sense it usually comes together well in the end, particularly if started off right. (See Chapter 17, Sibling Rivalry.)

Sibling rivalry

Parents who have only one child rarely realise just how much their life will change when they have two. Two together are usually the best of friends but they can also be fierce rivals. Most behave best when alone and are at their worst when competing.

Young ones resent not being able to do things as well as their older brother or sister. They feel that others get privileges they don't. They compete for attention and object when they think they have got less, be it love or a serving of pudding. Little ones taunt older ones and older ones taunt the littlies. This is what we call sibling rivalry and it is behind many an annoying display of bad behaviour. It is quite normal in toddlerhood, and probably will continue through to the age they leave home.

Adults who get in the way

When toddlers are taken out shopping they may resent the delays that occur when you stop to chat to friends. They wriggle, run off and tell you that it's time to get the show back on the road again.

During a long session on the phone, don't be surprised if your toddler engages in some well-planned demolition work, generally just out of eyesight, but with the right amount of noise to have you running to see what's up every two minutes.

When dad arrives home, it may be hard for the parents to chat about their day or impart important news to each other as toddlers

interrupt, so complex dealings are best left until after toddler's bedtime. Even a simple cuddle between husband and wife is often out of the question, as toddler will squirrel his way in between to get his share of the action.

When good friends drop round for a deep and meaningful discussion, they may be in for a disappointment. Most toddlers will regard this as unfair competition and may react by jumping up and down between you, asking to be taken to the toilet, or clambering all over you to ensure that coherent conversation is quite impossible.

The solution is to be selective, sensible and brief when interacting with other adults if toddlers are about.

Competition caused by other children

Toddlers generally enjoy the company of other littlies but they can still be very selfish when it comes to sharing their parents or their possessions.

For example, a visiting child is held by mum and made a fuss of, whereupon the resident toddler molests the cat, an act that miraculously regains his mum's full attention. Day care mothers can also find that their own child's jealousy may sabotage the work of looking after other people's children.

Time will soon cure this behaviour. Six more months can make all the difference.

Many toddlers resent others touching their toys. This is a quite normal reaction at this age and doesn't mean that you've bred someone who is destined to grow up as a mean and selfish adult. When faced with this behaviour as parents, encourage the child to share but by no means start a Holy War over the matter. A year down the track it will all be past history.

Frustration

Tiny toddlers have ideas way above their abilities and when things don't go as they have planned they can become mighty frustrated.

The 15-month-old loads food onto his spoon but the cargo shifts on the circuitous route to the mouth; and the $2^1/_2$-year-old's almost completed construction falls apart and the militantly independent toddler gets two legs stuck down one leg of his pants. It's tough being a toddler.

As parents we should accept that a certain amount of grizzling and tantrum throwing is due to frustration and not just bad behaviour. The toddler is trying to come to terms with the limitations of his abilities and at this time it is a cuddle and encouragement he needs, not punishment.

Fear of separation

Toddlers usually want to be close to their parents and get upset when separated. This is a normal stage of development and not a sign of sickness or bad behaviour. Anxiety over separation starts at

about 7 months of age, intensifies to a peak just after the first birthday, and gradually wanes over the next 3 years. This explains why some are so hard to leave with babysitters or in day care. Their protest is not naughtiness, they are just telling you that you are important and they would prefer to stay close to you. Usually this can be overcome gradually with gentleness, not scolding and punishment.

It has been said that children who wake repeatedly during the night do so due to separation anxiety. The children's point of view is that they love their parents and whether day or night, it is nice to call them in to check they are still there and get a bit of a cuddle. This has to be healthy, normal and nice for children but there comes a point when shattered parents must put their foot down. Separation anxiety is an interesting concept for academics but good rested relationships are more important in real life.

Illness and upset

When toddlers are sick, teething or have a temperature it is unreasonable to expect them to behave well. They feel uncomfortable and irritable, so why shouldn't they grizzle, dig in their heels and make a big drama out of life's trivial events.

In times of sickness, it is best to accept this all as inevitable, then freewheel for a while, establishing a firm hold again once they are better.

When the home is unsettled and routines disturbed, behaviour may also take a turn for the worse. Starting work, moving house, new babies, illness or death in the family, visitors, late nights, holiday travel and family fights can all cause upsets. With changes and turmoil, expect a little bad behaviour and work on the cause of the tension rather than combating it with the stir of punitive discipline.

Toddlers are not adults

Many non-problems are beaten up into big dramas by parents who expect 2-year-olds to act like adults. Toddlers have little sense, live for the here and now and certainly do not behave like grown-ups. Trying to make them grow up before their time is painful, pointless and a common cause of friction.

No sense

Very young children have very little sense. They may have acquired a smattering of it by the time they reach three, but before that age it is in extremely short supply, and between 12 and 24 months there is almost none at all.

For example, a 1-year-old doesn't know what he shouldn't be touching or why. 'Don't touch the video – that's a Sony which cost me $435 at David Jones!' – smack – 'I *said*, DON'T TOUCH THE VIDEO!' – smack. The child has no idea what you're on about.

By the time the child reaches 15 months the mountaineering instincts have usually kicked in. Up onto the kitchen bench he'll clamber like Hillary on his final ascent of Everest, not having the sense to realise that it is a long way down if he falls, and there's a very hard landing at the bottom.

It's not that they are being naughty. Little children under 2½ years don't have a bad bone in their body, they just don't have the capacity to think about the possible outcomes of their actions.

In just the same way, if you leave poisons, pills and sharp knives about, toddlers will not have sufficient sense not to harm themselves. It is up to parents to protect them, not punish them for their lack of maturity.

The message here then is:

- At age 1, children have zero sense

- At age 18 months, almost none

- At age 2, they have a little sense, but you need to watch them very closely

- At age 2½, they start to develop some sense

- At age 3, they acquire a good deal more sense

- At age 5, they begin to understand the details of cause and effect

Not thinking of others

In general, young toddlers are not renowned for their Good Samaritan attitudes. They tend to be jealous, self-centred and not talented in sharing or seeing the other point of view.

This of course varies from child to child and improves rapidly with age. Though there may be little thought for others at 2, this is much better by 3½ and by adulthood they may well have turned into selfless Christians.

Sharing is a particular problem. When someone else has the toy they want, it is quite likely that toddlers will grab it, push the other child over and in general lay on an utterly antisocial scene. Our role here is to encourage a more accepting attitude in the child without having a nervous breakdown in the process. Take heart in the fact that time will always cure this problem and if the worst comes to the worst, then just sit it out the best you can.

Non-adult values

Toddlers are often confused by their parents' behaviour. 'Why is Mum so angry, when last time she seemed really impressed with what I did?' The problem is that toddlers understand nothing of adult values, especially when it comes to expense, money, ownership and tact.

If you leave an open box of chocolates on the table, they will be eaten. There is no deception or dishonesty here. It is like climbing mountains. They do it because they are there.

Money may be taken from a purse but this is not a criminal activity. Toddlers are nosey, have no understanding about money and have no idea of the concepts of ownership.

When grandma's special toy gets broken on the first day of use, why is she so upset? Toddlers don't know the true meaning of $50.

As they 'hype' around the house, something is bound to get broken sooner or later. If it is an old pot, there is little reaction. If it is some priceless piece of porcelain, you have a seizure. They feel your displeasure, yet they cannot grasp the different values.

Children of this age behave just the same whether we parents are having a good or a bad day. When mum is tense, exhausted or has a headache, that is her problem and toddlers don't know to keep the volume down. Little children will be excited when dad comes home at night. They want to talk and play and certainly aren't interested in allowing him to sit down quietly and watch the evening news. It is their dad they want and they are wholly unimpressed by the antics of the Super Powers or the state of the economy.

Toddlers do not understand the meaning of the word 'Wait'. They cannot see why they should have to hang on until it suits mum to get going. Queues, or hanging around and waiting turns, are not in their way of understanding. And then there are the strange rituals that their parents seem to adhere to. Toddlers want to eat, for example, when their stomach tells them they are hungry, not at some fixed ritual mealtime which fits in with other people. When they think grandma's cooking tastes terrible, they tell her so. Honesty, as far as they are concerned, is the only policy and they know nothing yet of the diplomatic mistruths we adults use to avoid giving offence.

All this shows how normal little human beings think and behave. With time, they eventually conform to our strange adult attitudes. What happens in the meantime, however, should not be construed as naughty behaviour, and what they require at this stage is understanding and gentle guidance, not heavy-handed punishment.

Behavioural beat-up

I spend a lot of my life pulling parents and children away from each other's throats. The pattern is nearly always the same: child upsets mum. She retaliates and further upsets the child who, in turn, comes back even stronger, and so on and so on. Adults and children often treat those they love most with the least sensitivity and kindness. We can let so much tension develop between ourselves and our children that all it takes is a trivial trigger to plunge us into the bloodiest of battles.

Major wars have small beginnings. One bullet is fired and six are returned and in no time millions of people are involved. As parents, we are often so near the front line that we cannot see how we are creating an inevitable and unwinnable war. Both parents and toddlers can be very stubborn, but only mums and dads have the age and experience to know when it's best to back off. Try to muster all your insight and intelligence to see when you are causing harm and not helping a situation. It takes two to develop a behavioural beat-up and as 50 per cent of the combatants, we parents should aim for peace and a quick and fair solution. Life is quite tough enough without unwittingly damaging our closest relationships.

Conclusion

Most toddler behaviours start from a few predictable beginnings. Every child has an individual pattern and degree of those behaviours, but still they have much in common. The trick is for us parents to learn how to take a step back from our position at the front line to see who is making the gains and losses in the overall battle. Few toddlers do anything that is truly premeditated or aggressive. They simply behave like 2-year-olds.

When we understand what to expect and how to read the game, then we have a strong foundation, from which discipline comes easily. The techniques of discipline and how to put them into practice are covered in Chapters 7 and 8.

Summary: the 7 causes of toddler behaviours

Attention seeking Toddlers crave attention. If they can't get it by fair means they lower their sights, irritate their parents and grab it by some annoying act. This is by far the most common cause of toddler problems.

Jealousy and competition Toddlers can be pretty antisocial when others step into their limelight.

Frustration Toddlers' bodies cannot keep up with their brains. They become frustrated at their own inabilities.

Fear of separation Toddlers like to be close to their parent and can be difficult when separated.

Reaction to illness, tiredness, or emotional upset Toddlers can be irrational, irritable and hard to handle when unwell or upset.

Unreal parental expectations If parents expect a toddler to have adult values, they are in for trouble.

Parental dramas Parents bring problems on themselves by taking an unimportant event and beating it into a great drama.

Introducing Discipline

Every one of us, whether school child, toddler or adult, needs discipline. We all feel much happier and more secure when we have a disciplined lifestyle and know exactly where we stand. If you have ever worked in an office or been in a relationship where there are uncertain or unreasonable rules and limits, and where no-one encourages, notices or seems to care, you will be able to understand how some children must feel. Children are happiest when they know that their parents are united, consistent and concerned enough to care how they behave.

Good discipline starts in the home and spreads, eventually preparing our children for a smooth passage through school. When they start their education they will be expected to sit, settle, share and behave. It will impress no-one if their academic performance is like an infant Einstein and their behaviour like an infant.

Bringing up children may be no game but it will be more peaceful if all the players know the rules and have no doubt that the referee is both fair and in control.

The theories of discipline are easy to write about but they are not so easy to put into practice. Such are the individual differences of each of our children and such are the differences of opinion from the current epidemic of experts, that most modern parents are pretty confused. For what it is worth this is how I see it.

What is discipline?

When the word discipline is used many parents become flustered because they associate it with punishment but this is not what it is all about. The word discipline has a Latin origin which means teaching or training. The similar sounding word, disciple, comes from the Latin for 'a learner'. Discipline is a far more attractive concept when viewed as a learning experience for our children rather than one of pain and punishment. I like the idea of little children as disciples. They were the ones who learned through love and example – but in the background there were always clearly defined laws.

Discipline can be imposed on us from outside or it can come from within as self-discipline. Obviously young toddlers have no idea of self-discipline and at this tender age all direction must come externally from us, the parents. By pre-school age, children are ready to start taking some responsibility for their own affairs and this process can be helped if we loosen the reins and allow a little freedom of choice. This lets them feel the repercussions of their right and wrong decisions. By school age this loosening up process can be extended, putting them more and more in control of their own decisions. The ultimate aim is to have self-discipline firmly established by the time they up and leave home.

Attitudes towards discipline

At the beginning of the last century life was harsh. Almost one in five of all infants died before their fourth birthday and attitudes towards child rearing were pretty severe. Adults were seen as adults, children seen as children and there was no questioning the fact that the big ones were in charge. This approach started right from birth. Babies were fed and handled with rather frigid, rigid routines and children were brought up on a brand of discipline that focused on rules, obedience and punishment. This was a time where politeness and respect for the older generation was demanded.

By the late forties the pendulum had started to swing and by the seventies had overswung into an extreme of permissiveness. Then it was taught that babies should be fed, lifted and comforted the moment they cried. The older child received gentle guidance, not firm discipline, while home became a democracy where adults and children were almost equals. As the expectations of acceptable behaviour changed, some parents began feeling guilty and apologetic if they dared to use firm discipline.

In the nineties, this gentle, more permissive view continued to be promoted. It found favour with the best-selling academic authors. These experts read extensively in the university libraries but didn't work daily with difficult children. For them the thought of waving a wooden spoon, smacking, or marching junior off to his bedroom was utterly abhorrent. I like the theory of guiding with gentleness and love but the practicalities of implementing this approach are too vague. As I struggle down at the coal face of child care I don't need philosophy, I need hard techniques that work.

The more time I spend with families, the more concerned I become with the current view of child care. We have overswung from strict, to democracy, to a prevailing position close to anarchy. I believe now should be a time for a more balanced middle-of-the-road position: happy children who know where they stand with confident, together parents who are firmly in charge.

Strict or permissive

There are many ways to discipline our children and each one is as correct as the others. There are, however, two approaches that are universally wrong – the extremes of strictness or permissiveness.

Parents who are excessively strict and punitive can rob their children of independent thought and in the long term, when freed from this repression, there is a chance that the children will resent and rebel. At the other extreme, we impose no limits, which gives a poor foundation for both schooling and life. With excessive freedom, children may feel that their parents do not care enough about them to care what they do. If parents are as weak as water, this does not buy love, but loses respect.

If we keep away from the punitive and permissive extremes, this leaves a middle ground from which to choose the style that suits us. Each parent and each child is an individual with distinct needs for discipline and the style of giving it. The choice is ours.

And what of the future? Take as an example two happy, stable families, both committed to giving their best to their children. One uses discipline which is strict within reason, while the other favours a more laid-back approach. If you were to follow up these youngsters at age 20, you would have to look quite hard to see any difference in their behaviour, emotional adjustment or happiness. They will however have carried into adulthood quite different attitudes to child care which will resurface when they themselves become parents. The strict may tend to be strict while the permissive may favour that approach. As each adult enters marriage with some undiscussed but quite strong attitudes to child care, this will add a bit of interest to life when children arrive on the scene.

When to start

The view now is that infants in their first year cannot be spoiled. The overall aim is to establish security and closeness which glues parent and child together with an epoxy-like bond. Some of the older generation say that babies who get all this attention are destined to be more demanding but in fact there is now the suggestion that this may make them more secure and independent. Babies in the first year certainly do not need discipline. They need love, routine and closeness.

Toddlers are completely different little people. They are at that interesting stage when they flex their muscles and challenge all around them. They most certainly need discipline, the amount of which depends on the temperament of the individual child and the tolerance of the parents.

Those who have been blessed with an infant like a living saint will need to use little discipline before 20 months and even then an occasional soft whisper will produce a disgustingly perfect child. For those who have a toddler with the temperament of an urban terrorist, it is not as easy. These parents may have already had to deal with guerilla attacks on the guests at the first birthday party and this book will be well used by then.

Starting discipline is a very individual decision but the main message is to go gently at the beginning. Before the age of 2 our children do little which is devious, aggressive or nasty. Their actions just lack thought. Gentle firm guidance is usually sufficient, leaving the wrath-of-God-descending-like-a-thunderbolt, firmly in reserve.

SEVEN

Discipline – Making Life Easier for Yourself

Our children's behaviour depends on two competing factors: their God-given temperament and the environment they inhabit. This knowledge puts a lot of responsibility on us, the parents. While we are stuck with their temperament, environment is something we can always modify as we try to handle day to day situations better.

Many parents I meet seem hell bent on making their lives as difficult as possible. They are not driven by masochism but are so close to the situation that they cannot see how they are stirring things up.

This chapter is about some extremely simple ideas which we can all use to make life easier. Although most of these will be known, it is an unfortunate truth that when we are in a tired and demoralised state, commonsense is not too common.

Aim for calm and peace – don't stir them up

I see each family as a group of delicately balanced dominoes. If one is rattled this shakes those around, the chain reaction affecting all. As parents we can't stop our little dominoes rattling but we can stop them from rattling us.

Although most parents know the situations that bring out the worst in their youngsters, they continue to stumble into them with amazing regularity. Toddlers may not have university degrees in psychology but they still seem able to read us like a book. They plant little detonators which bring about major parental explosions. If we are one step ahead, sensible and calm, these detonations will be nothing more than a series of damp squibs.

Australian and New Zealand parents in the twenty-first century have many worries: jobs, relationships, and the major problems of money, mortgages and housing. I have no miracle cure for these troubles but we can work on minimising the damaging effects they generate. All I ask is that we become aware of just how infectious tension can be, then do our best to prevent it stirring up our children. There are many ways in which we can help the situation.

Don't nitpick

Some adults never seem to get off their children's back. In my office these parents nitpick non-stop. 'Look at Dr Green when you talk to him!' 'Say please.' 'Use a tissue.' 'Don't touch that toy.' 'Sit up straight.' There can be no peace in an atmosphere like this where every little gesture is used to generate tension.

This kind of over-disciplining is counter-productive. Notice what matters, concentrate on that, and selectively screen out the rest.

Avoid escalation

Many parents seem to seek out some trivial occurrence and then go over It again and again until it has escalated into a monumental hassle.

There they are sitting at home and their child drops a crumb on the carpet. 'Pick it up!' 'Pick it up now! This instant!' 'I am warning you, you will be in for big trouble!'

How can a crumb ever justify such a behavioural beat-up? If you had ignored it, the dog would probably have eaten it.

Once finished – forget it

Children may forget quickly but some parents just cannot let a matter rest. A child who commits a major crime early in the day should be punished then and the episode followed immediately by forgiveness and peace. Parents who are slow to forgive their children, write off days of their lives with a form of ongoing psychological warfare. This ensures that tensions remain high, bad behaviour is encouraged and maximum home unhappiness is guaranteed.

Holding grudges only produces parents with hypertension and ulcers – not stable, loving children.

They do it – you discipline – you forgive.

Turn down the volume

Loud music is known to make spotty teenagers want to dance and a mere fanfare of trumpets can move great armies to march off and fight. Likewise, toddlers will become greatly stirred up in a noisy situation. It is hard to discipline the young in a home where the adults are arguing, children are fighting and the television set is going full blast over the top of it all. Calm and peace are highly infectious qualities. Toddlers think and behave best when volumes are low and there is little distraction around.

Wind down overactivity

Activity is contagious and winds up all those around. When three children in a group are 'hyping' about, it won't be long before the fourth is compelled to join them. Toddlers love rough play and get very excited when springing around with a parent. If you spend time stirring them up, you must also allow for time to let them unwind.

A child who comes straight from frantic horseplay to the dinner table will not display the manners taught at finishing school. Any child who is overexcited and overexercised just before bedtime is unlikely to sleep.

Children's parties are dynamite to the active youngster. Parents assure me that this is due to the Coke, chocolate and sugar in the birthday diet. The behaviour would be just as high even if all they got was preservative-free bread and pure spring water. You don't need to be a genius to know that their bounce comes from being so close to activity, not food. If you are looking for peace and calm, don't 'hype up' little children.

Accept the inevitable

Tension may be minimised if you try to view life with a degree of philosophical acceptance. Some things happen to us and our children that are just inevitable. They are going to occur whether you burn yourself out with worry and tension, or lie back and adopt the philosophical approach of an Indian guru.

When our little ones are sick, they will wake just as many times at night whether we accept it as inevitable, or fight it. The wise approach is to salvage what sleep you can with thanks; the foolish approach is to so resent the situation that when at last your head hits the pillow you find you are too keyed up to sleep anyway.

In child rearing it is fairly difficult to view life from a calm plane of philosophy but on the other hand, beating your head against a brick wall is a futile exercise. The calm approach is not gained by sitting cross-legged, chanting mantras and chewing vegetarian delicacies. As parents, all we need to do is to open our eyes, stop blowing our tops and start using our brains.

Consistent discipline: 'There's only one set of rules in this house'

Children cannot live happily in a home where messages are inconsistent and conflicting. If one day they are allowed to get away with murder and the next punished for half the offence, they become confused and brainwashed. If one parent says 'Do this' and the other immediately countermands the request, then you have just witnessed the end of effective discipline.

It would be an unusual family where both parents agree completely about child-rearing but despite this, we need to become a coalition and present our children with a united front. In each home there can be one and only one set of rules.

If today the police let you drive on the right hand side of the road, tomorrow the middle and the next day you are summonsed for not driving on the left, you would become confused, insecure, angry and feel extremely vulnerable. The same goes for toddlers living in an environment of inconsistent, rapidly changing laws. They become angry, unhappy and unmanageable.

In some marriages, one parent is so pig-headed and has so little respect for the other party that each occasion of discipline becomes a dispute. The child is quick to spot the disagreement and will play off one parent against the other until the situation becomes intolerable. Where there is such major disagreement between parents, behavioural help is unlikely to work until the warring parties can reach a truce.

Angry, unthinking parents who use a child as a weapon with which to beat their partner are practising a form of legalised child abuse which can cause an immense amount of harm. In my experience, parents who openly disagree on discipline and use their little children as a means of hurting each other, have a relationship which is on such a downhill slide that separation is generally both inevitable and beneficial.

Don't use grandma as a scapegoat

Parents with uncontrollable children like to blame someone else for their problems. So often I hear parents say 'How can I discipline him when the next day he goes to his grandmother and she spoils him stupid?'. This is a complete red herring. You cannot go through life blaming child minders, teachers and others for your child's imperfections. The buck, as the saying goes, stops here, with you. Anyway, toddlers show an amazing ability to cope with the different disciplines in different loving situations. Of course they realise that there are different limits when at pre-school or grandma's, but they should also know there is one clear set of rules in their parents' home which will be enforced.

Parents are the majority shareholder and as such have the majority influence and responsibility for the standard of behaviour.

It takes two to fight

Fighting with little children is unproductive and on the whole it's best avoided. With toddlers, even the fight you win you lose. After 10 minutes the child has forgotten all about the fight, yet as much as an hour later steam is still gushing from the victorious parent's ears.

Every day parents tell me: 'He keeps fighting with me,' to which I invariably reply: 'Surely you mean you keep fighting with him?'

Obtuse as some of us are, no-one can fight by themselves, like a tango it takes two.

You know that when you've got your dander up and are spoiling for a fight the result will depend on how the object of your fury reacts when you meet. If they also explode and get out of control then you've got the makings of an intergalactic conflict. If, on the other hand, they refuse to be drawn into battle and remain cool, calm and collected, there can be no fight.

You alone have the power to enter or avoid fights with your children. You only have to go to the complaints counter of a major department store to find out what truly calm, collected people are like. As the customer's voice ascends in octaves of rage the only reaction coming from the other side of the desk is invariably 'Oh, I am sorry the blade flew off your new food processor and cut off your finger. That certainly has never happened before with this model.

I'll draw it to the manager's attention for you.' Parents too, believe it or not, have this power to encourage or prevent fights, depending on their reaction. Fighting with toddlers is futile, so exercise your veto in order to stabilise your blood pressure, maintain your sanity, and generate some domestic peace.

Structure and routine

Little children tend to be much more secure and happy when they live in an organised, structured environment. As well as knowing when they are going to be fed, when it is bedtime, and when it is time to go to pre-school, they also need to know the behavioural limits that their parents will tolerate. Most children thrive on routine and will immediately be thrown out of kilter by late nights, late meals, unexpected visitors or mum or dad going away on business. Wherever possible, parents should try to organise things well in advance so they can warn their children of what lies ahead for them. Disorganised parents can produce disorganised children, and the combined effect is a sure recipe for chaos.

Beware of the triggers

By triggers, I mean those situations that always seem to lead to trouble, like dragging their feet until they are almost late for school, refusing to bath, brush their teeth, eat their vegetables or being unable to pass an ice-cream shop. Minor triggers can create big repercussions and it is always better to avoid the trigger than to have to mop up after the 'Big Bang'.

If you stand back and try dispassionately to analyse your child's repertoire of tricks, you will find that it is in fact pretty small. You are probably being stirred up by the same trigger day in and day out but you are too close to see it.

Take a step back, open your eyes wide and see what exactly is setting off your child's bad behaviour. Then you can use a bit of cunning to steer around these triggers.

Positive is powerful

My toddler taming techniques are most successful when carried out by positive parents. First you must believe in what you are doing, then communicate clearly to your children. I refer to this brand of positive parenting as the evangelical approach – 'This is the way it is going to be, brothers!' This will be mentioned again and again throughout this book and if at any time your discipline seems to be slipping, stand back and check that it has been delivered correctly. Remember, positive parents are powerful people!

Beware the negative rut

Now it is all very easy for me to philosophise about being a 100 per cent positive parent but this is never quite so simple to put into practice. From time to time everyone hits a bad patch and with this, 'No!' can become a much over-used word. When things get really bad, each day of life becomes a negative battle of 'No', 'Don't', 'Stop it!' After existing through such a day parents feel demoralised and numb behind the eyeballs. As they crawl into bed they think, 'What good thing have I said all day? Is this what the joy of parenting is all about? I wish I had taken contraceptives three years ago.' But it is all too late.

Sinking into such a negative rut alters our attitude to everything. Next morning you greet the dawn with a negative sigh and the thought 'What awful thing will he do first today?'

A helpful technique is one used quite frequently with the families of children with disabilities in our care. We actively seek out good points in what at first appears an arid desert of bad news and general negativity. We look carefully for talents, skills and attributes and once they have been recognised, we build on them in the hope of lifting some of the despair and gloom that surrounds the family.

With toddlers, if all appears negative and full of unending bad behaviour, lift your sights and seek out some good. I have to admit that the behaviour of some of the children I see is so appalling that it takes a vivid imagination to spot anything that remotely resembles good. With the most difficult, start by rewarding the 'nearly

good' to build up a more positive attitude and, with this, better behaviour.

Trying to be more positive is an admirable but often impractical goal. If you fail, just try to be less negative. For example, instead of saying 'Don't walk so close to the road,' say 'Come and walk in the middle of the footpath with me.' In the long run this must have the same effect.

Sensible expectations

I believe that most of the major problems we experience would never surface if we had more sensible expectations of our children. The truth is that no 2-year-old is going to think or behave like an adult.

'Normal' toddler behaviour has been discussed in Chapter 3, so you should be under no misapprehensions about it. Try to readjust your sights and approach your toddler's upbringing with more sensible expectations. Some of the more common areas of conflict are mentioned below.

Mess and breakage

Toddlers by nature are noisy, dirty and messy. If allowed to pour their own drinks, a good proportion of it will inevitably land on the floor. In wet weather, mud and dirt walk into the house with your toddler, and toddlers are rotten judges of the dirt-resisting properties of your best quality Berber carpet. They have absolutely no sense of the adult monetary system and our strange values, failing to realise the difference between breaking a milk bottle and a priceless Waterford crystal vase. Animals they fondly cuddle yelp for release and ornaments they handle in genuine interest seemingly disintegrate in their fingers.

Toddlers aren't malicious, they are merely impulsive, non-thinking and often accident-prone. If you leave anything of value in their reach you have only yourself to blame if it is broken.

Broken toys

If you give a toddler an expensive toy there is a sporting chance that it will be broken before the sun has set. Toys do get damaged, and it is stupid to blame the toddler; it is probably you who should be reprimanded for spending too much money in the first place or buying poorly made articles. Little children do not need expensive, easily broken toys. They have such an imagination that an old cardboard box or the tube from the middle of a toilet roll can give hours more creative fun than any expensive plastic creation.

Parent's return

By evening, the toddler is bored with the parent who has remained at home. As he hears the other parent's (usually the dad) key turn in the lock he happily comes to life with renewed energy. Dad is viewed as an exciting new entertainment-giver, and the toddler has little respect for Dad's tiredness after a long working day and his wish to sit down, put his feet up and talk to his wife or watch the evening news. It's far from easy, but fathers must try to see life from their child's point of view and allocate a period of attention at the

65

time of their return each night. The child will expect it and is unlikely to accept rejection without a fight.

Social honesty

Children of this age have not yet developed the quality of 'social dishonesty', which is expected of any of us who wish to succeed in the grown-up world. Toddlers are not backward in pointing out different skin colours and people's disabilities, as well as informing people of their disastrous hairstyles or ugly features. When out visiting, if the cooking tastes rotten, the child will not beat about the bush, using the vague dishonesties of an adult; he will say it plainly for all to hear.

Whether we should change the toddler's honesty or the adult's dishonesty is an interesting philosophical point that we will not argue here.

Toddler proofing your home

Life can be made so much easier if you live in a suitably fortified home. Child proofing becomes a necessity just after the first birthday when the toddler is becoming extremely inquisitive and much more mobile, with sense at a standstill. I have seen some parents take child proofing so seriously that they crawled around the house on their hands and knees doing a trouble shooting survey from toddler level. This is a bit over the top but however you do it, toddler proofing is important.

Fiddly fingers and the collapse of the dream home

When newly weds move into their first home they love to display their prize possessions, usually at toddler height. It comes as a rude shock when a little terror bursts on the scene and starts fingering the ornaments and taking the house apart. Now a major rethink is called for.

Some stubborn parents adopt the attitude that 'We were here first and he will have to live here on our terms'. Sure you can leave those tempting trinkets lying around and if you say no and divert enough, he will eventually learn not to touch them, but it is rarely worth the hassle. Sensible parents keep temptation out of toddlers' way, gradually reintroducing things several years down the track. Without toddler proofing, parents need eyes in the back of their heads. Once home is secure we can relax, a little.

Latches, locks and prohibited areas

If you have a fast-moving, inquisitive toddler, child proofing is not just advisable, it is a necessity. You cannot be expected to fortify the whole place like a suburban Fort Knox but a few modifications are well worth the effort. Keep breakables in a child proof cupboard or up high on a shelf. If you have good furniture in a good room with a snow white carpet, it is often best to declare this out of bounds. If your teaspoons are flushed down the toilet – put a latch on the cutlery drawer. Some cupboards will need to be latched and out of bounds, while others are open to play in and explore. Cupboards with saucepans, vegetables and thick-skin fruit are always popular and safer, while those with sharp knives, detergents and drain cleaners are an absolute no-no.

One way to prevent inquisitive little fingers getting into cupboards and drawers is to buy one of those rolls of wide super sticky tradesman's tape. A short length stuck across a drawer, cupboard, or fridge, dissuades all but the most determined toddler, yet it can be easily peeled back for adult access. As the stickiness wears out new lengths are introduced. The aim is that by the end of the roll sense will have arrived.

Immobilise the refrigerator (if necessary)

Some parents come to me with what they believe to be a really profound question. 'Dr Green, how do you stop him taking the lemonade from the fridge?' The simple answer is not to keep it there, or ask the manufacturers to design child proof lids. It is not so easy when it is milk they are taking and spilling.

Little people can be kept out of the refrigerator with a remarkably simple technique told to me by a parent. Take a short piece of elastic cord, the type used to hook articles onto the roof rack of a car. Clip the hooks around the back of the fridge and you have a spring-loaded door. This opens only a short distance and will slam closed before the toddler can extract the goods. This method usually allows parents easy access, while providing the child with exercise equipment not unlike a chest expander. Although this works very well, we worry a lot about injury when using elastic cord. Some rope, a length of sticky tape or a wooden wedge between the door handles may be equally effective.

Make-up and indelible markers

Many toddlers have wonderful artistic talents, particularly when it comes to finger painting on bench tops, the floor or mirrors.

Lipstick, nail polish, make-up creams and indelible markers should be kept well out of reach. Any pen with ink that is not easily and instantly washable must be kept under the tightest security.

Dangers, dogs and sharp edges

Houses with glass doors or windows that come down to floor level pose a danger to the child. If he falls through the glass he will suffer severe cuts and even greater injury if he rides his tricycle through an unprotected first floor window to the ground below. Block such dangers with furniture, fit temporary bars across the window and use safety glass where possible.

Safety plugs should be fitted over power points as young children have the sort of fascination with electricity that a fly has with a zapper. It is essential to have a commercial circuit-breaker fitted to your junction box outside, and then at least you can rest safe in the knowledge that even if he does poke a knife into the electric toaster he should survive to poke another day.

Furniture and household items with sharp edges that are likely to cut or damage either him or something else are best removed altogether or a soft material can be taped over them. It is imperative that all medicines are stored safely in a securely locked cupboard high up out of harm's way. It is a common mistake for people who are very conscientious about storing medicines to leave even more dangerous products within easy reach in the kitchen, laundry or garden shed. Bleach, rat poison, weed killer, drain cleaner and dishwashing detergent are the sort of offenders that must be locked well away.

Pets and toddlers generally mix well but there is no place in the same house for a savage dog who bites when teased, however important his role as a guard dog may seem. Such animals should be sent back to the jungle where they belong.

Fortify the compound

Coping with an active toddler is always easier if you have access to a secure garden. They need the space but you can never relax unless there are fences and gates to prevent escape onto the road. Where there is particular danger, some parents find chicken wire is a cheap form of fencing and though it does not create a compound as escape proof as Colditz, it is an affordable start.

Where fencing is inadequate and roads are busy, all doors leading from the house must be immobilised. The best methods are a high-level latch, security chain or deadlock. If you have one of those quiet, angelic, predictable children or are surrounded by acres of gently rolling parkland sweeping majestically to the horizon, this will all seem a bit unnecessary.

The playpen

The playpen seems a marvellous invention for keeping active children out of mischief. Although sound in theory, it rarely works in practice, because extremely active children need space and protest if put in a playpen.

Some parents tell me that the playpen is for their own use. Inside it they place a comfortable chair, then sit back and read a book, while the child runs around the house.

Apathetic, helpless parents

Never a week goes by without a brilliant mother telling me of a new child proofing technique she has invented. Other parents seem to have no imagination, initiative or motivation to improve anything. They are apathetic and helpless, as they sit there and tell me 'It is impossible to lock the door' or 'It is impossible to immobilise the gate' or 'It is impossible to stop a 2-year-old drawing on the walls'. This is ridiculous. Astronauts can be blasted from the earth to fly for weeks through space before landing back where they started so it seems unbelievable that in this super-scientific world, an intelligent 30-year-old cannot devise some method to prevent a 2-year-old child from opening a door. We do not need the high technology of computers, space suits and rocket fuel; a latch, a piece of elastic, or a length of string can all produce dramatic results.

Fighting with children is such a waste of time and emotional energy, it is important to toddler proof your home, for your child's safety, the security of your belongings and your own peace of mind.

Absconders and reins

Toddlers need to be supervised closely as they have no road sense. Fortunately most do not like to be separated from their parents when out of the home and tend to stay close by. Others have no such worries and bolt at the first sign of open space. Some of these children enjoy being chased after, others have no fear of separation from their parents and get lost with monotonous regularity. Here we go again in the supermarket as they announce 'Will the mother of the grubby 2-year-old with a faded yellow T-shirt collect him immediately'.

This period of attempting to abscond is generally quite short lived, and though I dislike the use of reins, there are some instances when they are literally life savers.

Parents can use a short length of rope with a boy scout knot around the waist or one of those lightweight ties, like a telephone cord. If your child pulls like a Melbourne Cup mount at the starting gate a full heavy duty harness will be necessary. Reins may raise some eyebrows with your friends whose perfect children stay clamped beside them every moment. They are welcome to their opinion but for me, reins are preferable to exhausted parents worrying themselves and the local constabulary into nervous break-downs every time they venture out.

Avoid no-win situations

Beating your head against a brick wall is a painful and unproductive part of life. If you seek a peaceful existence, it is wise to reserve time and energy for the worthwhile causes and avoid at all costs those that cannot be won. The clever parent is quick to spot when they are on a losing wicket and extract themselves gracefully.

The main no-win areas involve feeding, toileting and sleep. Other problems arise when time is limited, the venue is very public or there are too many interfering adults around.

We parents have to be sensible. Sometimes our children chuck a boulder before us as we go down the highway of life and when this happens it is easier to steer around it than hit it head on and cause a major confrontation.

Feeding

It is easy to sit a child at the table and place food in front of him. What is difficult is to get it down the 'big tube' if he has decided it is not going to happen. Medical science is advanced but I am sure there is a Nobel Prize awaiting the person who discovers the switch that makes the reluctant toddler eat.

Fighting over food is a complete waste of time, which entertains children and ages their parents. Remember that no toddler has ever starved to death through stubbornness and forcing food down a child's throat is a cause of feeding difficulties, not a cure.

Toileting

You can take your child to the toilet, you can encourage him to sit there, but no amount of parental jumping up and down will make something drop out if junior has decided it is not going to happen. This is yet another case when you must accept that he may be small but he has the ultimate veto.

Sleep

In exactly the same way as you can lead the proverbial horse to water but cannot make him drink, parents can put a child to bed but there is no way that an unwilling child can be made to go to sleep. If the parent demands sleep immediately, the little rascal will generate unbelievable powers of wakefulness, just to show who is boss.

Parents can put them in their beds, keep them in their bedrooms, but have to accept that they cannot make them go unconscious. That is of course unless you fire tranquillising darts through the keyhole or pump anaesthetic gas under the door.

Limited time

It's a hot summer day and the 2½-year-old is romping around naked under a hose in the back yard. In exactly ten minutes you need to have him dressed, in the car and up at the school to collect big sister.

The toddler knows this and is darn sure that there is no way you will get him dressed and there on time. You could be bloody-minded, but it's all a bit hot and humid for that. Why not avoid the boulder, forget the clothes and put one naked toddler wrapped in a towel in his car seat and hope you don't have a breakdown?

There are times when confronting the toddler is just not worth the trouble.

When the going gets tough – get out!

Despite all the best behavioural advice in the world, there comes a point when some children's behaviour becomes unbearable. This usually happens on those wet, windy days when the single bedroom apartment seems oppressively small. When the whingeing starts, it seems to reverberate around the walls and ceilings, going right through your head and jangling your nerves. At this point, discipline becomes difficult and I believe it's best to cut one's losses and run. Take the children and head for the wide open spaces. Noisy children never seem quite so loud when their efforts are muffled by the great outdoors, and the movement of the baby buggy is usually very soothing to the active toddler. It's worth getting wet just for the peace of mind.

One mother of a particularly difficult child recently told me: 'When I am losing control, I get outdoors straight away. There, things never seem quite so bad, and even if I was driven too far, we are both much safer, I could never harm him in public'. Now there is a piece of wise, honest advice.

Out of control and birth control

I am often asked whether I believe the first, second or third child is most difficult. My answer has no research backing but it is my belief that the last child is usually the most difficult. It seems to me that if you have a really difficult child you make sure that this is going to be the last. A difficult child is the ultimate contraceptive.

When I see parents who cannot cope with their children, I always ask what are their plans for further additions to the family. Some whose children are completely out of control tell me that they may or may not have more, as 'It's all in God's hands'. Far be it from me to interfere in other people's affairs, but if we as parents cannot cope with our present brood, it is absolutely certain that an extra child is only going to make matters worse. Perhaps these parents should seriously consider some reliable form of avoidance rather than leaving all the responsibility in God's hands.

Summary: simple ways to make life easier

- Stay one step ahead and try to remain calm. Don't nitpick, avoid escalation, accept the inevitable and once finished, forget it.
- Both parents need to keep discipline consistent.
- Give your toddler structure, routine and clear limits.
- Have realistic expectations of your toddler's behaviour and avoid the triggers that set off bad behaviour.
- Toddler-proof your home.
- Avoid battles that cannot be won.
- When all else fails get outside.

EIGHT

The Techniques of Discipline

So far we've looked at introducing discipline into your child's life and some ways of making life easier for yourself. Now we need to explore some of the techniques of discipline.

'Here it comes,' you're thinking, 'he's going to tell us about smacking, and locking them in their bedrooms, and taking the front wheel off the tricycle – all that sort of nasty stuff.'

Well, I'm not. That's not discipline. Discipline is not about punishment, it's about encouraging, rewarding and moulding the child to behave in the correct way. On the whole, discipline is a very positive thing.

A behaviour which pays off for the child will generally be repeated, so what we want to make sure of is that the pay-off comes for the right behaviours, not the wrong ones.

It's all in the voice

The best way to discipline a toddler is through your tone of voice. 'Good boy', 'Good girl', 'That's right', 'Well done', all that sort of thing, coupled with the way you look at your child when you say it. Transmit love and approval in your eyes. Let them see the twinkle in your eye. Brush by them as they play, giving them a little pat on the shoulder and saying quietly, 'Love you'.

It's these kinds of tones and actions that we should mainly use to encourage the behaviours we want from our children.

When they aren't behaving the way you would like them to, then we can transmit that message, again with our voice. This time you use a firmer tone, a tone of disapproval, and they will instinctively know that they have done something wrong. They may not understand what, but they know you are not pleased.

This time the twinkle in your eye has been replaced with a deadpan look on your face. You move away from them, signifying that they have done something you don't like and you don't want to be a part of it. In this way you are subtly moulding their behaviour. See 'Behaviour modification therapy' later in this chapter for more about moulding behaviour.

The six top tips of discipline

Let's look now at some practical ways in which you can discipline your child without having to resort to the 'go to your room this instant!' method.

1. **Attention** is the greatest reward of all and most of the attention we give to our children is subtle. Cut off the attention when things aren't going well and you don't want that behaviour repeated. You want them to know that you're not pleased.

    Watch out for the trap however. If the greatest reward is attention, and the greatest punishment is no attention, be aware that shouting at them, arguing with them or even smacking them qualifies as attention. So you may think that you are punishing a child when you get all wound up with them, but in fact you may be giving them a reward. Better to cut the attention off altogether.

2. ***Don't analyse*** your child's behaviour. Don't try looking for logic in it, because you won't find any. There's no point saying 'She's doing that deliberately to annoy me', because the chances are she isn't doing anything of the sort. She's just not thinking too much about what she is doing.

    'He's deliberately disobeying me,' you say. 'I told him just a few minutes ago not to do that.' It's not disobedience. It's just that he has a very short attention span, and in any event, he's not really quite sure what you're on about anyway.

    Parents can get themselves into a lot of trouble in this way, grounding their 2-year-olds for long periods of time for alleged disobedience. It's to no avail. The debate about good and evil is an utter waste of time at this age. Leave it until they're over 5.

3. ***Diversion*** is your greatest weapon. All little children are very easily diverted, so when a child is about to touch your favourite ornament or embark on some form of behaviour of which you disapprove, you can say something like 'Look, there's a dog in the garden, oh, it's gone round the corner'. This often works. It may be dishonest, but it can save your sanity!

4. ***Know the triggers***. I bet you know all the ways to have an absolutely rotten day with your child. There are certain things that are guaranteed to wind your child up – for example, going to the supermarket. Some children just don't cope with super-markets very well. I have had parents say to me: 'Why is mine the only child who behaves this way in the supermarket?' What they don't know is that about 20 per cent of all other children of similar age never ever go to the supermarket because their parents know exactly how they'd behave and so deliberately avoid the experience.

    So if you know the situations which trigger off bad behavi-our in your child, then avoid them at this early age.

5. ***Clear communication*** is one of the tricks of positive parent-ing. It isn't a matter of saying to your child 'Would you like to

pick your toys up now?' but rather looking the child straight in the eye and saying 'John, pick up your toys. Here, I'll give you a hand.'

Toddlers play you like a poker machine. They try you out, because they know that if they play for long enough you will eventually give in and they win the jackpot. Well, the trick is never to allow the jackpot to be won. The news is that from now on the big people are back in charge!

6. ***Ignore the unimportant.*** So many parents I talk to nitpick over all sorts of irrelevant stuff, wind themselves up like cuckoo clocks and get the children so stirred up that they behave really badly.

The trick is to concentrate on the 20 per cent that really matters and ignore the 80 per cent that is irrelevant. This is important. Don't forget, however, that when you are choosing to ignore certain behaviours which you may not like, do it firmly but calmly, cut off your attention and don't get drawn in to what's happening.

Selective deafness is very useful. When your child says 'I love you, Mum,' you can reply 'Yes, darling, I love you too.' But when John shouts 'I hate you, Mum!' stay calm, don't buy in to it and don't get into a debate about it.

As I have often explained to parents, when you are standing in the lion's cage at the zoo, you don't take a stick and poke the lion in the backside. It is more sensible to say 'Nice Mr Lion, I'm not going to stir you up today as I would like to get out of here alive'.

It's the same with little children: don't go stirring up the wild animals, it doesn't get you anywhere!

Behaviour modification therapy

When I mention behaviour modification therapy, parents cringe as it suggests some sinister brainwashing technique. They have a vision of secret police moulding an unwilling dissident to another way of thinking. Even worse, others have heard that behaviour modification has been used to train dogs, pigeons and all sorts of circus animals. But don't panic, this is not some dog doctor's piece of animal psychology. It is old, it is effective and I am sure that even though your parents had never heard the name, it was the way they brought you up.

Encouraging the good – discouraging the bad

The theory of behaviour modification therapy is remarkably simple. It simply states that any behaviour that is reinforced by rewards will tend to be repeated. We have already talked about using voice tone, actions and attention to reward desirable behaviour. The latter is what happens at the end of the concert when the audience applauds enthusiastically. Such is the reinforcement that the group gives an encore – you get a repeat performance.

Behaviour modification also has a reverse side which states that any behaviour that is not noticed, encouraged and reinforced will probably disappear. This time the concert finishes but the audience is bored senseless and the applause silent – tonight there will be no encores.

Imagine the scene: your 2$\frac{1}{2}$-year-old stands up, smiles, then in front of the visiting church committee, with perfect articulation, says 'Bum!' Mother blushes and there follows a fireworks display. With such reward and reinforcement, before long all you will hear is 'Bum!' 'Bum!' 'Bum!'.

This could have been handled differently. When the child said 'Bum', mum could have remained distinctly unimpressed, yawning quietly and continuing to chat. Now junior stomps off muttering 'What a bummer – no audience – no show'.

In young children behaviour modification will work best if the good behaviour is rewarded quickly. Even a minute after the event the reward will have lost some of its power at this age. The technique must be used consistently if it is going to be effective. If a behaviour is going to be ignored and underplayed this must happen five out of every five times it occurs. If the ignoring is restricted to four out of five occurrences it will always be worth trying you out.

It is like feeding a poker machine; if you play long enough, odds are that eventually you will score a jackpot.

What sort of rewards?

Rewarding children for performing is not degrading, it is part of our Australian way of life. I get rewarded with money for working, and I get no pay if I don't. If I give a successful lecture people thank and flatter me and before I know it I have agreed to give another. If rewarding adults is thought appropriate, then children deserve the same.

In behaviour work there are two styles of rewards. There are the soft or social rewards and then there are those which are hard and tangible.

Soft rewards

These refer to giving attention, praise, smiles and touch. Of these, attention is the main reinforcer and, as will be seen later, when used wisely it can be very powerful. When misused, however, it can promote some mighty unwelcome behaviours. Both children and adults are very sensitive to soft, subtle boosting of behaviour techniques such as being noticed, or by the warmth of your voice, or that twinkle in your eye.

Hard rewards

These are the more tangible items like a smiley stamp, a gold star on a chart, a 'Thomas the Tank Engine' sticker, or a host of little toys. Then there are all those sweet rewards that tend to turn both your child's teeth and the dentist's bank balance black.

Rewards and bribery

There is a very subtle difference between reward and bribery. Most behavioural experts get quite upset at the thought of bribing children and encourage rewards. A bribe is seen as a form of blackmail, where the child is told that he can only have something after he has performed a certain task. The behaviour modification reward is given when there is no talk of what will happen until after the good behaviour has appeared and then the reward comes as an immediate and unannounced bonus. Very often the difference between bribes and rewards is far from clear and though I would prefer rewards, if a bit of good old-fashioned bribery achieves the desired effect, then go for it.

Soft or hard rewards?

When deciding whether to use soft or hard rewards, the child's age is an important factor. Most toddlers are very happy with soft rewards, particularly attention, whilst older children are more aware of the value of objects and may do better with hard rewards, especially those that jingle in the pocket.

Getting it back to front

These behaviour techniques allow us to steer a stubborn toddler around trouble without becoming drawn into any futile fights. Behaviour modification, however, does have one great weakness. It is far too easy to get back to front. The technique has no safety lock which makes it boost only the good, while selectively filtering out all that we do not wish to see.

Though we use behaviour modification every day, many times we unknowingly get it so reversed that it becomes an enemy, not an ally. Most of the behavioural difficulties which confront us are actually created by us. We fuss over trivial little problems thereby producing big ones.

Some years ago I was examining a little boy as he lay on his mother's knee. When I felt his tummy he quite involuntarily straightened one leg and kicked me. As a bit of a joke I jumped back, holding my knee and made a great fuss. A few seconds later my foolishness was rewarded by a sharp kick on my other knee and this time it really did hurt. Again I jumped and by the end of the interview the little terror was tramping on my toes, kicking my shins and having a ball. A week later I was working quietly at my desk, my office door burst open and before I knew it he dashed in and gave me a kick.

Now admittedly this seems a particularly silly way for a paediatrician to behave, but it illustrates clearly what happens when we make a fuss over some trivial event. If the first unintentional kick had been ignored, that would have been the end of it. But I made a big deal out of it and created a rod with which I was beaten. I should have done it differently, or purchased shin guards.

A common example of getting behaviour modification back to front would be with feeding. You put food in front of the toddler, he takes one look at it, and says 'yuk!'. Immediately the adults start to act like toddlers. Mum makes aeroplane noises, dad juggles oranges and the dog probably performs circus tricks. With so much reward for not eating, the mouth remains shut, tight as a Scotsman's purse. Now you have created a feeding problem.

Start again. He looks at the food: 'Yuk!' You ignore this. He either eats or ends up with hunger pains, but you maintain your sanity and have no future fights over food.

Changes come gradually

Some parents leave my office with a behaviour plan, convinced that if it does not work within an hour, my techniques are a ripoff. Behaviour modification gradually moulds the way a child behaves. It is time, cunning and consistency that bring results. There is no point expecting that a child will touch the hem of Dr Green's garment and be instantly cured. After all, they have been practising their particular performance for months and it seems reasonable to allow a few weeks to bring about change.

Things can get worse before better

For some time your child has studied his parents well, knowing your every raw nerve and point of vulnerability. If you suddenly smarten up your act, close the chinks in your armour and cease to respond, he will feel he is losing his touch and will have to turn up the pressure. Militant toddlers may initially try more of the same but with even greater persistence. When your defences remain strong, they go back to base to re-plan the campaign and attack on a different front.

If after a short while you show clearly that there is a new you who is in charge and really means business, then peace will soon return.

In life we often have to put up with a bit of extra pain on the route to a long-term cure. Before embarking on any major behavioural change, be sure you have the strength to handle that dark which comes before the dawn.

Behaviour modification is not some dubious new technique but a well-tried method of moulding behaviour. When this technique is used properly much can be achieved without recourse to raised voices, tantrums, force, threats or parental insanity. Consistency is important and so is care, not to get it back to front.

Smacking – let's be sensible

Smacking is a sensitive subject with a whole army of people lined up on both sides of the argument. My views on this topic may be out of step with most modern child care authors, but I suspect my opinions to be very much in tune with how many parents think.

I would like to make it quite clear that I do not condone 'hitting' children. However, I object to the philosophical hype that surrounds the push for legislation to make the physical punishment of one's own child a criminal offence. I worry that those who push this particular political barrow have not fully grasped the subtle difference between an occasional smack in a normal, happy home environment and severe, frequent beatings in a disturbed family.

Whether it is a good or bad way to treat children, it is a fact of life that some parents will smack their children at some time or other.

Smacking – don't get the wrong end of the stick

I don't like smacking children. This form of discipline is generally unhelpful and frequently makes matters worse. I certainly would not support any family that uses smacking as the main form of discipline – this is very wrong. Having said that, I feel that the anti-smacking brigade cause an unnecessary amount of alarm to thousands of good parents who may resort to the occasional smack.

The research quoted by anti-corporal punishment groups, if taken on face value, certainly shows that children subjected to corporal punishment have a greater chance of becoming child and wife abusers at a later age. But if you study the statistics more carefully, however, it soon becomes apparent that these academics have got the wrong end of the stick.

We know that all children are very sensitive to the emotional happiness of their home. Those who are reared in a disturbed setting often have trouble experiencing close and loving relationships with their parents. This sets a poor example and gives an unstable foundation to all relationships which follow. It also puts them at greater risk of contracting unsuitable marriages, which can all too easily bring the same problem straight to the next generation.

It is well-known that children of emotionally unhappy homes are much more frequently exposed to excessive corporal punishment, child abuse and domestic violence. There is now a proven link between excessive beating of children in one generation and pathological relationships, with abuse, in the next. I believe, however, that beating is not the cause, but rather the symptom, of the pathological relationship, which can go from generation to generation in a disturbing vicious cycle.

If lobby groups genuinely want to improve the emotional well-being of children, it might be more useful, I would suggest, to first address some of our present forms of *legal* child abuse. Maybe they should be lobbying for a law to give more protection to the children of heroin addicts or the families of alcoholics. And what about parents who upset their children by continually fighting and abusing each other in front of them? Perhaps they should face criminal action! And I'd like to see parents and lawyers who use innocent children as point-scoring pawns in messy divorce cases charged with abuse.

'What has all this to do with smacking?' I hear you ask. Well, in the big picture of things, the occasional corrective smack is pretty harmless, though it still remains a pretty ineffective form of discipline. It usually falls flat because it has been doled out in a fit of temper, following which our little ones capitalise on all our guilt and weaknesses and use them to their own advantage.

84

Smacking – the rights and wrongs

In as much as there is a right way and a wrong way to smack your toddler, if you have to resort to it, then you might as well have some idea of the possible outcomes.

Smacking not followed through

Most smacks seem to descend when we parents are angry. This may make us feel better at the time, but it is often ill-aimed discipline, both badly timed and inappropriate. The problem for most of us comes about two minutes later, when, after the child's flood of tears, our anger turns to guilt and then the game is lost.

Imagine the scene. You have had it up to the back teeth, but John still persists until – smack! He starts to cry – you feel bad. John knows you feel bad, so cries louder – you feel even worse. He knows how you are feeling and cries louder still, sensing that victory is within his grasp. You give up and John gets a cuddle.

A quick smack may diffuse a situation and regain control, but unless we follow it through properly it is all too easy to blow it.

The last straw smack

Most of the smacks we parents dole out are at times when we have had a gutful and can take no more. Often the smack arrives after a long series of annoyances and is precipitated by some trivial, unimportant event which becomes the last straw that breaks the parent's back. This certainly releases a lot of anger for the parent, but it tends to confuse the child. There are better ways of handling this situation than to become so angry that we need to smack the child for such a trivial misbehaviour. After all, we adults are supposed to be more intelligent and in control than the average toddler, though at times I'm not so sure!

Smacking back

Another occasion when smacking gets you nowhere is when the smacked child immediately smacks the parent back. The blow is returned and the toddler reciprocates. Soon you have been drawn into a minor war that will be much harder to get out of than it was to get into.

As the battle heats up, the parent gets increasingly angry and although the toddler is receiving a few minor 'flesh wounds', it becomes the best game for weeks. Toddlers are negative, stubborn and have little sense. If their parents are even better endowed with these qualities, the fight can go on endlessly. Unless you are obsessive almost to the point of autism, you don't have to cast the last blow.

I never felt it!

Some 3- to 4-year-old toddlers have the most amazing theatrical talent. When smacked they stand stoically like Rambo under interrogation, look you straight in the eye and, with the dumbest of dumb insolence, say: 'That didn't hurt!' Of course it really did hurt, but they know that this reaction will infuriate the smacker (and besides, thinks the toddler, how dare someone lay a hand on me!).

Believe it or not, I once had a child referred to my clinic with a note saying, 'Please investigate the nerves in his legs. He appears to feel no pain!'

Smacking used correctly

Smacking must be one of the oldest and best tried techniques known to man. Has it damaged our ancestors? Was it good for our parents' generation or are they a rather disturbed bunch? You be the judge.

Best in the younger child

Smacking has its main usefulness in the younger child. At this age words are less effective than some decisive action. You can debate all day with a defiant 2-year-old. You can explain about the finer points of love, example and character building and even your evangelical views against corporal punishment, but the chances are that words may miss the mark, while a gentle gesture of a smack may land centre bullseye, right on the target.

Quick results

Smacking has one major advantage over most other forms of discipline in its ability to bring a rapidly deteriorating situation to a quick resolution. A firm, positive rebuke and Time Out (see later this chapter) are also quick and effective but the rebuke is often ignored and Time Out is only of use when there is a suitable room available, which limits it to use at home.

Registers limits clearly

A well-considered smack registers a firm message. It states that these are the limits, you are in charge and you will be extremely firm if there is any further challenge.

Aborts escalation

Most behaviour wars start with some minor trigger. Some relatively unimportant decision sets in motion a train of events which seem to run rapidly out of control no matter which tack you take. In the end there is such a blow-up that the whole house is tense and unhappy for hours. A smack delivered at the right moment may occasionally curb this frightening escalation.

Resolves a stalemate situation

Smacking is also useful when toddlers and parents find themselves locked in a hopeless stalemate situation over some issue that must be seen through to the end. When all else has failed and our authority is on the line, either a short period of Time Out or a gentle smack will usually bring resolution and peace within minutes.

Deterrent to danger

I believe that smacking may be a worthwhile deterrent to ensure that a dangerous life-threatening act is never repeated. I see nothing wrong with giving an immediate smack which will strongly reinforce the message that whatever has just taken place must never happen again. Cats may have nine lives, but as those of us who work in big hospitals know, this does not extend to children. Children only escape once or twice when dismantling electrical appliances, playing with fire or running across busy roads. Even if a painful smack did produce minor emotional trauma, this must be a small price to pay if it prevents the major pain of injury and keeps our children alive and healthy.

Imagine your toddler climbing onto the edge of a high balcony. You can debate democratically saying 'Dear Cedric, that is rather dangerous. It is fifty metres onto the road below and you might sustain a nasty injury'. On the other hand, a smack might do more to engrave the message that this must never happen again.

Conclusion

The purpose of this book is to promote a peaceful life. For some, smacking may be a part of this. It is a form of discipline which, be it good or bad, continues to be used by many good, loving parents. I believe that smacking is a poor form of discipline, but it is used by real parents in real life and I can accept that. It certainly has an effect on a child with a fairly easy-going temperament, though I believe that there are far better forms of discipline for these children.

Parents with a difficult child need all the means of discipline they can muster. However, when discipline is most needed, smacking becomes both ineffective and dangerous. Desperate parents resort to a smack, and when that fails, they smack harder. In no time the situation has escalated to a war footing. Anger, resentment and loss of control set in and the potential for abuse may not be far off.

The firm cuddle method for treating tantrums

Some writers view tantrums differently from you and me. They do not see them as symptoms of militant little people trying to challenge the umpire's carefully considered decision. They believe the tantrum is the sign of children trying to find their inner selves. Instead of ignoring all the wriggling and crying, they recommend that children should be held close against their parent's body until their inner rage subsides. I believe there is too much academic hot air in this textbook technique for the real world people I work with. Of course it has a place when the little one is frightened or frustrated, but in the deliberate limit-testing tantrum, it is not only useless but also dangerous.

When mums are devastated, tired, run down and past thinking about scientific child care, few are capable of being asked to stay locked closely to a wriggling angry child. If methods like this are promoted for the average parent, one might see the incidence of child abuse escalate.

Parents need to remain calm, sane and emotionally in control. With major tantrums, it is best to separate the warring parties so that each has a chance to calm down.

Diversion

Diversion is one of those good old-fashioned remedies that has stood the test of time and still comes out with flying colours. Think back some years to when you were at grannie's, just about to deleaf her pot plants like a dose of Agent Orange. She says quietly, 'I just remembered I have those lollies in the big jar in the kitchen'. With this your hands disengaged from the plant and you were off to the kitchen with the speed of Phar Lap from the gate. With all this never a voice was raised, peace was restored and the plant continued to do its bit to combat the greenhouse effect.

Today's parents can use the same technique with equal success. It is particularly useful with younger children. When it seems you are about to run headlong into a bit of bother, it is often easier to quickly divert the child's attention before the obnoxious behaviour has time to take hold. There is an exact psychological moment that the clever parent can sense and if grasped, the situation is saved before control has been lost.

Some parents take exception to the use of diversion as they believe it deceives children, is dishonest and downright degrading. My answer is simple, it has been used and proved effective for centuries. It works. It prevents fights and helps people live in peace. Anyway, if it is so degrading, why do our politicians use the same technique on us intelligent adults.

Imagine the scene: the talented tantrum-thrower is just about to stage yet another amazing Oscar-winning performance. 'Sesame Street is just about to start,' you say. With this the faint-hearted performer diverts. The militant tantrum-thrower is another matter, dealt with in Chapter 9.

Selective deafness – selective blindness

Peace-loving parents must be careful not to notice and punish every trivial offence. When we overdo discipline, home becomes a place of, no! stop! don't! no! With this we become tense and get into such a negative rut that we wonder what happened to the pleasure of parenting. To keep sane and happy it is best to install a sort of filter in front of your eyes and ears, one that lets you see what matters and shuts out all the rest. This extension of behaviour modification is called selective deafness and selective blindness.

I first discovered this as I watched how husbands react when their wives talk to them. It seems that a line like 'Did you put the garbage out?' often fails to register whilst 'Would you like a can of beer?' seems to squeeze itself along the hearing nerve and be clearly registered by the brain.

I have to admit that I was once troubled by this problem but my medical wife soon sorted it out in her own quiet way. She just booked me into the Hospital Hearing Clinic to get my ears tested and at that point I heard what she was trying to tell me. Selective deafness is of particular use when our little ones abuse us verbally or try out some of those words that were heard, but not taught, at pre-school.

Imagine a 3-year-old militant who is not getting everything his own way. He turns to his mother: 'I hate you'. Now the upset mum gets flustered, feels that the hate is genuine and responds with such effusive assurances of love that it is like a soap opera.

It would have been much better to hear nothing, or if a reply was needed, it was kept short, e.g. 'Well, I love you' and then leave it at that. You don't need to be a psychoanalyst to know that he really does love you. There is no doubt who he wants close by him when he is sick or frightened.

The basis of behaviour modification is to boost the best behaviour so that it will be encouraged, whilst the rest is ignored and underplayed in the hope that it will gradually fade out. Ignoring is one of those things that experts find easy to write about, but we parents find hard to do. I am sure it would be different if I were writing for Wonder Woman or Superman but in the real world we get tired, cease to see clearly and then shoot with both barrels blasting at any behaviour that moves. Parents do best when they aim carefully and shoot only at clear targets. Of course it is impossible to ignore all irritating behaviour but we must try. This is helped along by a bit of selective blindness.

Imagine a 2½-year-old boy who wants to overdose on chocolate biscuits. After three, his mother says, 'That's enough!'. He knows she is a softie and puts on an interesting bit of theatre – he stands running on the spot, in one of those 'vertical type tantrums'. Now, despite all this huff, puff and stamping of feet you must stand firm and put on an even better act. Play this one completely serene, calm and in control like the Mother Superior in *The Sound of Music*. 'That's interesting,' you say as you take a pile of washing, walk out and hang it on the line. Now there are few actors who like seeing the audience walk out in mid-performance and even the most thick-skinned toddler will tend to get the message.

Time Out

Time Out is an excellent technique which quickly brings an escalating situation to an end. It brings rapid results and is useful and calming.

Getting the warring parties to separate

The aim of Time Out is to remove the child from a deteriorating or stalemate situation and place him, for a short time, in another room. This takes the child from his position on centre stage to a less prominent place, where his antics pass unnoticed. He has time to cool off and this also permits the parents to calm down. It takes two to fight and if either party can regain their cool, the exercise has been worthwhile.

Time Out is probably one of the more useful techniques I give to parents who are having great difficulty. It is a safety valve that lets them know what to do when their back is hard-pressed against the wall.

Time Out is probably most effective in the 2 to 10-year-olds but it still can be helpful in those who are very much younger. When all your best discipline has been tried and is getting you nowhere, when you are rapidly losing control and your little one knows it – don't snap, don't smack, use Time Out. Once you shout, argue, become irrational and behave like a toddler, the game is lost.

As with all well-proven techniques, this one also has its critics. Some parents with 'God-given' angels or heads full of theories find it offensive. They also make all sorts of excuses as to why it doesn't work.

That is their business but in my experience Time Out has been a life-saver for thousands of families who are close to snapping. Don't forget, real parents with difficult children do have their breaking point and it is never smart to see how close you can get to this very dangerous situation.

Which room?

The ideal Time Out room would be a dull, quiet place, of easy access but far from all excitement. This is nice in theory but in practice the nearest we can provide is often our child's bedroom.

The experts are quick to tell us that use of the bedroom is a mistake. They believe that the child will associate this room with punishment which develops fears and results in sleep problems. This response, though sound in theory, in my experience has not been proved correct.

If putting a toddler in his bedroom will put him off sleeping, then presumably putting him in the bathroom will put him off washing, the dining room, off eating, the lounge room, off sitting, the kitchen, off dishwashing and so on. I choose the bedroom because it is sufficiently soundproof and far enough away from the rest of the living area to give both parties the space they need to calm down.

The technique

The main purpose of Time Out is not to punish the child but to separate the warring parties and give enough time for both to cool off. As said many times in this book, big bangs start with little triggers and it is much easier to use a method like this to defuse the situation in its infancy than wait so long that you have to mop up after an incident of international proportions.

The technique is simple. When the child reaches a pitch of crying, aggravation or limit-testing that can no longer be ignored, this is the moment to decide whether to plunge into full scale battle or use Time Out. There shouldn't be a moment's hesitation: Time Out it should be.

Calmly take him by the hand or carry him, then decisively put him in his room. Be gentle, and in no doubt that you are going to see this through. Once inside, state clearly in your 'this is the way it is going to be' voice that you are not going to argue but he will stay there until he has calmed down. Then shut the door and move quickly from the scene. For children over the age of 3, a kitchen timer may be useful to show the child the time they are to remain in their room.

Don't lock the door

Time Out in the bedroom must never be mistaken for that unfortunate carry-over from the early 1900s of locking children in their room. This is more likely to terrify than help. It is part of the outdated view that little children should be punished, seen, and not heard, and has no place in day-to-day discipline now.

The naughty corner

Making a child stand in a corner may have worked well in our own school situation but in my experience few parents find it effective in present-day homes. The 1 to 2½-year-old will not understand what it's all about, while with the older toddler, no sooner than your back is turned, the child sneaks out, gaining great pleasure as he winds up his parents. On the other hand he may stay in the corner and gain even more attention with a flow of rude noises, or obscene 'taxi driver' type gestures. For most parents this is a useless form of discipline, which provides the child with little more than an enjoyable game. Time Out in the bedroom is real Time Out.

When Time Out does not work

Sometimes when I have suggested Time Out, parents return saying that it did not work. When I hear this, I know that it has failed for one of a few reasons.

Immediate reappearance

The main complaint is that of rapid escape. The child is put securely in his room and before you have taken five paces he is out the door like a bullet from a gun. I find this can usually be overcome if the parents harden their hearts and are 100 per cent firm at the time of banishment. Little children are very quick to sense when disobedience or a course of whingeing will get them what they want and they are equally aware when their parents are serious and not about to give an inch.

Other parents complain bitterly that the child won't stay in the room. When I ask them where they are at the time of the child's reappearance, I usually discover that it is directly outside the door. Children are not stupid. If they know there is a welcoming party ready to greet them, of course they will come out – anything for a bit of fun and attention.

Other pathetic parents complain that the child is out of the room before they have even turned their back. It seems unbelievable to me that a 2-year-old can run across a bedroom, manipulate a door handle and escape faster than a fit adult can sprint from the scene. If this is the case it might be better to stop complaining and enrol immediately in a fitness class.

In my experience, if the parent puts the child in the room with commitment, closes the door firmly then clears off quickly, reappearance is extremely rare.

Occasionally an escape artist does need some heavier guidance. At the first escape he is put back with complete firmness. The next time the door may need to be immobilised for a short period. It sounds tough but remember Time Out is the bottom line safety valve. This is where you go when everything else has failed.

Screaming and kicking

'Oh, I put him in his bedroom and he screamed and screamed until I had to let him out' is something I often hear. When I ask where

the parent was standing at this time, again the answer is 'Outside the door'. Your toddler may be only $2^1/_2$ but he is exhibiting considerably more intelligence than the parent who hangs around in such a position. Obviously if there is a captive audience listening to every whimper there will be a Royal Command Performance inside. Put him in the room – close the door – go away quickly.

Now and then I hear that Time Out is unsuccessful because the toddler forces the door handle. 'What were you doing at the time?' I say. 'Oh, holding the other handle!' Toddlers love this; it's like being a big game fisherman and hooking a whopper.

Sometimes parents complain that their very young children lie against the door and kick. Generally they only do this if you are within earshot and anyway if a bit of paint is displaced, this is always easier to repair than a parent's shattered nerves.

Wrecking the room

Many parents tell me that they cannot put their child in his room because he is liable to wreck it. In fact most are speculating that this will happen and it is extremely unlikely that they have put it to the test. Over the years I have seen very few children do this when their parents act as though they are in charge.

It is important not to have dangerous or destructive items left lying about. Paints, Textas and anything that makes a mess should be put away.

When a child shares a bedroom with a brother or sister, parents may find it hard to relax, fearing that the angry, attention-seeking toddler will reorganise the other's property. When this is a problem it may be necessary to use another 'neutral room'. When space is really limited, on occasion we have had to resort to a bathroom.

When the captive child does wreak havoc in his own bedroom you are left with three options. You can pretend (with great difficulty) to be completely unimpressed with what has happened and later, when the air is calm, tidy up together. You can pass a firm comment that you are far from happy, and then insist that he should tidy up. Finally, the wrath of God can descend on junior and a message is firmly engraved which states that this is not acceptable behaviour. I would favour the first option but it is best to go with the one that suits you and works.

Example. At about the age of 4 I find some children are bored with being toddlers and make life extremely hard for their mums. One wilful young girl had studied the art of tantrums and was now practising it with savvy. When put in her room she would cool off but then do a bomb job.

When I heard that the very necessary Time Out was being so effectively sabotaged, I started by getting the parents to clear the room of all breakable objects, pens, paint and any other messy substances. The next time she was placed in her room, she did not bother to cry as she knew that a little rearranging of her belongings would have much more impact on her mother. Ten minutes later she came out of the room in perfect control looking extremely pleased. Her mother steadied herself as she glanced in the door to see the bed wrecked and clothes out of every drawer on the floor. But mum had got the message and as she walked past merely remarked 'Oh dear, that looks a bit of a mess'.

The little madam was taken aback as she was sure this would have scored a direct hit on mum's rawest of raw nerves. As she sensed a 'change in the balance of power', she was extremely careful to avoid any tantrums for the rest of the day. Now when bedtime arrived she was sent in to get her pyjamas but returned complaining that she could not find them. 'I think they may be under that pile of clothes,' said mum helpfully. She then asked how she was going to be able to sleep in her unmade bed. 'No problem,' said mum, plonking one blanket from over there and another from that corner over her. The same procedure was followed the next morning when the girl looked for her clean clothes. Again the untidy pile of clothes was pointed out and a message came across in the clearest of terms: wrecking one's room got no major reaction from mother but was a complete pain to the wrecker.

I talked to the mother by phone first thing the next morning and we decided that mother and daughter should set about tidying the room together in an enthusiastic and positive way. All the clothes were gone through and those that were too small were set aside to be sent to the 'needy children'. The toys were tidied and mother and daughter made out a list of possible presents for Christmas, which was fast approaching.

I was impressed with the control and strength of this mother and delighted that the habit which in the past had prevented the effective use of Time Out was quickly extinguished. In the wake of such a showdown, mother and daughter were able to salvage the situation, build a much closer relationship and turn a disaster zone into a fun place to live. The room was never damaged again and surprisingly the tantrums were greatly reduced with less need for Time Out.

While occurrences like this are exceptionally rare, Time Out is an excellent safety valve for all of us parents and if carried out correctly is seldom sabotaged.

Unrealistic expectations

Time Out is often said to have failed when, in fact, it is the parents who have failed to realise what they are trying to achieve. Five minutes in a bedroom does not guarantee angelic behaviour for the rest of the day. No method I know, other than possibly a straightjacket, could ever give such a guarantee.

Many parents expect the child to walk out, head bowed, to stand before them and say, 'Dear mother, I have done wrong and will behave perfectly for the rest of the week'. Others refuse to let the matter rest and constantly remind the child of how naughty he has been. This maintains a high level of tension which is guaranteed to destroy everyone's ongoing happiness. The purpose of Time Out is to allow both parties to cool off and thus prevent major fights.

The child does not have to apologise. The only expectation is that he should re-enter in a more reasonable frame of mind.

Other parents claim that Time Out does not work because the child repeats the original behaviour. If he walks straight out and immediately and defiantly does the same, then he must be put straight back in the room. When parents complain that their child repeats the same behaviour they generally mean that it recurred, an hour later.

Time Out is a technique that defuses a rapidly escalating situation at one particular time. Once this has passed and peace is regained, the method has shown itself to be effective.

Some parents feel they have been cheated when the child goes into his room in mid-tantrum and remains there to play happily with his toys. I must repeat that Time Out is not a punishment; it is a technique aimed at separating two people who are hell-bent on a 'barney'. Whether the child plays with his toys, stands on his head or sings Waltzing Matilda in his room is utterly irrelevant, just as long as he cools off and parents are allowed a little time to relax.

Conclusion

Time Out is a very effective technique when used properly. I use it with toddlers, the disabled, and even some quite difficult older children. It is a powerful method of maintaining peace in the home and if used in the way mentioned, it reduces a lot of emotional tension without frightening or upsetting the child. As the tension settles and the child understands clearly the limits placed on him, this leads to a closer and happier life for all.

Team effort

If you want an adult to do something in the workplace, you use diplomacy. If I ranted and raved at my staff, I would be ignored and then quietly told to 'Take a tablet', if not worse. The diplomatic way is to give a goal, set an example, and lend a hand.

The same applies to the toddler who, after all, is a little adult but twice as stubborn. Often a straight demand will be greeted with a paralytic lack of movement, whereas if you say 'How about us picking up these toys together?' you are in with a sporting chance.

When working with very young toddlers it becomes obvious that they love things to become a game. At this age they may be blind to stains on the carpet, finger marks on the wall and rooms in a mess but they love to help mummy scrubbing, wiping and tidying, as it is fun to be in the centre of activity and attention. It is best for them to be helpers and play friends, an approach which makes for fun, not fights.

With the older toddler and early school child, you can often smooth things along by following a request for action with a consequence they wish for. 'You tidy up your toys and I will get that milk-shake ready for you.' 'You help mummy with the dishes and I will fix the puncture on your bike.' Whether dealing with toddlers or adults, diplomacy, team effort and carrying them along with you, brings about quiet achievement.

Debating, arguing – is there a place for democracy?

With the modern move towards democracy for children, many of today's parents believe that every little detail of what is going on in life must be explained to their toddler. This is a commendable and charitable action but it often leads to trouble when a highly intelligent but functionally blind parent is unaware that he is being manipulated by an infant, barely the height of his kneecap.

An amazing amount of parental energy is consumed each day, arguing, debating and being democratic with little children. It has certainly hit almost epidemic proportions in my practice and seems about as useful as discussing differential calculus with a Masai warrior.

Three- to 4-year-old toddlers love attention and one of the main ploys to guarantee a constant flow of this commodity is to ask endless questions. When you examine what is asked, you will find that their range is remarkably small, little interest is shown in the answers and the same question is repeated again and again, as long as we parents rise to the bait.

Now, to ask lots of questions is a rather quaint characteristic of the young child and should be encouraged up to a point but when debating, questioning and arguing goes on and on, bearing no relationship to the quest for knowledge, that is a different matter. When this verbal ping pong starts, parents must ask themselves 'Is this getting us anywhere or is the real reason for the exercise to stir us up?'.

Take for example the case of an acrobatic toddler who bounces up and down on your new coffee table. You communicate clearly and convincingly that he must get off but he immediately asks 'Why?'. If you are more into democracy than preservation of property, it is all too easy to embark on a long dissertation concerning the lack of strength of modern chipboard furniture, or possibly mention Mrs Smith who lives in the unit downstairs, outlining the characteristics of her nervous disorder that account for her intolerance for loud overhead noise and her sensitivity to large sections of plaster landing from the ceiling onto her lounge-room carpet. All this will avail you nought, when the sole object of the question was to hijack your attention. I believe the question 'Why' can be answered once and after this it is better to divert, become selectively deaf or pull rank and say 'Don't – because I say so!'.

Many of our toddlers are at this moment playing games with their unaware parents. With so many words and so little action, all this verbal incontinence does nothing but stir the home. Educate and listen to little people but when the sole object of the exercise is to wind you up – drop democracy.

Shouting

We all know that we shouldn't shout at our children, but we do. You don't need to have a university degree in communication to know that a bit of volume helps grab a toddler's attention. The trouble is that shouting stirs and often makes behaviour worse.

Young children are extremely easily wound up by noise, activity and tension in their environment. Pre-school directors often tell me that their class becomes almost airborne with the noise and movement of a windy day. At home the more tense we become and the more we shout, the worse our children behave.

Toddlers don't think before they open their mouths, but parents should. Calm is infectious and spreads to those around, so for peace in life, let us aim to keep the decibels down. Communicate important messages clearly and firmly but don't get into a shouting match.

I have to admit that there is an opposite extreme of controlled communication that makes me cringe. Some parents talk to their children with every word carefully articulated, considered and brainlessly boring. It is almost as though they were afraid to relax and act naturally for fear of dislodging a suppository they were trying to contain.

Toddlers are so charged with enthusiasm for life, they need enthusiastic, fun-loving people around them, even if we do occasionally go over the top and shout.

Threats

Thinking back to student days in my home town of Belfast, I clearly remember bus travel to and from the hospital and two things stick in my mind. I will never forget the winter rush hour with its over-crowded buses, their interiors smoky and thick with brown globules of condensation dripping from the roof. The occupants only took their pipes or cigarettes from their mouths to embark on a spasm of coughing that would have done credit to a tuberculosis ward.

Equally vivid is the memory of mothers on buses with their uncontrollable offspring. The trip from the city centre was punctuated with 'Stop that,' 'Do that again and I will smack you,' 'I am warning you,' 'I'll get the conductor to put you off'. Threats, empty threats, are a common and usually futile form of discipline.

Children should know the limits of acceptable behaviour and the consequences if they overstep the mark, but this should not be constantly told to them as a form of threat. It is also important that when you say something is going to happen, then it should be carried out as promised.

On those Irish buses, the children knew their exhausted mothers were all talk and no action. They had heard the threats often before, it was all water off a duck's back, a daily ritual that stirred up the mother and did nothing for the child.

Waving the wooden spoon

Parents who use a belt to threaten their children are a big worry. Though they would have fitted in more comfortably in the early 1900s, I still see a disturbing number and this form of discipline is too close to child abuse for my liking.

Waving the wooden spoon is a more benign pastime and still surprisingly common. From my academic background I don't like the idea but from my pragmatic perspective, if you wave it occasionally and it works well, then I am not going to have a tantrum.

It seems that in Australia, the fly swatter is almost as popular as the spoon. Parents tell me it makes a most impressive swish as they wave it about but it does little other harm, unless you are a fly.

Don't forget that waving spoons and swatters are both forms of threat and there must be so many better ways of helping behaviour without descending to this level.

Negotiated settlement

The technique of negotiated settlement is common in sorting out industrial disputes when the union members may agree to build an extra car a day in exchange for say, longer smoko breaks, and ten weeks' holiday a year. Bargaining with toddlers is usually a complete waste of time but the early school-age child is often interested in coming to such a settlement.

With children over the age of 4, I sometimes get the parents to draw up a list of behaviours they would dearly like to see changed and then balance this with a list from the child. Though we rarely revolutionise the child's behaviour with this method, there is always some improvement.

The youngest age I would use this negotiated settlement is just below the 4-year mark. Most recently I saw a girl of 3 years and 11 months, whose parents were greatly upset that she still liked a dummy with her by day. Now they should have just taken it from her which would have been most appropriate at this age, but they didn't. Instead they went for a gentle negotiated settlement. She was a bright little girl and clearly aware that we lived in a consumer society, so we negotiated this contract in her presence. On her fourth birthday she was to be taken to a large toy warehouse where she would be allowed to choose a special doll. What happened after this had been fully negotiated and went exactly to plan. Both girl and doll would come to the checkout where the shop assistant wrapped the doll but did not hand it over until the dummy had been carefully posted in the nearest rubbish bin. In this case a negotiated settlement passed off without a hitch.

I have to admit it does not always go quite to plan. Trying the same technique on a 3-year-old girl recently wasn't quite as successful. The dummy had been given to the local chemist in exchange for some much wanted item. The next day the little lady woke up and felt that the new item was no compensation for the dummy. While out shopping she whinged and whinged and at the chemist shop demanded to go through the rubbish bins and abused the chemist when she discovered it had gone for good.

Delayed punishment and the removal of privileges

Young children do not have a very far-reaching view of life. For toddlers, an hour ahead, tomorrow or next week is all quite beyond their understanding. Discipline and rewards for the toddler must, therefore, be immediate. Withholding some treat tomorrow or waiting until dad comes home is both unfair and ineffective. If the toddler has to wait until the evening he has long forgotten his misdeed and the delayed punishment will come as a thunderbolt from the blue. This will do more to frighten and confuse the child than it will to improve his behaviour or act as a long-term deterrent. With young children, punish immediately and make that the end of the episode. Young children do not think much about the future or future events, so removal of privileges is a pointless exercise. By the age of 4 or 5 the situation changes when a clear statement can be made as to the standard of behaviour expected and what will happen if it does not occur. The older child who won't do his homework, stays out late, or commits some major transgression can have his television viewing restricted, the front wheel taken off his bicycle, or the productivity bonus removed from his pocket money. (Note, for this older age group, see my book *Beyond Toddlerdom: Keeping five to twelve year olds on the rails*.) In toddlers this is pointless and should not be attempted.

The reign of terror

The reign of terror is an old-fashioned philosophy based on the belief that any child can be battered into shape if the parents are firm enough. This method was popular in Victorian times and many a drawing room echoed to such sayings as 'Little children should be seen and not heard'.

Some parents still believe that a house run on strict, authoritarian lines can create the perfectly behaved child. On the surface this may appear to be the case but underneath such forced compliance lies resentment and potential for rebellion.

Model children produced through intimidation continue to behave well just as long as the threat is present. Once it is lifted they rebel: going wild, getting boozed up or having super orgies when their parents go away for the weekend. They usually leave home at the first possible opportunity, making a rude departing gesture as if to say 'Thanks for nothing'. Like government by intimidation, discipline of children by the same method is only good as long as the repression continues. It never creates respect, long-term stability, independence or happiness.

When on top – keep on top

In my work I watch many parents with young children move from a position of power to one of definite defeat, often within the space of five short minutes. What is worse, these parents usually bring this deterioration on themselves.

At the end of a lengthy interview with a family, all their tired toddler wants is to be shot of my office and get out quickly. At this point there is peace, the parents have been given some practical ideas and their attitude is positive – but then they blow it. 'Shake hands with Dr Green.' 'Say thank you to the nice doctor.' 'Pick up all the toys.' 'Park the tricycle over there – No! move it even further over.' After this the parents drag their feet, fiddle about looking for their car keys and chat to the secretary about the weather before they leave.

By this time the child is protesting, the parents are rising to the bait, the air is full of tension and those who were in charge have carelessly thrown away their previous position of advantage.

When I finish a family session with a twitchy toddler, my door opens and they are out and away immediately. When you are handling material that can sometimes be unpredictable or highly explosive, you don't hang around looking for trouble. Don't release your grip; keep little ones interested and on the move.

When on top – keep on top.

Summary: The techniques of discipline

- Use tone of voice and actions to encourage desirable behaviours.
- Remember the six top tips of discipline:
  1. Reward good behaviour with attention and withdraw it from unwanted behaviour;
  2. Don't over-analyse your child's behaviour;
  3. Divert unwanted behaviour;
  4. Avoid the triggers of unwanted behaviour;

5. Communicate clearly;

6. Ignore the unimportant.

■ Use behaviour modification therapy (behaviour that is reinforced by rewards will tend to be repeated).

■ Smacking is a poor form of discipline, but it is used by real parents in real life.

■ Selective deafness and blindness.

■ Time Out.

N I N E

Dealing with Tantrums and Other Tricks

N ow, after three chapters cram-packed with theory and techniques, it is time to see how all this works in practice. How do
we stay calm as the toddler performs theatrically on the lounge-
room floor? How can you get through to a child who turns deaf the
moment you ask him to help? What about those spectacular
tantrums in the supermarket?

In this chapter we'll look at putting practical discipline into action.

Tantrums

Tantrums are the trademark of the toddler. They start around the first birthday, but generally by the age of 4, most children have learnt that there are better ways to get what they want. As we look around at our adult friends, it seems that a few never grew out of tantrums, lapsing into the most childish behaviour when they do not get their own way.

All children are born different: some are quiet and controlled, with a great frustration tolerance; others come with a remarkably short fuse. To discipline them is like juggling with sticks of unstable gelignite. You are never quite sure when things will go well and when they will blow up in your face.

In the hands of the skilful toddler a tantrum is an art form which can be brought about by a number of different stimuli. Not all tantrums are caused simply by a parent thwarting a wilful child in mid-activity. Some come from the inner frustrations of the toddler himself, who is being stirred up, or is impatient with his lack of ability.

The treatment of the tantrum depends on the age of the child, the reason for the behaviour and where the performance is being staged. In the first year of toddlerhood, before the second birthday, behaviour often just happens, without much thought or reason. Where possible at this age it is best to guide, and be gentle. It is different when you have a 3-year-old who uses a tantrum to openly defy his parents' authority. This is absolutely not on. When authority is challenged, the parents must be consistent and stand firm.

Some toddlers play their parents like poker machines. If their efforts still score jackpots, then they will continue to play. If the parents review their discipline and rig the odds so the toddlers never win, they may crank away but all to no avail. At this point even a 2-year-old should see that it is just not worth the effort.

If a young one becomes frustrated and throws tantrums because he has plans and designs which are way ahead of his technical ability, then it is not punishment he needs but a helping hand and comfort. Any child who is sick or in a home which is upset needs the gentle approach.

Tantrums – the major league

The highest quality toddler tantrums come with all the skill of a Broadway stage production: every detail is designed to elicit the very best audience reaction. Once the tantrum starts, its length and intensity depends on the sort of feedback the actor receives from the audience.

On centre stage is a wilful toddler who is being prevented from doing something or other that seems immensely important to him. He quickly sizes up the situation and makes instant preparation for a spectacular tantrum. First he takes a quick look over his shoulder, to check that the proposed area for a crash landing is clear of hard and potentially hurtful objects. Next he takes a look at the audience, checking that they are well positioned and watching and that the lighting is adjusted to the best effect. Then quick as a flash, he is off. Crash! He hits the floor and the performance has commenced.

Tackling tantrums is easy in theory but never quite as simple in practice.

- The $2\frac{1}{2}$-year-old music lover decides he wants to fiddle with big sister's Walkman. This is not wise; you take it gently from him and place it safely on a high shelf.

- Explain calmly, clearly and in three words or less why he can't have it. He is not satisfied with the situation.

- He ignites his engines and they start to rev up in preparation for take-off.

- This is a good time to divert his attention. 'Here is Dad home early,' you say as you look out the window. 'Oh no, it was another white Ford.'

- This hasn't worked, he is now revved up almost to full thrust. Now a tantrum is inevitable – CRASH! – he hits the deck, arms and legs going with all the grunts, groans, hype and genuine hurt of a professional wrestler.

- Now even the most serene and best adjusted parents are severely stressed. Hands tremble, palms are sweaty, blood pressure has surged, you are close to having a stroke.

- This is the time you should ignore, but this is not easy. Luckily it is sufficient to pretend to ignore.

- Stay calm, don't fuss, don't notice, don't argue, go about your business.

- Move away to a different room. Wash the dishes, peel the vegies, hang out the laundry, get outside for a breath of air.

  Note: *Now think for a moment what is going on in the mind of a tantrum-throwing toddler. Here he is having put on his best Oscar-winning performance and in mid-act the audience has upped and walked out. With most actors if this happened, they would stop there and then, but of course they are not toddlers.*

- Now that the audience has moved away and is ignoring him, the faint-hearted toddler gives up, waves the white flag and with a sniff and sob, goes for comfort. If this happens forgive, forget, don't lecture, be gentle. Don't be over-effusive; after all the victory was the parent's and the tantrum must not gain a great reward.

- Meanwhile, back on the lounge-room carpet, the militant is still in full flight. 'This is a bit off,' he thinks, stomping out after mum and putting on twice the tantrum at mum's feet.

- The volume is now rising, your heels are being kicked and you are rapidly losing your grip. Don't forget that we parents are the big people who should stay in control and in charge. While still on top use Time Out. Lift the little one gently, without anger or hate, and put him firmly and decisively in his room.

- Do this with complete conviction, leaving him in no doubt that you are 100 per cent serious.

- As you leave, say very firmly, in few words, that he must stay until in complete control, then extract yourself rapidly to a distant part of the house.

- Whether he comes out in one minute or in fifteen, the time is irrelevant, as long as the tension has eased and the unwinnable confrontation has passed.

- Forgive, don't point score, don't hold a grudge and get him moving along to some new and interesting activity. Loosen up and leave the tantrum and tension in the past.

The supermarket special

Tantrums are not usually difficult to manage when at home but are a different matter when thrown in some prominent public place. When outside you are much more vulnerable and there are always crowds of interfering people, watching to see how you will extract yourself from some unpleasant situation. What is worse, whatever you do, half the people who watch will think it is wrong. Tantrums whilst out shopping are a real pain. Probably one in six of the parents I see find shopping stressful. Many are ashamed when they are out in public, convinced they are failures who can't control their children.

Don't be fooled, what you see out there is modified by a form of natural selection. Yours may appear the worst in the shop, the mall or even the entire city but there are always many more difficult little ones, whose mothers have learnt from experience not to take shopping. While you are being embarrassed in public, crowds of similar children are left with a neighbour, casual care, or maybe even in a heavily fortified dungeon at grandma's place.

Designers of modern supermarkets have much to answer for as they have created an exciting environment, designed to bring out the worst in a difficult toddler. It starts on the walk from carpark to complex where one finds all those coin-operated rides. For a small sum they will bounce and shake your child but never to the point of complete satisfaction, they must always have another ride. It is best to avoid ever putting a coin in one of these mechanical highway robbers, as once it has been primed, it becomes almost impossible to walk past without fuss. It's like puffing your first cigarette; after a few goes, the habit may be hard to break.

Once inside the shops, the noise and bustle stirs up most children. It is an exciting place and a great learning experience, if they behave. Each child has an individual time limit for shopping and once it has expired every effort must be made to gather up your business and get out as soon as possible. Getting out of supermarkets is never easy, at the best of times, because the checkouts tend to be slow and crowded. To make things worse, the management takes great care to leave rows of sweet stuff beside the queue, strategically placed at knee height.

As you wait, it is not surprising that junior grabs a Mars Bar. He may not know that it is new, improved and 15 per cent bigger but he is quite convinced that he wants it, 'Now'.

You say 'No! – put it back'. He glances at you, now at your most vulnerable with arms full, purse open and surrounded by an audience holding their breath just waiting to see what will happen.

The little one grizzles a bit and you repeat 'No!'. CRASH – now you have a full blown tantrum and if the other shoppers held scorecards this would rate at least 7.6 for style.

Now you have three options:

1. Give in to this blackmail and buy the bar.

2. Try hard to ignore the antics.

3. Deliver a sharp, well-aimed smack.

The trouble is that whatever you do will have its problems:

■ If you weaken and buy the bar, each visit that follows will cost you.

■ If you pretend that you are deaf and walk on quite unmoved, you can hear half the audience mumble 'Disgraceful. A woman like that shouldn't be allowed to have children'.

■ If you smack, the other half says 'Shame, that's a child basher if ever I saw one'.

Your hands seem tied but there are some things you can do. In my experience, most children who throw a tantrum when outside do the same at home. It is sensible to focus first on the tantrums at home and once these have been tidied up, this control usually spreads to outside. If this fails and you still have the supermarket terror on your hands, then only seven options remain:

1. Suffer stoically, buy a rinse to hide the grey hairs and wait for age and maturity to bring about some better behaviour.

2. Use grandma, a neighbour or occasional care, to allow tantrum-free shopping.

3. Use late night shopping or bring your partner on a Saturday as an extra pair of arms, a minder and entertainer.

4. Choose supermarkets that have a chocolate-free checkout and use it.

5. Set up a distraction before you get to the section of the super-market where you know the problem lies. 'Look, there's a man with funny-looking hair!' is always a good ploy.

6. When all else fails, opt for smash and grab shopping. The S and G shopper knows exactly what she wants to buy before leaving home. She enters the supermarket, toddler in tow, with sparks flying from the trolley wheels. She speeds round, scooping products off the shelves, with direction, determination and not a shred of hesitation, then through the checkout, pay and away. If you are lucky, this leaves the stunned little spectator still revving up for his usual supermarket performance, but it is all too late.

7. Get your child to a quiet corner. Crouch down to toddler level, get eye contact and make sure you have junior's attention, then say 'I will NOT take any more of this behaviour.'

He won't do a thing I say

One of the most common complaints I hear from parents is, 'When I ask him to do something he doesn't seem to hear. Could he be deaf Dr Green?'. Well if he is deaf he seems to be able to become 'undeaf' again with ease. Though he does not hear what he is asked, there is no difficulty picking up the hiss of an opening Coke bottle at one hundred paces.

This is not the case for a hearing aid but some simple behavioural encouragement:

- If you don't get a response, don't make a fuss of the event unless you are sure that it is a message which must be registered. (Don't fight over trivia.)

- Communicate clearly – gain their attention and eye contact, then transmit a short, positive statement. Don't nag, otherwise nagging will always be needed to get action.

- Don't slow the pace of life to allow excess time for arguments and debates. Jolly them along, help them, keep the show moving.

- When obedience is really important, repeat with conviction. Then when all gentle techniques have failed, Time Out will clarify who is running the home.

Tidying up toys

Some children seem to be born tidy, while others are quite oblivious to the disaster area they inhabit. The former are easily trained to be neat, the latter will pose a problem, but things can always be improved and made easier:

- Have sensible expectations. Cleanliness and tidiness are possible but not usual in the under 3-year-old.

- Restrict the number of toys on offer. Little children don't need an entire warehouse full of playthings. Put some away, then rotate and reintroduce bringing new interest in forgotten toys.

- Avoid any product which comes apart into twenty tiny pieces. If you don't you will write off weeks of your life, looking for the lost bits.

- Have a big cardboard box for toys and try to establish a habit which encourages it to be filled at the end of play.

- Give a positive statement that it is time to tidy. Softly reward their efforts to help with appreciation. Then move on to some rewarding activity.

I have to admit that teaching tidiness was never successful with my own children. At one point I got so frustrated that I went out and bought a plastic garden rake. This allowed a room to be cleared in seconds, then with a quick burst of the vacuum it looked like new. This was finally sabotaged when an interest developed in glass marbles. These seemed to slip through the rake and then hit the innards of the Hoover like a landmine.

Behaviour – discipline questions

As I have talked to parents over the years, the same questions seem to come up time after time. Many are about sleep, toileting and feeding (see Chapters 10 to 13), whilst the vast majority concern behaviours which are really non-problems which would not arise if we had more enlightened expectations of our little ones. Here follows a list of quick questions, most of which are best answered with understanding, not discipline:

'I tell him no. He stops momentarily, then when I have turned my back he does it again.' This is an example of a toddler who is determined to find out how far he can stretch the limits without getting hurt. If the toddler is clever and his parents lack insight and are blind, it is fun and rewarding to watch us grab the bait.

- Ask yourself if this behaviour is worth noticing. Probably it would be better left ignored.

- If you do respond, be clear, concise and convincing.

- Divert, move them or yourself from the situation, keep little bodies busy.

■ If really important, warn again, then use Time Out.

'Every time I raise my voice to discipline, he disintegrates into floods of tears.' This is a common situation where correct and appropriate discipline backfires leaving the parents punished, confused and feeling guilty. Of course there are a few children who are truly sensitive and must be treated with gentle discipline. Others are little Mata Hari's who use their seductive talents for reasons of subversion. They know they have a losing hand but use tears to trump their parents.

■ With a genuinely sensitive child – stay close, be gentle.

■ Tread carefully in times of separation or family stress.

■ If these antics become a major form of manipulation, stand your ground.

'If I say no, he whinges until I give in.' Little children are extremely clever at getting what they want from their parents. Some have developed whingeing into an art form, which so grates on their parents' nerves, that the most convincing No! can be turned to a yes with only two minutes of torture.

■ Was the issue worth fighting over? Next time don't rise to trivial triggers.

■ Be firm, consistent and convincing. Don't ever give in to the whinge. Divert. Move away.

'Our 2½-year-old grizzles, kicks and complains when putting on her shoes to go out.' This is yet another piece of limit testing, attention-seeking manipulation. They know you have to be up at the school in ten minutes and every delaying tactic is certain to get a good response. It may not be as much fun as being cuddled or read to, but at moments like this they still have 100 per cent of your attention.

■ Be organised, be ready, then move gently but with single minded determination. Transmit clearly who is in charge.

- Be decisive, produce the shoes, put them on.

- Don't allow diversion with complaints about the colour, the style or the socks.

- Don't hang about. Get the show on the road.

'My 2-year-old screams and pushes if any visiting child dares touch his toys.' Young toddlers are not heavily endowed when it comes to socialisation and sharing. They believe they are important people, they know that the toy is theirs, so they expect all intruders to keep their hands well clear.

Don't panic, the fact that your children do not socialise or share at the age of 2 years does not indicate that they will still be mean and antisocial by their twentieth birthday. At this young age they need gentle guidance, after which time and maturity will bring about some major miracles.

- Briefly mention the expectation to share. Don't force the issue, don't make a scene.

- Compensate the empty-handed visitor with the majority share of attention.

- Introduce another area of entertainment. Time Out is not appropriate here, unless there is a repeated heavy assault on the visitor.

'No matter what I say he disputes my decision and argues.' Toddlers will always argue black is white if it gains good attention from their parents. Fighting with little children is pointless and one of those things one learns to avoid. It takes two to fight and if either party stays calm, there is usually peace.

- Communicate positively, clearly and mean it.

- Become deaf to dispute and debate.

- Stay calm. Do not show upset or emotion.

- If the situation escalates, try Time Out.

■ Arguing and debating will not depart overnight, it will take consistency and time.

'You tell us to ignore undesirable behaviour but you cannot ignore him when he is fiddling with the television or video.' Toddlers see adults adjust their electronics and as apprentices to the big people, they copy what they see. To prevent breakages, this must be discouraged and where possible keep vulnerable valuables secure and out of reach. When this is not possible there are several options.

■ Persuade gently that touching will not be accepted.

■ If the gentle approach fails you may need to be tough. Where touching is being done not through natural curiosity but as a deliberate attempt to defy, gain attention and wind up, be 100 per cent firm.

■ Use Time Out as the absolute bottom line.

■ For the very young use a playpen. Put the video, not the toddler, inside. This acts as a palisade to protect your property.

'When out shopping my 2-year-old often attacks other children.' We know by now that many 2-year-olds are lightly loaded with social skills. When out in public some push, nip or throw insults at some innocent infant they pass. This does not come with premeditated malice, it just happens. It may appear a great worry at the age of 2 but don't despair, it will not last long. Socialisation will usually have set in within 6 months or a year at most.

■ When concerned keep the toddler tightly in tow.

■ If this is minor and occasional it may be ignored or given gentle correction.

■ If major hurt is inflicted and repeated, intervene early, warn clearly and be tough.

■ Quickly extricate and don't philosophise.

'When I say no, he goes to his father, hoping to be told yes.' If mother and father are united, no child will bother to play this game. If a toddler ever gets wind of a split in the leadership he will hone in on this and prise it wide apart. Like political parties close to election time, there is room for different opinions in private but the public profile must always be one of complete unity.

■ Remember, united we stand, divided we fall.

Non-problems need no discipline

'He uses the pen by the telephone to scribble on the wall.' Put the pen out of reach.

'My 3-year-old is not as tidy as his twin brother.' Don't compare children. If they were all the same, life would certainly be pretty boring.

'When visitors come I cannot get my child to go to bed.' This seems very sensible. When there is so much excitement around, they want to be part of it. Give them time, have a later bedtime or get a baby-sitter.

'My toddler won't say please or goodbye and cringes when kissed by grandma.' That all sounds pretty normal, they are a bit young to understand these empty adult utterances and kissing probably spreads germs.

'I tried your behaviour techniques but they made things worse, not better.' When children find their old antics don't get results, they have to switch up the volume, which is generally the sign that you are starting to get through. Stick at it for success.

'When dad comes home tired my 2-year-old won't let him watch the evening news.' Why should he? After being apart all day toddlers want to talk and play with dad. Toddlers see the affairs of the family as more important than the affairs of the world. What's more they are right.

'What do you do with a toddler throwing a tantrum in the car in rush hour on the Sydney Harbour Bridge?' This is the sort of impossible question that exhibitionist parents ask in a crowded meeting, knowing quite well there is no answer. Tantrums in the car are often associated with tantrums in the home and these should be treated before focusing on the untreatable.

'My toddler keeps taking chocolate from the fridge.' Don't keep chocolate in the fridge.

'How do I take comforters and cuddly toys from my toddler?' Why should you take comfort from a toddler? There is a move afoot to prise thumbs, pacifiers, cuddly toys and comforters away from children at the youngest age to promote independence. We all need our comforters; why rush children and rob them of their childhood.

'At the end of each meal my toddler throws food on the floor.' He is telling you it is time to wipe his hands, clear the dishes and put him down. Food is for eating and not entertainment. Don't let these aerial food drops be used as attention-seeking antics.

'When his father is away from home he comes to my bed at night.' This sounds sensible. When one parent is away the child often wants to stick close to the other, just in case. Try to return him to his own bed, but go gently. Be really firm when dad returns.

'When I put him to bed he immediately asks for a drink, a wee wee, a brighter light, etc.' Many children procrastinate at bedtime in an attempt to keep those they love close as long as possible. Give lots of attention before you put them down, then be decisive, firm and go.

'On a wet, miserable day their behaviour is awful.' Active little children cooped up with tense parents in bad weather are hard to manage. Try to entertain more, divert and when it gets too difficult, rug up and get out.

'My 2-year-old seems to want snacks all the time and does not eat big amounts at mealtimes.' Toddlers eat when they are hungry and are not governed by our artificial adult mealtimes. Healthy snacks can provide excellent nutrition. If they are thriving, healthy and energetic, with a reasonable diet – relax.

Summary: effective discipline

- Have sensible expectations. A 2-year-old will not behave as an adult.
- Keep temptation away from inquisitive infants. Child proof your home.
- Don't over-discipline. Don't fight over trivia. This makes home negative and causes tension.
- Encourage and reward the good. Ignore and underplay the undesired.
- Don't get this back to front. Take a pace back and check that you are not boosting the bad and missing the good.
- Steer around trouble. Divert. Keep fiddly fingers and busy bodies entertained and active.
- When you mean it, say it with conviction and see it through.
- When losing control use Time Out.
- Some parents will find that an occasional smack will let a child know exactly where the limits lie or abort an escalating, unwinnable situation.
- Avoid no-win situations. Be quick to retreat and regroup when on a losing wicket.
- Remember, tension at home, conflicting opinions and parental point scoring sabotage effective discipline.
- If you love and enjoy your children, then use a form of discipline that feels right and works for you. You can't do better.

TEN

Toilet Training

Despite anxious parents, grandparents, the interfering neighbour and a host of other people who think they know better, children become toilet trained when they, and only they, are ready. No child can be trained until the appropriate nerve pathways have sufficiently matured, a process that is completely outside the influence of even the most brilliant parent or doctor. Once sufficiently mature, the process is controlled by the child's will to comply or his determination to defy, which, in turn, is dependent on the child's temperament, as well as the skill and cunning of the trainer.

It seems that at the beginning of the twentieth century children were trained much earlier than today, with the process starting at about 3 months, and there are many reports of children being completely trained by their first birthday. There was a lot to be said for early training in those days of cold water, poor detergents and washing by hand. It was also a time when people had a great obsession with bodily functions and the clockwork regularity of bowel movements. It was vigorously drummed into new mothers that if the baby was started off on the right path in his earliest months, he would be saved in later life from the scourge of constipation. Most of what was labelled as toilet training was in fact an unrecognised, involuntary bodily reflex – Toilet Timing. Although we are now 100 years on, the myth of early toilet training still confuses and worries parents.

Most toilet training difficulties today are really non-problems caused by unrealistic expectations and misleading advice. Parents often start training too early, motivated by ideas more akin to the 1900s than to the 2000s. Turn a deaf ear to all those well-meaning but interfering friends and family. Do not start too early: this invariably leads to unnecessary problems. Remember that the child alone has the ultimate power to go where and when he wishes. Don't hurry, don't fight, just relax.

Toilet timing, toilet training

Babies, from their earliest days, tend to empty their bowels or bladders when their stomachs are full after a feed. This is a completely reflex action, being no more clever or voluntary than a knee-jerk reaction. If a child is put on the potty after a meal there is a sporting chance that something will 'pop out'. This is most interesting but it is nothing to get excited about. This is toilet timing.

Toilet training is something completely different. Here an older toddler uses his brain to decide whether he wishes to go to the toilet and then makes a deliberate attempt to oblige. This is a voluntary action and the child is in full control.

Most of the crazy ideas concerning early training are put about by those interfering know-alls who mistake toilet timing for toilet training. No child is toilet trained at the age of 1 year, and children who give this appearance are just demonstrating a particularly strong toilet timing reflex. The effect may reduce the load on an overworked washing machine but this is a temporary lull, often relapsing as soon as the child starts to exert voluntary control.

Toileting: normal development

During the first $1^1/_2$ years of life there is no proper bowel or bladder control, just the toilet timing reflex. As the child approaches 18 months this reflex appears to weaken and voluntary control begins to take over.

It is pointless to consider serious toilet training until the child knows at least when he is wet or dirty. The realisation rarely dawns much before 18 months of age. In the months that follow this discovery, the child becomes aware of his toileting needs before the event rather than after. This great breakthrough occurs somewhere between 18 months and 2 years of age, but with urine training there is one unfortunate flaw. Although warning is given, the child's alarm system is only adjusted to tell of the impending puddle 5 seconds before it arrives. By the age of 2, the amount of warning has increased and you can start to notch up a few successes. At about this time bowel control will also become established, in some children before urine control and in others after it. By the age of $2^1/_2$ years, over two-thirds of children will be dry most of the time; the majority can take themselves to the toilet and handle their pants without too many mistakes. At this age night-time wetting also starts to come under control, the child initially needing to be lifted onto the toilet in the middle of the night, and later holding on unaided. Although most children are dry and bowel trained by the age of $2^1/_2$, the whole procedure is still surrounded by a great sense of urgency – the child needing to go 'now' rather than when it suits the parents.

In toilet training development, there is a great variation from child to child. There is a strong relationship with family history, and parents with late bladder training, especially at night, frequently find that their children are endowed with similar characteristics. Girls tend to become trained slightly earlier than boys, possibly because of their slightly more advanced development, different anatomy or, perhaps they have a more compliant personality at this age. Early training is no more a sign of intelligence than early development of teeth. As far as I am aware intelligence comes from the brain, an organ somewhat distant from the bladder.

Our teaching today is clear:

■ Eighteen months is the earliest age to consider toilet training.

■ Two years is probably a more realistic time and if you wait till 2¹/₂, it won't worry me.

■ The average young Australian will be night trained at 33 months.

■ The normal young Australian will become night trained somewhere between 18 months and 8 years.

■ One in ten of all normal 5-year-olds still wet at night. That is three in every kindergarten class at school.

■ If one parent was not night trained before the age of 6 years, 40 per cent of their children may follow suit.

■ If both parents were not night trained before the age of 6 years, 70 per cent of their children may follow suit. (Children – please choose your parents carefully!!!)

■ Forcing little children causes tension and tension causes little humans to clamp closed all bodily openings. Don't force – relax. Relaxed little children find toileting easiest.

The fundamental rules

1. A child must first learn to sit on the toilet before he can learn to open his bowels on that toilet.

2. A child must know the difference between the feeling of wet and dry before he can be bladder trained.

3. A child must be able to produce some dry nappies at night before you can expect a dry bed.

These are my basic rules for toilet training children. It seems pretty obvious that you have to sit before you can perform on a toilet. Seagulls may be able to do it as they fly over Sydney Harbour, but little humans need to be firmly in place if they are going to hit the target. It is equally obvious that you are wasting your breath trying to convince a youngster that he should have done his wee wee in the toilet when he is quite oblivious to the fact that he has just done it in his pants. If the nappies have been consistently wet every night, it stands to reason that if you remove them the bed will become wet every night.

Bladder training

Some time after 15 months of age little children start to realise when they are wet and they don't like the feeling.

The majority just set to and bladder train themselves. They see mum doing it every day, they love to copy their mum. They sit, then one day they surprise themselves.

There is, however, a certain sub-group who seem quite oblivious to the feeling of wet, much to their parents' despair. We do have a simple cure – trainer pants. Now if you get rid of the well-insulated nappy and trade it for a pair of these thin towelling pants, you are in with a chance. They may do little to protect your best Berber from seepage but when wet they evaporate and cool. As the wind whistles off the high hills, the chill factor increases in the lower regions and brings icy feelings to sensitive spots! Now they know they are wet and you are in business.

Pants have the added advantage of being quick-release. This is of great benefit given the precarious state of toddler urgency. Now they know they are damp, it is time to encourage them to sit regularly each day, if they are not already doing it. Put them on the pot at times of coming in and out of the house, as well as all major meals and minor snacks.

Some children will be enthusiastic and keen to oblige while others with a negative streak will use it as an excuse to exert some of their excess power. Forcing is a complete waste of time.

If they sit you encourage, if they rebel you ignore. If something happens you praise, if they do nothing you keep going with patient optimism. When handled in this gentle way, bladder training will rarely cause problems.

The plan

- Are they old enough to start training?
- Do they know the difference between wet and dry?
- If your carpets can cope, use pants.
- Sit regularly before mealtimes and as a double act when toileting yourself.
- Don't force, don't stir, drop subtle hints of encouragement.
- When it eventually happens, notice and reward.

Bowel training

There are many different ways of bowel training a toddler. Most are effective as long as they are not started too early and not pushed too hard. There are three methods that you might consider:

- the 'grunt and catch' method;

- the 'broody hen' method; or

- the 'sit and wait' method.

The 'grunt and catch' method

This method is self-explanatory. The parents do nothing until they hear a grunt, and see that strange look which appears at times like these on the toddler's face. This is accompanied by an ominous silence, an odd posture and finally a characteristic smell. At the first sign, the child should be rushed to the pot in anticipation of the big event. This may be easy in theory but it often fails in practice. Firstly, the parent needs all the speed of an Olympic sprinter to reach the toilet on time and the dexterity of Houdini to untangle the obstructing nappy. Then, if all goes smoothly and the child reaches the pot on time, there is a sporting chance that he will then announce he has changed his mind. It is not a bad method to try, but I suggest it be used only as a back-up to the more reliable sit and wait method.

The 'broody hen' method

This is my term to describe one of the common but perhaps slightly bizarre training methods. When the child dirties his pants, he is immediately taken to the potty instead of being changed. Here, his offering is placed in the sacred chamber, and the child is made to sit above it like a hen incubating a newly laid egg. This is a form of conditioning, getting the child to associate bowel motions with the toilet. I know many parents who swear by this method but I find it a bit weird.

The 'sit and wait' method

This is the best way to train all toddlers, whether they are malleable or militant. The method is not very scientific but is just a large chunk of good, old-fashioned commonsense. Start with Green's first rule of toilet training – a child must first learn to sit on the toilet, before he can learn to open his bowels on that toilet.

Initially you use gentleness and guile to achieve a regular sitting habit. Once this is established you give a discreet emotional nudge of encouragement which plants the seeds of success. If you establish these good routines, encourage and don't force, eventually it will happen and then you set off the fireworks.

Don't commence training until both child and parent are ready. Eighteen months is the absolute earliest, 2 years is more sensible and a 2½ year start would not worry me, though it might wear out your washing machine.

Like so much in this book, this is not going to work unless the parents are fully committed and prepared to persevere with the technique. If you don't feel strong enough to see it through at present, then wait a while. If home is in turmoil with visitors, a new baby, holidays, illness or family tension, there will be more success if you postpone until the dust settles.

The method starts by getting the toddler to sit happily and regularly on the potty. Aim for three sits a day, preferably after meals. The secret of success is to make this fun. 'How about sitting on the potty? I'll read you that story we had last night. Once upon a time there was a girl called Goldilocks who went into the wood one morning . . .' Maybe at such a young age they don't understand the finer points of Goldilocks but they sure understand the meaning of being the focus of all attention at centre stage.

This is another application of behaviour modification, the technique that is behind most of the methods in this book. The idea is to encourage the desired behaviour – sitting, and not make a fuss of the undesired – refusal to sit.

The trouble is that it can be all too easy to get this back to front. Fighting over toileting often backfires on us parents. Imagine the scene, you have dragged him to the toilet, and say sternly, 'You will use the toilet at once!'. With this the eyes twinkle with devilment and a little smile comes onto his face, as he says to himself, 'That's what she thinks!' You force him to sit for five minutes before realising you are beaten. It is unfortunate that this is often not the end of the saga. Ten minutes later junior reappears, a coy smile on his face, nappy at half mast and an interesting manurial odour in the air. Now you have got your just reward. Getting worked up over toileting leaves the child with a trump card that can be used mercilessly to batter the parents when the spirit or bowel decides to move.

As for the length of sitting, that will depend on the child. Some active toddlers find it almost impossible to sit for two minutes, while others are content to remain in an almost catatonic state for most of the day. The law of diminishing returns operates here, however, and if there has been no sign of action after five minutes, then there is little point in prolonging the process.

Once the sitting habit is firmly established, it is time to engage in a little amateur psychology. Gentle hints are dropped to get them thinking positive thoughts about a bit of action. 'Gosh, you are almost 2 and big 2-year-old girls do poos in the potty.' 'We could give all the nappies away and get new pants.' 'Grandma is going to be pleased.'

What you say is nothing more than a gentle emotional nudge. It must never suggest anxiety, frustration or impatience on your part. Remember, you can only make them sit, they have the ultimate control over what happens and they know this. Even if two minutes after leaving the pot empty they dirty their pants, this must be dealt with calmly, saying nothing more than 'Next time you may do a pooh on the potty – Daddy would be proud'.

If the child sits regularly, is relaxed, encouraged and not forced, eventually something has to drop out in the pot. At this age soft rewards of fuss, attention and praise are best. Grandma is contacted and dad dragged to the phone at work to hear the piece of earth-shattering news. This may seem a bit over the top but it works.

Once training is established there remains an air of urgency for some time before it becomes more stable. Relapses are very rare except in times of diarrhoea, constipation or sickness.

A mother once told me how she toilet-trained her son. Her husband worked at the North Head Sewage Plant in Sydney where the sewage is treated and collected before being pumped out to sea. The mother would say to her son, 'John, sit on the toilet and do something – pass a message down the pipe to Dad.'

The plan

- Start after 18 months of age at a time when both parents and child are ready.
- Sit the child three times a day after meals. Make it fun. Never force. Don't make a fuss over defiance.
- Once sitting is established give a gentle emotional nudge and then wait patiently.
- When the big day arrives – set off the fireworks!

The untrained 3-year-old

As the author of *Toddler Taming*, I get hundreds of requests for help each year. One of the most common is from the parents of the 2½ to 3½-year-old child who refuses to use the toilet. These parents often feel that they are the only ones in Australia who cannot toilet train their toddlers. 'What have I done wrong?' they write. The truth is they have done nothing wrong and thousands of other parents are in exactly the same boat.

It is very difficult to deal with children who scream and protest if you as much as take them near a toilet, then wriggle off in seconds, or sit stubbornly but don't deliver. After a year which started out gently and degenerated into forcing, pushing and punishing, the tension level is now running extremely high. At this point both toddler and parent have dug in for a siege and while in that position, neither they nor their bowels are likely to move.

The best course to steer now is to back right off, cool down and put all the fights and failures of the past year behind you. Defuse the tension by suspending all attempts to train, as a first step. Once calm is established, all attention must focus on sitting. Gently and cunningly build up a good sitting habit, then sow the seeds of success, stay cool, wait and reward when the big day comes. This approach will work with both the child who has never been trained and the one who has regressed. With this latter group a medical opinion is wise, to ensure they are not overloaded and constipated.

When refusal to sit has become an insurmountable barrier to training, it is easy and possibly correct to interpret the show of hysterics as a sign of tension or fear of a painful toileting experience in the past. Whether this is true, or whether they just got off on the wrong foot, an alteration of attitude usually secures success.

The majority of these apparently impossible toileters start to sit when there is calm and their parents approach them in a confident and convincing way. Occasionally one needs to resort to a little desensitisation. This starts with the potty in front of the television, the child seated with trainer pants in place. From here there is a gradual move to no pants, no television and no nonsense.

Toddler bed wetting

Most doctors say that bed wetting (nocturnal enuresis) is so common in the toddler that it is a 'non-problem'. This may be scientifically quite sound but it offers little comfort to parents who know that their child is still wetting the bed, whereas their friends' children were all dry by the time they were 3.

The average age of attaining night-time dryness is about 33 months, but 10 per cent of 5-year-olds still wet their bed regularly. After this age, about 15 per cent of them are cured of the habit each year, until it becomes relatively rare in the teenager. The parents of the 5-year-old who wets his bed must be reassured that, although other parents are not openly declaring the fact, two other children in their child's class will also be regular bed wetters.

Delay in bladder training at night seems to have an extremely strong genetic relationship. Some studies show almost 70 per cent of wetters have a parent or sibling with a similar problem. Bed wetting is also more common in boys; while I find that day-time wetting in the older child is almost completely confined to girls.

Some doctors get very worked up when they hear of a dry child who regresses to becoming a wetter again. They believe that this secondary enuresis is caused by infections or emotional trauma. Certainly infections can cause a relapse but other unmistakable symptoms such as urgency or pain are usually very much in evidence. As for emotional trauma, it may well be a triggering factor but in most of the children I see, I doubt whether even Sherlock Holmes could find the real trigger.

Treatment for bed wetting

The best time to start night training is when a few nappies have made it unannointed through the hours of darkness. Attempts can be made before this but it tends to be a long uphill battle.

When you move from having a couple of dry nappies each week to using no nappies at all, this change often acts as a catalyst to speed up the night training process. Though getting rid of the nappies at this time usually brings training together, some toddlers seem to stick with watery beds with no relief in sight. Now you have to make a decision whether to reintroduce the nappy and relax or try some other tricks.

Some parents believe that restricting the fluids you offer in the early evening will do much to reduce the wetting. Unfortunately most experts claim this does not work, but experts are not necessarily right. From my simple way of thinking, it seems that what goes in must eventually come out and if it doesn't go in it is less likely to leak out. I am told that this is faulty logic, but for your child you must be the judge.

Many parents find that if they get the toddler up and put him on the toilet late at night, just before they go to bed, this greatly increases the chances of a dry night. This is a sound idea, just as long as the child doesn't become too distressed and as long as it works.

When the toddler has a dry bed, that is the time for encouragement and praise. When the bed is wet, notice is made of it but there is no fuss, punishment or implied blame. I remember asking a rather silly mother if she punished her child when he wet the bed. Her answer was: 'No, I don't punish him, I just rub his nose in it'.

We know that when you start to get a number of dry nappies you stop using them altogether, but what do you do if you never see a dry nappy? Whether dry or wet there comes an age when nappies have to go. This is some time about 4 years of age, but it depends on how the child handles the wet nappies and how you handle wet beds.

When 4 years old, out of nappies and still untrained, there is little more to do but wait. Some suggest star reward charts to encourage them to 'think dry', but in my experience soundly sleeping children have little interest in my stars. It used to be popular for paediatricians to prescribe a medicine for the older wetter, which had some effect. This is out of fashion at present and even though it often works, the effect only lasts as long as the prescription.

However, a new preparation, desmopressin, is becoming much more popular. This is an antidiuretic hormone that acts through the pituitary gland in the brain and reduces the amount of urine released by the kidneys. It has a relatively short period of action so it is given last thing at night.

Initially desmopressin was used to provide temporary protection for sleepovers and camps. But there is now a body of research that shows good results with no side effects for periods of six or even twelve months. As with imipramine, those who have not resolved spontaneously in this time will relapse when the drug stops.

Desmopressin is currently given by a nasal spray but an oral preparation will soon be released. The dose needs to be adjusted to suit the individual child, so it must be trialled well before the child departs for camp. Most but not all children get a good response.

At the age of 6 years, a bright light appears at the end of the tunnel. This is in the form of the electronic bedwetting alarm. This gadget has two electrodes in the bed, kept apart by a thin dry sheet. When the bed gets wet the sheet shorts out and bells start to ring. With this, parents descend like a swarm of chamber maids, sheets are stripped, bed remade, new pyjamas supplied, alarm set and off again. No-one seems sure why this works but in children 6 years and over, more than two-thirds will be dry within a month. If you have a wetter of this age, don't psychoanalyse the situation, book in for an alarm and get results.

When a child is ready to train he has no respect for the seasons, but when possible try not to begin in a cold wet snap. For a start the sheets will be hard to dry but also it is less likely to be successful. When a warm child lies in a warm bed, he sweats and loses fluid. When a cold child lies in a cold bed, there is little reason to sweat and the fluid may choose another route for escape. This leads to a full bladder, probably a wet bed and cold parents who have to change the clothes.

Summary

- The time to night train varies greatly from child to child. The average is 33 months but the range of accepted normal is anything from 18 months to 8 years.

- When you find a number of night nappies make it through to morning still dry, it is time to take them off. For most this accelerates the training.

- If bladder control remains unreliable, lift and take the child to the toilet before you go to bed. This suits some and helps them stay dry.

- If you have no success by the age of 4 years, night nappies must soon be withdrawn, leaving the load on the washer.

- Medication is known to help some but the effect is temporary.

- Star charts are more use for astrologers than night wetters.

- When 6 years and still wet, get a bedwetting alarm. The results are excellent.

Potty or toilet?

A decision that parents have to make is whether to train toddlers to use the toilet or a potty. There is no right answer to this; the method of using them is more important than the equipment itself.

Most parents start their child sitting on the potty, and most toddlers prefer this to the toilet. It has the great advantage of being portable, so it can be taken from room to room and even out in the car. There are, however, a number of independent little toddlers who are bored with being children and who wish to use the toilet like grown-ups. If this is the case, I offer the following suggestions.

Sitting perched high on the toilet with legs waving in mid air is not the physiologically ideal posture for moving one's bowels. If the child is using a toilet, I recommend bricks or a step under his feet. This makes it easier for the child to climb up, and gives support for his legs when pushing down. A small child's toilet seat should be put inside the adult one which gives more stability and dispels any fears of falling into the bowl. Whatever you do, don't flush when they are still sitting, or they will think they are about to blast off and join the astronauts.

Chain flush toilets are pretty obsolete now but I remember in one old hospital where I used to work there were vintage toilets in the children's wards, which gave one adventurous toddler a most terrifying experience. After using the toilet, he climbed on to the seat, just managing to grasp the dangling chain before losing his balance. The toilet started to flush, and still holding on tight, he hung like Indiana Jones over the raging whirlpool below. Eventually, as his strength ebbed, he fell, becoming wet to the knees and having his toilet training delayed by at least six months.

The right thing in the wrong place

Some children have good control of their bowels but they insist on displaying the fact in various places around the house and garden. This can cause anxiety and anger in parents, many of whom believe that it is an early sign of deviant behaviour. All that needs to be done is to quietly mention to the child that this is not welcome, and give great rewards when the right thing is done in the right place.

Boys: should they sit or stand?

Some experts philosophise painfully over the pros and cons of whether little boys should learn to wee standing or sitting. It honestly doesn't matter one little bit. If you opt for standing, urine training may come fractionally faster due to the rewards of hearing so much tinkling water and also being in charge of one's own equipment.

There are, however, several drawbacks. Toddlers at this age are prone to what I call the 'Fireman Syndrome' – they are hellishly inaccurate and spray water all over the place. In addition, some get so carried away with this new skill that it's almost impossible to ever get them to sit. So you've promoted urine training but delayed the bowel habit.

In the first edition of *Toddler Taming* my only cure for inaccuracy was to remove all carpets from the bathroom, after which you had to call in the plumber to insert a big drain and then all you had to do was hose the scene down with great regularity. I have now discovered a better, and dare I say, more scientific, way. Tear up some bits of paper and roll them into little balls. Drop these into the pan and there before your very eyes floats the entire Australian navy just waiting to be bombed into oblivion by the better aiming toddler. Alternatively you may drop a ping pong ball in the bowl and encourage your little bomb-aimer to sink the *Bismarck*.

If your child gets locked into standing and resists sitting, don't worry, this is only a temporary problem and easily rectified by using one or other of the methods outlined in the next section.

The reluctant sitter

I have seen children from 2 to 12 years old who refuse to sit on the toilet. This bad habit may be due to pure stubbornness, to being too busy to spare the time, to fear of toilets, or to the pain of trying to move constipated bowels.

No child of any age should be forced, but rather encouraged. With the very young, I get the parent to read to the child as he sits on the potty, initially with his nappy on. Once the sitting has become an established pattern, then the nappy can be removed. If he leaves his seat prematurely, there should be no fights, but the reading and the attention simply stop. Most young children respond very well to this simple technique.

For those who are frightened of being left in the toilet, it is best if the mother initially stays near by, gradually moving away until eventually the child learns to 'fly solo'.

Other children will establish a good sitting pattern if rewarded with praise and attention when they comply. In the older child (over 4 years), I use a star reward system which is very effective, or I negotiate a simple, no-fuss agreement such as, 'You go and sit and I will have a milkshake waiting for you when you come out'. Strong-arm tactics do not work on toddlers. There are much easier ways of getting things done. If the child has been constipated and possibly also has a small tear in the anal area, there may be great fear of using the toilet. Laxatives and faecal softening agents are useful, as well as a little lubricant gel for the tail end.

139

Toddler urgency

When you are out shopping with a toddler, you learn very quickly that when he says 'Wee wee, now,' he means *now* – and not in five minutes. At this age, parents are forced to throw modesty to the wind, aiming the child towards the gutter or helping him water the flower arrangement outside the Town Hall. Car travel is also difficult, with frequent stops often being required, usually in places where it is impossible to pull over.

Urgency is normal in toddlers. Small patches of dampness appear, particularly when the child is excited or engrossed in play. Major accidents also happen for at least a year.

Rituals

Some children will engage in quite extraordinary parent-manipulating toilet rituals. A stubborn little 3-year-old girl I saw recently had it down to a fine art. She had been bladder trained long before but when it came to bowel motions the fun really started. When such a motion seemed imminent she summoned her mum. A warm, freshly laundered nappy had to be brought and carefully pinned in place. The little dictator then gestured the family to assemble at the dining table. She sat in her chosen chair, her favourite doll seated on her right-hand and mum on her left. Then her favourite book was opened at a special page and placed in front of her. Then, when all was exactly to her liking, she gave a great heave and peace was restored for another day.

The cure for all this followed a rather bumpy course. As a first shot I got all her nappies donated to a newborn baby down the road. Our little lady's response was swift. She entered a stage of concrete constipation. A large dose of laxative was administered which worked like a dream, the trouble was that the resultant movement was in her pants. At this point mum and I wondered if dirty pants were really any sort of improvement on the ritual. But we were pursuing greater goals and persevered, and with a great deal of guile and gentleness a good sitting habit was started and in three weeks we had achieved a complete cure.

The obsession with regularity

Parents' concern over what goes in the feeding end of their child is rivalled only by their obsession as to what comes out at the other. It is best to interfere as little as possible with toddlers' bowel patterns; there is a wide range of normal, which nature usually takes care of quite adequately. An eminent doctor once claimed that the normal toddler's bowel habit was between five times a day and once every five days. This may be a rather extreme view, but it is probably more sensible than many parents' over-concern.

The two common conditions that upset parents most are constipation and diarrhoea. Some children are born with a 'sluggish' bowel and always tend to be constipated. Others become constipated as a result of bad toilet habits, and others have problems that started following a feverish illness. Whatever the cause, parents need reassurance that, though it is best for bowels to open every day, this does not always have to happen. A bowel pattern as irregular as, say, once every three days, does not cause headaches, bad breath or lack of energy. Constipation does, however, lead to a vicious circle in which the more constipated the child becomes, the more difficult it is to pass a motion, and the more reluctant the child is. If this is associated with a small tear in the anal margin, the resultant pain may cause a major problem of withholding.

Diarrhoea can occur as a result of the slightest variation of diet or even minor illness. There is a strong relationship between the extremely active child and an extremely active bowel. There is also a condition known as 'toddler diarrhoea'. The child passes many motions a day, which are often very watery and usually contain undigested peas, carrots and other bits of fibre. Toddler diarrhoea is benign and temporary. Treatment for it is covered in Chapter 12.

Conclusion

You can't go far wrong, just as long as you don't start too early, don't force the child, and just take your time. As the poet said: 'They also serve who only stand and wait.'

ELEVEN

Sleep Problems – the Answers

Toddlers who don't sleep well can be the cause of great unhappiness to their parents. Sleep deprivation, as any well-practised torturer will avow, is a sure method of breaking your spirit, determination and ability to think clearly. The mother who says, 'He's not getting enough sleep,' is in fact talking in code. What she really means is, 'Forget the kid, I'm a walking zombie'.

The night-time antics are really only half the story. It is the aftershock the next day that causes the real harm. Then a tired, irritable mum with a befuddled brain has to struggle valiantly to manage a tired, irritable and unreasonable toddler. The result is often complete disaster.

As far as my work is concerned, sleep problems are probably the speciality of the house. My interest started in 1974 when I became disturbed at how many parents were suffering because of their little insomniacs and how hopeless most of us professionals were at helping.

At that time there were four popular ideas on treatment. Some childless doctors suggested that you let the hysterical child cry all night, whilst others recommended a strong sedative. Philosophers believed it was a mother's duty to be up all night, every night, with her crying child, no matter how it disturbed her. Then there was the psychodynamic view that all sleep problems were caused by separation anxiety and if we improved the relationship with our children by day, the sleep problems would disappear.

Of these the only idea that worked consistently was to let them cry for long periods. Unfortunately this also unnerved the parents and as the children became hysterical it did no good for them either. In the end it was this method which I modified, taking its strengths and discarding its upsetting elements, to become the foundation of my controlled crying technique.[4]

If you are an exhausted reader, with a sleepless toddler, relief is now in sight. The methods that follow offer a 90 per cent chance of cure within a week.

The science of sleep

Let us start by getting the science of this straight. Sleep is not one consistent state of unconsciousness, it is a cycle of deep, light and dream sleep punctuated with regular brief periods of waking. Brain-wave studies (EEGs) back this up. These show a different electrical pattern for each stage. First we drift off to sleep, then hit the deepest plane of unconsciousness, we dream for a while, then lift to a lighter state before coming briefly to consciousness, to stretch, turn over then drift off again for a re-run of the cycle.

These electrical tracings indicate that the average newborn has a sleep cycle of just under 1 hour, a toddler about $1\frac{1}{4}$ hours, whilst we adults go about $1\frac{1}{2}$ hours between awakenings. Other studies confirm this. One of particular interest recorded children with a video camera as they slept in their own homes[5]. Parents of the children studied believed that their little ones were sleeping soundly right through the night, but the recordings showed otherwise. It appeared that even apparently good sleepers may wake a number of times to sit up, look around, play with their toys, kick off their covers, then perhaps have a quiet grizzle before slipping back to sleep. We have to accept that all humans will wake regularly each night, but we do not have to accept that human children should disturb their parents when they do wake. As adults we surface regularly to hear a window rattle, notice it is still dark or that the clock say one minute past three. We register this then turn over and zzzzzz, we don't kick our partner and say 'Hey, it's one minute past three. How about getting me a drink?'. The same must apply to children. They can kick, wake, grumble and make some noise but they cannot expect you to share in their nocturnal activities. Waking should be discouraged, not encouraged, but we often get this back to front.

Think for a moment from the toddler's point of view. You are 16 months of age, you dream, then lighten a bit, and as you come near the surface you stretch and grizzle. A minute later as you open your eyes there out of the darkness a breast approaches. That's great, then, zzzzzz, down once more to the deep. An hour later you come to the surface, grizzle, the eyes open and there it is again! You have learnt that a good grizzle or a grumble makes a breast appear, and now you believe in the Genie of the Lamp. If mum can do this and still feel rested, that's fine. If not, she now has a problem.

It is normal for children to wake briefly throughout the night but toddlers should be encouraged to act like adults and learn to settle themselves back to sleep.

The statistics of sleep

No two studies have ever shown exactly the same incidence of sleep problems in a population but a few figures are shown in Table 2 that give some insight into how other people's children behave at night.

Table 2: A profile of some sleeping habits[6]

Problems	Percentage of age group				
	1 year	2 years	3 years	4 years	5 years
Wakes once or more every night	29	28	33	29	19
Wakes at least one night each week	57	57	66	65	61
Requires more than 30 minutes to fall asleep	26	43	61	69	66
One or more 'curtain calls' before settling	14	26	42	49	50
Requests comforting object to take to bed	18	46	50	42	20
Goes to sleep with lights on	7	13	20	30	23
Nightmares at least once every two weeks	5	9	28	39	38

The Chamberlin study in New York found that 70 per cent of 2-year-olds, 46 per cent of 3-year-olds and 56 per cent of 4-year-olds regularly resist going to bed; 52 per cent of 2-year-olds and 3-year-olds and 56 per cent of 4-year-olds regularly wake up during the night; 17 per cent of 2-year-olds, 18 per cent of 3-year-olds and 36 per cent of 4-year-olds regularly have nightmares.

By comparison, studies in the United Kingdom gave lower figures for waking at night with only 27 per cent of 1 to 2-year-olds and 14 per cent of 3-year-olds doing so. Another survey in the United Kingdom found that 37 per cent of 2-year-olds living with their parents were waking up at nights. These were compared with children of the same age who lived in a residential nursery and found that only 3.3 per cent awoke at nights.

This lends weight to my own belief that the more readily available the comfort at night, the worse the sleep pattern of the child. Certainly when the child enters a period of semi-wakefulness, he is more likely to roll over and go back to sleep if he realises, from past experience, that crying does not bring rapid Grade A attention.

When is waking at night a sleep problem?

What appears to one family to be a massive sleep problem may not concern the next. A problem is, therefore, only really a problem if parental well-being and happiness are compromised. A child who wakes up four or more times a night may not necessarily have the worst sleep problems. He may merely wake, cry briefly and go straight back to sleep after a reassuring pat on the back, and the parents may return to sleep within seconds with no real problem occurring. Another child may only wake once or twice in the night, but each awakening may be followed by considerable difficulties before sleep returns. By the time the parents have paced the floor and bounced the child up and down, the child may be fast asleep again but the parents are wide awake, wound up and incapable of further sleep.

It's not the number of times a child wakes up at night that constitutes a problem but the effect this disturbance has on those around.

I am constantly criticised by influential experts who found their own children no hassle at night and from such a fortunate position judge my methods as unnecessary and extreme. They are welcome to their views but if your experience is different and sleep deprivation is removing much of the happiness of life, ignore such opinions, read on and the chances are you will soon have a complete cure.

Just who suffers

I used to think that it was only parents who feel the effect of sleepless nights, but that is wrong. The shock waves are felt by all around. They influence the mother, father, other children, the neighbours and most of all, the child himself. Each year hundreds of parents write to me, with a simple message: 'Since sleep returned, home life is ever so much happier. Once again I am enjoying my children'.

Parents

Mothers who have not had enough sleep tend to be tired, irritable and less patient. As a result, their ability to look after their children both by day and by night may be affected. Many get so tired that life with a toddler is viewed as a form of penance to be endured, with child care giving little joy. I have seen wonderful mothers in tears because they are genuinely scared they will hurt their children unless they get some sleep. Others have slipped past coping and sunk into a pathological depression. It seems crazy that the toddler is often the instrument of his own destruction. He has the power to greatly damage his mother or father, who, unintentionally and unavoidably, then transfer the wound.

The marriage

A tired mother makes a tired wife, who needs the help and support of an understanding husband. Where this is not forthcoming a great strain is placed on the marriage. I see many husbands who deliberately spend as little time as possible in the disturbed atmosphere of home, while others have to put up with being ousted from the marital bed to make way for a sleepless, kicking child. Husbands and wives need to have some time alone together if they are to communicate effectively and remain a strong team. If a child stays up half the night, destroying all meaningful conversation, this is almost impossible.

Brothers and sisters

Most brothers and sisters of sleepless toddlers develop an amazing ability to sleep through most of the night-time antics. A few are, however, sufficiently sensitive to noise to become sleep-deprived, just like their parents. They cop it twice, which is most unfair: once from having their sleep disturbed, and again next day when they inevitably suffer unjustly from the wrath of tired parents.

Neighbours

If you live in a double-brick, detached residence set in the middle of nowhere, you can afford to ignore the neighbours. Unfortunately most of us don't live in these ideal circumstances, and complaints from irate neighbours always add to parental harassment. Even worse I have known excellent parents who have been reported to the police and local child welfare agencies by their intolerant neighbours. It seems grossly unfair that these parents are accused of child abuse, when in fact it is the sleepless child who is abusing his parents.

The child

I used to reassure parents that when the toddler would not sleep, they were the only ones who suffered, as the child always got all the rest he needed. Recently, I have altered my opinion. I now believe that the child who sleeps all night becomes more settled, happier and easier to control by day than the child who has sleep problems. An even stranger phenomenon has come to light with some of the younger children I see.

Once the night-time sleep pattern improves, there seems to be a lengthening (or reintroduction) of the daytime nap. This is a paradox but it appears that more night-time sleep encourages more daytime sleep as well. It must be due to the combined effect of both child and parent being more relaxed and calmer, thus producing a sleep-inducing environment.

Sleep problems – the main offenders

When it comes to sleep, there are three strategies children use to pain their parents. By far the most damaging is that *middle-of-the-*

night wakening, where the child cries once or many times night after night and month after month. This can turn happy smiling people into the 'living dead'. Then there are those who *won't settle when put down at night.* This does not exhaust parents or deprive them of sleep but it robs them of valuable time alone together. Lastly, there is the child who goes down alright but then in the wee small hours *wriggles his way silently into his parents' bed.* By itself this is a fairly innocent habit but as many night visitors also kick and push parents out the side, this is not much fun.

Children wake on other occasions when they are sick, teething, frightened or when home life is disrupted and of course these are not sleep problems. At times like this children need comfort, not discipline.

Repeated middle-of-the-night wakening

The night wakers I see are of two sorts. Most have had a reasonable sleep pattern at some time in their lives and have now slipped from the straight and narrow, while a few have been appalling sleepers right from birth. Generally those who were good and then slipped lost this sleep skill at a time of teething, illness or home disruption. What happens is that ill children wake, are comforted and enjoy the attention. When they get better they think 'That was a bit of alright, let's keep calling for comfort,' and they continue to wake every night thereafter.

As a rule of thumb I can cure almost all of those who at some stage had a reasonable sleep pattern, whilst the born insomniac poses a greater but not impossible challenge.

When children wake at night their cries are often interpreted as a sign of sickness or fear. Now I can never be completely certain but if the disturbed sleep has gone on for some time, it is likely to be a bad habit, not an illness. With just a few days of waking you should always give the child the benefit of the doubt but if it goes on, and on, blaming teething or sickness would stretch the limits of credibility.

Over the years a procession of parents has come, complaining of sleep problems which really don't need treatment. If a child wakes once at night, gets a gentle pat or even a drink, and everybody can get straight back to sleep, then no harm is done. It is a different matter when middle-of-the-night wakening starts to damage the happiness of both parents and children and that is the time to come on extremely strong.

There are some parents who come to me seeking a cure but they are only interested if it involves no effort on their part. They speak as if they are motivated, then make innumerable excuses to ensure that anything I suggest fails. I must stress here that as a prerequisite to any attempt at treating sleep problems, parents must be absolutely certain that they want a cure. They must be determined to see it through, and have the strength to put up with a short period of greater difficulty that usually precedes the complete cure. If you have that sort of commitment, let's look at the method which will do this: the Green Controlled Crying Technique.

The controlled crying technique

We have seen that all humans have a sleep cycle that brings us close to waking almost every ninety minutes. All adults and most children learn to wake, roll over and put themselves back to sleep without disturbing the household. When toddlers are comforted, fed and fussed over every time they come near the surface, the chances are that they will wake regularly to capitalise on so much good attention. When comfort is not readily available to toddlers, they generally decide it is easier to settle themselves and go back to sleep.

We also know that leaving wakeful children to cry unattended dissuades them from waking in the future. Having said this, we don't let children cry for long periods in the 2000s. This is an old-fashioned idea which causes children to become confused and hysterical, while few parents are insensitive enough to put up with so much upset and crying from those they love.

Controlled crying refers to my method of letting children cry for a short period, then coming in to give some, but not full comfort, letting them cry a little longer each time, giving more incomplete comfort, gradually increasing the crying time between comforting until eventually they say: 'I know she loves me, I know she will always come but it is just not worth all the effort'.

In 1974 I would only use this method on children 18 months of age and older. By 1980, I found that 10-month-old babies could be treated and in the 2000s we know it is useful right down to the age of 6 months.

We recently ran a research project with this technique in which over a 12-month period 140 children were treated. The results showed that over the age of 2 years, 100 per cent of our group responded, usually within 3 days; between 1 year and 2, 93 per cent were cured, usually within a week. With those children 6 months of age to 1 year, 80 per cent got better, though it often took as much as 3 weeks and often needed some modification to the method.

The technique

- Toddler wakes at 3 a.m. Initially there is gentle crying, which soon turns to a noisy protest.
- Leave them crying for 5 minutes if you are average, 10 minutes if you are tough, 2 minutes if you are delicate and 1 minute if you are very fragile. The length of crying depends on the tolerance of parents and how genuinely upset the child becomes. Don't give in easily to grumbling or noisy crying with dry tears, but genuine upset with fear and hysteria needs quick comfort.
- Go into the toddler's room; lift, cuddle, comfort. Occasionally you can get away with patting them as they lie in the cot, which is all the better.
- When loud, upset crying turns to sobs and sniffs, this is the God-given signal to put them down and walk out decisively.
- They are taken aback that you dared to walk out. Immediately they start crying again in protest.
- Now leave them to cry 2 minutes longer than the previous period (10 + 2 minutes, 5 + 2 minutes, 2 + 2 minutes, 1 + 2 minutes).

- Go in, lift, cuddle, talk, comfort. At the moment the crying comes towards control, put them down and exit immediately.
- Once again increase the period of crying by 2 minutes. Then comfort, increase period of the crying again, comfort, increase, etc.
- Be extremely firm, continue for as long as it takes. It is pointless starting this technique unless you are prepared to see it through.
- Once they fall asleep, get yourself back to bed and try to get some rest. If they wake again, once more be completely firm. Do the same tomorrow night, the night after and for as long as it is needed.
- If no success is in sight and you are approaching the limit of your endurance, don't give up, combine the technique with a small dose of sedation for several nights.
- After half an hour of unsuccessful controlled crying technique, give sedation. This will take a further half hour to act and in this period, keep the technique going with firm resolve. With sedation you are guaranteed to get your sleep after an hour and the child still hears a very firm and consistent message before finally dropping off. Sedation is strictly short term.
- It can be helpful to get a friend to act as a 'sponsor'. As you struggle away at 2 a.m. trying to be tough, it is a whole lot easier to be firm if you have to report your efforts to someone outside the combat area in the morning.

Common questions

Each year I talk to thousands of parents and questions about my sleep technique always top the list. Here is a selection of the most common.

'I have tried your controlled crying technique and it does not work.' I hear this every time I talk and when I get exact details

of what has been done, the questioner has usually missed the point of my method. If you are going to use this technique it must be carried out correctly. You must be committed to a cure and be totally firm, especially in the middle of the night. When you appear to be getting nowhere, short-term sedation in association with the technique is necessary. This allows parents to remain rested and resolute even through a quite prolonged campaign.

When performed properly, it is extremely rare that a cure, or at least a significant improvement, cannot be achieved.

'My child wakes to grizzle, grumble and fuss but doesn't really cry.' Remember that each of us and each of our children will come to the surface repeatedly throughout the night. If they wish to grizzle and grumble at that time, that is their business and we should not interfere. Children who call out or want you to come and play at 2 a.m. are also best ignored. Children who behave like this in the night can be left unattended, as they are neither frightened nor truly upset. The controlled crying technique is only for use with those children who cry consistently to grab their parents' attention.

'My 18-month-old wakes and demands a feed. Is this necessary?' Toddlers may enjoy little snacks delivered during the night but these are not necessary for their nourishment. We adults might like our partner to get up and make us a hot drink on several occasions during the night but we have more sense than to ask them. Drinking, nibbling and sucking may be nice for children, but they are more interested in the comfort than the calories. If you are going to use the controlled crying technique, no bottles, breasts or high class comfort can be offered between dusk and dawn.

'What do I do? His father works very hard by day, he needs his sleep and I cannot let the toddler cry.' I hear variations of this feeble excuse almost every week. I feel it is an insult to mothers, implying that they can be up all night because what they do during the day really cannot be classified as work. Husbands were very generous as they shared at the time of conception and it seems only fair to me that this sharing and caring attitude should continue. The controlled crying technique usually brings success within four nights and any husband genuinely interested in his family's psychological well-being should be helping, not hindering.

'We live with my in-laws and they refuse to let the toddler cry.' There is no answer to this statement; you are powerless while in that position. If they obstruct yet are genuinely interested in their grandchild's welfare, maybe they should offer to do the night shift.

'He shares a room with his sister and if we try your crying technique they both will be awake all night.' It is surprising how many siblings are able to sleep through all this crying. When the disturbance is genuine and not being raised by the parents as a red herring, I suggest that the other child is moved to a different bedroom and if this is not available, to the furthest corner of the house. Having isolated the offending party, you are now able to perform my technique properly and within a week, two sleep-loving children will be together again.

'He cries at night and if I go in immediately and insert a dummy there is instant peace. Should I use your technique?' If we were being completely sensible about discipline, the dummy would be removed, the controlled crying technique used and the problem would be finished within a few days. Having said this, it is often easier for most of us to insert the dummy, knowing that minor disturbances like this are remarkably short lived. We don't need to bring our children up exactly by the book. If we are reasonably rested, happy and peaceful then that is good enough, without worrying about minor infringements.

'I have used your technique effectively in the middle of the night, but what do I do when he wakes at 5.30 a.m.?' This is a common question which is hard to answer. If you are tough at this hour and use the controlled crying technique, by the time he falls asleep you are ready to get up for the day and it all seems a bit pointless. Sedation so late also leaves hangovers during the day. (More on this later in the chapter.)

'What sedative do you suggest?' This should be prescribed by your own doctor and it is his decision. In my practice I usually favour brands such as Vallergan.

'I have used sedatives and they don't work.' Most parents who tell me this have unrealistic expectations of these drugs. Firstly they need to know exactly what they are trying to achieve and then if the right dose is given at the right time there will be few failures.

If parents are at the end of their tether and it is imperative that they get one good night of sleep, there are two ways of achieving this. You can use a suitable dose, given at bedtime, which will take the toddler through the night in most cases. Unfortunately a few toddlers will sleep soundly until 3.30 a.m. and then disturb you until dawn. This is overcome by the second method which is to withhold all sedation until the first time they wake. When given at this later time (e.g., 11 p.m.), there are usually no further disturbances before the dawn.

Most of the sedation I now prescribe is in conjunction with the controlled crying technique. Here we can use a low dose as the aim is not to propel them into twelve hours of unbroken sleep but to break a stalemate situation. In this instance it is now the middle of the night, the child is tired and all the crying has made him even tireder. Often it takes little more than the smell of the uncorked medicine bottle to send them to sleep.

'Many experts say you should never use sedatives.' Sedation as suggested is used for the purpose of making a highly effective behaviour technique work and in this instance is rarely needed for more than three or four nights. Sedation which is prescribed independent of a sleep technique is generally unwarranted, except when parents are close to collapse, when it gives them several nights of rest and allows them to recharge their batteries. My main concern with sedatives is that some people prescribe them for long periods with no attempt to introduce a sleep programme. This application does not provide a long-term cure. The main side-effect is that sedatives may produce a hangover in some children which leaves them slightly below par the next day. When used correctly, sedatives are safe and effective.

'Is this technique effective on the 3½ and 4-year-old?' Yes, it is often so effective it seems like a latter day miracle. Children over the age of 3 are a joy to work with. Over half of those I see are cured as they leave my office without ever 'a shot being fired'. Once I have

told the parents exactly what to do, I then explain it again, this time in the child's hearing. Children at this age are compulsive sticky beaks and though they appear somewhat bored as they play or look out the window, they are taking it all in. As they leave they know the score and their parents are committed to seeing it through. When the parents ring me in the morning, most of them are amazed at what happened. 'Dr Green, you won't believe it, he never woke last night!' We all know that something simple yet powerful has happened. The children know exactly where they stand and can sense that the big people are in charge, and going to see this through. It is not worth a challenge.

'Are you sure your technique does not cause some psychological damage to sensitive children?' There are many things we have to do in paediatrics which cause considerable upset to the children in our care. We frighten them with X-rays, examinations, immunisations and hospital investigations. Then there is the pain and trauma of life-saving surgery. Whatever we do must always be a balance of the benefits against any emotional upset. I cannot be certain that my controlled crying technique does not cause upset to children but even if it does, it would seem that the amount is minimal. Balanced against this there is no doubt that sleep deprivation can do immense harm to parents, who in turn bring stress and emotional harm to their children. I am convinced that the benefits of my technique when used correctly greatly outweigh the theoretical objections.

When they won't go to bed at night

Over half of all toddlers will play up when it is time for bed if they know they can get away with it. They seem to be designed with a sleep clock whose bedtime is considerably later than the setting their parents would wish. Some are tired but still obstinately refuse to go to bed, while others infuriate their parents by popping in and out of their rooms like a Jack-in-the-Box. Other, more subtle toddlers, create a smokescreen of requests for drinks, the toilet and various comforters, which succeed in keeping parents on the hop and gain them great attention. Most bedtime problems are simply bad habits which can be avoided with routine and rules adminis-tered by gentle but determined parents.

Refusal to retire is a much less damaging problem to parents than the antics of the middle-of-the-night wakener. All this in-and-out drama is a pest and though the parents may be irritated, at least they are not losing any sleep. Parents deserve the chance to have some time alone together, so their children should be expected to go to bed at a reasonable hour – a nice notion, although sometimes sabotaged by our little children.

One group of reluctant settlers are those who require less sleep than the text books tell us. These children will probably grow up to be prime ministers, leaders of industry or other irritating insom-niacs. For them, no matter what we do, bedtime will be later than we want. Then there is another group who like an afternoon nap, but this so recharges their batteries that they continue to run on full power half the night.

Of these the first need a later bedtime and when put down they must be made to stay in their room, even if not unconscious. The others may need to lose their afternoon nap or at least make it shorter.

Some fortunate parents have the luxury of a child-free period each afternoon, followed by the same each evening. However, many of us can't have it both ways.

Medical science is not sufficiently advanced to make non-sleepers take more sleep but we are in no doubt about how to put children to bed and how to keep them there. Here are some suggestions.

The gentle approach

Good routine Try to follow a regular routine in the lead-up to bed, then put them down at a constant bedtime. Where settling poses a problem, a later bedtime may be introduced on a temporary basis. Once this is well established it is quite easy to bring it forward a few minutes each night, until an acceptable level is achieved.

Calm them down Don't fight, stir, run, chase or play wild games near bedtime. Olympic athletes do not finish the race and then go straight to sleep and we ourselves need to unwind before bed. Bath, talk, tuck up, cuddle and read a soothing story.

Leave decisively When it is time to go, say goodnight and leave as though you mean it. Do not rise to requests whose only purpose is procrastination.

If they come out If they reappear you must be firm. Don't feel guilty at being tough, after all you have given them your absolute best attention before bedtime. Never encourage Jack-in-the-Box behaviour. Over the years some parents have told me in all serious-ness: I put my child back twenty-four times last night. This is not discipline. You are playing a fun game with your child and only one party is appreciating it. You put them back once, no questions are accepted, you know you are in charge, they know where they stand and that is it.

The even gentler approach

Good routine, calm down As above.

Sit until they sleep The gentlest approach is to stay until they slip off to sleep. You finish the story, cuddle, kiss, tuck up then sit beside the bed until they start to snooze. This is a very loving way to do things but many parents find it backfires as their child prolongs the process with a lot of questions and manipulations.

You sit quietly in the room either reading to yourself or just relaxing. All you are offering is your presence, not an evening of entertainment. If they lie quietly you stay but the moment they question or climb out, this gentle approach has failed and you must leave decisively.

The tough option

Good routine, calm down, leave decisively As above.

If they come out once Put them back immediately. Leave them in no doubt that you are not going to tolerate this and will be extremely heavy if they reappear.

If they come out again At this point there must be no misunder-standings. You dearly love them but you have given them a more than generous amount of your time and attention and if as much as a nose pokes out again, you will descend like lightning from Mount Olympus.

If they come out yet again At this point a serious challenge is being staged and you can either stand up and be decisive or decide to abdicate your position as a credible leader. If you mean business, you must block all routes of escape, or, if you believe in giving a warning smack, this is the time to do it.

Green's patent rope trick If parents realise that they are rapidly getting nowhere, I strongly recommend the rope trick. This is one of my better inventions, which came from the drawing board when I was trying to curb the escape-artist antics of my own children. All that is required is a short length of strong rope.

Before you get worried, I am not going to suggest that you tie your child to the bed, tempting though this might on occasion be. What you do is loop one end of the rope around the inner handle of the bedroom door and attach the other end to the handle of a nearby door. Carefully adjust the rope so that when the bedroom door is forced open, the aperture is just a little less than the diameter of the offending child's head. As all of you who have had babies know, if the head is not going to get out, nothing is. It is not that they are locked in, they just cannot get out.

With your child safely in his room, he may resort to crying to break your resolve but once again this ploy will fail as you use the controlled crying technique. A light should be left on in the passageway outside the bedroom, so that the child can see and hear what is going on around the house. This means that the child will not become frightened, yet at the same time he is made very aware that bed is the place he is meant to be.

Before you all rush out to the nearest hardware shop, ordering up metres of rope, let me relate one cautionary and somewhat embarrassing tale. One late evening it had become quite apparent that there was no way our active superboys were going to stay in their room, so a loop of rope was attached in the approved manner. Following this, there was a bit of gentle crying which then dramatically increased in decibels. My wife and I knew we had to wait five minutes before we came and comforted (it had to be true because I had read it in my book) but when we eventually arrived we got a nasty shock. The boys were still in their room but unfortunately I had made the rope a fraction too long and the older boy had skilfully pushed his younger brother's head into the crack in the door, where it was firmly jammed. Extraction almost needed an obstetrician with forceps. Life is not without its troubles, even for child care experts. Don't let this put you off, though, as the patent rope trick works well.

If you must smack, then most children realise that the game is up and remain firmly in their room. Unfortunately many change the rules of the game and start to cry vigorously in another attempt to break the resolve of their parents. This of course will not work as the parents have already been instructed in the controlled crying technique and if this is used the battle is all but won for them. On first reading this may seem a hard way to treat children but bearing in mind that a complete cure can usually be guaranteed in under a week, it is a small price to pay for peace.

The results
Whichever of these approaches you take, if you are determined to achieve a cure this can be guaranteed in under a week for at least nine out of ten cases. Whatever you do, have sensible expectations. This is not a way of making children go to sleep, it is only a means of ensuring that when you put them to bed they stay there.

The child who comes to his parents' bed each night

Many philosophers extol the joys of a family sleeping together in one giant, bed-bound commune and in fact I receive many rude letters if I dare suggest eviction. This may be a terrifically enjoyable state of affairs for those who are deep sleepers or are lucky enough to have children who do not wriggle or kick. If you enjoy having children in bed with you all night, every night, that's your decision. If you are all happy, let them stay there until they are ready for high school as far as I am concerned.

In my experience, about 75 per cent of mothers and 95 per cent of fathers wish their bed to be a private, peaceful place. They greatly resent intruders making a regular appearance in the small hours of the morning.

Nocturnal wanderers tend to be the more active members of the child population, seemingly incapable of lying quietly in the

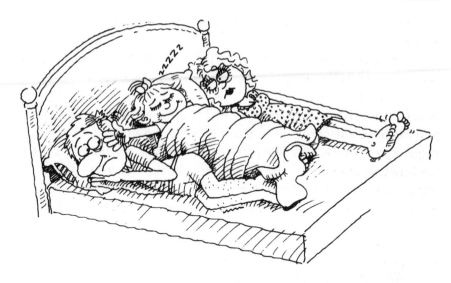

parental bed. It is almost as though they had different magnetism, while mother and father lie North/South they are almost drawn to the East/West position in which they can simultaneously kick one parent and poke the other. Many mothers can tolerate this intrusion but fathers, I find, are less long-suffering. The prospect of a busy day after a disturbed night's sleep will force them to flee to the peace and comfort of the lounge-room or take up position in the child's vacated bed, probably with their legs hanging out the bottom.

Many lonely mothers, whether alone because their husband is away on business, or because of a marriage break-up, subtly encourage their children to come into bed with them each night as company. This is probably quite good for both parties but it may cause problems when life returns to normal.

A child who is sick or genuinely frightened, will always have a rightful place in his parent's bed, though it is important to evict him once his health has returned. All children are entitled to that enjoyable early morning romp in their parents' bed, just as long as the sun is up and the cock has crowed. Sleep is very important to the sanity of us parents and I believe that children should be excluded from our beds if at all possible. Peace and privacy are important to people and that includes parents. Of course it is up to you but if you want a good method of evicting the most determined toddler from your place of rest, read on.

The technique

1. ***The moment the child appears he must be put back immediately.***

   On a cold night, a tired parent must be very strong to resist slipping the little intruder into bed, but such an action only reinforces antisocial night-time behaviour and must be discouraged. Some unwelcome little nocturnal prowlers can slip into their parents' bed with all the stealth of a cat burglar and lie there unnoticed for quite some time. If you are determined to stop this habit, I suggest putting a wedge under your bedroom door, which allows it to be opened a short distance but causes an obstruction that alerts you to the child's approach.

2. ***If the child returns, give a stern warning and, if possible, have the other parent return him to bed.***

   More democratic parents give the child a stern warning, leaving him in no doubt as to what lies ahead if he is seen again, and then put him back to bed (preferably the other parent than the one who dealt with him the first time). I must admit, however, that most parents feel that this degree of civility is quite unwarranted at that time of the night, and they move straight to the next stage.

3. ***If he returns a third time, immobilise doors or if you must, give a light smack.***

   In this case, various doors should be immobilised with the patent rope trick or a therapeutic little wedge or, if you must, a symbolic smack should be used before returning him to his bed, Following either of these, the controlled crying technique is used.

4. ***The results: ten out of ten cured if that is what you really want.***

   Coming to the parents' bed in the middle of the night constitutes the least damaging of the three major sleep problems of toddlerhood. It is up to the individual parent to decide whether to tolerate their behaviour or have a showdown. The methods outlined may seem rather harsh but the middle of the night is no time for playing games, and it is worth being firm, because the chances of a quick and permanent cure are excellent.

Other sleep-related problems

Most young children, once asleep, are dead to the world and would not wake even if set down in the middle of the 1812 Overture, cannons and all. Some, however, are uncommonly sensitive to sound, which leaves the parents tip-toeing round the house at night, frightened to run a tap or flush a toilet.

The light sleeper

Problems with light sleepers are easily overcome by placing an ordinary household transistor radio beside the child's bed. On the first night, turn the radio on with such a low volume that the sound is barely audible to all but a passing bat. As the nights pass, gradually increase the volume over a period of two weeks. Most children are well and truly desensitised by this time. From there on, most children should sleep through garbage collections, car horns, the football final on television and the odd cannon.

What station should your child listen to, I hear you ask. Assess his interest. Budding merchant bankers should be tuned to the station that gives the best stock market reports, punk rockers in the making will be happy with a rock station, and a possible candidate for the clergy is probably happiest listening to hymns. Of course, I am joking. It really doesn't matter which programme the radio is tuned to. In fact some tune to FM and then go slightly off station, thus leaving the radio with a crackle not unlike Niagara Falls which gives background noise constantly without the quiet spots at the end of records or talking.

The afternoon sleep

Children in the first two years of life enjoy their daytime nap – and not only the child, I may say. Mother looks forward to this time with equal glee. Unfortunately, this peaceful event disappears some-where between the ages of 2 and 4, and every parent mourns its passing. But in the final days before the changeover, parents are in a dilemma. If the child does not get an afternoon nap, he is unbear-ably irritable in the late afternoon but he goes to bed early and sleeps soundly. If he does sleep in the afternoon, the peace is enjoyed but it is paid for when the revitalised child romps round the house until all hours of the night.

There is, I'm sorry to say, no answer to this problem. Parents simply have to make a choice. I favour the sacrifice of the already waning afternoon nap, believing the good night-sleeping pattern to be more important.

The right bedtime

There is no universal 'right' bedtime for all children. In my experi-ence, 7.30 p.m. appears to be the accepted time that most toddlers should assume the horizontal. This may be the case for the sleeping majority but a significant minority won't settle to sleep at this time in a month of Sundays. The offenders are usually those difficult children who have been poor sleepers from birth. They are mostly active boys, which is surprising because one would expect them to need more sleep considering the massive amounts of energy they use up during the day.

All we can do is accept that children, like adults, have different sleeping needs and be thankful that most toddlers are snoring by 7.30 p.m. As for the late settlers, they need a later bedtime, and although they cannot be forced to sleep there are at least ways of keeping them in their rooms, which must surely increase the chances of them inadvertently falling asleep.

The procrastinator

Little children who do not wish to be parted for the night from their loving parents have an immense repertoire of procrastinating techniques. 'I want a drink,' 'I feel hungry,' 'I want you to lie beside me,' 'I want a different pillow,' 'I don't want a pillow at all,' 'I want two pillows,' and so on. This is a genuine wish to hang on to the parents' attention for as long as possible and put off having to go to sleep. This is all part of the charm of these tender years but it must not be allowed to get out of hand. A little procrastination is fun but if handled badly it can turn into a major case of manipulation. Know your child and know when to say enough is enough.

The early riser

Some children love to sleep late while others are up and on the go from the first chirp of the dawn chorus. Once again, this tends to be the prerogative of those over-active members of the toddler population. I have to admit that I have never been of much help to parents with this problem. In theory, if we suggest a later bedtime, this should cure the habit, but I find that its only effect is usually to turn a happy, early riser into a tired, irritable early riser. Cutting out the daytime sleep leaves them hard to live with in the late afternoon but they still seem to wake equally early. Some may be helped by blocking out all light from the windows.

One approach which sounds sensible but rarely works is to ensure that the room and cot are filled with quiet toys which will let them entertain themselves and play in the early morning. In theory this should enable the rest of the household to remain asleep, but few toddlers are interested in this. They want to get up, move, be fed, and share the full beauty of the sunrise with their parents.

When the early morning habit becomes a major hassle, the controlled crying technique can be extremely effective, but it often leaves you in the ridiculous situation of soothing a child off to sleep just in time to wake the rest of the family up for the day's activities. Sometimes it is easier for the adults to change their sleeping pattern, going to bed earlier and waking in harmony with their youngster. I fear that with early risers sometimes the most I can offer is sympathy, not a cure.

The night prowler

Some children wake up in the middle of the night wanting something to eat, or to play or explore the house. Recently I was brought a 3-year-old who had discovered that getting up at 2 a.m. and turning on the vacuum cleaner had quite an effect on his befuddled parents. Another 3-year-old of my acquaintance loved to play with his toy cars in the middle of the night. As he could not reach the light switches, he had to find an alternative form of illumination, which he achieved by setting up his automobile collection in front of the refrigerator, then pulling open the door and playing by its cold, bright light. This would have been a quite innocent pastime, except that he was often overcome by sleep in mid-activity and would be found in the morning in company with piles of defrosted vegetables.

If children are determined to play in the middle of the night, that is fine, just as long as they are quiet and do not damage themselves or other people's property. It is usually safest to deal with night prowlers by resorting to the patent rope trick, as well as making sure there are deadlocks on all the exterior doors and wedges on others to limit the child's access to danger.

The shared bedroom

Often, with the midnight screamer, parents are defeated before they ever start. They are quick to point out that my techniques will never work as they are too disturbing for the other children. I can assure you, however, that if you are really keen on finding a cure, then a shared room, although inconvenient, is not an impossible hurdle.

All I ask for is one week of absolute firmness, during which most families should be capable of rearranging themselves for a short while. Older children who share the crying toddler's bedroom usually have a much higher tolerance for nocturnal noise than their parents anyway. The controlled crying technique can usually be used without causing any great disturbance to the other room occupants. If this is not possible, a temporary sleeping arrangement must be organised and the other children moved from the bedroom to the comparative quiet of the lounge room or off to granny's for the weekend. This will leave the toddler pretty well soundproofed for the duration of the treatment, and once a good sleep pattern has been established, the children can be reunited.

It's only when the entire family live in one bedroom that my technique falls sadly apart. In these difficult situations parents simply have to give in to the child in the interests of the family's peace.

The cot in the parents' bedroom

Many newborn babies sleep in a cot close to their parents' bed, taking some of the effort out of the night-time feed. Some parents with older children prefer, for a variety of reasons, to keep them close to their bed at night. This may be fine if the parents are sound sleepers and the child remains quiet at night. But it may not be such a good idea for light-sleeping parents who are stirred to consciousness every time the child coughs, turns over or passes wind. Even children with epilepsy or other medical problems should be encouraged to sleep in a separate room, as unbroken sleep has great curative powers for the entire family.

The lost dummy

Some young toddlers can only survive those wakeful periods at night with their mouth firmly plugged by a dummy. If it becomes disconnected, help is summoned by loud wailing and gnashing of teeth, and the cries will only subside once the missing piece of junk is replaced. Many parents get sick and tired of this constant midnight drama, but they don't know how to rid themselves of this offending object. Some disposal suggestions are mentioned later in this book, but one way of keeping track of the thing is to tie a short tape onto the dummy and pin it to the child's night clothes. Children of an advanced age, who shouldn't have a dummy in the first place, are thus able to locate the lost object. Unfortunately young children seem to be unable to make contact with the tape and, even if they can, find it well nigh impossible to reel in and plug their mouths.

The only reliable cure for repeated wakening as the result of a lost dummy is to get rid of the object completely. Certainly this may lead to several difficult nights but in the long term, it is well worth the momentary inconvenience.

Night feeds

There is a major relationship between night wakening and night feeding. If night-time breast feeding continues after the first birthday, there is a strong likelihood that this will be accompanied by multiple nocturnal wakenings. So great is the comfort from breast feeding, that the child will demand the breast as an adjunct to sleep – comfort rather than sustenance is the object of the exercise.

When breast feeding and sleep are both wanted, toddler breast feeds should be given by day, on going to bed and on wakening in the morning. A strict curfew must be imposed during the hours of darkness. Bottles and beakers give less comfort. When compared to a warm breast, there is minimal joy to be gained from sucking a cold rubber teat that has been steeped in some nasty, antiseptic solution. But these should also be suspended during the hours of sleep if night wakening is to be cured. When given, they establish a bad pattern, which once again encourages the half-asleep child to cry out for sustenance rather than turn over and go back to sleep.

A basic law also decrees that 'what goes in must come out'. The more fluid the child drinks, the greater the number of wet nappies, wet beds, discomfort and excursions to the toilet.

Don't be fooled by advertisers' attempts to encourage you to combat 'night starvation'. Toddlers don't starve at night. For the sake of peace and quiet and an undisturbed sleep, all midnight snacks, be they from breast or bottle, should be discouraged.

Of course if night-time feeding is no major hassle, please continue. That's always a gentle, comforting and charitable way to go.

The cot escaper

Long before they reach their first birthday, some children have developed strong mountaineering skills. They lie quietly in their cots for months, planning their escape route down to the final detail. The time of the first successful escape attempt varies greatly from child to child, and from cot to cot.

No matter how energetic and ambitious the young child may be, he is unlikely to scale a high side that has no horizontal stepping bar from which to take off. The first effort usually ends in a hard fall, as he finds the climb up considerably easier to control than the journey down the other side. Some children never consider climbing out of their cots at all and would probably remain there happily until school age.

Parents often ask at what age the child should be moved from a cot to a proper bed. This often happens precipitantly when a new baby arrives, but on other occasions it is a well-planned move. If the child has a good sleeping pattern, little harm will come from the change. The trouble comes with the child who sleeps poorly in his cot, and parents misguidedly think that the move to a bed will help. All it does is transfer the bad sleeper from one mattress to another with no attendant benefit. I am all in favour of toddlers remaining in their cots at least until well into their second year. There seem to be few advantages in an early release programme.

When the toddler starts climbing out of his cot, parents are usually terrified that he will fall and hurt himself. At this point, they have to decide whether to leave the side of the cot down or put him in a bed, both of which allow easy escape and will possibly lead to night-time problems. If they leave him in the cot, it should be situated against two walls with a soft floor covering under the exposed side. It may seem a rather callous thing to say but in my experience most young children who have a tumble from their cots usually have the sense to postpone further attempts until they have become sufficiently mature to guarantee a soft landing.

The nocturnally deaf husband

This is a fascinating phenomenon, which I have studied assiduously for years. My observations show that when the child cries at night, most husbands appear to become suddenly stone deaf, and thus their wives are forced out of bed to cope with the problem. I don't believe this is, in any sense, true deafness, but rather a conveniently learned response to an unpleasant situation. My wife claims that, when our children cried at night, she found that my hearing could be toned up with the aid of a sharp kick. Certainly in these enlightened days, I believe there should be more sharing of the less pleasant parts of parenthood, and if kicking is what it takes, then that is as good a method as any.

Fears

When a child starts to cry at night, many parents worry that he may be frightened and thus will not allow my firm methods of control to be used. Certainly younger children do have fears but when they wake once or more every night, that's a bad habit, not fear.

Separating from parents at night can cause anxiety in some toddlers, but it must be coped with if both parents and child are to get any sleep. To help with this separation, it is quite a good idea to use comfort items, such as a favourite teddy bear or a security blanket.

Fear of the dark is common among older toddlers, and indeed in quite a large number of adults. A dull, low-wattage light is a small investment that will relieve a great deal of stress. Some academics dispute the value of night lights, believing that the shadows they throw make the child even more frightened. This certainly doesn't seem to be the case with any of the children I have ever seen.

Nightmares

Nightmares are much more common at an older age, but they can occur in toddlers. As the child wakes from active dream sleep, he may still be in the midst of some alarming escapade. He has an unmistakable frightened cry and is easily soothed by the rapid appearance of a parent. He quickly becomes aware that it was a dream, not a real event, and in some cases he can even remember all the details. Nightmares may occur quite regularly, and although there is some association with stress and anxiety, it is usually the sort of normal stress of life that we cannot change. The most loving, attentive, angelic parents, who have the best possible relationship with their child, will find that the child still has nightmares. He's probably dreaming in this case that he has become separated from them.

The treatment for nightmares is simple. Go quickly to the child, hold him, talk soothingly and stay as the child slips quietly back to sleep.

Night terrors

These occur in a slightly younger age group. The child wakes from a deep, sound sleep in a state of utter terror. He sits up in bed, looking through glazed, staring eyes and cries profusely. His parents run to his aid and are confronted with a difficult situation, as the child seems almost paralysed and stuck in a different world that they cannot reach. The parents always feel that they want to cuddle the child but the current thinking is to observe the child and only intervene if they are likely to be hurt. In the morning, the child will have no memory of the previous night's events, although the parents will find it much harder to forget.

Once again, there may be repeated episodes but it is extremely rare that any treatment is required other than letting time do the healing. As with nightmares, it is unlikely that there is any treatable anxiety-provoking event that causes night terrors.

Sedation

Sedative drugs are abused and over-used by many parents. In some families, they are almost a nightly routine, being used for sleep problems that could be more effectively and safely treated by simple behavioural methods. I disapprove of sedatives being used unnecessarily, but there are three situations in which I think their use is justified:

■ in conjunction with my controlled crying technique;

■ as a safety valve for fragile families to use in times of crisis when sleep is imperative to maintain sanity and stability; and

■ to sedate the severely disabled child who is extremely irritable by day and is awake crying all night.

The secret with sedation is to give the right dose at the right time. Most doctors quite gratuitously write the instructions 'to be taken at bedtime' on the bottle. It is, however, unrealistic to expect that a sedative given at 6 p.m. will miraculously ensure sleep right through until next morning. When I want a child to sleep, I give the drug, in its correct dose for the child's body weight, on the first occasion that he wakes in the night. This is more effective than administering it before the child goes to bed, because he was probably going to sleep perfectly well for the first few hours anyway, but when given later the effect will extend to protect those golden hours between midnight and dawn.

Over the years I have seen children who have never in their life ever slept more than six hours a day. With these and other families who are exhausted and fragile, sedation not only brings immediate relief but gives them the strength to see through one of my behaviour programmes. When parents are really shattered I may prescribe a few days' sedation for the child to allow everyone to get back onto an even keel before embarking upon a more permanent cure by more effective methods. There is no harm in having a sedative in the house as long it is used with sense and as a last resort when an unbroken night's sleep is vital for survival.

Sedatives are not without their problems. Some children become quite hung over the next morning whilst a minority may demonstrate some unexpected paradoxical effects. These children become irritable, overactive, unreasonable and poorly co-ordinated. They adopt all the worst characteristics of an obnoxious drunk, staggering around the house, slurring their speech and walking into door handles. Be careful before administering a large first-time dose on a car, train or especially a plane trip. The thought of being trapped at 10 000 metres with a drunk, belligerent toddler is somewhat mind boggling.

Sensitive neighbours

Parents with children who sleep poorly are often sabotaged in their attempts to implement controlled crying by complaining neighbours. I recommend the direct approach in these instances. On returning home from my office, the parents go straight in to see the neighbours and tell them that the child is now in the hands of a specialist doctor from the Children's Hospital who has designed a new treatment for sleepless kids. They explain that this is quite revolutionary and the doctor has insisted that they let the child cry a number of times at night, but that the cure will come inside a week. On most occasions this super-scientific approach, blaming everything on the doctor, has worked. So far I have had no reports of parents being set on by the neighbour's dog, but despite all my best efforts, some have been verbally abused and even reported to the police and welfare agencies.

Summary: toddlers and sleep problems

- Sleep problems can affect the whole family – and sometimes the whole neighbourhood.
- Ask yourself 'Is this sleep problem worth the effort of changing?' Remember many problems will settle with time.
- There are three main kinds of sleep problems:
  1. Middle of the night awakening – use controlled crying technique;
  2. Getting children to bed on time – have a regular bedtime routine, keep calm and leave decisively. Be firm if they reappear. Use the patent rope trick;
  3. Coming to the parents' bed during the night – use controlled crying technique.

TWELVE

What Should Toddlers Eat?

Food is the fuel that powers our young children. It makes them grow strong, gives them pleasure and provides them with many opportunities to wind up their parents. We can choose the healthiest designer diet, put it on a plate, even get it into the mouth, but if they decide that's as far as it is going: checkmate – the game is over!

When animals feed their young, it seems such an uncomplicated affair, yet humans, with all their nutritional advisers, find it is downright difficult.

As parents, let's aim to loosen up a bit, stick to realistic expectations of diet and never let food become a battle. We should also set a good example, and where better to begin than at the start of toddlerhood. There we have complete control over the available diet. After all, we are the ones who buy the stuff.

Occasionally an uptight parent tells me, 'My 2-year-old seems to eat nothing but chips, chocolate, chocolate biscuits and more chips. What can I do?'. Is this parent telling me that junior gets up in the morning, takes the keys of the Volvo, drives down to the supermarket, loads up a trolley with chips and chocolate, drives home and eats them? I think there is a message in this somewhere.

What is a balanced diet?

Adults and toddlers need six different types of nourishment to survive: protein, carbohydrate, fats, vitamins, minerals and water.

Protein is present in meat, eggs and cheese; lesser quality vegetable proteins are found in beans, nuts, etc. In our affluent country we tend to eat considerably more protein than we need.

Carbohydrate comes in simple forms as glucose, sucrose (cane sugar) or more complex form as the starches in cereals, bread, pasta, vegetables, fruit, nuts and so on. The simple sugars are easy to eat, and often come partnered with fat, making an irresistible taste combination, so it is easy to eat too much. Complex carbohydrates have much more bulk than the simple sugars, which means it is not so easy to over-indulge and thus become overweight. Complex carbohydrate, once the in-food for athletes, is now reckoned to be the in-food for all of us.

Fats are present in meat, cooking oils, milk, butter, cheese, nuts, etc. There are two types of fat, the saturated sort mostly found in animal products and the unsaturated type more often derived from vegetable sources.

Fats are an important source of energy, providing double that of the same amount of sugar and putting on twice the amount of weight if we are not careful. Though reduced fat diets are important for adults and older children, young toddlers burn up so much energy with their activity and growth that a reasonable amount of fat does not seem a problem.

Vitamins are required in small quantities if we are to remain healthy. Once we have the desired amount, doubling or trebling these levels does not make us twice or three times as fit; in fact it does nothing. There are various vitamins such as vitamin C which is found in fruits and juices, and vitamin D which is present in eggs and butter as well as being manufactured by sunshine acting on our skin. There is a great deal of misleading advertising about vitamins. Australian children who do not have some major bowel or other medical condition will be getting all the vitamins needed if they are given a half reasonable toddler diet. My understanding is that natural vitamins come from natural foods, not from a pill laboratory.

Minerals are required in small amounts. Iron and calcium are the two we think of most. Iron is found in large quantities in meat and lesser quantities in fortified cereals, bread and some vegetables. Toddlers who do not eat these can become short of iron. Calcium comes mainly from dairy foods and it may be low in a child who takes absolutely none of these in any of their varied forms.

Water is required in large amounts and what better way to take it than straight from the tap. In this form it has even fewer calories than Diet Coke and your dentist, no matter what his religion, will bless it. Most of our water is now fluoridated and despite various ill-informed pronouncements, this is safe. As for other pollutants, we can protest about discolouration or too much chlorine, but the water we use must be purer and safer than that available to 90 per cent of the world's population.

He doesn't eat enough

So often parents tell me, 'Dr Green, he hardly eats a bite'. I look up and there stands an infant heavyweight about as puny and malnourished as King Kong. You cannot get this build from swallowing air. A few calories must have slipped down along the way.

Most children who seem to eat too little are in fact getting a very adequate and healthy diet, if only we realised it. When in doubt, note down all the food eaten as snacks, milk, juice and half-finished main meals. When this is added up you will be surprised at just how much goodness has gone down the big tube in one day.

If our children are growing well and are healthy, there cannot be too much wrong with their food intake. Health in a toddler means boundless energy and a mischievous zest for life. The healthy toddler has bright little eyes full of devilment that twinkle as if he is thinking: 'Let's go home and put a bat up grandma's nightie'.

The hunger striker – cracking the code

When parents say their child just won't eat, one starts to wonder how these little hunger strikers manage to survive. Over the years I have thought long and hard about this and now believe I have managed to crack the code. Children who eat nothing, usually eat plenty but it is just in an invisible form, taken as some inconspicuous nourishment.

The milkaholic These children bring joy to the dairy producers as they live and thrive on milk. Each day they consume litre upon litre which leaves no room for solid food. Milk is of course a good food but alone it does not provide a balanced diet for a toddler.

If our children are taking a reasonable diet as well as all this milk, then there is no cause for concern. If they are eating an inadequate amount of solid food and overdosing with milk, now is the time to cut the volume by half. This will produce some hunger and a renewed interest in other food.

The grazer It is not just Australian sheep that nibble away all day; whole flocks of little children also graze. They may not be eating three major meals a day but the food still seems to get in. Children thrive well on this regime as long as we ensure that the pasture they nibble is of reasonable quality.

Unorthodox eaters Often children eat plenty but it is not registered by parents as proper food. Toddlers can get an excellent, well-balanced diet without eating sliced beef, potatoes and two vegetables of different colours. Of course it is important to encourage variety, as long as our children get the right balance.

It doesn't matter how food is presented, as once it hits the stomach it is irrelevant whether the meat was lamb, pork or beef, whether it was minced or carved and how many vegetables were served. The body is more impressed by nutrients than Nouvelle Cuisine.

He won't eat his vegetables

Modern nutritional science has proved something that we all know anyway: vegetables are very important foods. They contain not only fibre, complex carbohydrates and vitamins, but also many protective factors that prevent chronic diseases in adulthood. Unfortunately vegetables turn out to be children's least favourite food. And, let's face it, many adults do not find them particularly mouthwatering.

When it comes to vegetables and toddlers, the story is quite simple. Try to introduce small amounts, different tastes and lots of variety from the earliest days. If your little ones enjoy them that is great, if not don't force the issue. Experiment with the full spectrum of vegies, from greens to beans and back again. If all this is a non-event, don't worry, fruit (and fruit juice) can substitute for vegetables. But remember, keep offering small amounts of vegetables without any force. Research has shown that persistence without pressure is the key to success.

He won't eat any meat

Parents often tell me, 'He won't eat any meat; he just eats chicken, hamburger and sausage'. We should remember that all meat does not come in a thick slice of cow or sheep. There are many other animals and presentations, one of which will usually tempt the appetite of the toddler.

The main need for meat is to give protein and iron. When the toddler meat embargo is total it would be extremely unusual for them to also refuse dairy products like cheese, milk and yoghurt. Eggs are always another excellent source of first-class protein.

Beans, lentils and nut products (e.g. smooth peanut butter), when used wisely, can keep vegetarian children healthy, but usually those who refuse to eat meat will be equally militant when it comes to accepting these alternatives.

He won't drink any milk

Dairy products provide by far the most important source of calcium to the growing child. It is not uncommon for children to go off milk, but thank goodness they rarely go off all dairy foods. When milk is not being taken, cheese is the great standby. Cheese has plenty of calcium and protein and what's more is one of the more universally popular toddler foods. In fact some years ago we surveyed parents and found that cheese and chocolate were equal favourites behind the number one food, ice-cream.

If cheese is not eaten, there are other popular products such as yoghurt, dairy desserts, milk-based ice-creams and sweet flavoured milks.

It is extremely rare for a child not to take some form of dairy product and if this were a genuine concern, it would be wise to seek some professional advice. There are times when there is a true milk allergy and in these cases a calcium fortified alternative product would be suggested. If you want to go the natural way you could always try spinach and sesame seeds. They would be sprouting out your toddler's ears before he got even the calcium of half a glass of milk, but oh what a feeling!

A toddler relies heavily on the full cream dairy products that would cause spasms in the adult heart watcher. At this young age they need all those fats to fire up their furnace, to keep them going and growing.

Healthy diet – healthy example

It is unrealistic to expect our young children to have a healthier lifestyle than that of the adults whose example they follow. If parents are chain-smoking, overweight and under-exercised without a sniff of self-discipline, then it is not going to be easy for the next generation. Diet and healthy living are a family affair and that must start with us, the parents, getting our act together.

The best way to start toddlers along the straight and narrow is to try to introduce them to as wide and varied a diet as possible. They need to be offered many different tastes and textures in the hope of broadening their feeding horizons. This is the way to go but be warned – some little militants will be immovable in their quest for monotony. Another important aim is to avoid establishing foods that are either too sweet or over-salty. There is nothing wrong with the occasional potato chip or chocolate but when it becomes a regular part of diet, this habit may be hard to shake.

The healthy diet of today is not one of don'ts, nevers and definitely nots. Some nutritional extremists forget that food is for enjoyment and turn it into an unhealthy obsession. Our children are just as entitled as we are to have moments of indulgence, as long as the general balance is on track.

The aim for healthy eating is to:

- Increase the complex carbohydrate intake.
- Reduce all fats, particularly those which are saturated.
- Cut down on highly sweet and refined foods.
- Reduce salt intake.

In practice, this means maintaining a balanced diet.

- Eat plenty of pasta, cereals, bread, fruit and vegetables.

- Eat moderate amounts of lean meat, fish, nut products and, once past toddler age, low fat milk, low fat cheese, low fat yoghurt. (Toddlers should have full cream dairy products, the rest of us should not.)

- Eat small amounts of fried foods, sweet drinks, butter, margarine, cakes, lollies, honey and sugar.

The varied diet – often a dream

Some children take to new food like a duck to water; others are much more stuck in their ways. For this group the daily diet is: Weet-bix, Weet-bix, Vegemite sandwich, Weet-bix, a sandwich, then goodnight! This of course would never be a hit on the a la carte menu at the Ritz but some toddlers love it today, tomorrow and forever.

We should aim for variety but it is pointless fighting about it. It is better to introduce small amounts of new foods from time to time until a varied interest is achieved. Remember that persistence, not pressure, is the key.

Another common area of confusion is toddler taste as opposed to adult taste. Parents may feel that toddler foods lack salt or have an unpleasant texture but that is none of our business and we must not pollute them to our palate. Likewise, parents who themselves dislike liver, beetroot and brains will never give these to their child. In fact the toddler may be quite happy with these foods, but parental hang-ups prevent them from being tried. Let's face it, adults have some pretty odd tastes of their own, such as oysters, anchovies and chilli sauce. Toddlers have a right to their own tastes.

Diet and teeth

Our toddler's teeth are calcium-filled pearls surrounded by a tough enamel shell. This protects them from almost everything with one major exception: acid. Unfortunately this acid is never far away as we all have bacteria in our mouths which ferment any passing carbohydrate food to form enamel-eating acid. These bacteria are natural and otherwise harmless lodgers which we cannot get rid of. Two ways of protecting our children's mouths are to give fluoride to strengthen the teeth and to keep contact with acid producing carbo-hydrates to a minimum.

When fluoride was added to our water supply the incidence of dental caries in children took a 60 per cent nosedive. This provides a good reason for fluoride to be given to all children. If it is not in your water supply, drops or tablets can be ordered from the chemist. It is now recommended that young children should also use a toothpaste with added fluoride but at low levels. Children's toothpastes are formulated with the correct amount of fluoride.

Teeth should be brushed regularly. A soft toothbrush should be first introduced at the age of 2, with the parents guiding it around the mouth. The best way is to wait until they're in the bath and then give them a toothbrush more to chew on than anything else. It helps them to get the feel of a toothbrush in their mouth. Then you can add a tiny bit of some child-friendly toothpaste – not some super blast stuff that burns their mouth. After the child has had a go the parent should brush the teeth property. If they don't get the hang of it soon, it doesn't matter because all those teeth are going to drop out by the time they reach 6 anyway. But you've got plenty of time to get it right so that they can take extra good care of their next lot of teeth. Those will not be so easily replaced. The child could go solo about the age of 5. Toddlers should visit the dentist in their pre-school years, even if they do not have cavities.

Trying to keep carbohydrates from teeth is a pretty tall order. After all, food is not much use to us until it has touched the teeth on its way down to the stomach. The best protection is to keep the mouth free of carbohydrates for as much time as possible and this means that children should not be encouraged to eat sweet foods or drink sugary fluids non-stop throughout the day. Also beware the sweet bottle at night! The other point of protection is the realisation that certain carbohydrates appear to be enjoyed more by the bacteria while others seem largely left alone and produce little tooth damaging acid.

Everyone knows that sugar, lollies, sweetened milk, cakes and lemonade are bad for teeth. What is generally unrecognised is that some so-called health foods can be almost equally damaging. Honey would do as much harm as sugar, while many natural fruit juices are just as damaging as lemonade. The breads, vegetables, and some fruits are much less of a problem, but to some extent all carbohydrates can be fermented to make acid. Remember that it is the simplest sugars that make the biggest impact and the longer these simple sugars are in contact with the teeth, the greater will be the damage.

Cheese and other dairy foods, especially milk and yoghurt, are believed to have a protective effect for teeth.

In conclusion, don't be a party pooper and ban all sweet pleasures but if we cannot protect our children's first teeth for six short years, what hope have the second teeth in the seventy years that follow? Moderation is important.

Tonics to stimulate appetite

In Ireland, I trained in a hospital that was particularly sensitive to the happiness and well-being of its elderly patients. Each night a well-known black, alcoholic Dublin beverage was handed out to help wash down the hospital food. Some believed this helped to stimulate the old peoples' appetites; others were more realistic in thinking that it merely stimulated their feeling of well-being. I am often asked for a tonic to stimulate a child's appetite. It would create quite a stir if I were to prescribe the black Dublin 'medicine' but it would be just as effective as any other proprietary brand tonic. There is no such thing as an appetite-stimulating tonic for children.

Vitamins and iron

Children who are on any sort of halfway decent diet don't require any extra vitamins or iron. Though many parents swear by the beneficial effects of their favourite multi-vitamin preparations, there is really no scientific evidence to back up their claims. I recently read an article in which the author said he had gathered together all the papers ever published on the beneficial effects of vitamin C in preventing the common cold. For every paper that claimed it was effective, there was another that presented proof to the contrary.

Occasionally I prescribe a vitamin preparation when I am confronted by an over-worried mother who is sure her child is malnourished, sickly and in need of such things. As I write a prescription I smile as I tell the mum, 'You know this is not going to help your child in any way but my God, it is going to make you feel better'.

Diet and bowels

There is as much variation in the bowel habits of toddlers as there is in the bowel habits of parents. Some children seem to be born with normal bowel regularity; others have lazy bowels, and some are definitely overactive. We are stuck with the equipment we have been allocated, and it can only be regulated by introducing certain dietary changes.

Roughage is definitely an 'in' substance these days. It is said to exert a 'normalising' effect on the bowels, speeding up the sluggish and calming the hyperactive. When a child tends towards constipation, more dietary fibre is encouraged. This roughage can be increased with selected palatable breakfast cereals, vegetables and more fibrous breads and biscuits. Even the baked bean is an excellent form of fibre, having exerted a regularising effect on an entire generation of cowboys who won the west. Fruit and fruit juices provide a most palatable and effective way of giving the sluggish bowel a push.

The term toddler diarrhoea is applied to a condition where a healthy child tends to have a very active bowel. Parents worry over the apparent diarrhoea and, as the children are also generally very physically active, they put on little weight, which further concerns the parents. Gastroenterologists treat this problem by restricting the fluid intake to mealtimes and increasing the fibre and roughage the child eats. Sugars in the diet are reduced, fewer snacks are given, and the child is steered towards the adult pattern of three meals a day. Toddler diarrhoea is a temporary condition; these suggestions just keep it under some form of control until it is cured by time.

What makes a fat kid fat?

Children, like adults, become fat when they have a genetic tendency to lay down fat and then take in quantities of food greater than their body's needs. For years, the experts have debated whether it is the over-eating or the heredity factor that predominates. Despite years of discussion, no-one is any clearer about the answer.

Over-eating

Certainly the amount you eat has a significant bearing on weight gain. Overweight toddlers often have overweight parents as well, but whether this is hereditary or simply the parent inflicting the same over-eating habit on the child is unclear. A great many parents set a very bad example to their children with the type and quantity of food they consume. Others spoil their children with food, sometimes giving it as a poor substitute for proper love and attention. Some parents seem to take a delight in fattening up their offspring, like a cattle farmer preparing beasts for market. To parents, fat may be beautiful but when the competitive teenage years arrive, few children give thanks for obesity, and by that time it is often hard to do anything about it.

Heredity

No-one can become fat without eating but there is no doubt that all children and adults react differently to identical food intakes. Some could be locked in a chocolate factory all weekend and still come out looking like a famine victim. Others only need to see a Mars Bar and they have already gained a kilo.

The statistics relating overweight children to overweight parents are interesting. If neither parent is overweight, there is only a 10 per cent chance that the child will have a weight problem. If one parent is overweight, this increases the child's risk to 40 per cent. If both parents are overweight, the child's risk increases to 70 per cent. This would appear to give all the evidence we need to show that the child's weight is predestined by heredity. One humorous piece of research, however, has rather shattered this view. One group of researchers successfully showed that fat parents had fatter children. Meanwhile, another group came up with the added discovery that they also tended to have fat pets! This rather threw a spanner into the works of the heredity lobby and once again we are left in some confusion. In reality, both diet and heredity are important factors and still no-one is quite sure which plays the stronger role.

Do glands cause obesity?

Many children are referred to endocrine clinics of big hospitals by parents who are convinced that their child is overweight because of a glandular problem. This is a widely held view. This may be true but only to the extent that obesity is related to the salivary gland, with the child's mouth watering whenever he sees any food. Other than this, a connection between glands and obesity in children is extremely rare.

Puppy fat

At the end of their first year, babies have a very different shape from that at the end of their second year. Before children start walking, they usually have rolls of fat on their thighs, arms and abdomen, with few muscles visible. Once they start to exercise, the puppy fat generally disappears and the more grown-up muscular body proportions appear.

Many parents become concerned at about this time, being unaware of the different weight gain rates of different ages. The baby in his first year of life gains weight at a remarkably rapid rate but this reduces markedly after the first birthday, often becoming stationary for a period. At the same time as this fat starts 'burning off', many children become fussy, negative eaters, which causes even more worry about weight.

Over the past decade, numerous articles have been written expressing concern that fat babies become fat toddlers, who in turn become fat children and finally fat adults. The most recent work, however, shows that there is minimal connection between fat babies and fat adults. After the age of 1 year, there is an ever increasing relationship between the ageing child's weight and his adult build. For the fat teenager, it is far easier to put weight on than to take it off, which can be the start of a weight problem that will dog them all of their adult lives.

The importance of exercise

As a nation we are getting fatter. But, strangely we don't appear to be eating more. The problem is that we don't do as much exercise as we used to. Children are particularly 'grounded' these days. Good habits start early, so from the toddler years onwards exercise, activity, getting out and about should become a priority. This is not a message to start training your toddler for the Olympics, merely a reminder to turn off the television more often.

Special diets

Over the last 2000 years doctors have tried to relate health and behaviour to foods in the diet. Although you might think this is sufficient time to have gathered the evidence, I have to report that conclusive data is still not yet available. Certainly there are some specific conditions in which food causes ill health, for example, the allergy of wheat found in coeliac disease, but there is also a great deal of confusion between fact and theory in this matter.

Some children and adults have true allergies to certain foods. A child may eat eggs, seafood or oranges and then have an attack of itching and swollen eyes or diarrhoea. There is little doubt as to the offending substance, as the symptoms appear each time it is introduced into the diet.

There are, however, claims that milk, wheat, corn, malt and yeast are responsible for many conditions, ranging from asthma through to runny noses, dyslexia, sleep problems, clumsiness, and just annoying one's mother. Judging from figures released each year from the asthma clinic in my hospital, it is extremely rare for milk allergy to precipitate or worsen asthma. For most, therefore, this must be regarded as a myth. Our experts also dispute the claim that milk causes runny noses. Folklore has it that milk causes the human body to produce mucus, but scientific evidence to support this is scant.

Much of my work is with disabled children, an area in which constant claims are made that diet improves intelligence and behaviour. I recently saw a mildly mentally-disabled boy whose parents had been assured that if he ate one kelp (seaweed) tablet a day his intelligence would rise to normal within six weeks. This would have been harmless enough, except that each tablet was about the size of a pigeon's egg and tasted like something found in a sewage farm. The child had the insight and was clever enough to remain mildly mentally-disabled.

Other parents have been told that a vitamin B preparation would cure dyslexia but while this preparation is of enormous benefit in the treatment of pellagra, beri beri and possibly even premenstrual tension, it has no beneficial effect whatsoever on reading difficulties.

I have been told that zinc cures autism, which is not true. It is also claimed that artificial colourings, preservatives and some natural foodstuffs have a major detrimental effect on the concentration and on behavioural problems of the hyperactive child. Occasionally this can be true but its effect is much less common than generally believed.

Parents are bombarded by the claims of special diets but it is wise to remember that real medical breakthroughs do not take 2000 years to gain acceptance. From the first dose of penicillin administered, there was never any doubt of its amazing effect. Kelp tablets, artificial colourings and milk, despite all manner of extravagant claims, are simply not in the same league. (See Chapter 18.)

Junk food is not all junk

Junk food is a term created by some media writers to describe all those fun eats like chocolate, soft drinks, lollies, thick shakes, sweet biscuits and fast foods. Now I am not the sort of killjoy who believes that strict avoidance of anything pleasurable is the only way to health and holiness. I do however worry that if taken in excess, these foods have far too much fat, salt and sweetener.

I am a great believer in the therapeutic powers of McDonald's restaurants. It seems to me that these are the best places for any demoralised mother to eat. You just have to walk in the door and immediately you know that there are other children even worse-behaved than your own. For many parents that trip through the golden arches brings the realisation that they are normal, which lifts the morale with probably as much effect as a year of visits to a psychiatrist and all for under ten dollars!

Health foods may not be all that healthy

I have to admit that I do suffer from an allergic condition. I am allergic to the advertising agents who promote health products. Bending of the truth with phrases like, 'no added sugar', 'naturally decaffeinated coffee', 'healthy, dairy-free milk', 'the vitamins to cure colds and stress', 'the magical properties of glucose and honey', make me go pale, cringe and start to stutter.

Don't get me wrong, I have nothing against health foods, in fact my family often eats brown rice, potatoes, vegetables, bread, fruit, baked beans and even drinks water. What is more, when weak and in the need of an occasional glucose lift, my health food is something nice that is sweetened by natural Queensland sugar.

My objection is not to the much needed promotion of healthy diets. It is just that trendy words and truth get somewhat tangled when financial advancement is a major part of the message.

Overdosed with orange juice As I see parents struggle out of the supermarket, weighed down with litres of natural fruit juice, I wonder if this is all quite necessary. Off they rush pouring glasses of it into the line of open little beaks that look over the edge of the nest as they get home. These juices have become almost a sacred part of life and you could believe that the mothers will be testing the teeth for the wobbles of scurvy if they miss a few days. If our children eat real fruit, of the sort that comes from a tree, fruit juices become nice but not necessary.

Orange juice is encouraged as there is still the belief that excessive amounts keep children healthy and fight off the common cold. Despite years of study there is no evidence to back up this idea. The body does not store excess vitamin C, which is flushed out the kidneys and down the toilet as quick as you can say ascorbic acid. It astounds me that some parents will give up to five glasses of orange juice a day to their children. If each glass were to contain three oranges, you have just seen fifteen oranges disappear. That would be enough to turn me inside out.

The perfectly balanced breakfast cereal It would be very smart to eat a low fat, low salt and low sugar cereal if our children were like battery hens who lived on nothing else. But for them this is only a part of a big balanced diet. It all seems a bit pointless, if this perfect product is then submerged in full cream milk and sprinkled with sugar until it looks like the alps in winter.

The juice with no added sugar So often the advertisement says, 'This juice has no added sugar'. The truth is that it probably doesn't need any more, it already contains quite enough sugar in its natural state. There are many ways of getting sugar into contact with delicate teeth other than spooning it in from sugar cane.

Sometimes juices have no added sugar but that is not to say that artificial sweetening and other chemicals have not been included.

Glucose, honey and health Glucose is a simple, highly refined sugar, similar to sucrose (cane sugar). Its absorption into the blood may be marginally more rapid but it is no more nutritious than its cheaper brothers.

Honey is a natural product which many believe has almost mythical properties. In reality it is just a blend of simple sugars refined by the intricate innards of a bee. Though it has a pleasant taste, it is less pure than glucose or cane sugar.

Glucose and honey have no special health-giving properties. *As sweeteners they have no advantage over cane sugar and when made into a health drink they are no kinder to teeth than lemonade.*

Health bars If health bars are going to be popular, they generally need to be sweet, fatty or full of fruit. The fact that the product gets its sugar from fruit, honey or glucose, instead of sugar cane, does nothing to promote health. There are of course some genuinely healthy exceptions but most children would not be tripping over each other in the rush to eat them.

Healthy natural vegetable milk I find it hard to come to terms with vegetable milks, as my old-fashioned mind believes that milk is something that comes from a mammal and not from a vegetable-processing plant. Cow's milk is good for little cows and not too bad for little humans either. Soy and other milks may be beneficial when our children have true milk allergies but for the average child they have no special health-giving properties.

Bran – good for horses Processed bran is popular with both health enthusiasts and horses but toddlers are not without wisdom, and dislike eating something that tastes like sawdust. If you want to get bran into little children, some of the high roughage breakfast cereals or fibre rich loaves are the best answer. For most young children it is better to leave bran in the stables and rely on the more enjoyable fibre that comes in fruit and vegetables.

Vitamin enriched health drinks Blackcurrant, rosehip and other syrups are advertised as a healthy way to tank up on vitamin C. They are no better than the cheap vitamin C tablet, readily available from your chemist. The main concern with these syrups is that some contain an unhealthy excess of sugar for safe, regular use.

Dried fruit and nuts Raisins, sultanas and dates are a popular form of toddler snack but they are sweet and stick to the teeth to some extent, causing the same sorts of problems as chocolates, toffees and other confectionery. Peanuts and toddlers are generally a bad combination. Peanuts are quite nourishing if eaten but hospitals spend many hours each year removing inhaled ones from little children who have sent them down the wrong tube.

An enormous industry exists out there producing health drinks, health bars and healthy breakfast cereals but these products bear some investigation. Certainly added roughage and complex carbohydrate is to be encouraged but if the product is then smothered in honey, glucose or some other high carbohydrate food then the benefit is lost. Some products are advertised as containing no salt and sugar, but these will only be of benefit if the child is going to continue on this diet right through the day. It is pointless if it is followed immediately by a highly sweetened milk shake and some salty salami. Health drinks that contain all natural ingredients may contain these in unhealthy proportions. Milk is a true natural food, if it is not tarted up with additives.

Perhaps I am a trifle cynical about the advertised advantages of health foods. A substance may be natural but this does not mean it must be healthy. You can rot teeth, become fat and poison your system just as well with natural substances as with factory produced ones. Tobacco and opium are two very natural substances.

Conclusion

There are many ways to get a good diet into our young children, it just takes a bit of ingenuity, calmness and commonsense.

Example is important and that is where we, the parents, need to smarten up our own act. Sensible parents who give a reasonably balanced diet have little to worry about. If the children are growing, healthy and happy – relax, you have got it right.

THIRTEEN

Feeding Without Fights

Parents use up an enormous amount of energy forcing stubborn but otherwise well-nourished toddlers to eat against their will. All these parental antics are a great source of mirth to the child but, when the final score is taken at the end of the meal, not an extra pea has been eaten. Playing aeroplanes, dive bombers, singing, dancing, crawling round the floor barking, and threatening that they won't grow up 'big and strong like daddy' are a complete waste of time. Just as adults don't eat bigger meals while being entertained at a theatre-restaurant, toddlers' consumption won't be improved by all this entertainment either. What they really need is gentle encouragement.

Some children take their food extremely seriously, never lifting their eyes from the plate until they have almost scraped the pattern from it. Others dawdle, play, and escape at the first opportunity, finding food a complete bore. Some children are thin, some are fat, some are fussy and some are walking garbage bins. Don't force. Remember, no child has ever starved to death through stubbornness. At a recent lecture I made this statement and almost before the words had left my lips a militant mum at the back was on her feet complaining. 'Dr Green, you are wrong. My child once went for twelve hours without food and if I hadn't forced him he would certainly have starved.' 'Do you know how long it takes the average hunger striker to die?' I asked. 'No I don't,' was the frosty reply. 'Well it's about sixty-eight days,' I said. 'Do you mean that at the Children's Hospital, Westmead, you recommend only feeding the children every sixty-eight days?' was the answer. With this, the dietitian sitting beside me could control himself no longer. 'If you are really worried in the future, how about giving Dr Green a call on the morning of the twentieth day?' I think she got the message.

Normal feeding patterns

Most babies in their first year are in no doubt about what to do with food. They don't mess about, generally getting the food to where it belongs with a minimum of fuss.

By 9 months, the food goes down with relative ease, and the chewing pattern becomes well-established. At this stage, the first teeth are just tiny, ornamental pearls that do little damage to the food as it hurries past.

By 1 year, the teeth are used more for chewing, and the child eats a diet similar to that of the rest of the family. Many children at this age undergo a dramatic change of attitude to food, halving their intake and becoming extremely fussy. At this time, too, the child's weight gain may slow up, stop or even go down, while activity burns up the puppy fat and stubbornness restricts food intake. From this age onwards the negative streak is always just around the corner, so with most children, forcing them to eat becomes unproductive.

At 15 months, independent children are keen on holding a

spoon, although few can keep it level between plate and mouth – the contents usually slip off as the arm tries to negotiate the bends. Children will also hold a feeding cup and, after 18 months, most children will suck rather than chew the end of a straw.

At 3 years old a knife can be used by them to cut soft foods and attempts to butter their own bread will follow soon after. By 4^1/$_2$ the child should be able to use a knife and fork in a sort of way, and it is just before this age that Chinese children generally learn to use chopsticks.

Feed – don't fight

Toddlers have minds and tastes of their own. The dining table must never become a battleground.

The ten-point plan for problem-free meals

1. Avoid disorganised, disturbed, noisy mealtimes. The toddler should sit and eat with the rest of the family, but if this is impractical then a parent should sit next to the child and feed him before the main family meal.

2. Although the toddler should ideally be given a variety of well-balanced foods, if he dislikes variety, then a repetitive but nutritious diet is perfectly acceptable. After all he's the one who has to eat it, not you.

3. Adult eating habits should be encouraged, but it is no disaster if a child decides to return to the main course after having polished off his pudding.

4. Use labour-saving cooking ideas, because it is hard to stay calm when the wilful toddler refuses a dish that has taken hours to prepare.

5. Gently encourage the child to eat, NEVER force.

6. Once it is obvious that the child is not going to eat any more,

Choking on food

Young children do not have the back teeth needed to chew and grind lumps of food properly; these may not be fully developed until around 4 years of age. Young children are still learning to eat solid food.

Food swallowed in large pieces is more likely to get stuck and block off the airways. If it goes 'down the wrong way' this can cause young children to choke.

If young children run, play, laugh or cry while eating they are more likely to choke on their food.

How to make eating safer for young children

Food:

■ Do not give food that can break off into hard pieces.
■ Avoid raw carrot, celery sticks and apple pieces, for example. These foods should be grated, cooked or mashed.
■ Sausages, frankfurts and other meats should be cut into small pieces. Tough skins on frankfurts and other sausages should be removed.
■ Do not give popcorn, nuts, hard lollies, cornchips or other similar foods to young children.

At eating times:

■ Always stay with young children and supervise them while eating.
■ Make sure that young children sit quietly while eating.
■ Never force young children to eat, as this may cause them to choke.

What to do if a young child chokes on food

Check first if the child is still able to breathe, cough or cry.

If the child is breathing, coughing or crying, the child may be able to dislodge the food by coughing:

- Do not try to dislodge the food by hitting the child on the back because this may move the food into a more dangerous position and make the child stop breathing.
- Stay with the child and watch to see if their breathing improves.
- If the child is not breathing easily within a few minutes, phone 000 (111 in New Zealand) for an ambulance.

If the child is not breathing:
- Try to dislodge the piece of food by placing the child face down over your lap so that their head is lower than their chest.
- Give the child four sharp blows on the back just beween the shoulder blades. This should provide enough force to dislodge the food.
- Check again for signs of breathing.
- If the child is still not breathing, urgently call 000 (111 in New Zealand) and ask for an ambulance. The ambulance service operator will be able to tell you what to do next.

Courtesy, Women's and Children's Hospital, Adelaide.

wipe his hands and face clean and allow him to get down from the table. Whether this is after five minutes or half an hour, don't worry about it. If the child is dawdling over his food, leave him to dawdle without an audience.

7. Display no anger if food is not eaten. Put the untouched plate in the fridge and bring it out later on request.

8. It is the child's right to eat or not to eat his food as he pleases. Parents have a perfect right to fight with their child if that is what they want, but they should have the sense to avoid battles over food. If a child refuses the meal, he must not be allowed to immediately top up on milk, chips and the like.

9. Don't fuss if children prefer picking foods up with hands rather than using spoons or other eating utensils. Hands are fine and minimise washing up.

10. Never let children run around eating. Make sure they sit down. Choking on food is a real problem. (See Box: Choking on food.)

Make food fun

When serving fine food to adults, a chef prides himself not only on the taste but also on the presentation. The same should apply when feeding toddlers. For a start, portions should not be massive. Various garnishings should be used, such as a square of cheese, some raisins and a few fingers of fruit. Vary texture and colour wherever possible and make food look appealing. Bread can be cut into fun triangles and homemade biscuits can be baked in animal shapes.

When feeding problems continue, then try varying the venue. Wonders can be achieved by transporting stubborn feeders to the balcony or the garden, where they can drink milk through a straw and eat little sandwiches out of a lunch box.

I think we have to rid ourselves of some of our rigid and old-fashioned ideas about feeding toddlers. Within reason, try to give them what they want, where they want it, and when they are hungry. They are going to have to learn adult eating habits sooner or later, but to begin with it is more important to get them enjoying the process of eating.

Nibbling can be nutritious

Toddlers have none of our funny adult ideas about food. When they are hungry they want to eat. When they are not hungry they don't. Rigid fixed mealtimes are more appropriate to top restaurants than to the toddler. We should encourage the main meal habit but when this is obviously failing, cut your losses and let them eat when they're hungry. Now is the time for snacks.

Healthy snacks don't mean thick milkshakes, chocolate or salty chips. Ideally, they should include raw grated carrots and finely chopped celery but few children have read that book and remain unconvinced. It seems that the 'in' food now is complex carbohydrate. Bread is pretty complex, especially if fortified with some extra fibre, so sandwiches are healthy. All that's needed is a bit of imagination with the fillings. Surprisingly, there are substances other than Vegemite to put on bread. What about egg, or peanut butter? Chewable meat or even baked beans are good too. Add a glass of milk to the baked bean sandwich and you'd have most nutritionists smiling.

Finger foods make ideal snacks for the busy toddler. Cubes of cheese, slices of fruit and sliced, cooked vegetables, are all fine. Of course there is also banana and chopped cold sausage, both of which are highly portable. Anything that you can both eat and poke the dog with has got to impress the average toddler.

We might as well face the fact that between-meal snacks are here to stay, so they should be treated as seriously as the main meals they often replace. Properly orchestrated, this 'alternative' diet can improve rather than damage children's health.

Labour-saving food preparation

I'm sure that at some time or other in your life you've slaved over a hot stove for hours preparing a delicacy for your dream child, only to find he takes one look at it and turns his nose up in disgust. Times like these tempt you to child abuse! Rather than taking this drastic course of action, may I recommend a bit of labour-saving cooking instead.

A liquidiser or food processor and a freezing tray are all that the parents of babies need for food preparation. In one morning you can cook carrots, cauliflower, pumpkin, steak, chicken, fish and apples, pop them in the liquidiser (one at a time), and then put them into individual ice-cube trays for freezing. When mealtime comes, all you have to do is look in the freezer and decide on the menu, defrost it, and there you have a small portion of an instant, but freshly made meal. This idea can be carried through to toddler-hood as well, using slightly larger containers and of course non-liquidised food. Food can be prepared as quickly as it takes an ice-cube to melt and, when refused, can be returned to the refriger-ator (not the freezer) as quickly as you can say 'See if I care!'.

Feeding the militantly independent child

From their first birthday, some children are hell bent on feeding themselves without any outside assistance. Unfortunately the most independent children are usually the most impatient, which is a sure recipe for trouble. These children should be given a spoon large enough to allow them to load the food with some accuracy. To cope with the spillage on the long journey from plate to mouth, a 'pelican' bib, one of those strong plastic bibs with a large catchment area at the bottom, is recommended. As the drop-out food is caught in the bib, it can be quickly recycled, cutting down on mess and wastage.

To further help the impatient and hungry child determined to have a go at feeding himself, it is best to give him one spoon while feeding him with another. But remember, if children want to feed themselves with their fingers, that's fine (if messy).

The toddler who's hooked on bottles and baby food

If after 8 months of age the child's diet is still milk and bland, untex-tured baby foods, it may be extremely difficult to change him over to a proper mixed diet. Prevention is obviously better than cure, so parents must be encouraged to provide a variety of textured solids after 6 months, avoiding milk as the sole source of nourishment.

For those who are hooked on milk and refuse solids, it is hard to give effective help without cutting down dramatically on the milk intake. Some people are extremely tough on these toddlers and exclude all milk immediately, substituting less calorific fluids until the child gives in and starts taking a reasonable diet. I prefer a gentler approach, which in the end achieves exactly the same results. The milk intake should be reduced by about half and other fluids and a variety of interesting nibbly things introduced. This is usually all that is required, but if it does not work immediately then the milk can be further reduced. Like all such procedures, the parent must not weaken mid-way.

Firmness is also needed with toddlers who have remained on slushy baby foods for too long. These children often refuse to chew and the slightest lump causes them to gag. Somehow, however, they seem to exert some hidden strength when a piece of chocolate is popped into their mouths. Once again, prevention is better than cure, as these children will often put up quite a fight before you can get them onto a normal diet. To cure these children, I start again by halving the milk intake so that it cannot be used as a substitute food. Then I gradually start polluting tinned baby food with homemade liquidised products and, as the days go by, I make the food more and more homemade. Gradually a normal diet is achieved in a matter of weeks.

What is enough food intake?

Children have different food requirements. They eat like birds: some like sparrows, others like vultures. There is no correct amount of food for all children to consume in a day. Food intake and growth are not the only indicators of good health, energy is also important. If my car used only half the manufacturer's recommended amount of petrol to cover a given number of kilometres, I would not complain. I would be grateful that I had an efficient machine that was obviously tuned to perfection. Forcing toddlers to feed is futile. We need more sense and less food.

Consider the toddler's point of view

It is a very special occasion and you are booked to eat at the best restaurant in town. Out comes the food, immaculate with those cordon bleu sauces flowing off the meat. Your mouth is watering at the very smell.

Then up marches the head waiter, looks you in the eye and with a stern voice says: 'Just one thing, madam. You will not be leaving the table until you've eaten every bite. What's more there will be no dessert until your plate is completely clear.' Would it not make you choke?

A minute later there beside you is the chef, complete with beard and big white hat. He takes out a large carving knife and fork and proceeds to cut up your meat into little pieces, mashes it all up with the vegetables and then starts spooning it into your mouth.

Just put yourself in your child's place. Why should he like it any more than you would? Get off their backs and don't fight over food.

Conclusion

Most toddlers whose parents claim that they never eat are in fact getting a very adequate food intake.

If children wish to eat three good meals a day, that is highly commendable, but for those who don't, it is usually better to provide nourishing snacks rather than fighting with them. Time and peer-group pressures will eventually force the toddler into more traditional mealtime habits; in the meantime, be flexible and use your imagination.

Remember, food is not just for nourishment, food is for fun.

FOURTEEN

Nasty Habits in Nice Children

In those dreamy days before toddlers, I bet you never saw yourself reading and recognising your children in a chapter like this. Now you may well have found that the nicest of nice children can display some of the nastiest of nasty habits. Let's look at a selection of these.

Biting

The residents who man our hospital's busy Emergency Department once asked me if I would come and lecture to them, and I presumed they wanted to hear me expound on some high-powered medical topic. To my surprise, I found that what they wanted to hear, more than anything else, was how to manage children who bite! It seemed that in our city biting had reached almost epidemic proportions, which was upsetting not only our emergency officers but also parents, playgroup leaders, and any child or adult within biting distance.

In my experience, biting is purely a playgroup habit found mostly in the 1 to 2½ years age group. It is not a premeditated, spiteful act, just a symptom of this age of little sense. Your little biter doesn't get up with the lark, sit there and hatch a plot to get into playgroup early, hide behind the door and ambush Freddie Smith when he enters, sinking his teeth into his arm like a demented piranha. It's more a case of Freddie happens to be passing, your angel is a bit overexcited and not thinking. He bites him as an impulse. It just seems like a good idea at the time.

Experts who have written on this topic state that it is a symptom of a tense, anxious child and although this may occasionally be the case, in practical terms I find it a great deal easier to stop a child biting than to stop a child feeling tense.

Many babies in the first year of life suddenly sink their teeth into whoever is carrying them, unaware of the pain they may cause. Although this is not a malicious act, it is important that the baby be taught that it is not an acceptable form of behaviour. Rather than shouting, becoming angry or slapping the baby, it is preferable to put him down on the floor immediately. It does not take the average baby long to work out that, if he wants the pleasure of a cuddle, he shouldn't indulge in cannibalism.

With the toddler, it is usually a piece of brother or sister that finds itself wedged between the closing teeth and as this is a sort of family feast, it is much easier to discipline, as you own both the biter and the bitee.

When it is a neighbour's child that has been nibbled, the parents may expect you to instigate some sort of major retribution. If justice is not seen to be done, friends may ban their little children from your house and it can lead to family feuds more vicious than that of the Montagues and Capulets.

How you react to a bite will depend on the circumstances. If just a minor nip in times of excitement, a gentle warning is all that is needed. If it is repeated, premeditated or major and a stern warning has been ignored, then use Time Out or, although it is not politically correct, some parents will give a short sharp smack to register the limits of acceptable behaviour.

When your toddler bites another at playgroup, this is a different matter. Now you are in the full public view, without Time Out to fall back on and if you smack, half the audience will criticise. It is particularly embarrassing when your loved one has become known as 'Jaws' to the other mums. The best you can do is to watch carefully, warn firmly, divert when an impending attack is anticipated and then, if a bite occurs, ignore the biter and give the best toys and attention to the injured party. This may sound rather wishy-washy but when outside the home, your hands are tied and in truth your child probably has more teeth than any technique I may suggest.

Many parents view all this warning and diverting as pathetically weak. For them there is only one answer. If their child bites, they bite him back. This is the eye for an eye and a tooth for a tooth approach that was probably pretty modern 2000 years ago. I think that there are better ways of doing things now.

Don't despair – remember that biting is only a habit of the first 2½ years and be reassured that they will not be going round biting others as adults, unless they take up rugby.

Finger up the nose

Little noses are to little fingers like a burrow is to a bunny. It is a comfortable place to explore when there is nothing better to do. Though most toddler fingers find toddler nostrils at times of tiredness or boredom, occasionally an older child with an easily baited parent will do it just to annoy.

Finger in nose – dad explodes. Finger up again – dad explodes again – great fun for child! Soon this little arm is going up and down like a fiddler's elbow. When this happens, it is best to ignore, divert to something more useful and if you decide to take notice, don't make a game out of it, be 100 per cent firm.

The gentle poke of boredom is another matter. When recently I was on a lecture tour in the United States it seemed that every time

I talked on air some parent asked about fingers up noses. Such was the concern, you might have thought this habit to be exclusive to North American nostrils, but it isn't; this is a universal toddler pastime.

The toddler watches the TV, is bored, his mind slips and with it a finger, ever upward and inward. You can only sympathise with the problem, such is the standard of today's television.

With toddlers, the aim is to divert them and keep those little hands and minds fully occupied. I believe we should not be too tough with our youngsters; after all we adults have some pretty nasty and not dissimilar habits ourselves. The next time you stop at a red traffic light, take a look at the car beside. You can see where one hand is, but you have no idea what is happening with the other. That's why film stars have tinted glass in their limousines.

Head banging

Head banging is a habit which can occur for one of two reasons. Usually it is part of a tantrum in the senseless 1 to 2-year-old, though it may be a form of innocent entertainment in the child of a slightly older age. Parents fear that a bit of banging will damage their child's brain but when you look at football players and boxers, you realise that even the most persistent toddler's efforts are pretty trivial by comparison. Other parents believe that this is a sure sign of disability or mental disturbance, but if the child is normal in every other way, head banging is not a sign of significance.

When senseless young toddlers do not get their own way, they may fall to the floor and bang their heads. They rarely hurt themselves and if this does happen it is certainly not intentional. They are usually careful to seek out the surface with the greatest noise potential and the lowest pain-inflicting factor.

Head banging tantrums are short lived, as the child soon develops sufficient sense to realise that self-inflicted pain is a poor way of punishing others. It is as silly as a robber who enters the bank and says, 'Hand over the money or I will poke myself in the eye with this stick'. Head banging is quite self-limiting and all you have to do is divert attention elsewhere. If that's difficult, just let them go for it. Toddlers may have little sense but they are not stupid. Whatever you do, this habit will be well away by the age of 2 years.

Some children head bang when bored or tired. This is usually the speciality of active children who enjoy rocking and gentle head banging, particularly in the cot. They do it because it is enjoyable and sends them to sleep as reliably as counting sheep. Though it may be soothing for children, the rhythmic thump is far from soothing for the adults of the house. There is not much you can do about it other than padding the edge of the cot, or in extreme cases, putting a pillow under each cot leg to deaden the transmission of sound. This sort of head banging is not a sign of bad behaviour but a form of innocent entertainment that gives as much pleasure as thumb sucking or nail biting.

Breath holding attacks

These are among the most alarming of all toddler behaviour traits. Some children have been reported as having up to ten attacks a day, others one a month. Luckily the vast majority of toddlers never indulge in this nasty habit in their lives.

Breath holding comes in two forms, the more common cyanotic (blue) type and the rarer pallid (faint) type. With the cyanotic attack, the child voluntarily holds his breath to the point of passing out; it is a kind of super-tantrum used to stir up anyone preventing the child from getting his own way. Although less common, the pallid form is associated with a painful experience. For example, the child sustains a minor hurt and passes out rapidly in a form of fainting fit.

The cyanotic (blue) attack

These attacks most commonly occur from 18 months to 4 years, although they may occasionally be seen before the first birthday in the really negative child. This is not a new behaviour pattern brought about by the hectic life-style of the twenty-first century. Hippocrates described something very similar happening among the terrible toddlers of ancient Greece.

What normally happens is that the child is thwarted in the midst of some action that is vitally important to him and, reviewing his repertoire of reactions, he decides that breath holding will be a more effective reprisal than one of his lesser tantrums. He then gives about three long cries, the last going all the way until his lungs are completely empty of air. The audience waits in anticipation for the next breath but the ensuing silence is deafening. No breath is heard. Over the next fifteen seconds the child voluntarily holds his breath, which inevitably leads to him going blue in the face and passing out. Once unconscious the child loses voluntary control of his breathing; the body immediately switches over to 'automatic pilot' and breathing restarts, with full consciousness returning about fifteen seconds later. Occasionally the episode may end in a minor short convulsion, leaving the parents even more upset.

Breath holding attacks terrify parents but do not harm children. Although the treatment is extremely easy for a doctor to prescribe, I realise it is very difficult for a parent to administer. If breath holding is to be stopped it must be viewed in the same light as a tantrum or any other challenging behaviour. It must simply be totally ignored, as making a fuss about it will only ensure that it is repeated.

Firstly the parents must be quite certain that this is a breath holding attack and not some quite different medical problem which they are misunderstanding. After this, the techniques of diversion and ignoring must be used. Diversionary tactics will usually fail, so when the child stops breathing, he must be left to his own devices. Difficult as it is to do, parents should watch carefully while the child is briefly unconscious but the moment consciousness begins to return, move away immediately. With this he will open his eyes and look around for the appreciative audience, but he has wasted his time because they have just walked out.

Some experts suggest splashing cold water on the child's face as he starts to hold his breath. This may be effective, but it will only work if done in that first fifteen seconds of voluntary breath holding. After that it is pointless and probably dangerous once unconsciousness has occurred.

I have no illusions that this is an easy treatment but I know that firmness and ignoring the child, although hard, are the only effective methods of curing this behaviour. After the child reaches the age of 4, breath holding becomes extremely rare.

The pallid (faint) attack

This is not the true breath holding attack, as it is more like a simple fainting spell than a form of attention-seeking tantrum. Children who have pallid attacks seem to be particularly sensitive to pain or fear, either of which may trigger off an attack. (They are generally thought to become the sort of adults who faint at the thought of a hypodermic needle or the sight of blood.)

A 2-year-old may be walking under a table when he hits his head hard on the edge. In the pallid attack, he would not cry out or hold his breath but will simply go limp and fall to the ground. His heart rate drops dramatically, and he looks very pale. This is the child's equivalent of an adult faint, and recovery is usually quite quick.

As for treatment, if the child is lying flat nothing else needs to be done and nature will remedy the situation. If the attacks are genuinely the result of some involuntary reflex in a sensitive child, then the child should be cuddled and fussed over upon recovery. Although this seems quite logical, most authors on the subject in the past seem to have doubts about whether or not there may be some minor attention-seeking component in this action, and it is suggested that the parents maintain a low profile and do not fuss too much over the child.

Let me reassure parents with children who suffer from breath holding attacks, however, that it is not a serious condition. It is the parents, more than the children, who need consoling.

Playing with their private parts

Most toddlers play with their genitalia at some time or other. They may touch, rub, rock or move their legs, all for the pleasurable effects these motions afford. It is normal toddler behaviour, and it has no true sexual overtones.

Historically, so much fuss has been made over children masturbating that even the most broad-minded parents still have a twinge of concern when they see their children doing it. Tales of how it would send you mad or deaf, or both, still ring in their ears. It was even claimed in Victorian times that it sent you blind. This of course is utter rubbish, but even if it were true most of our children would opt to do it a little and wear glasses.

These days, parents are encouraged to relax, ignore it and not let their own hang-ups get in the way. Playing with the genitalia occurs in both boys and girls. It starts in the second year when the nappy region is unveiled and a new area of discovery is made available. The treatment is to completely ignore what is, after all, a perfectly innocent habit.

Now it is all very easy for me to say ignore but what do you do when the child is standing in church with his hands down his pants, or when the grandparents are visiting? In fact it is probably more realistic to gently divert the offending hand or interest the child in something more sociable. I emphasise that at toddler age this has no sexual connotations and it almost exclusively happens when they are tired, tense or bored. Ignoring, diversion and keeping them active is the answer – not humiliation or punishment.

Sometime later in the pre-school years, children discover that little boys and little girls are not identical. This leads to a certain amount of innocent interest which is a quite normal and natural stage of development. This needs to be viewed with a broad mind and a relatively blind eye.

When I was recently in the United States one talk show host asked an off-the-air question about little boys and little girls. She was quite embarrassed, as her own $3^1/_2$-year-old boy had the day before been found naked with the neighbour's 4-year-old girl. I said that this sounded all pretty normal to me and she agreed, but it appeared that the neighbour had taken it as a serious form of assault. I said it was not the children but the neighbour who had the problem and maybe she should consider seeing a psychiatrist. Quick as a flash my host replied, 'The trouble is she is one'.

Concerns of sexual abuse

The statistics vary from study to study but, at the most conservative estimate, one in ten adult women and one in twenty adult men have suffered sexual abuse in childhood. The extent of this varies from an incident of touching to major repeated sexual activity.

The worst part of sexual abuse is that the perpetrator is usually a trusted adult or adolescent who is well known to the child. They can be a relative, family friend, stepfather or even father. In sexual abuse, power is inappropriately misused and children are made to feel guilty and the older child may be frightened to speak out.

As a paediatrician, I find this an extremely difficult diagnosis to make. In its most clear-cut presentation, abuse shows as obvious physical damage or there is an unmistakable history. More commonly, the only sign is a change in behaviour. The child may withdraw into themselves, become angry or display inappropriately explicit sexual behaviour. When an astute parent sees this change they may pick up clues of the assault, but often the school-age child feels so guilty and confused they maintain a code of silence.

I often see another side to this when parents are incorrectly reported and investigated as abusers. In my experience this usually happens with older children who have a major developmental problem that results in some disinhibited, inappropriate sexual behaviour. There is no evidence of abuse, just out-of-step behaviour that prompts the diligent child care worker to make the report. Often the families are already struggling to stay afloat, and while this assault on parents may be legally necessary, it is extremely destructive. Abuse damages children, but false claims of abuse can pull apart stressed families.

The main message for parents is to gradually educate but not terrify children about the possibility of abuse, stranger danger and the importance of saying no. A 2-year-old will not understand much of this at first, but by school age they will get the message. We must be on our guard when there is any unexplained, inappropriately explicit sexual behaviour.

One of the saddest aspects of abuse is that the child can no longer trust the adults who are supposed to protect them. The sad part for me is that I probably diagnose only a small proportion of the children in my care who are abused.

Whingeing

Whingeing is one of the most parent-destroying activities that any child can indulge in. Naturally we expect children who are tired, sick or teething to whinge but there still remains a great band of healthy, well-rested children who continue to devastate their parents. As practised by some children, this habit is equal in potency to the Chinese water torture. In my experience, boys generally take the prize for overactivity and really bad behaviour but when it comes to whingeing, the fairer sex usually gets the gold medal every time.

There is a great variation in a child's ability to whinge. Some never whinge at all, others wind up to full volume at the drop of a hat, whilst some work their way up in fits and starts, prolonging the agony as skilfully as any torture in the Spanish Inquisition.

The trouble with whingeing is that we can unintentionally make it into a much repeated behaviour by the way we act. The 4-year-old is not allowed out to play because it is raining. He complains and whinges. This gets particularly painful after ten minutes so you repent in order to preserve your sanity. Now you have blown it. You have set a precedent that a definite 'No' can be turned to an equally definite 'Yes' if you whinge long enough. This is not a wise way to run things.

Skilful mothers can divert lesser whingers back to the straight and narrow by noticing something around the house or setting off on some interesting activity. This strategy can be of some benefit in the not-very-determined whinger.

If diversion does not work, the child must be ignored. Mortal man has only a limited ability to actually ignore whingeing, so pretending to ignore it is probably the best we can hope for. It still gives an equally strong message to the offending party. When the parents can no longer ignore the irritation, and the situation is coming close to a blow-up when somebody is going to lose control, this is the moment to employ the Time Out technique. This avoids a loss of control when everyone would become very unhappy, and little would be achieved.

As a last resort, when diversion, ignoring and Time Out have all failed, mother must sweep up the offending party and head for the great outdoors. Most children suspend hostilities as soon as they escape from the restrictions of the home battleground, and with the minority who continue, the whingeing never seems so bad when competing with bird song and noisy motor vehicles.

The absconder

Any toddler worth his salt, and who has read up on his child psychology, will realise that he is meant to be clingy and loath to be separated from his parents. A small percentage, however, seem ignorant of this fact, and they are forever running off and getting lost. Absconders are a real trial to their parents, who are forced to take part in high speed pursuits down the main street, hide and seek in the supermarket and the interminable wait for the voice to come over the loudspeaker informing them that the infant absconder has been corralled and is awaiting pick-up. If your child is an absconder, make sure he is wearing a luggage label like Paddington bear.

Luckily most absconders develop sufficient sense to stop the habit within a six-month period but some may take years to grow out of it. I have little success in treating children who run off. I am able only to suggest that the parents remain fit and vigilant at all times, or resort to toddler reins. I have fitted reins to many children including two who had the curious habit of jumping on passing buses. The first did it as a form of attention-seeking but was always extracted before the bus started off. The second child managed to get as far as the terminus, his mother following in hot pursuit in a taxi.

One mother told how, while shopping in a department store, her toddler became bored and wandered off. A search was mounted and the police were called. It later turned out that he had gone up the escalator to the next floor and found the bed department. He had tried out a few beds and was found fast asleep on a king-size deluxe Posturepedic.

Interrupting adults

One of the greatest sources of irritation with small children is their inability to refrain from interrupting when adults are talking. In some houses it is almost impossible for parents to talk to each other when there is an awake toddler around. Parents often find it hard even to communicate by cuddles and kisses without the star of the show trying to force his way in between them.

The child has three problems. He thinks his wise sayings are of earth-shattering importance and that everyone must immediately shut up and listen. He does not like others stealing his much enjoyed position centre stage, and he knows that if he does not say his piece immediately it will be forgotten and lost forever.

Some children become absolutely impossible when visitors call and want to talk at some length to their parents. The child interferes so much that tempers are lost or the visit becomes a complete waste of time for all concerned. Visitors who are real friends should realise that the toddler needs a lot of attention, and if they are not sharp enough to see this, their absence is probably not a great loss anyway.

Some children refuse to let their parents talk on the phone. They successfully prevent this by either making so much noise that reasoned conversation is rendered impossible, or create such havoc in the house that the call has to be abandoned.

Several years ago I looked after a young disabled boy whose favourite trick was to wait until the phone rang and then set off at high speed round the house, turning on every possible electrical appliance he could before the call was terminated. When his mother got off the phone the house was buzzing with the noise of vacuum cleaners, food mixers, hair dryers, while lights blazed like a crystal palace on a Saturday night, and the electricity meter raced round and round like a Grand Prix car.

Now the bad news . . . I have no answers to help those whose children behave in this way, except to assure you that it is perfectly normal behaviour. I suppose that visitors who try to monopolise parents are pretty boring to a toddler, who tries to discourage them. Long telephone calls are fairly antisocial at the best of times and should be reserved for the evening. The constant interruption of conversations will resolve itself by the end of toddlerhood, by which time the child will have a better short-term memory, be less impulsive, and will have learnt to wait his turn. It is sometimes useful to have some special toys on a high shelf which can only be used while mum is on the phone. This can be especially useful if working from home. A cordless phone could be considered a neccessity in this situation.

Teeth grinding

The noise of grinding teeth sends a shiver down any parent's spine and conjures up all sorts of thoughts of madness. Grinding the teeth during sleep is a common, normal occurrence. It doesn't indicate that the child has worms or is suffering from any form of lunacy. There is little to be done to help the situation, although in very extreme cases dentists have been known to intervene.

Normal toddlers occasionally grind their teeth noisily by day but, in my experience, it is almost exclusively the behaviour of a child with a major disability. Some people report success with these children, but it has not been my experience that any therapy has lessened the amount of nerve-shattering noise.

Bad language

Even kings and queens use rude words, but only in private. Our children are different from royalty – they hear words in private and repeat them in public! However, bad language is not a major problem in toddlers. Much of the obscene language they know is learnt at pre-school, along with all the other trappings of a normal education, and is regurgitated parrot-fashion at home. Indeed, parents tell me that all bad language is from school, but some must come from a source nearer to home. Toddlers are great mimics and they have mighty retentive memories. Just remember that the next time you hammer your thumb instead of the nail or express your opinion of someone else's bad driving.

A mother once told me the following story. Her husband loved his garden. When the dog from next door kept digging it up, he got very angry and called the dog a 'bloody mongrel', not noticing their toddler was nearby, all ears. Later, while walking to the supermarket the family passed a beautifully coiffured poodle. The toddler pointed to the poodle and announced to all and sundry, 'bloody mongrel!'

The problem with swearing is not so much the words used, but where our children use them. A lot of bad language involves religious figures and references to 'begatting' but despite this it doesn't sound good in church.

Toddlers also have an extraordinary interest in 'lavatory' talk. Bottoms and bodily functions seem to make fascinating topics of conversation, probably because in the toddler's world of limited experience, these are subjects that they can talk about with real authority. The bodily function fascination usually disappears of its own accord before the age of 5, and before that it can be gently doused, generally by diverting the child's attention to something else.

When new, undesirable words come from the toddler, the chances are that he does not know what they mean but is aware of the interesting effect they have on his parents. In handling this problem some degree of selective deafness is suggested and a quiet caution, like 'we don't really want to hear that'. If the parents throw a tantrum every time the child uses a certain word, it again gives him a potent weapon to stir up the household any time life begins to look a bit boring.

Undesirable language shouldn't be allowed to upset the parents, but it should be gently moulded out of the vocabulary. A major confrontation will lead to nothing but trouble and will probably only suffice to implant the behaviour even more firmly.

If a household is run on democratic lines, it is only fair that if parents are allowed to use excessive bad language, then the toddler has the same right. If you don't want your toddler to use bad language, then watch your own words.

Won't buckle up

Experts tell us that when we are going out in the car we should put the child into his car seat and we should not drive off unless the seat belt is done up. But there are some children I work with who refuse to stay in their seat.

If your child won't stay in his seat, pull over to the side of the road and don't move off until you have him back in the seat and buckled up. Look your child in the eye and speak firmly: 'This car will not move unless you have your belt done up'. If it happens again, give another warning. After several warnings you have run out of options.

A child roaming around in the car is very dangerous. If there is an accident the child may be killed. If the police pull you over you will be fined heavily. The police won't be impressed when you tell them 'I can't make my 2-year-old stay in his seat'.

I don't like smacking children but now is the time you may choose to use one. Give a clear warning, 'If you undo your belt one more time I will smack you'. Be firm, don't feel guilty, and carry it through.

Stealing

To a child under 5 years of age there is no such crime as stealing. However, adults are obsessed with who owns what, and they spend thousands of dollars guarding, insuring and locking away all their treasures. Toddlers are fortunate in not having reached this stage of life; they are totally uninterested in all the hang-ups of possession, titles and deeds of ownership. Although they may collect items and money, this is not done with any malicious intent. All that is required, therefore, is a gentle reminder, when objects are taken, that they should really be left alone. Nothing more should be said.

When out visiting, a slightly firmer line is required, more for the benefit of the person whose house you are visiting than as a genuine reprimand to the toddler.

Vomiting on demand

When I am feeling weak there is nothing I dread more than dealing with a child who vomits on demand. This problem certainly can be cured but the method of treatment can be extremely tough. Some children have a weak valve at the top of their stomach which allows them to regurgitate their food frequently and effortlessly. Others have completely normal anatomies but still find that profuse crying or coughing can result in a return.

The last, and luckily the rarest, is that group which vomits on demand for the sole purpose of manipulating and punishing their parents. These children present one of the greatest challenges that we behaviour experts ever meet.

Children of the first group, with the weak valve, need proper diagnosis, medical treatment and review. Those from the second group who find that coughing or crying leads to vomiting, need firm but sensitive handling. They may be left to cry but once this changes from gentle to upset and hysterical, you must intervene quickly if disaster is to be averted. With these children the controlled crying technique is useful (see Chapter 11) but the period of crying must be kept short and if vomiting is used to manipulate the parents, firmer action is needed.

I see quite a number of children in the third group who quite blatantly vomit when they don't get their own way. These children are usually in the 1 to $2^1/2$ year age group. A frequent problem is when parents need Time Out for discipline but it is sabotaged by vomiting. Without some form of 'safely valve' technique, the parents find it hard to control their children and are now left completely impotent.

With such children, Time Out can first be tried combined with my controlled crying method. They should be put in their room and allowed to cry for a brief period, then given a small amount of comfort to keep them very aware of what is going on but not good attention. If this gives an effective form of Time Out and there is no vomiting, that is great. If there is too much comfort for it to be an effective form of discipline, or if they vomit, you now have to be extremely tough.

When put in the cot, they vomit. You are upset and feel a heel, but today you must not give in to this form of blackmail. Calmly take the soiled child and place him in the bathroom. Close the door.

Quickly change the cot without the child being able to see you and your obvious upset. Return to the bathroom, remove the clothes without fuss, sponge off using cool water, then dry. Put the child in a nappy or pants and return him immediately to the cot. This must all be done in a matter-of-fact way, without anger, emotion or any good quality attention.

I must emphasise that it is extremely unusual to be driven to such lengths but when it is necessary, this method certainly works.

I recently worked with a brilliant mother and her 2-year-old twins. These little girls were unbelievably militant and unfortunately they could also vomit with the greatest of ease. One had quite severe asthma which required inhaled medicines and the other went hysterical when put down to bed. When either of these young madams was pushed, they didn't argue, they just threw up.

Fortunately, their mum was way ahead of them. When it was time for medicine, she handed this girl a bucket and then produced the pump. With the other the bucket appeared at bedtime after which stories were read, kisses and cuddles were given, but it was made obvious that vomiting was not going to be tolerated. Within two days, this awful problem, which would have floored many of us was past history. In my job, I am constantly amazed by the strength and wisdom of the parents who find remedies for seemingly impossible situations, like this one.

Smearers

The unpleasant habit of smearing is mostly seen in young mentally disabled patients, although occasionally normal toddlers aged about

18 months will indulge in it. It is usually restricted to the early morning – the damage is done to the accompaniment of the dawn chorus. The toddler wakes before the rest of the household, is bored and has a dirty nappy, so to wile away the hours he engages in some 'finger painting' on the walls.

This ghastly behaviour pattern sickens and depresses parents, so we use two methods to cope with the problem. First, the parents must get up and change the toddler's nappy the moment he wakes in the morning. Second, the child must be prevented from getting his hands near the nappy area, which is achieved by dressing him in high overalls or similar 'high rise' garments, fastened firmly in place with safety pins. If the right style of garment is used only the infant Houdini would be able to get his hand into mischief. And even then he couldn't extract it loaded! Luckily, smearing in normal toddlers tends to be a very short-lived problem.

Conclusion

So there you have it, even the nicest children can develop some nasty habits. Most of these problems are innocent and pass with maturity. While waiting for this to happen, focus on the light at the end of the tunnel and steer calmly in that direction.

FIFTEEN

Children Who Are Hard to Love

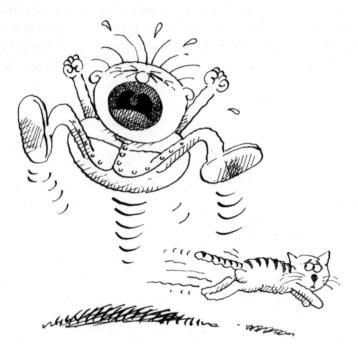

As we prepare for the birth of our first baby, we expect a soft, cuddly, easy-going infant. For some of us, this ideal remains nothing more than a dream. The infant we get cries inconsolably, demands every kilowatt of our energy and by toddlerhood we are worn out and at war. Those who have only experienced an easy angel have no idea how other parents feel. The truth is that difficult children can make themselves extremely hard to love.

The constant crier

Quite a number of babies cry and are hard to console. Some start right from birth, others turn it on for their tired parents once they arrive home. Though a few of these irritable infants have some medical cause, most cry for no apparent reason.

Doctors often use the term 'colic' to describe this irritability. The symptoms are reasonably consistent. It generally starts in the first two weeks of life and is usually over by the fourth month. These babies are unsettled after most feeds but they are at their worst in the late afternoon and evening. They suck a bit, then look unhappy, stiffen and cry. We lift, burp, and comfort but nothing really seems to help. Though the cause of colic is uncertain, the result is well known to anybody who has been there, confident loving parents soon become confused, unhappy and stressed. Unfortunately for some the crying continues until around 12 months.

How to cope

- Seek support from your early childhood sister, doctor or paediatrician.

- Remember there is light at the end of the tunnel. Most irritable infants are over the worst by 4 months of age.

- Try to find the most comforting posture; for example, over an arm, a shoulder, on a pillow.

- Sooth with gentle movement, walking slowly or wheel the pram over a slightly uneven bump in the carpet.

- Take them with you as you sit in a warm, deep bath.

- When all else fails, put them down, get outside and phone a friend for help.

- For more information, see my book *Babies!*

The demanding infant

Though most of the early criers soon settle, some go on to be irritable right through to toddlerhood. Though they may cry a lot after

6 months of age, they can be comforted at a cost. These infants are amazingly demanding; they need to be entertained every waking minute. It hurts when your friend's baby is so placid and self-contented, yet you can't move a metre without your child crying. Some parents accept this as inevitable, they give constantly and remain close and happy. Others resent, complain and try to change the unchangeable. It's at this point they can fall out of love.

How to cope

- We can give quality attention which stops most crying or we can resent and end up at war. At this age, giving is the best course.

- Carry, use a sling, buy a backpack, sit them beside you as you work.

- When friends visit, entertain the awake babe on your knee.

- Try to get grandparents, friends and family to provide some respite.

- When things are really tough, a short time in family daycare maybe a lifesaver.

- Be reassured that most of these demanding infants become much easier once they get on their feet and become mobile.

The out-of-step toddler

We expect little children to be busy, exuberant and into mischief, but some parents get a child who is right over the top. The two behaviours that cause most trouble are extreme over-activity and zero frustration tolerance. The over-active hits like a tornado. The moment they walk they are into everything and unless entertained every minute, they create havoc. These pacy children demand, run, touch, fiddle, break and when they see open space, they're off.

The intolerant children are less active, but more difficult. They tend to be irritable, rarely satisfied and the smallest trigger sets off an unbelievable bang. They want up on your knee, then they want down, they want out, they want in. Nothing is ever right and unless things happen immediately they blow up. They intrude, demand, object and brainwash their parents. Keeping the peace with these children is like juggling gelignite.

Whether the toddler is active or explosive or both, these children put immense strain on their parents. When shopping they run off, protest or stage a tremendous tantrum. At family get togethers, they upset, damage, grizzle or explode. Parents can't understand why their friends with other small children have such a normal life, while they have become isolated and exhausted.

A mother I look after has the most difficult twins. They cried all through the first year of life. They have always been irritable. They haven't slept and now at about 18 months they are always dissatisfied. Everything is wrong: when they are up they want down, and when they are down they want up and when they are being fed they don't want food. The mother told me, 'Recently I went to the dentist for root canal therapy. It was wonderful having an hour to myself'.

I see many excellent parents with one such child, who are 100 per cent certain they will never consider another pregnancy. Some are angry and resentful, enduring rather than enjoying their children. Others steer the most peaceful path and remain close.

How to cope

- Ensure that development is normal. Do they hear? Do they speak well? Are they clever? If there are any doubts see your doctor or clinic sister.

- Fortify the home, make it childproof.

- Volatile toddlers are best handled by anticipating, diverting and steering around trouble.

- Avoid all but short shopping expeditions.

- When tantrums are extreme, it is safer to separate than to risk doing something stupid. Put them in their room.

- Restrict visits and social life to secure situations with friends who understand.

- Get out to the wide open spaces when possible.

- Accept any help or respite offered by friends and family.

- Get their name on the preschool waiting list. When that time comes you will be glad of a break.

- Don't become brainwashed by those whose children are all angels.

- Difficult children will be difficult whether we accept or resent. It does get better with age, so hang in there and keep loving.

SIXTEEN

Fears, Comforters and Security

All small animals know fear and small children are no exception. Some of these fears may seem quite 'off the beam' to parents, and some children's comfort habits may seem distinctly strange. Parents are never quite sure what is acceptable for well-adjusted offspring. In fact, it would appear that just about anything seems possible at an early developmental stage and in this chapter we look at some of these fears, as well as security and various methods of comfort.

However foolish a child's fears may seem to an adult, they are very real to the child, and they must not be put down or ridiculed. Talking openly about anxieties helps to keep in clear perspective the division between fact and fantasy. The best way to treat childhood fears is by good parental example, lots of support and comfort, and then gradual desensitisation. There is usually no reason to get too

227

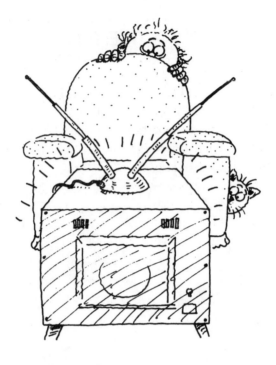

worried, as most fears at this age are temporary problems that evaporate with the passage of time. Looking back one year on, it is hard to think what all the fuss was about.

Different fears for different years

Children have very fertile imaginations that are capable of generating great uneasiness as a result of hearing stories or watching television. The result is that they conjure up visions of ghosts, long-legged beasties and things that go bump in the night. It's all part of growing up. At birth, babies are relatively immune to the fears that beset the rest of us. This is probably a mercy, when you think what the inside of a modern neonatal nursery looks like, with all that space-age gadgetry attached to the poor little, underweight scraps. The only things that startle the newborn are sudden movement and noise. Forty babies will leap in unison when a clumsy nurse drops a tray on the nursery floor. From birth to 6 months there is little progress in this department, until somewhere around the seventh month the baby suddenly becomes inseparably attached to his main caretaker, usually his mother. After this, any attempts to separate him from mum will precipitate distress and floods of tears.

At 1 year this separation is still a major problem, and the child will also often react badly to loud noises, such as doorbells, vacuum cleaners or food mixers. As the decibels rise, he will cuddle in tighter to his mother for protection. Strange people, strange objects and sudden movements can also cause him distress. At the age of 2 the fear of separation still exists but it becomes slightly less intense and more predictable than in the 1-year-old. Loud bangs still cause upsets, as will the unexpected screech of brakes, ambulance sirens or the violent barking of dogs.

Between 2 and 4 years that obsessively tight attachment to mum weakens further and a whole new package of fears starts to emerge; animals and the dark featuring prominently in this array. The fear of animals hits its peak around the age of 3; fear of the dark usually peaks nearer the fifth birthday.

Between 4 and 6 years the child develops a highly vivid imagination, with fear of the dark constantly worsened by regular visits from ghosts, bogeymen, monsters and travellers from outer space. After the age of 6 some children are said to worry about being injured, or they may even start to fear death, although they still do not have the adult picture of either of these possibilities.

By the age of 10, the child has been lumbered with most of the burden of adult fears, which he will carry for the rest of his life. These are compounded during adolescence with the major fear of not 'making it' as a fully accepted member of the peer group.

Some specific fears

All young children have one overwhelming fear in common: the fear of being separated from their parents. Other fears come and go and are either of the child's own making or instilled into him by transference of anxiety from the parent. Whether we like it or not, fear has always been a major part of life, both for adults and children, and nothing I can say is going to make it go away.

Separation

The fear of separation is common to all toddlers from the age of about 7 months, until it wanes by pre-school age. It is at its most intense in the early years, its ebb varying greatly from child to child and family to family. Initially, the child resents being handled by anyone except his mother, but this quickly eases to allow all the other members of the family and close friends in on the act. When playing, he is never far from mum, and if outside or playing in another room, he reappears every few minutes to reassure himself of her presence.

Most parents need babysitters at one time or another so that they can maintain some outside life. The ideal babysitter is a grandparent, other relative or close friend. Leaving the child with other babysitters may be difficult initially, with profuse tears being shed on departure and again at pick-up time. Between these times there is usually relative happiness which can be confirmed by one quick phone call. The child should be accompanied by his cuddly toys and security items, and he should never be left in a great rush, preferably being given a little time to acclimatise, after which the parents should leave decisively, not weakening to his cries when halfway out the door.

Although most toddlers do well in the care of a good child minder, a few are immensely unhappy and never really settle. If this happens, the parents must ask themselves if separation is really necessary and if it might not be kinder to wait several more months before continuing. Of course, in our modern world many parents are forced, for a variety of good reasons, to leave their child with a babysitter whether they like it or not. But some parents seem particularly blind to what they are doing to their children. An intelligent mother recently asked me for advice on a problem that was worrying her. For the past 6 months she had attended church each Sunday morning, placing her toddler in the church creche, where he cried inconsolably throughout the entire separation. What could be done to make the child less unhappy? I explained that I was certain that an understanding God would probably much prefer to see a happy child than a pew occupied in His church.

By the age of 3 most toddlers are able to separate and settle quite happily at pre-school. As this is his first major separation, the child must know what is going to happen to him when he is left, and he should be gently introduced to his new surroundings before being abandoned. Parents are never sure, when they bring their child for the first time, whether it is best to sit with him for an hour or so or leave immediately. This advice is probably best left to the individual pre-school director, who has a great deal of experience with this problem. What I do know is that once the parents have made up their mind to go, then go they must, decisively, without lurking in the bushes to spy on the child.

Occasionally the child will not settle happily, nevertheless parents will insist on his going, believing that non-attendance will cause him to miss out in the warm-up heats for the academic rat race. Once again, where the child is very unhappy, there is little point in forcing him to go on. Better to wait 3 to 6 months and then try again.

A band of philosophical child raisers believe that it is important to rush through the stage of separation, to prepare a child for schooling and later life. I believe that toddlers were designed to remain close to their families for a number of years and in a normal 80-year life span, rushing a child out into our far-from-perfect world any earlier than is necessary seems rather unkind and pointless. When I am irritated by bureaucrats, bullied by bank managers and forced to read continuing evidence of man's inhumanity to man, I secretly would love to regress to those blissful toddler years with a loving mother to protect me from all this stress.

Baths

Most babies like water and enjoy splashing in their baths. But for unknown reasons, after their first year some take a strong dislike to this and the very word 'bath' or the noise of a running tap will set them to arching their backs, crying and complaining bitterly. Once again you must use the technique of gradual desensitisation and reintroduction to the bath.

A good start for the toddler who absolutely refuses to bath is to stand him in an empty basin in a warm place and sponge him with warm water. After a time of this, some water may be put in the basin and, when he is rather braver, he can be sponged in a bath with a maximum depth of water of two or three centimetres at the deep end. From here he will sit down, and you can start increasing the water level until you have a child who baths in the right place, at the right time, and with the right attitude.

To prevent bath refusal, it is important to avoid frightening the young child with such things as spluttering taps, gurgling plugs and slippery baths. Place a rubber mat in the bottom of the bath if there is any chance of the child slipping and losing his balance. The bath can become one of the best playtimes of the day, and this should be actively encouraged, filling the bath with boats, submarines, rubber duckies and discarded detergent bottles, which double as excellent water squirters. A bubble bath is always fun and is easily provided by a quick squirt of dishwashing liquid, if you don't want to go to the expense of commercial preparations. Be warned, however, that happy aquatic toddlers and carpeted bathroom floors do not go well together – a tiled floor with a big drain is definitely preferable.

Once again fears of the bath are generally short lived and, if handled sensibly with gentle desensitisation, they are quickly overcome.

Genuine fear of the bath should not be confused with the theatrical antics of a manipulating, attention-seeking toddler, who, out of principle, refuses to bath when told. Recently I saw a $3^{1}/_{2}$-year-old girl, who greatly upset her mother by refusing to do anything she was asked whenever her father was home in the evenings. She would never bath unless the water was turned on by her father, and she had to be carried to the bathroom and undressed by him as well. When father was out, the child would never take a bath, because her mother thought it was never worth the fight.

This situation was cured in a rapid, though slightly devious, manner. Father continued to show great love and attention, running the bath, undressing his daughter and putting her in the water, but one minor adjustment was made to the routine. 'Absentmindedly', he consistently forgot to turn on the hot tap when he was running the bath with the consequence that the water had an Arctic chill – the balance of power was immediately redressed. Mother's care at bathtime was once again in equal demand.

Toilets

Some children are afraid to sit on the toilet, which obviously makes toilet training well nigh impossible. This fear may arise from a number of causes – maybe the association with a severe pain when passing a particularly hard motion or fear of being sucked into the toilet when it is flushed and being washed out to sea down a big pipe. Some children are frightened of gadgets, like the extractor fan in some bathrooms that starts automatically when the light is switched on and which, in a confined space, may sound like a jumbo jet about to take off. Other children refuse to sit on the toilet purely out of attention-seeking, toddler stubbornness.

I recently saw an irate mother who complained that her 3-year-old daughter had lost all her previously excellent toilet training skills as the result of a stupid action by the girl's father. Browsing through a shop one day he came upon a poster of a gorilla climbing out of a toilet bowl. So impressed was he with this piece of visual art that he brought it home and stuck it up on the back of the toilet door. Well, the little girl walked in, sat on the toilet, kicked the door shut and, after seeing this horrific vision, absolutely refused, not surprisingly, to sit there ever again.

With children who will not sit on the toilet for one reason or another, we once again must introduce gentle desensitisation. For the most resistant, they should start sitting on a pot with their nappy still on. There should be no forcing but lots of rewards given. From here progress to sitting without the nappy; sitting on the pot beside the toilet with mum close by; sitting on the toilet with mum close by; sitting with mum outside giving encouragement; and finally going solo while mum rustles up some interesting treat in the kitchen.

This may all seem rather cumbersome and excessive but often you will find that some of these steps can be bypassed. The important message is that children should not be forced; give them good security and gently desensitise them.

Noises in the dark, monsters and other assorted beasties

It is perfectly normal for toddlers to be frightened of a great variety of noises, even such common ones as household appliances. This does not mean that the child is hypersensitive or emotionally disturbed, and the phenomenon in any case is usually very short lived. Sensitivity to some noises never goes – dentists' drills and the screeching of car tyres are two that are guaranteed to make my hair stand on end, for instance. I presume that, although these noises worry me, the perpetrators have long since come to terms with them. Fears are very real to the person who suffers them. No amount of explaining will convince me that dentists' drills are a form of relaxation therapy. We must accept the fears of others, whatever the age, give comfort and not belittle their beliefs.

At an older age, somewhere between 4 and 5 years, fear of the dark usually hits its peak and then largely disappears by the child's seventh birthday. A low wattage light is much appreciated by many children at night. When the sun sets and darkness appears, this is the time when the older child's vivid imagination conjures up visions of robbers, monsters and other assorted bogeymen. It is popular for authors to attribute this to the 'junk viewing diet' that we feed our children on television but children have been terrified at night-time for centuries, long before Mr Logie Baird's ingenious invention became freely available.

Children listen to stories told to them by their parents, grannies or friends or read books full of varying degrees of mayhem, terror and violence. Ali Baba's offsider was so mutilated after his murder that they needed a leatherworker to sew him up for burial. Hansel and Gretel and Snow White were all taken to big, black forests and abandoned. Snow White was poisoned by a nasty old woman. In 'Struwwelpeter', the boy who sucked his thumbs had them cut off with a large pair of scissors. The Pied Piper took all the town's children hostage and never returned them to their parents. Humpty Dumpty had a most violent accident, relived in gory detail at a thousand breakfast tables daily, and what about those three mice who, despite severe visual disability, had their tails so cruelly severed from their bodies. Even the Bible tells us of some exceedingly nasty people and punishments. So let's not blame all these childhood fears on modern films, television, cartoons and comics. The element of fear in childhood upbringing is as old as childhood itself.

Imaginary fears are all part of childhood development and only too soon fears move out of the area of fiction into the realities of the adult world, fears that unfortunately will not go away. It is important, however, to be a little selective with the type (and amount) of viewing matter your child is exposed to, and constantly remind them of where fact ends and fiction begins.

In theory parents should always watch television with their children but in reality we all know that at times children will be left to watch unsupervised as parents need a break to cook dinner, for example. In theses cases, select the programme your child is to watch, or choose an appropriate video.

Dogs

It is common for the under 4s to fear animals, especially dogs. Naturally, we don't want to encourage the toddler to poke passing German Shepherds or pat every surly mongrel in the street, but those who fear dogs are usually quite unselective, being terrorised by even the most benign ball of fluff.

Most commonly the child who fears dogs will sight the offending beast, stiffen, then hold on tight to his mother and start to bawl. Rest assured if your child reacts this way that it is a normal developmental stage for many children and, even if you do nothing, it will pass in a short time. One way of helping overcome the fear, however, is to talk quietly to the child about 'nice dogs' and introduce him to some of the gentler of the species.

Very few children have such great fear of dogs that they hardly dare go outdoors in case one appears. Once again, you should gradually introduce the child to dogs, possibly starting with a small, newborn puppy or a securely caged dog in a pet shop window.

Some therapists I know introduce stuffed dogs into their treatment, but I feel that once you go to those lengths you're only a hair's breadth away from turning serious therapy into a sketch worthy of Monty Python.

Whatever else you do, be confident, talk openly about the animals and try to get a toe in the door with some distant dog contact. From there build to full desensitisation and cure.

Doctors

As a paediatrician, I have learnt the hard way that busy days surrounded by anxious, crying, unco-operative children are extremely stressful. It is, therefore, important for our own sanity, as well as the happiness of the children we serve, that doctors' surgeries are made as friendly and non-threatening as possible.

As mentioned, most babies up to the age of 6 months don't mind being separated from their mum, so it is easy for a doctor to lift them up and examine them on a couch. From about 7 months until pre-school age, however, this separation is a problem, and I find that examinations are best done with the child sitting relaxed and secure on mum's knee.

Some parents – and doctors for that matter – are amazingly skilful at stirring up a child the moment they enter the office. The child is bundled through the door and not allowed to touch anything, move or even talk in some cases. A nervous mother will wrench the child's clothes up and twitter in his ear in an unnatural way like a bird warning of impending danger. Utterances such as 'doctor is not going to hurt you' are counter-productive, since the thought of getting hurt had probably never even crossed the child's mind.

Children should neither be restricted, nor over-stimulated by anxious parents when taken to the doctor. They should be allowed to sit quietly on mother's knee to allow the doctor to make the initial examination. As far as the doctor is concerned, the introductory touch is best with arms and feet being wobbled in a fun way, which introduces the doctor to the child as a human being and not an ogre. Thereafter, examinations should be quick and confident, accompanied by quiet, reassuring talk. The doctor should engage the child's eyes, communicating gently with him and watching carefully for those early signs of distress that appear in the eye seconds before the first tear is shed.

Painful and uncomfortable procedures, such as throat examination, should be left until the end, followed by a cuddle and release. Neither parents nor doctors should insist on things like painful blood tests unless they are of indisputable diagnostic and therapeutic value.

Doctors are really very nice people, as long as they keep their scalpels, syringes and tongue depressors away from the child. A visit to the doctor should not be a fearful experience for either child or mother. Most of us enjoy working with children, otherwise we wouldn't be doing it.

Hospitals

In the not too distant past, hospitals were places of dread, run purely for the business of curing the sick and without much interest in protecting the emotional well-being of the patient. This was particularly horrifying for children who had to go into hospital. Between the ages of 7 months and $3^1/_2$ years the young child grieves deeply when separated from his mother and is too young to understand the reasons and temporary nature of the separation. The unhappy toddler may feel abandoned, as if his parents had walked off, leaving him on the steps of an orphanage.

Initially the child will protest, crying his little heart out as his parents leave. Usually he will settle within five minutes, only to greet his parents on their next visit with copious tears, giving the impression that he has been crying non-stop since they departed. Hospitalisation may be upsetting for toddlers, but it is often even more upsetting for the parents.

Generally speaking, hospitals are not places to be feared by children, and it is important for parents to talk openly about them should they pass one in their daily travels to let the child realise from an early age that it isn't some dreadful institution. Each day we have pre-schoolers from some of our city schools visit our wards, and they have a ball, realising that it is really quite a fun place run by 'good guys'!

In the last ten years hospitals and their routines for the care of children have changed greatly. Now if a child needs to be admitted, there is open visiting for the parents and in most cases some form of bed for the mother if she wants to stay.

If you get some warning that your child may have to be admitted to hospital, it is important to prepare him, discussing openly what is going to happen and encouraging medical pretend play with dolls and teddies. If you can, take him to visit the ward before admission and make sure that when he does go in he has all his favourite cuddly toys and comforters with him.

'Day only' surgery is encouraged now, so that the child can go home to the care of his parents as soon as possible. When the child goes to the anaesthetic room, he is accompanied by his teddy bear and his mother, and he will find both waiting for him in the recovery ward after the operation. Anaesthetists who specialise in children's anaesthetics have thrown out all those cruel, old ideas that children don't really feel pain. Now, in a good children's hospital, any child from birth upward is afforded the same, or an even greater, standard of post-operative pain relief than we might expect for ourselves.

In short, hospitals are no longer places for children to fear. Talk to your children freely and openly about them, for one day they may have to visit one.

Comforters and security blankets

Little children love their cuddly bears, their rugs which they carry around with them and a variety of other objects. I think these comfort objects are one of the really cute things that little children have and I love them. This clearly gives them a feeling of security and as far as I am concerned they can carry these objects with them right up to school age if they feel happier doing so.

These objects are what psychiatrists call 'transition objects'. All that means is that when the child goes to pre-school, she doesn't have her mum with her, but she does have her teddy bear or her rug, and these objects remind her of her mum. It's a bit like taking a photograph of

your loved one with you in your wallet when you go overseas.

Children are not the only ones to enjoy comforters. Adults enjoy them too, relieving their tensions by sucking on a cigarette, a cigar, chewing gum or their fingernails, or holding on to a can of alcoholic beverage. Toddler comforters are probably a great deal less harmful to health, generally consisting of thumbs, dummies, teddy bears and security blankets. There's nothing intrinsically wrong with any of these, as long as the habit does not last too long.

It's a perfectly harmless behaviour, though your child may get some funny looks if she is still lugging her teddy through high school!

Thumb sucking

Despite Sigmund Freud's inevitable emphasis on the sexual connotations of sucking one's thumb, modern thinkers believe they are sucked because it seems a natural and good thing to do at the time. If there were not some comfort and satisfaction in sucking the thumb, I doubt whether children would bother to do it. Thumb sucking is a worldwide phenomenon, although some writers claim it is less frequent in some races; apparently little Eskimos hardly ever do it at all, but I presume this is a practical move on their part, keeping their hands in mittens to prevent their digits falling off through frostbite.

Children certainly seem to suck their thumbs more when they are either tired, bored, frustrated or tense, and it is a good way of getting to sleep, particularly for those children who have not yet attained the mathematical skill to count sheep. In times of stress, and particularly when a new baby arrives, many toddlers regress to this old habit.

By the age of $3^1/_2$, most children have spontaneously removed their thumbs from their mouths, although some studies suggest that up to 2 per cent still have this habit in their early teens. Most experts now believe that there is no harm in the habit.

It is not a sign of a scarred psyche or emotional insecurity. Little children do it for only one reason: they enjoy it.

If there is even a smattering of justice in this adult-run world, before any thumbs are plucked from the mouths of innocent infants we should first get our grown-up act together. For a start, cigarettes should be totally taboo, adult nail biters should be kept in mitts and gum chewers should be viewed as a trifle wanting. Once the big people have set the example, it would then be time for the young to follow.

The only worry with thumb sucking is that it can cause teeth to become displaced and stick out. This is of particular importance to today's parents who seek the perfect alignment of a Colgate commercial, yet know that getting wired up with an orthodontist comes mighty expensive. Certainly before the age of 6, thumb sucking does not damage permanent teeth and after that, it takes more than just a few minutes of thumb in mouth at bedtime to cause harm. There appears to be only a very slight risk of the continuing habit altering the position of children's teeth.

Kicking the habit
Thirty years ago, splints were attached to elbows, mittens put on hands, and the fingers dipped in bitter substances to prevent children from putting their thumbs in their mouths. Some dentists,

fearing a misshaped bite, used dental plates, which blocked the ability to suck the thumb. For a child's emotional well-being, there is much to be said for leaving nature to cure this habit rather than engaging in these antisocial activities.

Below the age of 4 years I believe that sucking should be totally ignored. After this, hands can be subtly diverted and bodies can be busied onto something more productive. Rewards for 'grown up behaviour' can be given, but whatever happens it must never become the cause of a fight or the child will continue it, just to annoy.

Before 6 years of age thumb sucking cannot harm the permanent teeth as they are still busy burrowing their way up to the surface. After this I don't mind a little gentle sucking to help soothe to sleep but if it is more major, you should discuss it with your dentist.

It is hard to know whether protruding teeth were caused by thumb sucking or just designed to be that way. Some parents believe that their own teeth were displaced by sucking but I often wonder if this had nothing to do with the thumb. Maybe they were born to have horizontal teeth and as the thumb slipped in and out so smoothly they decided to garage it there permanently.

Dummies, pacifiers and comforters

Most doctors have an inbuilt dislike of these plastic or rubber devices, but no-one has ever found any evidence to indicate that they really do any harm. Objection to them is more on aesthetic grounds than medical ones. It is fashionable in some quarters to claim that they are unhygienic, but so for that matter are the ten dirty fingers that would be inserted in the mouth if the dummy was not there. Many parents who are determined never to resort to these pacifiers relent when confronted with an extremely irritable, difficult child. If the dummy helps in those situations, then good luck to them.

I dislike the way a dummy can make an intelligent child appear dull, delayed and a dribbler. I also worry about them being used at bedtime because, although they undoubtedly precipitate sleep, they also have an unfortunate habit of precipitating wakefulness when they become disengaged in the early hours of the morning (see Chapter 11).

Kicking the habit

There are no long-term side-effects from sucking these comforters, as long as they are not of the sort that has a built-in bottle which constantly irrigates the teeth with a sweet tooth-rotting solution. When the time comes to discard the dummy, it is usually best to be brave, throw it away, and then brace yourself for the repercussions. There will inevitably be some hours, or even some days, of trouble but the dummy will soon be forgotten. Those who do not have the courage to discard it so abruptly may try a gradual withdrawal by losing it or accidentally damaging it. After $3^{1}/_{2}$, the child may well be reasoned with and the dummy given up after some hard bargaining.

Although I do not like dummies, I assure parents that they do not cause any harm. When a child is under stress for any reason he has the same right to his dummy as his parents have to their cigarettes – the difference is that thumbs and dummies are not proven health hazards. When the time is right, preferably before $2^{1}/_{2}$, discard the object nevertheless. It has to go some time.

Teddies, cuddlies and security blankets

Most youngsters have some object that they seek out and cuddle up to when tired or upset. This can be some exotic imported stuffed animal, mum's own battered but much-loved teddy, a sheepskin rug or even a rapidly disintegrating bit of old fabric. Whatever the 'real-world' value of the object, in the eyes of the child it is priceless. As I noted earlier, these items are often referred to as 'transition objects'. They give security, continuity and comfort to a child when the environment and those in it are changing. At the day-care centre, at granny's, in hospital, although the environment has altered and mum may no longer be there, the child has a beloved familiar object to hold on to. It is his link with his home base; without it he feels a stranger in a strange world. No wonder ET wanted to go home.

As the child becomes more and more attached to his blanket, greater is the distress when it falls apart or is mislaid. To the toddler, this is a disaster of major proportions, not unlike a death in the family. But surprisingly, despite the great attachment, a bit of high-powered salesmanship from an enthusiastic parent will steer a toddler towards another, reserve comforter.

Security blankets of the type favoured by Charlie Brown's friend Linus get progressively grubbier and grubbier, until eventually they simply must be washed. This needs to be planned with all the precision of a military operation to ensure that they are in and out of the washing machine and returned dry to the owner with the minimum of time wasted.

When a blanket is wearing out, it may be wise to remove a part of it to keep in cold storage until the fateful day when the original is in irretrievable tatters. Even without this foresight, a minute, disintegrating patch of material may be reincarnated if clever mum sews it onto the corner of some new material. This is rather like the horticultural grafting of roses and, when properly achieved, ensures years of continuing pleasure.

Comforters and transition objects are normal, natural and healthy. They promote, rather than postpone, security. Like Christopher Robin and his trusty bear, Pooh, the young child armed with his blanket can accomplish many a daring feat that would never have been possible alone.

Tags and touchers

Parents can spend big bucks on a top-of-the-line toy, but all that interests their infant is the maker's tag. Some twist this round a finger as they settle to sleep, while others love to rub the silky label against their skin. The ultimate comfort experience is to clutch a teddy, suck a bottle and twiddle a tag, all in unison. Other children are touchers – as they drift off to sleep, they fiddle with their mother's hair, or rhythmically stroke some skin. A few little people have an alarming interest in thrusting a hand down mum's front to find a breast. This type of behaviour is acceptable in infancy, but it can cause extreme embarrassment in the preschool years, especially when the front they've selected is not their mother's.

Some children can't be bothered with them, while others have an inseparable relationship with their teddy. Parents have been known to drive halfway around the city to retrieve lost bears; others find that when they wash this dirty animal, the child watches the window of the machine and/or drier, glued like a soap opera addict.

Pretend friends

After the second birthday, little children start to develop a vivid imagination. By the age of 4, this has become so intense that sometimes there is a blur between real and pretend. These are the peak years for pretend friends.

Some preschoolers are greatly comforted as they discuss the meaning of life and the universe with an imaginary mate. Others are befriended by strange animals, but don't worry, they are not going mad – it will pass before they get to primary school.

Some children even talk to inanimate objects. The daughter of one of my friends used to talk to the Sydney Harbour Bridge. Soon her dad joined in the game, both conversing with this structure every time they crossed.

Recently, he told me he was driving with his mother-in-law in the car. As Dad talked knowledgeably to the bridge, Grandma asked the girl, 'Who is your father talking to?' 'Beats me if I know,' was her reply.

Summary: fears, comforters and security

- Children's fears are very real to them, and they must not be put down or ridiculed.

- The biggest fear for most children is the fear of separation from their parents.

- Most fears at this age are temporary and evaporate with the passage of time.

- Toddler comforters generally consist of thumbs, dummies, teddy bears and security blankets. There's nothing wrong with any of these, as long as the habit does not last too long.

SEVENTEEN

Sibling Rivalry

Sibling rivalry refers to that competitive streak which makes children squabble, fight and accuse their parents of impartial treatment. I do not see this as a pathological condition but just as a very normal human trait.

Probably the greatest problem our children have is that they are too like the grown-ups they live with. If you come to think of it, adults are remarkably competitive and jealous beings. Most humans seem to have a strong drive to get more and do better than their mates, even if a few people get trampled along the way.

Imagine the secret elation if we were awarded a 20 per cent pay rise and our colleagues got none. Then think of the disappointment if we unexpectedly were granted a 100 per cent rise and everyone else got 120 per cent. If adults are competitive to the point of starting wars and taking advantage of their fellow man, then what's wrong with a toddler having a few skirmishes and shows of strength?

All little animals love to taunt and fight. This builds up their bodily reflexes and muscles, while it drives their mothers mad. In common with most child care experts I find it easier to philosophise about sibling rivalry than to come up with sure-fire ways to stop our children fighting. Anyway for what it's worth, here are some of my ideas. (For more suggestions see my book, *Beyond Toddlerdom*, Chapter 13.)

Two toddlers – double trouble

When the Greens had just one toddler, I thought I knew all about children's behaviour. When we had two, I realised how little I knew. Two toddlers are never difficult when separated by a distance of at least a kilometre; it is when they come together that they set each other off.

The creative genius of such young people is always astonishing. A duet of toddlers can devise ways to get into mischief well beyond the imagination of any adult or child alone.

When we talk of sibling rivalry in the toddler, the presentation depends very much on the child's age. The very young are keen to protect their home pitch from interfering intruders. Older toddlers have a different but equally difficult style – they squabble. The young behave badly when their toys are touched by brothers, sisters or visitors and they hate anyone monopolising their mum's attention. Older ones just bicker, bait and complain of inequality. This is a strange age where they can't bear to be apart but when together, they show their affection in a very odd way.

True equality – fine for fairyland

We all know that each of our children must be treated with equal love, limits and discipline. We also know that this admirable goal is often quite out of touch with the reality of life in our own homes.

The discipline and expectations may be equal but the children we discipline are not.

It seems to me that there is little true equality in our adult world. He who is strongest and shouts loudest generally gets the most. Parents of twins are often the first to realise this. No matter how high their ideals at the start, the docile may miss out while the difficult noisy half hijacks an unfair slice of the action. Time and attention may not be divided fairly but our love is still transmitted with complete equality.

Try hard to be totally fair, but when this is sabotaged by two children with dramatically different temperaments it may be necessary to tone down our expectations for once, steer round trouble and not force unwinnable issues. I apologise about this apparent double standard but if you are going to survive at the front line of child care, you have to be a realist.

Taunting

At the end of toddlerhood our children start on the school-age special of taunting, squabbling and grumbling. There are of course great differences from child to child. Some are so good that you wonder if they are training for a place in the Peace Corps, while others could start a fight in an empty room. The most skilled taunters will always appear innocent, it is just that a trail of trouble seems to follow in their wake. Their brother's homework book mysteriously falls to the floor. The TV channel changes in the closing minutes of the movie. While all this goes on, children are poked, tripped and insulted.

Boredom brings out the worst in a taunter as they pace around the floor like a hungry lion on the lookout for a Christian. At moments like this it is best to keep them occupied and divert their attention as they position themselves for the pounce. Try to keep out of children's squabbles and if you do intervene, lay down the law quite firmly. There is no place for debating and democracy and, if they are unhappy with your decision, let them take their case to the Human Rights Commission.

Fighting

Fighting between our young is one of those universal but irritating parts of family life. Over the years I have talked to hundreds of parents trying to find some foolproof peace-keeping methods but so far they remain elusive. I do have, however, some suggestions that may help to secure an uneasy sort of truce.

- Turn a deaf ear and a blind eye to as much squabbling as you can.

- When siblings start to spar, divert them onto something more innocent and interesting.

- Bundle squabbling children into another room or banish them out the back door. Fighters like an audience.

- It would take a team of detectives to find who started the fight. Don't waste your time. It is usually the one who protests loudest who is most guilty.

- At the first grunt don't rush in like the United Nations peace keepers. Children have to find their own equilibrium.

- It becomes a different matter when one child is being unfairly and continually victimised. Now firm action is needed.

- When we do intervene, it must be decisive, without debate and with 100 per cent firmness.

- When all else fails, separate the squabblers with a brief period of Time Out in different rooms.

The main mistake we parents make is to get drawn into our children's battles. If they know that you will always intervene, you may still be intervening when they are 18. If the moment they start you rush in like the anti-terrorist squad, gas grenades and guns at the ready, soon they will squabble just to see you in full action.

Another observation I have made is that few fights take place without an audience. Can you imagine Ali, Tyson or other boxing champs, holding the World Title in their back room, watched only by the cleaning lady and her dog? It seems to me that if there is not an interested audience most fights will fizzle out. When our children squabble it is best to either move away from the ringside, or move the ringside away from us.

If you are eventually forced to become involved, do so properly. Don't hold an enquiry into who fired the first shot as, at the height of any conflict, it is peace not recrimination that is needed. Don't enter the squabble yourself. Pull rank, say 'that's it!' and leave them in no doubt that you are not going to take sides or tolerate any more. When this fails it is time for the warriors to be separated then banished for a while to their different rooms.

The toddler and the new baby

The way our families seem to happen, there is usually a gap of about $1^1/_2$ to $2^1/_2$ years between our first and second child. Now you don't need a degree in psychology to know that this spacing spells trouble. The unsuspecting baby is going to drop in on top of a self-centred toddler at the peak of his militancy.

If you pause to see it from a 2-year-old's view, he thinks he is the most important person around. He likes having his mum's and dad's undivided attention. He doesn't understand the meaning of the word share. Anyway, no-one asked his permission to bring that thing into the house and in fact it should be sent back to the hospital with instructions to reinsert it.

I used to think that toddlers did not get upset until the new baby arrived. But in fact, parents tell me toddlers start to act differently when mum is pregnant, even before the toddler has been told to expect a new brother or sister. They just sense change in the air – they don't know what is happening, but they feel it.

Sometimes children may seem to regress when the new baby arrives home. They will suddenly start behaving like a baby them-selves. They will want a bottle, want to be on mum's breast again and may even start talking like a baby. Children who have been toilet trained may start to wet their pants again.

'Why is he doing this?' asks the frustrated mother. Well, he's just following the example of the baby as the baby is getting most of the attention. It's nothing to worry about. It will last for a while, then go away again.

I have to admit that despite all this potential for problems, if the toddler is handled sensibly, few will occur. We do however need to be careful. With the arrival of the new baby, the toddler has been provided with the most potent weapon he has ever held in his armoury. Before long he discovers how sensitive and overprotective his mother has become. For some reason she cannot accept that a grubby, accident-prone 2-year-old should be allowed to manhandle her newborn piece of perfection.

When life becomes boring, all that is needed is for the toddler to walk a few paces and poke the baby. The result is quite dramatic, but even this effect can be surpassed by jumping on the infant or tipping up the pram. The *pièce de résistance,* however, is reserved for very special occasions: a dirty digit is poked within a few centimetres of the baby's eye, which is usually quite close enough to guarantee an emotional eruption from one's mother.

If parents have been strong enough to get rid of other antisocial, attention-seeking behaviour, there is no reason for them to surrender now to strong-arm toddler tactics. It is important to protect but not overprotect the baby. If the toddler is scolded for going near the baby, who then receives cuddles and comfort, this is the surest way to sow the seeds of an unhealthy sort of sibling rivalry.

I believe that in general babies are pretty unbreakable. Within certain limits the toddler should be allowed to play with the new arrival and poke him just as long as he does not cause significant hurt. While all this is going on the parents must try to act nonchalant and keep off the stage. It is best to stand a short distance away and out of the corner of one eye to watch that the baby suffers no harm.

As for putting fingers near the baby's eyes, I don't believe that this is often done with any malicious intent. It may be done to reward an over-fussy parent who jumps every time a finger starts to move. More often it is just an innocent exploration; after all, the eye of an infant is a beautiful and fascinating structure. It interests me, so why should it not interest a toddler?

Are only children disadvantaged?

This can cut both ways, depending on how you look at it. In some ways only children are advantaged. They get more of their parents' time and tend to get more education. On the other hand, they miss out on playing with peers and, as a result, often have rather more adult attitudes. They can be out of place in the company of adults or other children. This means that they may find it harder to settle down when they get to pre-school.

But when you add it all up, I don't think there is any great disaster in being an only child and parents shouldn't worry if that is the way things are.

Making the right introductions

- When pregnant, talk to the toddler about a new brother or sister and how mum will need a little helper if she is to cope. Discuss possible names for the baby. Mention the impending arrival of all those dirty nappies. Toddlers can relate to this, as they are world experts on bodily functions.

- When mum is in hospital, leave the toddler with someone he knows well, where he will feel secure, e.g. dad, grandma or a good close friend.

- These days toddlers are encouraged to visit mothers and new babies in the post-natal ward. It should be a fun time with lots of fuss over the toddler and a few little presents on hand to sweeten the occasion.

- Visitors who come to see the baby must first fuss over and notice the toddler. After all toddlers see themselves as the main attraction.

- Though tired and overprotective of the new infant, try hard to give the appearance of equal attention. This can be achieved by what I refer to as 'sidestream attention'. As you feed the baby, use the toddler as mother's little helper, talk or read a story. If you don't do this they will hijack your attention by demanding to latch on to the unoccupied breast, or stalk away and do such demolition that you have to give in.

- Of course mums are sensitive and highly protective of their newborn infants, but this must never be permitted to put a wedge between the toddler and baby. If you cuddle the baby and scold the toddler every time they come together, this is the surest way to create resentment and unhealthy rivalry.

- If handled well, most toddlers will accept their baby brother or sister without the slightest hiccup. A few will accept initially but when the baby is around the age of 6 months, there may be a backlash. At first new babies are seen as interesting animated dolls but at 6 months, when they sit up and start to do other clever things, they then become a great threat to the balance of power.

■ Be reassured that most new babies and toddlers will come together well if we parents are sensible.

Summary: sibling rivalry

■ Rivalry and competition are to be expected in both big and little humans.

■ All young animals squabble and fight. It improves their reflexes and tones up their bodies, preparing them for a 'grown up' life.

■ Our children are going to fight whether we like it or not, and it is best to keep out of their battles.

■ Keep taunting toddlers occupied.

■ Divert impending trouble.

■ Don't take sides.

■ Put little skirmishers in another room or out the back door. They can fight but they cannot expect an audience.

■ When forced to intervene, use few words and the gentle tones of a regimental sergeant major.

■ When all else fails, separate the two fighters with Time Out in different rooms.

■ Life is much easier if we introduce toddlers to babies carefully and give attention to both in a way that appears to be equal.

EIGHTEEN

Attention Deficit Hyperactivity Disorder (ADHD)[7]

CLASS OF 2001

Many parents think their child is hyperactive when in fact they just have a normal, very active child. Parents also think that ADHD is just about hyperactivity. However ADHD is actually a mix of a number of troublesome behaviours which may include hyper-activity. ADHD causes children to underfunction intellectually and under-behave for the quality of parenting they receive.

It is unusual for a child to be diagnosed with ADHD before school age but it does happen. In my work with these children the complaints I commonly hear include low frustration tolerance, lack of sense, demanding, generally dissatisfied, busy, noisy, and launching unthinking attacks on other children. It is the degree and the combination of these behaviours which causes the problem.

Overview: ADHD in all ages

These behaviour and learning problems are caused by a subtle difference in the fine-tuning of the normal brain. This mostly affects those parts of the brain which control reflective thought and put the brakes on ill-considered behaviour (the frontal lobes and their close connections).

ADHD affects at least 2 per cent of the school-age population, and some quote figures as high as 5 per cent. Boys are more commonly affected than girls. The first behaviours of ADHD are usually apparent before 3 years of age, but few of these children require treatment before they start school. ADHD is a chronic condition and it is now believed that approximately 60 per cent of those affected will take some of their symptoms with them into adulthood.

Until relatively recent times, professionals blamed the parents' attachment or relationships for causing ADHD behaviours. Others said that ADHD was due to additives in food. Now we know that neither of these is the cause, although the standard of parenting and some food substances may influence already existing ADHD. Two things are certain: firstly, ADHD is strongly hereditary and, secondly, it is a biological condition.

Heredity of the condition is obvious as so many sufferers have a parent or close relative with a similar problem. If one identical twin has ADHD there is almost a 90 per cent chance the other sibling will also have the condition. If one sibling has ADHD there is about a 30 per cent chance that another sibling will also be affected. The majority of children who present with ADHD will have a parent or close relative who has experienced many of the same difficulties.

The presentation in the under-fives

In the preschooler two problems make diagnosis difficult. Firstly, at this age there is such an extreme of behaviour which is accepted as normal, it is hard to know where the 'terrible twos' merge with ADHD. Secondly comes the problem of parental misperception.

Some of us enter parenthood with the expectation that our

preschoolers will be obedient, self entertaining and behave like little adults. Sometimes at this age it is hard to determine whether a problem of ADHD is real or a parent's misperception of a normal, high spirited youngster.

There are good academic ways of documenting the diagnosis of ADHD, but the most reliable measure comes from the experienced eyes that see and ears that listen to what parents say. In simple terms, ADHD should be considered when a certain package of behaviours cause a child to be significantly 'out of step' with others of the same development, age and equal quality of parenting.

A diagnosis of ADHD will only be considered when the out-of-step behaviours are causing difficulty. A child can be active, impulsive and explosive, but if everyone is happy there is no need to consider the diagnosis. 'A behaviour is only a problem when it causes a problem.'

At this young age diagnosis also involves excluding ADHD looka-likes. We frequently see young children diagnosed as ADHD when in fact their restlessness, low frustration tolerance and lack of sense are due to intellectual disability. Of course ADHD and delayed development can coexist, but in this case the child must be 'out of step' with the extreme that is accepted at that developmental age.

It is often said that the autistic or Asperger child is indistinguishable from ADHD but this is not so. These are distant, detached children, with a robotic quality to their language, which is totally different to the mischief-loving interest and energy of ADHD. The most difficult children in our care are those with ADHD and a major degree of language delay-disorder.

The Parents

Parents of extremely difficult young children become 'brain-dead' and bewildered. They can't understand why the behaviour techniques that work so well for their friends are so ineffective with their children. They feel criticised by onlookers, friends and family. There seem no easy answers and they wonder what happened to the joy of parenting.

With a difficult ADHD child of any age, parents seem to adopt one of three approaches.

- They accept this temperamental difference, make allowances, relax and parent from the heart.

- They become overwhelmed, feel failures and lose direction.

- They try to drive the bad behaviour out of the child and force them to comply.

Most parents at some time try the third, firm, confronting approach, but fortunately back off when it is seen to fail. Some get stuck in the middle ground, being overwhelmed and unable to move ahead. It seems that those who are successful in managing ADHD eventually find the first approach, then accept, nurture and parent from the heart.

In the USA it is said that 60 per cent of ADHD children will become oppositional and defiant, with 20 per cent showing the severe, almost amoral behaviours of conduct disorder. Where I work the figures for these problems are much lower. It may be a simplistic view, but I believe these conditions are exacerbated – if not in part caused – by the forceful, confronting approach. When parents decide they are going to 'make' their child conform, a conflict of Bosnian proportion often results. At the end of the day the peacekeepers may be in place, but hateful relationships and lifelong distrust remain.

Turning around discipline

When simple behavioural techniques are ineffective its time to re-evaluate all available methods. Parents must not expect a miracle, instead they find what techniques bring them some success, then dump the rest. Parents find it hard to let go of usually effective methods which, in their child, are clearly not working. *'Are you telling me we should stop punishing his bad table manners?'* they ask. 'Is this working?' I respond. *'No, it makes things worse.'* 'Well, why do it?' *'Are you telling me to let him away with everything?'* 'No, but if it's not getting you anywhere, let's back off.'

As a rule:

The best chance of success comes from anticipating problems before they hit, steering around the unimportant, clear convincing communication, diversion, Time Out, getting outside, putting on a favourite video, avoiding escalation and keeping young children moving.

The ways we make things worse are generally: nitpicking, escalating, addressing the unimportant, confronting, debating, shouting, smacking, withholding privileges and over-use of the word 'no'.

Parents who do not accept the ADHD child as different, and make no special allowances, are in for trouble. Those who are hell-bent on bringing up their children with the same rigid discipline of their parent's generation are also heading for failure.

In academic circles the thought of smacking is taboo, but in the real world it is an extremely common form of punishment. For children with an easy temperament smacking may occasionally work but there are much better forms of discipline. In the challenging child, smacking is ineffective, escalating and dangerous. Parents smack to 'make' their child conform. He defies, they smack harder; he resists, and things get out of control.

Parents who live with a demanding, difficult young child feel trapped and have no space. If putting on a favourite video gives a short period of peace, this must be encouraged, despite current criticism of child-minding by television.

Medication can be a miracle

There are a number of medications used in ADHD but the two most commonly used are the stimulants Methylphenidate and Dexamphetamine. Paediatricians and parents are uncomfortable with the use of stimulants under the age of 5 years, however, having stated this, it is my experience over the last 10 years that stimulants can be surprisingly safe and successful in 3 and 4-year olds. In our clinic, stimulants, with their quick action and clearly documented effects, remain the first choice. Remember that drugs are only used when the problem is severe.

Medication is only trialled with informed consent and on the parent's request. We trial both stimulants, as these two preparations are definitely not equal for each child in effect and side-effects. After an initial three-week trial no drug will be prescribed unless the parents, with feed-back from the preschool, are certain of the benefits and freedom from unwanted side-effects.

Some young children seem to metabolise quickly and rebound as their level drops. To combat this some are maintained on four, or occasionally five, small doses to give an even response throughout the day. A few who are extremely difficult will get their first dose the moment they wake.

Ten years ago we were reluctant to use medication in young children, but have now realised that with drugs we can first reach, then teach. This makes our behavioural techniques much more effective. It also helps parents communicate with their children and become closer in their relationship.

Survival Psychology (for the very difficult child)

Its not fair, it shouldn't happen, but the child is there and no one is going to miraculously change their temperament. Over the years we have moved from proposing clever behavioural programmes that rarely work, to regroup and promote the art of 'survival psychology'.

The first step is to accept the reality of the situation, then become committed to a few firm rules, then steer around the strife. If lengthy time in the supermarket is a nightmare, avoid it; instead use late-night shopping or bundle the child in the trolley and use the 'smash and grab' approach. If gatherings with friends and family cause embarrassment, drop in for a high quality half-hour and leave before the bomb blows. If travel is a torment, stay near home. If the child is a runner, fortify the compound. If ornaments get broken, lock them away. If the video is being reprogrammed, put it in a playpen.

It's not the way it should be, but it is easier to spend time playing with the child than getting nothing done as you squabble and resent. They enjoy getting out, but don't let two hours of fun in the park be destroyed by an argument on the way home. We are not looking for conflict, our aim is peaceful coexistence and a child who is still close to their parents at the age of 18. The general rule for all our ADHD children is: when in doubt use an olive branch, not a stick.

The end result

Children who present with extreme ADHD behaviour at preschool age will probably continue to be a challenge for many years. We can't wait until the age of 6 to take this seriously, if we don't get it right at the start, relationships can become permanently derailed.

Recently I worked with an explosive ADHD 3-year old and his defeated mum. I asked if his behaviour was as difficult for everyone, to which she replied, 'Even our German Shepherd guard dog is frightened of him!' With redirecting the discipline, survival psychology and a successful trial of medication she returned for review. When asked 'What's different?', she was quite clear: 'Now I love him'.

For information on the essentials of ADHD in children and adults see Appendix VI. For children over the age of 5 years and more information see *Understanding ADHD* by Dr Christopher Green and Dr Kit Chee.

Summary: ADHD and the under-fives

- ADHD is a strongly hereditary condition.
- ADHD is a mix of troublesome, out-of-step behaviours such as low frustration tolerance, lack of sense, demanding behaviour, being generally dissatisfied, busyness, noisiness and unthinkingly attacking other children.
- It is the degree and the combination of these behaviours which causes the problem.
- A diagnosis of ADHD should only be considered if out-of-step behaviours are causing difficulty. Remember, 'a behaviour is only a problem when it causes a problem'.
- Parents who are successful in managing ADHD accept temperamental difference, make allowances, relax and parent from the heart.
- Keep behavioural techniques that work and dump the rest.
- Ten years ago we were reluctant to use medication in young children but have now realised that with drugs we can first reach, then teach. This makes behavioural techniques much more effective, helps parents communicate with their children and become closer in their relationship.

Playgroups, Preschools and Early Learning

Eighty years ago children lived out their earliest years in an extended family of mum, dad and grandparents. They watched, listened and learned as they served a sort of apprenticeship for adulthood. Nowadays, in our more mobile society, there seems to be a move away from this natural approach towards formal, structured learning. Children from the earliest days attend day care, playgroups and preschools.

Obsessive, driving parents arrange swimming and gym then cram in reading, number work and music lessons on top of all that.

Is this really a great step forward, or is it a misguided stagger to the side? As a doctor who spends much of his time trying to support extremely sad parents with disabled children, I admit I am heavily biased. I think that those of us who are privileged enough to have normal, healthy children should give thanks for what we've got, give them the best love, attention and example we can provide, and not seek to turn them from normal children into something super-normal. Happiness and success in life depend on many things other than academic tutoring. These efforts often do more for the parents' own egos and hang-ups than help the child to cope better with the real, harsh world they will have to live in.

Playgroups

Here young children come along with their mothers, play, attempt to mix with each other and, while all this is going on, the mums chat, socialise and watch. This has advantages for both children and parents. The toddler experiences a little bit of independence yet is never far from mum. Although he is too young to play with other children, he plays happily alongside them and generally enjoys their company. Often children have strange ways of showing their enjoyment, as this is the peak age for biting, kicking, pushing and not sharing. They are also directed in some simple structured play and get their sticky hands on a multitude of new toys.

By attending playgroup the isolated mum avoids becoming entombed in her own home. She hears what problems other mothers are experiencing, then sees she is normal and not alone. Playgroups are great places to compare notes and pool resources with one's fellow toddler tamers.

Preschools

Preschools take children from about 3 years old until school enrolment. The child stays at the centre, where all care and teaching is in the hands of the preschool staff. The directors of our preschools are constantly being sniped at by pushy parents who think that they provide too much play and not enough 'learning'. Despite this, the staff hold firmly to their beliefs that this is the time for the child to enjoy and to develop a wide spectrum of skills needed for life and school. They provide an opportunity for gentle separation in a child who has previously been close day and night to his parents. They also give a quality of child care that is in most cases as supportive as the child would receive at home, thus making the transition a bearable one. This is particularly reassuring to those families who by necessity, or through choice, have to leave their children during the day while they work.

The best way to describe the activities of preschool is 'learning how to learn'. The child is taught basic skills necessary for life at school. These include sharing, mixing, sitting, settling, listening and sticking to a particular task. Many children find this immensely difficult at first but the skilled, trained teachers know how to hold a child's waning interest and encourage him to sit and finish a task, bringing some structure and gentle discipline into the child's life. The skilled teacher builds on the child's natural curiosity to develop an enthusiasm for learning and a quest for knowledge, as well as encouraging the child to both make and be a friend.

In preschool, the child learns to communicate not just in speech but in all sorts of other ways. Using imaginative play their little bodies tell stories just as skilfully as their mouths. Speech accelerates at preschool, as all those busy little beings chatter among themselves. By speech, I do not mean that regurgitated, parrot-like repetition of clever sayings and nursery rhymes they will come up with, but the organisation of thought to produce appropriate original expression. I think that preschools provide some of the best speech therapy available in the Southern Hemisphere.

The child also mixes, learns to share, to take turns and to respect other people's property and wishes. He learns much about structure and discipline, which will prove invaluable when he enters school. As he separates from his mother, he starts to experience a little independence.

The child is not the only one who benefits from preschool. At last mother has some time to herself to 'recharge her batteries'. If there is a younger child in the family, he will now receive some valuable one-to-one care, which he deserves without competition from the older child. Not only does preschool prepare the toddler for the separation of going to school, it also prepares the mother for her feelings of separation when she views the 'empty nest' after the child has flown to school, never again to be a toddler.

Hints for starting preschool

Usually by the age of 3 years and certainly by 4 years our toddlers are ready for preschool. At such a young age there is however a great variation in each child's ability to separate. Some who are militantly independent will cut loose from mum at the gate leaving her empty-handed as they target in on the main action. The majority will be more tentative, being more clingy and cautious for the first week or so. Then there are a few for whom the start of preschool will be very stressful.

Whatever sort of child you have, separation will be smoothest if you prepare in advance and don't rush the first day. When you leave, do so decisively and if in trouble listen to the advice of the class teacher.

In the months before, talk about preschool, visit, walk past and mentally prepare. Get them used to their new gear, the kindy bag, the lunch box, etc. Be sensible with clothes, taking care to avoid those high fashion designs with stiff belts and buttons that take on the style of a straight-jacket when toilet urgency is at its peak.

The food you send should be simple, nutritious and easy to eat. You don't have to compensate for your guilt about leaving your child at preschool by giving out chocolate and other unsuitable pay-offs. Make sure that it is clear which packet is for little lunch and which is for the big lunch. Food should be packed in an easily opened lunch box with the child's name clearly marked. Don't triple wrap in some film that may be environmentally friendly but even the infant Harry Houdini could not find the opening.

On starting day set out in good time, don't rush and try not to transmit your uneasiness to the toddler. It has to be a bit stressful for them. Remember how you felt the last time you changed jobs or came cold into a party to face thirty complete strangers? If we big people get tense, it is likely the little ones will do the same.

Go in with purpose, hang up the bag and take a tour of the premises. The toilets should be first stop as these will be much used in the year that follows. Many little people find the lack of privacy and so much collective flush a bit mind boggling but will get used to it. On the subject of toilets, don't worry if there are a few wet pants. The preschool staff will have been there many times before; they know that recently trained toddlers are prone to leak in times of stress. Put a spare pair of pants in the bag and leave the staff to do the worrying.

Don't rush your departure on the first day. Sit and play and give them time to settle. If a working mum, arrange some cover for that day so as not to drop off and rush away. When it is time to go, be sure they have your contact number, say goodbye and then leave decisively.

Like General MacArthur, say 'I will return,' and like the General, keep the promise. Explain, 'John, you will play, have lunch, a little snooze, more playing and then I will be back'.

Don't use transparent untruths like 'I am just going out to move the car'. Even a 3-year-old knows it's a mighty poor car that takes five hours to move! If in doubt about settling, be guided by the staff. After you've left, if you are worried about your child during the day, ring the preschool – they are used to it!

If leaving does pose a problem, ask the teacher for advice. Most children will settle well, though for a few it sometimes becomes necessary to postpone preschool for a few months. Some will settle well but after a couple of weeks they start to drag their feet as the novelty wears off. This is rarely more than a minor hiccup.

At home be prepared for a tireder toddler. In some instances their behaviour may be worse as they use their mum as a whipping boy to work out their tensions of the day. Beds that were dry may become temporarily wet but this is usually only for a few days. Generally, preschool brings a maturity and better understanding of sharing, mixing and living at peace with one's fellow man and that includes mothers and fathers, though possibly not brothers and sisters.

When to graduate from preschool

Modern parents suffer from a speedy condition called hurry sickness. Life is lived at such a pace there is no time to savour the present. From the moment of birth they are pushing their children on the fast track to independence. If the local law allows their child to start education at 4 years and 7 months, that's when they will begin.

But there is no need for such a rush: school enrolment is usually not compulsory until the age of 6 years. Young children vary greatly in their social and emotional maturity. Some are ripe for an early start, but others need more months to develop.

If your child is eligible to start young, look carefully at their social readiness. Discuss next year with their preschool teacher. They know how your child compares with the others who are preparing for school. When the teacher says no, take it seriously.

Many parents have no choice as, for them, school provides the only affordable form of child care. But if you have concerns and finances will support it, take the safe option and hold back. A late start will never do harm, but starting too soon can cause problems that don't go away.

Producing the infant Einstein

The word 'advanced' means different things to different people. Playing the piano at 4, or being two years academically superior to one's peer group at 5 are all signs of being advanced. But will this necessarily continue and be a help in later life? Being a vivid communicator, resourceful, reliable, sensible, determined, proficient at sport, popular with one's peers, and a keen observer and lover of life, may be much more desirable qualities to help a child struggle through his three score years and ten in a difficult world.

Children who enjoy learning should be encouraged but not pushed to ridiculous lengths. Parents must also be cautioned that many apparently clever tricks are in reality much less spectacular than they would appear.

Rote rituals

Rote learning (learning by memory) has some benefits but it does not always indicate brilliance or academic success. I often see a child whose parents ask him to stand up and count to a hundred for me. As these are rote learned skills they cut little ice with this singularly unimpressed doctor. The child may sound very impressive until asked the simple question: 'If you pass a field in which there are two cows and open the gate and let one out, how many cows would now be in the field?' – Silence! Rote learning is of no benefit in answering real-life problems unless you can think laterally.

Other parents ask their child to recite nursery rhymes, which is promptly done with all the skill of a trained parrot. Having heard about the three blind mice, I might then ask how many tails were cut off by the farmer's wife. Again rote skills are seen to be 'all show and no action', when it is obvious the child does not know what I am talking about. This lateral thinking is important in becoming a creative, intelligent person.

By lateral thinking I refer to the ability to be given one piece of information and use it to generalise for other situations. It is like a dog I know. Now Jake is a mad Rhodesian Ridgeback who has no lateral thinking, that is if he thinks at all. Last year poor Jake ran out on the road and was hit by a bus. He was badly hurt but recovered. Recently I asked his owner, 'Is Jake now more sensible on the road?'. The answer was that he was terrified of the spot where the bus hit him but was just as mad on every other road. Jake is a rote learner, he doesn't use his knowledge to generalise.

One 6-year-old autistic boy I work with has no speech, lives in a world of his own, and is severely and permanently handicapped. Despite this, each time I see him he takes a sheet of paper and as I talk to his parents he writes down with complete accuracy the name of every street he has passed on the way from his home to my clinic. He has an astonishing photographic memory but sadly this is no compensation for the multitude of real-life skills he does not possess.

General knowledge is another skill, most valuable for television quiz shows or to be dragged out as a party piece to impress, but it is more often than not rote learned information.

Our aim in life must be to teach children the basic skills of learning, then encourage and enthuse them to work from there. Computers may indeed store an amazing amount of information but the human brain is infinitely superior when programmed in the right way.

Flash cards, sight words and early reading

Many parents ask me when I think they should start reading to their children. The answer is early, early, early. Twelve to 15 months is a good age to start showing them books. At first they'll probably only fiddle with the pages and look at the pictures, but soon they will start recognising images.

Start reading to them at an early age and keep reading. They won't understand much of what's being said, but it's a good habit and the ultimate aim is to get them to read for themselves.

Some parents with a certain upbringing and philosophy of child rearing can't wait to secure a place for their children in the academic rat race. Reading is one skill they wish to promote, and although they generally receive little encouragement from preschool directors or infant teachers, they undertake the task themselves.

This generally does little harm, and although there is no doubt that at the age of 6 some of these children read much better than their 'uncrammed' contemporaries, there is little evidence that at the age of 8 or 10 these gains will still be apparent. There is also the very real danger that being forced to read and pushed too hard at too early an age can turn some children off the whole idea, and a definite resistance will appear which might hinder an otherwise normal approach to the subject.

In many cases, it is just about impossible to teach active young toddlers to read anyway, as their interests lie more in the areas of running, playing, helping mum or dad, and just enjoying the fun life of being a toddler. Let them have that time, it is all too short as it is.

One may ask why giving a 4-year-old the reading skills of a 6-year-old wouldn't be beneficial. Once again, it is because it is a photographic memory, rote learning exercise, which does no long-term good. These skills can be left until a much later date.

Some young children may be taught to recognise 'sight words' at the age of 3. This is a skill that greatly excites most parents, who are convinced that their child is a reincarnated Einstein. In fact, this skill can be imparted to any child who is prepared to settle and concentrate and has a good photographic memory for differences in patterns. This is the same skill that is used in recognising trade names or a favourite chocolate bar. To encourage this skill, flash cards are used (little cards on which the words are written), and when the appropriate response is given the child is immediately rewarded. Pigeons and chimpanzees have been taught to recognise shapes using very similar techniques. Of course the animal experiments can only reach a certain point because, although it is possible to reward a pigeon for recognising certain shapes, it is impossible to teach it to use its knowledge to work out unfamiliar shapes not previously encountered.

To read properly, recognising patterns is only the beginning. The real skill is in being able to look at a word, sound out its letters, apply a multitude of rules, short cuts and exclusions, and then come up with the right pronunciation. Once this skill has been mastered, words never seen before can be read with ease. Coupled with good reading comprehension, this is the real adult reading skill. Unfortunately, the human brain is not sufficiently mature to handle all this computation before the developmental age of 6, and it is then that we see who are destined to be the good or the bad readers. All this will probably have little relationship to the number of sight words the child could recognise at the age of 5.

Teaching a child to recognise words is not the same as teaching a child to 'read'. I believe that early reading is little more than a clever trick, but research could well prove me wrong. In a large group of toddlers, some are destined to do well academically, some will be average, and some will underachieve. It is known that parents who care and spend much time with their children will usually produce better academic results in their children than those who are uninterested. It is also known that the child who settles, concentrates and is receptive to learning at the age of 4 is more likely to succeed academically than the disorganised, over-active, poor-concentrator.

Although statistics may show that the recognition of sight words at an early age is associated with future academic success, I believe that teaching reading has nothing to do with it. To read successfully at preschool age, you must have some basic academic ability and be encouraged by an enthusiastic teacher. This prerequisite immediately excludes all those with a degree of dyslexia, developmental delay and children from non-reading households. Once these are screened out, it stands to reason that the academic future of this group must be more successful. Early reading is an imprecise indicator of ability, not the reason for that ability.

Swimming

Swimming is very good for toddlers, not only for obvious safety reasons but also because it provides a valuable and enjoyable form of exercise and family fun.

A 1939 study looked at the reactions of 42 infants when put in the water. In the first four months of life, a reflex swimming pattern was observed with the child moving his arms and legs in a rhythmic manner, with vague similarities to freestyle swimming. At 4 months, this reflex disappeared, and the child started to show totally disorganised movement in the water. This is the stage when little children splash and enjoy water but do little more than that with their arms and legs. It was well into the second year that the first, feeble attempts at real swimming, some voluntary semi-purposeful movements, were noted. From here it was only a matter of time, brain maturity and practice until the little children swam.[8]

Swimming from the earliest days of life is to be recommended, if it is used as a form of fun for the whole family to enjoy together. The little baby holds tight to his mother or father with one hand, and the other splashes in the water. Later they paddle by themselves under close supervision before being fitted with some sort of flotation device that gives them more independence. A form of 'dog paddle' swimming develops somewhere between the third and sixth birthdays, depending on the child's determination and the practice he gets. Swimming for older children provides a healthy sport, which children of all physical and intellectual abilities can enjoy equally.

There is a modern trend, perpetrated in the name of early swimming, to toss babies into the water soon after birth. This, like early reading, has little long-term advantage; a communal family 'splash clown' is many times more therapeutic.

Child wonders: who are we trying to help?

All good parents want the best for their children and put a great deal of effort into encouraging and helping them to achieve. This should, of course, be supported but it must never be allowed to progress to unhealthy extremes. Unfortunately, the efforts of some parents soon escalate from an admirable action into an obsession, and academic goals blind them to the realities of life. For some, this is a gradual and unintentional progression but for others, showing off a brilliant child is a crutch to prop up their own crumbling egos.

Recently I talked to a journalist who had just researched an article on teaching youngsters to read at an early age. In the process, she had come up against some amazing parents and their children. One 6-year-old boy was so advanced that his parents insisted that he was bored with school and arranged for him to be promoted to a class with 8-year-olds. Dad installed a home computer for his personal use and then arranged for extra home tutoring in the hope of widening the gap even further. Music lessons were also arranged and the child was largely withdrawn from activities that involved mixing with children of inferior abilities. Certainly he had become an academic genius but, as he had little exposure to anything that might loosely be termed 'fun', he was a pale, indoor child who was socially and physically backward. He was viewed by the school and his parents as an interesting showpiece and by his classmates as a boring nerd. To a sceptic like myself, it seemed that these parents were hiding from their own hang-ups in their obsessive crusade to produce a 'superchild'. Sadly, the other children in the family, who were 'only normal', were to a large extent ignored in the process.

Another family had a 3-year-old boy who was doing remarkably well in the second year of a reading programme. As this was so time-consuming, the parents hired an interesting lady from overseas to teach the child. Her daily task was to tutor the boy in reading, then to talk away to him in her native tongue so that the child would become at the same time academically advanced and bilingual. You might ask, where were the parents while all this was going on? Well, being busy professional people, they were out at work all day.

Just because pushy parents engage in these programmes, all you normal well-adjusted parents must not let yourselves be made to feel either inferior or guilty. Reading and jabbering away in a foreign tongue at the age of 4 may satisfy some parents' egos, but I can assure you children much prefer to learn through love and living.

Learning through living

The greatest educationalists our children will ever meet in their lives are their parents. The value of watching, listening, playing and just being around them must never be underestimated.

During the average day all manner of adventures take place in a toddler's life. A fire engine clattering by or a big, barking dog will spark off his imagination and he will want to verbalise his experiences to anyone who will listen. On the way to the shops he might recognise an advertisement previously seen on television, or he may want to talk about the shops, the cars and anything else of interest that passes. In the supermarket, he counts out the oranges, gets the bigger, not the smaller, packet, and learns to spot subtle differences on the labels. Once home, he will start matching and sorting as he helps to put away the groceries – all accompanied by non-stop chatter. In all this, the toddler looks to his parents for reassurance and guidance.

He listens to mum and dad, copying their sayings and asking innumerable questions. With this, his verbal abilities increase, and so does his general knowledge. He helps with the household chores, learning to run simple messages and generally being 'mother's little helper'. Unbreakable dishes are washed in the sink and helping with the cooking is a particular favourite. Pastry is rolled, cut and shaped and his rather grubby effort at a jam tart is ceremoniously placed in the oven alongside the family meal. While all this goes on, he feels very important and loved, and he develops a great interest in life.

He builds up his muscles, not in gym but on the arduous walk up to the park, sitting on swings, ascending the climbing frame and the sprint to chase some unfortunate pigeon foolish enough to land within a hundred metres of this active little bird scarer. Much of the day is spent in play, not with those expensive computerised inventions produced in Silicon Valley but with natural raw materials, such as boxes, chairs and paper.

Improvisation and free play produce an extremely inventive brain which is often lost in the 'spoon fed' child. One minute the chairs are all lined up, and money is collected and counted by the toddler conductor; minutes later he is piloting an amazingly noisy jumbo jet down the middle of the lounge room. The cardboard box becomes a garage for toy cars; later it is a rocket base from which the cardboard innards of a toilet roll blast off into space.

Academic education, like sex education, can be acquired in a number of ways. The child may be summoned to a room, alone with his father, and given a formal lecture on the facts of life. The relaxed parent usually abhors this approach, preferring to answer questions as they arise in the course of daily life. Similarly, toddlers may either be sat down and taught formally, or allowed to be apprentices to their parents and learn through the activities of everyday life.

Good parents must not let themselves be browbeaten by their friends who have adopted the role of high powered educationists. Being good, loving, caring parents, who teach their children through practical living, is to be commended above all. When viewed over a 70 year life span it seems pretty irrelevant that a child reads at the age of 4 or 6. Better by far to start life with a healthy, happy, balanced outlook. The trials and tribulations will come soon enough.

TWENTY

Working Mother – Effective Parent

Books about child care often censure mothers who have young children and yet go out to work. In an ideal world they might have a case but the world we all inhabit is far from ideal. What's more, though many have tried, no-one has yet shown that children of good, working mothers are damaged or disadvantaged in any way.

Today in Australia 51 per cent of mothers of under-5s will be back in paid work. For an ever-increasing number, there is now no choice, if there are not two wages the bills cannot be paid. The position is even worse if you are a sole parent. Others have trained hard to attain a responsible position and with prolonged absence they lose skills as well as prospects of promotion in a competitive workplace. There are quite a few mums who find that they were just not made to be 24 hour a day mothers and no matter how they try, the role does not suit. It is all very easy to criticise but in these times of supposed sexual equality, it seems to me that few men would be prepared to be 24 hour a day parents.

Though I accept the inevitability of the current trend and the complete absence of evidence of harm, I still wish the percentages could be lower. I worry that young mothers *and fathers* are both so busy in these fascinating early years. It is only in later life that one can see how quickly this time has passed and once gone, we cannot ask for a re-run.

Guilt

If mothers who either wanted to work or were obliged to work could just get on with it and stop feeling guilty, their lives would be much happier. Recently I attended a preschool parents' meeting where a bevy of home-based mums turned on the working mums in the group telling them that they had no right to have children if they didn't want to stay at home and care for them. Even without this unwarranted assault, most of those mums were feeling guilty at short-changing their children.

Let me reassure working mothers by quoting from the internationally respected writings of Michael Rutter: 'Although frequently blamed for their children's troubles it is now apparent that working mothers have children with no more problems than the children of women who remain at home. This has now been shown in a wide range of studies using different measures of children's behaviours'. A more recent study was done by Elizabeth Harvey at the University of Massachusetts.[9] She evaluated children's language development, academic achievement, self-esteem and behaviour problems. In comparison with children of mothers who did not work, she found no statistically significant difference in any of the measures.

It is increasingly clear that it is not the number of hours spent away from home that make the difference but:

- the quality of the child's day-care arrangements

- the quality of parent–child relationship

- Mum's emotional wellbeing

- extra attention given to the child when parents and child are together.

Choosing child care

Those lucky enough to be surrounded by family are fortunate indeed. If this help is not available, day care can be arranged, using either high quality approved centres or a local mother, authorised to take in three or four children in her own home. With these official carers you certainly will not go wrong, but there are at present only half the places needed and even then they prove too expensive for many parents.

With a private arrangement, the minder must be chosen with great care. You must have complete confidence in her ability so that you can relax when at work and concentrate on the job in hand. When choosing a care giver, it is wise to watch how she relates to your little one. Does she talk, listen, play and share genuine mothering gentleness and care, or is it a relationship based on an adequate injection of money? When the child is first left with a minder, enough time should be allowed so that this isn't done with a great rush and fuss.

The child should be clearly told where you are going and when you will be back to pick him up. Despite the explanation, the young toddler will not understand and may shed copious tears on your departure, as well as probably punish you by doing the same when you return.

The minder should be left with a contact telephone number and told to telephone you if she has the slightest worry. This will help ensure a better standard of care for the child and some early warning for you if anything goes wrong.

Illness and child care

After a year of living in the relative isolation of home, our children have little immunity to all the bugs that cause colds, coughs and fevers. When they start in child care they are at their most vulnerable and they seem to catch everything that is on the go.

Child care is not designed to cope with unwell toddlers and this puts a great strain on the parents and their employers. Some firms are reluctant to employ mothers with young children as they expect so much adult sick leave to be taken on account of childhood sickness.

There is no easy answer to this. It's only right that close family have to be there to comfort children when they are unwell. I should, however, mention that mothers do not have the monopoly when it comes to taking time off work, fathers should also shoulder some of this responsibility.

A fair deal for the child

The mum who works must make sure she gives good attention to her child in the time that they are together. The work-tired mum feels little enthusiasm to start washing, cleaning the house and cooking, let alone talking and playing with a toddler. But, however good day care is, it is only acceptable if accompanied by good night care and weekend care. Shopping, cooking and housework must not be allowed to consume all the parent's and child's time together, although if handled properly these can be a source of fun and education. If money allows, shop well ahead so that only occasional topping up from the corner store is needed. Prepared frozen foods are a good standby diet, but rather expensive and monotonous on a regular basis. Exotic, time-consuming dishes must be deleted from the menu and replaced by nutritious, easy-to-prepare meals. For those with big freezers and an organised brain, there is much to be said for a weekend cooking binge, in which dishes are mass-produced and frozen in meal-sized portions. This allows good food to appear with all the speed of melting ice. A weekly visit to the local restaurant or hamburger joint will give the cook a welcome break and provide great excitement for the toddler.

Working mums and a 'Home Beautiful' are not a compatible combination. Cleanliness, hygiene and relative tidiness are desirable but obsessive house pride is out. Family fun comes first. It is hard to communicate with a child over the roar of a vacuum cleaner and difficult to have a good, fun-filled romp around the house when an obsessive mother resents the slightest disturbance to even a cushion.

A fair deal for working mothers

Working mothers are often expected to do at least two full-time jobs, and only one of which receives pay or thanks. All husbands are generous to a fault. They give with absolute equality at the time of conception but, unfortunately, for many that's where all giving and equality seems to end. For some fathers, you might well ask, 'Is there life after conception?'.

In these days of contraceptive choice and the increasing need for mothers to work, discussion of shared care would seem sensible before, not after, the act.

When two tired parents and an excited child get home each evening there must be a fair division of labour and the child must not miss out. Weekends can have one parent shopping, cleaning or taking the toddler to the pool or park, while the other irons and prepares for the week to come. If fathers can have a night out with the boys or go off to soccer training, mothers must be afforded the same opportunity. Husbands have no serious form of impairment that prevents equal sharing of home and child care.

Conclusion

The trend is for an ever-increasing number of mothers with young children to return to work. These mums have taken on two full-time jobs, one at home and one at work, and without help the stress will start to show.

It seems only fair that if children are planned and conceived together, then care should continue together. In the twenty-first century, there can be no place for a sleeping partner in a two-wage family. Fathers must wake up to this reality.

Though many mothers worry and feel guilty as they leave their young, it must be stated that there is no evidence that working mothers harm their children in any way. Of course day care must be good and parents must not short-change their children after work and at weekends. In parenting it is not the amount of time, but how we use that time that matters most.

TWENTY-ONE

In Praise of Grandparents

Grandmas and grandpas are some of our most valuable, and least utilised, natural resources. Over the last fifty years, as a result of better housing and what is called 'progress', families have moved apart to live in relative isolation. This has brought with it all manner of problems. Mother-in-law jokes keep countless comedians in business but this brand of humour is lost on the toddler, who is not interested in squabbles about his grandmother's interesting, irritating ways. He just enjoys being in her company. I write here in praise of the older generation and their great value to us and our children.

Benefits

Historically, in families that lived together, the younger members would call upon the experience of the older ones for advice. Owing to the often self-imposed isolation of modern-day living, however, parents lack easy access to that sensible advice as well as that much-needed extra pair of hands in times of stress. Other young parents view the older generation as past it, out of touch and incapable of offering anything. This is a strange attitude, when you think that up until recently the world's most powerful countries were all ruled by people who are themselves grandfathers or grandmothers.

Life is lived at a more realistic pace as we get older, and it is viewed with that mature, 'been there, done that' approach. Most older people have lived through wars, financial deprivation and all manners of upsets, so they are in a better position to view the relative futility of the minor irritations that get blown out of all proportion in our day-to-day lives.

The older generation often has a more infectious, quiet gentleness that our fast-moving younger generation has not yet developed. Children who won't sit still are often quietened, as if by hypnotism, when in granny's care. Grandfathers may not be able to engage in high energy rough and tumbles, but they are streets ahead in other areas. The youngster will sit and listen to all manner of stories, viewing grandpa as the world's greatest wit and raconteur. They go out together on exciting safaris around the garden or the neighbourhood, and although perhaps never more than a hundred metres from base, there is so much of interest to see when helped by someone who can slow down for long enough to point it out.

There is no better form of temporary child care than that provided by good grandparents. This is really an extension of the parents, not least because genes and twenty years of brainwashing by grandma are bound to ensure that one parent will have much in common with her. Day care when the parents are at work, babysitting, care when sick – all these valuable services can be provided by grandparents. Some parents organise a regular afternoon or day a week when the child stays with grandma. Some take the occasional weekend mini-break, leaving their child with her, or take the grandparents on holiday to share the child care load. There are tremendous benefits for the parents, the child and the grandparents with this shared care.

Isolated mums should not be backward in befriending elderly neighbours, a good move for the old folk and also enriching for the young ones. This can provide much needed foster grandparents.

Laying down the ground rules

The main cause of friction with grandparents is when it is thought that they are interfering and criticising. Their interference is perhaps understandable, because they find it hard to sit back quietly and watch their own children stumble through life making all the same mistakes that they themselves made and later regretted. A forewarning of one's errors is often greeted with either a deaf ear or much resentment. Many fights occur over trivial matters, which are irrelevant when viewed against the background of the great benefits of care-giving that grandparents can provide.

To ensure a good relationship, the rules have to be set down, and both sides have to accept that the other has rights. When the child is in the care of the parents, then the parents are in charge of the show, and although advice may be tactfully given, it does not have to be accepted. When the child is being looked after by the grandparents, then they are in charge and should not be forced to adhere to the parents' often obsessive and irrelevant ideas. A child is like a chameleon, who can match in easily with an ever-changing environment.

Within reason, grandma should be allowed to feed the child whatever she wants and if, for example, the parents believe the sugar content will damage the child's teeth, this can be remedied with a quick brush of the teeth on returning home, rather than a family feud. Grandparents should be left to discipline the child in a way that feels best for them, and this should in no way damage the overall behaviour and discipline of the child. The parents are the main caretakers, and they cannot go through life blaming grandparents, schools or other children for their offspring's shortcomings. What shortcomings there are must be laid fairly and squarely at their doorstep to remedy.

Conclusion

It would be foolish to suggest that all grandparents are interested in being closely involved with the toddler. Come to think of it, some have had little enough time for their own children and, having screwed them up, should not be afforded the privilege of doing the same to the next generation.

But most of us under-use our greatest resource, tending to keep grandparents like Christmas decorations, to be brought out and shown only on high days and holidays. Both children and parents have much to learn from the older generation, whether it be grandma and grandpa or the old couple living next door.

For a happy partnership there are some simple rules. The younger generation must have some respect for age and maturity. They must not fight over pointless trivia, nor interfere with grandma's care, and they can, therefore, expect the same non-interference when the child is in their care.

TWENTY-TWO

Sole Parent Families

Today's statistics show that over one quarter of our children can expect to be part of a sole parent family before the end of their school years.

In my more philosophical moments I despair over us human beings. We can split atoms, explore space and create computers but often we can't chose a compatible partner and live in peace together. It seems that as science races ahead, human relations lag far behind.

There are a number of reasons for sole parenthood but sadly for most people the end result is much the same. Isolation, loneliness, little social life, money worries and frequently, aggravation from the absent partner.

It may be tough for us adults but usually we had some choice in the course we took, whereas our children are not so fortunate. They had no say as to whether conception or contraception was advisable and once born they are stuck with a situation outside their control. Adults can separate but children often have to live with arguing, unstable and unreasonable grown-ups, as so far, divorce of one's parents is not a legal option.

The sole parent situation is difficult for both parent and child but not impossible. If the custodial adult can remain strong and emotionally together the outlook for the children is excellent.

Special situations – their problems

Each sole parent situation comes with its own special package of problems. How these evolve and affect the child will depend on three things: the warmth and resilience of the custodial parent; the amount of support or destructive interference from outside; and the circumstances that led to the sole parent state.

When two parents are committed to separating in a responsible and amicable way it results in a totally different situation to the angry aftermath of a bitter break. The sole parent shattered by the death of a much loved partner is again in a very different state to that of the isolated teenage mum, hardly more than a child herself.

Separation and divorce – sole parents

This is the most common 'solo' situation I meet. Though these parents have many worries, the greatest influence on the household happiness is whether there was peace or continuing hostility after the split. (See Chapter 23, Tension in Families – Spare the Children.)

No matter how unhappy life was before the break, most parents find the final separation an emotionally shattering watershed. Studies show the next twelve months is a most difficult time, as parents readjust and toddler behaviour is often at its worst. Many questions deserve a mention.

Custody and access rights I may have an oversimplistic view of the law but I see little point in parents fighting over custody and access. In my experience, if the mother wants the children, she will be granted custody, unless she has some very major emotional or addictive problems.

Access is usually open but may occasionally be restricted but rarely is it totally blocked. I have been subpoenaed as a reluctant witness in a number of access cases and in all of these the infrequent successes could never justify the great emotional and financial costs.

Housing After separation, many families gather up their belongings and move home. This may be for financial reasons or as a result of an unconscious need to flee from a house full of bad memories. A word of caution: if possible make no hasty decisions. While the life we knew is falling apart, we need to grasp tightly to familiar places, people and routines. The house is like a nest which we can fly home to each night so we can feel the security of a place we know. Children are much the same, they have just lost one parent and if they lose their own home, this can add insult to injury.

Money For most mothers the solo state brings a drastic drop in their standard of living. This is all the more galling if they see their husbands parading around in relative abundance. When he visits, children may be feted and feasted, and then returned to the care of a mother, scratching to make ends meet.

Of course, not all ex-husbands are in this category. Many never wanted to divorce in the first place and are now struggling to maintain two homes. Many will also have money problems if they have remarried and have a second family to support.

The present pension is designed to support life but could never be classed as generous. Returning to work does much to boost a mum's flattened esteem and identity but by the time child care has been funded and the pension foregone, the job needs to pay well to be worth pursuing.

Fathers have both a moral and legal duty to support their young. Government has legislated that child support is taken directly from the salary. The self-employed can make out that they have little income so the ex-wife gets little or nothing. Life goes on – but life is not fair and often both parties feel bitter. (There are often no winners in a separation.)

Family and friends

Where a close network of family and friends exists separation is so much smoother for both adults and children. An on-side grandparent provides all the security of a safety net, there to catch the children when the parents let them slip.

Though there may be great benefits, it is not easy for a mother to return home to her own parents. It is not just the loss of an independent life, it is also the subtle admission of failure. This however is not a time to be difficult or choosey. The advantages of a return to a familiar friendly patch, with help in child care and an emotionally secure environment for children, makes diplomacy a course to consider.

After a marriage break-up it is never easy to get back into the social set you knew before. Friends have divided loyalties, they do not know who to support, so often they support no-one. Married couples cope well with other married couples but may feel uneasy with a single in their midst. Some keep their distance almost as though they see separation as some sort of contagious affliction.

Parents who have lost a partner and now have no close friends or family tread a very lonely road. They are emotionally most vulnerable and in this state it is all too easy to rebound straight into another unsuitable relationship. It never ceases to amaze me how so many wives escape from one alcoholic or uncaring husband and by year's end have sought out and married another the same or worse.

Don't divorce the grandparents

At the wedding celebration there were guests on the bride's side and guests on the groom's side. At the divorce the relatives are still seen as being aligned. But little children don't understand the dynamics of a break-up; they have no interest in branding people as good guys or bad guys. They are unsettled by the change in their parents' life, and they rely on relatives from both sides to provide a vital safety net.

A wife may divorce her husband, but there is no need to divorce his parents as well. Legislation now guarantees grandparents access, but until recently I met grandparents who had lost all contact with those they loved. And this was at its most malicious when an inadequate new partner had come on the scene. Often the grandparents phone calls were obstructed, letters destroyed and birthday presents returned.

288

One grandmother told how, after the separation, she had cared for the children every day for three years. But when the new partner arrived all access was blocked. Now the only time she saw the children was a glimpse from a passing bus or looking longingly through the bars of the school fence.

With break-ups children need the security of grandparents. If relatives are prepared to keep out of the politics and give support, they should have the most open of access. An amicable settlement involves being amicable to all friends and relatives who genuinely wish to help.

Access visits

Whether you like it or not these visits are going to happen. You have the option to be stirred, which also stirs the children, or take it like a Swami, with a divine aura of acceptance.

Of course it hurts when your children are out with your ex and his new friend. Of course it hurts when you don't have a cent to spare and they live in relative affluence. Of course it hurts when you wash, feed and care all week, while they come and go taking all the rewards, with none of the responsibility. That's life. No-one pretends it's fair but that's the rotten way it is.

Behavioural backlash

Children are not marriage guidance counsellors, and have no idea or interest in the rights and wrongs that led to the split. Little children cannot grasp the permanence of the situation and no matter how obnoxious and unreasonable the absent partner has been, they still wish to see them.

Due to the peak time that most marriages break up, preschoolers represent the main age group involved. Their problems vary in intensity but usually show up as insecurity, regression of skills and difficult behaviour.

Insecurity hits with a bang. They have lost one parent and are sure they are not going to let the remaining carer out of sight. They cling like a limpet and are reluctant to move far away without checking that their parent is still around. Day care and preschool may be difficult, with them protesting loudly when left and settling poorly through the day. Try to spend more time before leaving them and let the director know the situation so they may be even more supportive. Sleep may become disturbed as they wake at night demanding comfort, to check the remaining parent is still there. Many slip into the parent's bed, which is not a problem now but if a new relationship develops, it may pose quite an impediment.

Behaviour often takes a turn for the worse. They are angry at a situation they do not understand and they take this out on those nearest to them. They feel the sadness, confusion and tension in the air but are not at an age to tread gently, so instead they stir. For parents, bad behaviour is hard to take when in an emotionally weak state and feeling flat. We tend to forget that our little ones are also upset. They feel let down and need gentle guidance, not heavy and punitive discipline.

Mums and mental health

Although at the time of separation there may be a distinct feeling of relief, the year that follows will be one of confused emotions. Often there are regrets, doubts about self-worth, sadness, anger and confusion about whether the current difficult situation is any improvement on the one left behind.

I am not a psychiatrist but I believe that many mothers are clinically depressed at this stage and the mental health of the caring parent has an immense effect on the children. When we become sad, isolated, immobile, without drive or enthusiasm and emotionally flat, it is time to seek professional help. It is always easier to struggle on but this is not good for either parents or the little people who depend on them.

Remember, it is not only the grown-ups who are unhappy, the children are also confused and upset. Our emotional batteries may be depleted but our little ones are more than ever in need of an emotional jump start to keep them going.

Life will be easier if you accept the inevitable and don't waste energy on futile fights. Access, inequality of responsibility and general injustice are par for the course, whether you anger yourself into a stroke or accept it.

Try to get out, to walk, to play in the park, to meet other mothers. Work hard to keep both body and brain in shape with regular exercise and interest. Remember, one emotionally together mother is more important than having distant parents who happen to live together.

New relationships

Sole parents are in a social straightjacket. It is extremely hard to get out to meet interesting people when tied to the home with small children, no baby-sitters and a limited budget. If a new relationship gets going, this for many is where their toddler troubles seem to start.

See it from the child's point of view. They have just lost one parent and though there may have been a divorce, he's still my dad. They have been upset by one parting and don't really want to start down the same track again. Most have become extremely close to their mother and they don't want anyone coming between them – thank you very much. Then there are those who have squirreled themselves into the family bed to sleep with mum and any suggestion of eviction would warrant a protest rally.

In any new relationship the secret is to be conscious of the child's feelings, to move gently and not force the issue. At first it is best to keep the initial action outside the home, as it takes time for children to adjust to one they see as an intruder on their own pitch. Don't be punitive when they stand up for their rights or are downright unfriendly.

With new relationships often step-children arrive as a sort of package deal, which can cause additional problems of personality clashes, territorial claims and divided loyalties. Again move slowly, be sensitive to children's feelings and give it time.

Finally another word of caution. Isolated, lonely people may crave adult companionship but rebound relationships are often fraught with difficulties. It seems foolish to enter any permanent relationship until quite clear why the last one did not work out.

This is not a caution without backing. The statistics show that over half of divorced parents with little children will have remarried within three years. Unfortunately over half of these second marriages will not survive a full 5-year term. A second separation causes a double dose of disruption that no child, and few parents need.

Sole parents through accident or illness

As caring humans we feel particularly sad when we read of the untimely death of a young parent. This is much more upsetting to us than would be news of an angry separation or a damaging divorce. Often these bereaved families tend to fare better than many other solo situations.

Life is suddenly shattered but there is a funeral and in the next years the events of the past are put firmly behind. While this goes on, friends, family and the community as a whole tend to rally to support. In this situation there is no bickering over property, access or custody. The wounds are deep but they are allowed to heal without unnecessary interference.

Little children cannot grasp that death is permanent and to them it is as though their dad or mum had gone off on a long holiday. They usually need no counselling, play therapy or psychiatrist. They take their lead from those around. Their home has changed from fun and frolic to tension and tears. When the adults in their life get themselves together, the children will then follow suit.

One statistic always makes me sad. It has been shown that the young child whose father is killed in an accident stands to emerge emotionally many times sounder than the child of a long running bitter divorce. We humans have the ability to do much more harm to our children by our deliberate actions than through life's unavoidable accidents.

Teenage solos

It is not fashionable to talk frankly about teenage solos but few people who have a genuine interest in the long-term emotional well-being of our young, could be anything but concerned.

The group that worries me most are those children brought up in an unhappy, disturbed home, who have never seen a proper parenting example and have felt little warmth or love. Often the pregnancy for these teenagers is an attempt to find the love and purpose that life so far has denied them. Most cope reasonably well in the first year with a baby but often by toddlerhood they are in deep strife. The restriction to a life of 24 hour a day child care, the isolation from their young social scene, loneliness, poverty and for many the behaviour of a difficult, disturbed toddler make life far from happy.

Five years on, when I see these mums, some have done amazingly well, though I can't but worry that so many have had such a difficult and often deprived time. As the years go by and I get to know them better, it seems that with the hindsight that comes with age, many of these adults would have preferred to have done things differently if life would permit a re-run.

It is one thing mentioning this concern but what can we do about it? What is needed is support for the young parents of today and then to look at possible prevention for tomorrow. These young solos are extremely vulnerable and need a great amount of close, ongoing support. It is rare that the community can afford to provide this but bearing in mind the possible repercussions, one wonders if we can afford not to.

Prevention involves education and example.

Education is not just sex education. It involves the whole area of gaining a realistic perspective of relationships. This is hard to get across to the young who may see physical attributes and attraction as all-important in having a close and continuing relationship.

Education also involves encouraging teenagers to choose the course of their life not through indecision but by active decision. Contraception, termination and adoption, whether appropriate or not, all require very active decisions. Conception and continuing with a pregnancy may also involve carefully considered decisions but in reality, many enter sole parenthood through never facing up to the events that were happening in their lives.

Teenagers need to be made aware of the restrictions and limits to life that come with parenthood. It is hard to convince them of this; after all, most of us much older adults were never prepared for the change that our children brought.

In one Sydney school the headmaster was worried that so many teenage mothers were not finishing their education. He actively encouraged them to come back and finish their schooling. This has reaped a double benefit. First the young mothers got an education which hopefully helped them out of the poverty trap. Secondly it gave the other students at the school a lesson in life. They discovered how very, very difficult it was to be a parent – much worse than they ever thought. In turn this has decreased the number of teenage pregnancies in the school.

Example It is easier to talk about setting an example than to put it into practice. However, example is vitally important to every child whether they are part of a one or two parent family. The number of parents is not the issue here, it is the warmth, peace and togetherness of a family that have the greatest bearing on the children. At this moment, our little ones are tuning in to the atmosphere of their home, storing it away in their memories to draw from it when they enter their own adult relationships.

It is quite a sobering thought that our behaviour today will have a considerable effect on how our children and even grandchildren may behave in the future. Whoever said parenting was easy!

Conclusion

It is a fact of life that many relationships will fall apart and many children will feel the repercussions. Life for the sole parent is not easy, with many upsets and injustices in their path no matter what they do. It is not the fact of being a sole or two parent family that affects the children but the strength and emotional togetherness of the main carer and the peace of the home environment.

TWENTY-THREE

Tension in Families –
Spare the Children

Throughout the world today thousands of children live in the midst of war and conflict. We live in a peaceful country where our young are presumed to be spared such traumas – but are they? You don't have to live in downtown Belfast or Beirut to know the full feeling of tension and hostility. You can feel it right here, not on the streets but where it hurts most – in many of our homes.

This year another 50 000 Australian children will witness the break-up of their parents' relationship but this is only a small part of the problem. A great many more continue to live unhappily with parents who are geographically together but emotionally and behaviourally a million miles apart.

It is not just the alcoholics, the psychopaths and the violent who

295

upset their children; it is also the thousands upon thousands of normal parents who bicker, nitpick, hold grudges, escalate events and make little effort to maintain their home as a happy and peaceful place.

Tension troubles children

Not a week goes by without some parent telling me: 'Dr Green, our relationship is a complete mess, but it's all right, the children don't know'.

Don't fool yourself for a minute, you can never hide tension and unhappiness from children. You may keep your disputes and disagreements behind closed doors but the chill that comes with them will permeate to every corner of the home. Whether we like it or not, our adult problems soon become our children's problems.

Tension makes parents irritable, unreasonable, and emotionally tepid. Children, when they feel these vibes, may become insecure, demanding or just downright difficult. Tension must be one of the main triggers of bad behaviour and child unhappiness in our peace-loving society today. Most of this is quite unnecessary if only we adults could act more like adults and less like self-centred, inconsiderate toddlers.

Bitter break-ups (legalised child abuse)

It is not the breakdown of a marriage that does the damage. Rather it is all the associated aggravation and hostility that upsets our children. We may not like our partner but they still should be treated with the respect and civility due to another human being.

Many parents are shameless in the way they abuse each other and then recruit their innocent children to become pawns in their battle. Soon these unwilling conscripts are being used as weapons to cause pain to the partner. Disputes on child management are heated and open. When one parent doles out the discipline, the other contradicts, just for spite. You can see how confused and bruised our little ones become.

Access visits are used as an excuse to gain entry and disrupt the happiness of the home. The visitor deliberately does not come when expected, is obtuse and inflammatory on arrival, vague about the time of return and then once more abusive.

Mothers tell children that their dad is unreliable, while dads poison their young with equally spiteful untruths. Before long children dread the tension of the weekly visits as these become an endurance to be feared, not enjoyed.

Court battles are necessary to resolve genuine grievances. Sadly some cases are brought purely to cause prolonged pain to the other partner, and in this vindictive atmosphere there is no thought for the feelings of a child who is becoming increasingly disturbed.

It still seems strange to me that we, as intelligent, compassionate people, can so often set out to deliberately damage our children. These guerilla tactics, used both during marriage and through the break-up period, can keep tension and bitterness running high for years. I don't see this as a civil right of any parent. It is a form of legalised child abuse which should never be condoned in any country that genuinely believed in the rights of its children.

Amicable settlements (thank God for sensible parents)

Not only are amicable settlements possible between divorcing partners but thankfully they are also very common. Here parents split in such a way that they are both completely committed to cause the least amount of upset to their children.

In these families there will be no sabotage, no point scoring or trying to win affection over the other party. Discipline will remain consistent. Custody is not an issue, property is divided fairly and access is looked forward to and enjoyed.

Children of peaceful settlements usually bear no long-term emotional scars, a state of affairs greatly helped by close extended families, the support of good friends and the children staying in touch with those familiar faces and surrounds they know.

The toddler cannot be expected to fully comprehend the meaning of the separation but careful explanation is still important. This should be done using simple words, told without anger or blame. Words must be reassuring, as some little ones can feel they have somehow been responsible for spiriting one of their parents away.

Children must realise that though their parents will not live together, both still love them and will continue to care for them. They must know where they will live and it is advisable that they see where the absent parent will stay. This gives them a picture to store in their minds and assures them that their dad or mum has not departed from the face of the earth.

Access should be kept as flexible and peaceful as possible, with both parties committed to making it go smoothly. The best sole situations for our children are those where their parents, though they don't want to live together, can still be good friends when they live apart. In this amicable climate, peace is preserved while the children continue to have two caring parents who can work closely and constructively to ensure a secure present and future.

Conclusion: happy homes – happy children

It seems strange that most intelligent human beings tend to treat those near and dear to them with less civility than they would afford to those they hardly know in outside life. I find it hard to believe that the highly advanced ape called man is so often intellectually impaired when it comes to choosing a mate for life. Is this a human failing, or is our judgement quite sound, and our expectations unreal?

There are no perfect marriages, even the best will have their ups and downs. Don't expect roses and violins every day; in real relationships the roses go in and out of bloom and the violins slip in and out of tune. If it's going to work for us and therefore our children, we need to have sensible expectations and be committed to easing and not escalating the bumps.

All relationships will slip into a rut unless we work hard to keep them fresh and alive. You may be busy and tired but take time to

notice, to encourage, to communicate and to cherish. A bunch of flowers given today is better than a whole shopful to put on a loved one's coffin. By then it is too late.

Tension and needless bickering are probably the greatest and most unnecessary cause of upset to today's children. Nothing I say will stop relationships running aground. What I ask is that some thought be given to the children before you hoist the battle-flags.

Settling our disputes in an amicable way may not be as satisfying to our adult anger but it is important to the emotional well-being of our children. While parents have the right to fight, children have the right to be spared trauma.

Summary: split, sole, step: protecting the children

1. The main priority is always the emotional wellbeing of our children.
2. Never underestimate the detrimental effect of stress and hostility on children. Parents may feel angry, but that's their problem, not the child's.

3. You can't stop the break-up but you can ensure that it is as amicable as possible.
4. Children need as little change as possible.
5. Children show their upset by clinging close, acting out or withdrawing.
6. Young children are open and intense in their reaction. Their behaviour settles when the parents' behaviour settles.
7. Older children may carry a more chronic but less obvious wound.
8. Children need to be told what is happening, in a way that is appropriate to their age.
9. Don't draw children into adult battles. They don't understand the rights and wrongs; all they know is that it hurts.
10. Children need to know they will have two parents and both will continue to care for them.
11. They should know where they will live. Where the non-custodial parent will live. And when they will see each other.
12. Keep close to grandparents and any extended family who genuinely wishes to support.
13. You may divorce your partner, but your children do not want to divorce their grandparents.
14. Access must be encouraged and made easy. It's going to happen whether the parents make it enjoyable or a time of tension.
15. Don't spy on or slander the other parent.
16. When a child is out on access, it is up to the accessing parent what they do and whom they do it with. You can't prevent you child being cared for by a new partner.
17. Most custodial parents get a raw deal. No one said this is fair but that's the way it is, whether we accept it or not.

TWENTY-FOUR

The Disabled Child: Behaviour and Discipline

I t is very difficult to define clearly the behavioural problems of disabled children, because there are so many different degrees of disability affecting so many different children. There are a few generalisations that can be made, such as there being a somewhat higher proportion of restless, irritable, hard-to-comfort children among the disabled.

The best forms of behaviour and discipline techniques to use with disabled children are exactly those you would use with normal toddlers. The good is rewarded and praised. The undesirable is ignored, or pretended to be ignored. Time Out, where they are placed in their bedroom, provides a much-needed safety valve, to be used when everything else seems to have failed. The controlled crying technique is used with sleep problems, although sedation is more often needed in addition. One difference with all behaviours is that, try as we may, the cure rate is less spectacular than we would like. Part of the difficulty is that special children have special parents with special feelings. For many, it is hard to be as tough as is needed to get results. Another part is that many such children have bodies which are strong and advanced in their physical skills, while the brains which control all this power lack insight, sense and sometimes the ability to learn easily from experience. Bearing this in mind, it is often best to lower our sights and aim first for a percentage improvement rather than the full cure. This is not defeatism, merely realism. Any small improvement will bring benefits to the tired parents.

As a general principle, each child should be treated with the discipline and management appropriate to his developmental (mental) age, no matter what the actual age may be. Despite this, however, you will find that outside factors can take charge and make treatment less successful. For example, children who have epilepsy that is poorly controlled are often more irritable and diffi-cult than average. Their problems are often worse just before a seizure and in the days that follow it. Some of the medications used for epilepsy can also worsen behaviour, and some doctors do not seem to realise that the drugs they prescribe, although giving perfect control to the seizures, can make the child virtually impos-sible to live with.

Children with major expressive speech problems tend to get very frustrated and often display far from easy behaviour. Children born completely normal and later smitten by meningitis or head injury can develop many of the worst features of the hyperactive child. They may be of normal intelligence but so disabled by restlessness, poor concentration and negligible sense that their parents are driven to distraction.

Autistic children tend to have very obsessive, repetitive behav-iours and, hard as we may try, these can be very difficult to cure. We concentrate more these days on diverting these immovable problems to more socially acceptable presentations. The child who flaps his hands may be diverted to clapping, and the child who repeatedly flicks the light switch on and off can be diverted to a torch. Now that we have accepted our limited abilities we stop wasting time attempting the impossible and channel our full energies into what really matters – communication and socialisation.

Dealing with specific problems

Some severely intellectually disabled or cerebral palsy children are extremely irritable by day. To soothe them, we use movement and other techniques, although occasionally we have to resort to sedation.

In the really difficult child, it is often necessary to provide care away from parents for one or two half days each week so that the exhausted parents have time to recharge their batteries.

Quite a number of disabled children come to their parents' bed at night; others stay in their own but cry. Parents are often much softer with these children than their normal brothers and sisters, and they are reluctant to let them cry or to throw them out of the marital bed. The controlled crying technique can be used for many of these children although in some severely mentally-disabled children I have had no success with anything other than heavy sedation. If the parents are to survive the day, they cannot afford to be up all night with a crying child. The secret with sedation is to give the drug not at 6 p.m., just before bedtime, but when the child wakes up later in the night. This at least gives the parents some chance of gaining those golden hours of sleep between midnight and dawn.

Some young disabled children can take an age to feed, and mothers often spend up to two hours at mealtimes, leaving little time in the day for anything else. The best that can be done is to engage in sensible experimentation. For example, the child who takes his milk painfully slowly from a bottle may be given it from a spoon or cup, or given more solids instead. For the child who has difficulty with solids or lumpy food, different textures can be manufactured, and there are ways a skilled therapist can desensitise the mouth and encourage swallowing.

Toilet training may be difficult and sometimes toilet timing is all that can be initially achieved. Some children, particularly those with cerebral palsy, may get quite constipated. In these cases, it is a good idea to introduce a simple laxative or a 'depth charge' of extra fruit in the diet, which may ease the situation.

In the older disabled child, all my greatest failures have been with those who have the major problem of 'little sense'. Day after day, year after year, the same behaviour happens with these children, despite my best advice. The problem is that these children, although they may appear quite intelligent on being tested, do not learn from their experiences. Their poor parents try their best but as nothing helps, they soon begin to feel quite impotent. Unfortunately they may be further disadvantaged when they are in the care of some newly qualified 'whiz kid', whose university education never taught him that a child may have the severe disability of lack of sense. He will misread the situation, blame all the lack of success on the parents, and make their lives even harder than they already are. The parents should be given all the support and encouragement possible. If things are not going well, some temporary respite care should be arranged to keep the parents on the rails and to allow the other children of the family a more equal share of their parents' time.

Understanding and helping the parents of the disabled child

Many parents of a special child are determined to remain completely unchanged in their attitudes and expectations, but most do treat their child differently from his brothers and sisters. Many are overprotected, never allowed to cry, and usually given their own way. Behaviour techniques are often not seen through with determination, because parents find it hard to be tough on a child who has physical or intellectual problems. And even the most robust parent has considerable inner sadness and is under much stress.

I will digress for a minute and give a brief outline of the common reactions of the parent with a disabled child. Once these are understood then it is easier to give them help. Following the realisation that one has a disabled child, the parent may go through a form of grief reaction, not unlike the feelings experienced after the death of a loved one. Initially, when they hear the news, there may be a short stage where they feel stunned and disbelieving. This soon progresses to a long, painful stage where they try to come to terms with the situation they find themselves in. This may take months, years or even a lifetime. At this stage, the parents need to protect themselves from the harsh reality of the situation by closing the shutters of their mind and only letting a little of the realisation sink in each day. Denial, anger and activity are all methods they use to survive these difficult times.

With denial, the parents may refuse to accept the degree of the problem and shop around from doctor to doctor in the hope of hearing better news. Some deny they have even been told anything, and others embark on ill-proven miracle cures. Anger is a strange defence that we all use when under immense stress. It seems at times like this that displacing a bit of our anger onto those around us often makes us feel better. When the home football team has lost the grand final, you come home and kick the cat, not that the poor animal has done anything wrong but it just makes you feel better. Activity is a defence that we all engage in when under great stress. Sitting immobile and worrying only makes the problems seem even larger. The parents may take up a good cause, take on full-time employment, or work day and night for their special child. The activity will probably make them very tired but it does help them to feel better.

It is not clever for anyone to try to break through these defences. Once the shutters are torn down and the full light of the problem hits the parents, they may be precipitated into that state of immobility, isolation and guilt called depression.

I believe that with time, talk, friends and good practical help, most parents get through this need to defend themselves in this way. They may still feel the hurt but they can look past it to talk realistically and plan constructively for the future.

How can friends help?

The reactions I have mentioned are all normal and healthy. With good friends and good time, the presence of these defences will become unnecessary. With denial, friends should not force the issue but equally must not be afraid to talk gently and openly about what has happened. Pretending that the disability doesn't exist fools no-one and only serves to upset the parents. When parents are about to risk bankruptcy and destroy their other children's well-being all for the sake of some ill-proven miracle cure, they should be firmly encouraged to visit a top local expert beforehand rather than some dubious, expensive, overseas figure known to them only through the pen of a sensation-seeking journalist.

Anger is quite natural and may land on even the closest of friends. The anger is not really aimed at the friend; it is more a sign of the parents' tension and upset at their lot in life. Friends should be philosophical, and view it as a privilege that some of the anger that is probably levelled at the Almighty is landing on their humble shoulders.

Never criticise the mother who wishes to work or strive for some noble cause. She may well need this, and to suddenly remove it would be as ill-conceived as removing the crutch from a limping man. Activity is far preferable to immobility, isolation, guilt and the lack of enthusiasm that it generally replaces. Those who have become isolated need great understanding. They need encouragement to get out and mix, as well as practical help with child minding. Last, but most valuable, they need your listening and non-condemning ear.

The message is, stick with the parents. They may not say it in so many words but they need friends and will be grateful, if not openly then certainly in their hearts.

Conclusion

Such is the variety and degree of disabilities that there is no universal remedy for behaviour and management problems. As a general rule, use the same behavioural techniques with the disabled child as you would use with a normal child of similar mental age. Bear in mind that other factors will sabotage your best efforts, such as increased irritability, specific medical conditions, lack of concentration and lack of sense. Always remember how stressed the parents of a disabled child are, and how you can help by sticking in there with them.

TWENTY-FIVE

Common Toddler Illnesses

For the parents of a toddler it seems that hardly a day goes by without their child suffering from something, be it tonsillitis, an ear infection or the common cold. As part of growing up, the child goes through a whole series of illnesses, each one apparently more ghastly than the one before but nevertheless all quite common and in most cases nothing to be feared. To be forewarned is, as they say, to be forearmed. This chapter deals with the most common medical problems, and it is designed as a pointer to the parent. Naturally if you are worried by any of these symptoms, take your child to a doctor.

The common cold

Colds are caused not by one but by a number of viruses, which explains why one infection may follow straight after another, giving the impression of a non-stop nose run. As they are viruses, they do not respond to treatment with antibiotics but cure themselves, usually within four or five days of appearance. When the child first goes to day care or preschool, he is coughed over by a multitude of virus-splattering infants, and this is frequently his worst year for infections. Eventually some immunity is acquired, and the number of illnesses gradually decreases each year until adulthood. Most of the natural immunity which a baby inherits from his mother is lost by the age of 6 months, and the first winter thereafter is often a prime one for colds.

Average toddlers will get up to nine colds each year, with six being about the usual number, which you may have gathered works out at about one every eight weeks. Colds are spread by playmates and other people with whom the toddler comes into contact; they do not come from getting wet or playing out in the cold, whatever the myths may be. Despite years of trying to prevent colds with various vitamins and other treatments, there is still absolutely nothing one can reliably do to help.

A further area of confusion arises because the common cold often starts with a sore throat, slightly pink ear drums and even a slight cough. When all these symptoms come together it shows that the child has indeed contracted a common cold; individually they indicate tonsillitis, ear infection or bronchitis. There is no specific treatment for colds, although paracetamol (Panadol) preparations may make the child feel more comfortable.

Tonsils

It is almost impossible to find tonsils in anyone over 30 years of age, because in years past they were whipped out at the drop of a scalpel, being regarded universally as useless appendages. Nowadays, removal of the tonsils is relatively rare, and the operation is not performed unless there are some major reasons for doing so. Tonsillitis is not the sore throat found at the beginning of a cold; it is rather the specific infection of the tonsillar tissues at the back of the throat and their associated glands at the angle of the jaw. The tonsils are not just red but 'angry' looking with flecks of pus, and is usually caused by bacteria. Antibiotic treatment is needed and is usually effective.

The decision for surgical removal is not dependent on the size of the offending part but the number of genuine tonsil infections and the chronically infected appearance of the throat. Tonsils are minute in the young toddler, reaching their peak size somewhere around the age of 7 years. Large does not mean unhealthy, and large tonsils do not cause feeding problems. However, if your child has large tonsils, snores all night and is tired and irritable all day, check with your doctor, as your child may have obstructive sleep apnoea.

Croup

This is a juvenile form of laryngitis, usually caused by a virus, which creates an infection in the region of the child's voice box (larynx). Antibiotics are no help and probably the best remedy is the good, old-fashioned one of inhaling steam sitting in a steamy bathroom. The child with croup makes a characteristic and often frightening 'crowing' noise when breathing in, accompanied by a cough like the sound of a sea lion. In its mild form, it can be easily treated at home with humidity. A small minority of children can become quite seriously ill, and if their condition deteriorates rapidly or there is any other medical concern, seek help immediately.

Bronchitis

Bronchitis is another viral infection, which will probably start as a cough and go to the chest. This ailment will not respond to anti-biotics. Despite making quite a lot of coughing noise, the child should be relatively happy and show little sign of illness. When the coughing is associated with wheezing and shortness of breath, it may be wise to consider asthma as a possible cause. When fever and general sickness are also present, then it may be a more major chest infection and a medical opinion should be sought. Bronchitis may be the first symptom of approaching measles in some children, even before the very first spot has appeared.

Asthma

Asthma affects about 20 per cent of all children. Its hallmark is a musical wheeze that comes from the depths of the lungs, mostly when breathing out. It is made worse by exercise and viral respiratory infections, and it is often associated with periods of dry coughing in the middle of the night. Unfortunately the most common cause of toddlers coughing is exposure to passive smoke from smoking adults.

Many parents are obviously distressed when I diagnose asthma, thinking immediately of their schooldays when friends with severe asthma spent more time at home than at school, were excluded from sport, and were regarded as moderate cripples. This is not the case today. Most asthmatic children have the condition in a mild form, and they can live a completely normal, unrestricted life.

Treatment uses certain medicines to open up the air passages, and they are best administered as inhalants. These products are now extremely safe and highly effective, and they do not lose potency with continued use. Make sure the doctor has given you a step-by-step asthma action plan for intervention if needed. Milk withdrawal, chest exercises, antibiotics and restrictions of lifestyle are not prescribed for my patients. Allergy testing may be helpful for a small number of children, but let your doctor know about cats, dogs and birds in the house.

Late to speak

Development of speech varies dramatically from child to child. Most children will develop speech at 1 year. If a child is late developing speech the most important thing to check is the hearing. (See Hearing loss). If the hearing is normal and the child is bright alert and interested in their environment, and development and understanding are all right then you shouldn't worry too much about late speech.

Ear problems

At birth the baby is startled by loud noises and changes the pattern of his crying when comforted by his mother's voice. At 6 months, he will turn his head towards the direction of quiet sounds from objects he cannot see. Just before 1 year, there is much tuneful babble in some strange, unintelligible foreign language, which is soon followed by repeating appropriate words. At this stage we know there can be no gross hearing problem.

Hearing loss

Although most children who have severe hearing loss are now diagnosed between 6 and 9 months of age, I still see quite a few who have remained undiagnosed until 18 months. If the child does not respond to quiet, unexpected noises, if his speech development is slow, or if there is the slightest doubt in the parents' minds, a proper hearing test should be arranged.

Consider hearing loss if you talk comfortingly to a baby who is crying and he does not change the rhythm of crying to that of your speech. A child with normal hearing will respond when you walk into the room unnoticed and speak quietly. If the theme tune of The Wiggles is playing, a child with normal hearing will turn to the sound.

The middle ear

The human ear is made up of an ear canal, which often contains some wax and goes from the outside to the ear drum, and inside the drum is the middle ear, which is a small chamber filled with air. In this chamber a number of delicate little bones transmit the sound waves from the ear drum to the hearing nerve and then the brain. This middle ear is connected by a thin tube (Eustachian tube), which communicates with the outside atmosphere through the back of the nose. This causes the 'popping' of ears associated with the pressure increase of a vigorous nose blow or when landing in an aeroplane.

For the middle ear to transmit sound efficiently it needs to be filled with air, which gives it resonance, rather like some musical instruments. When full of fluid, the tone and hearing volume is diminished much in the same way as filling a drum with concrete would affect its musical quality. Fluid gathers in the middle ear when the tube from the nose gets blocked, as may happen briefly during a heavy cold. If the fluid in the middle ear is associated with infection, this may cause an acute ear infection (acute otitis media). If the fluid is present but not infected, it deadens the hearing in a chronic manner, and the condition is generally referred to as 'glue ear'.

Ear infection (otitis media)

Following a cold, a swim, or diving into a pool, bacteria may enter the middle ear, and if the tube blocks, an infection can develop. The child becomes sick, irritable, has ear pain, partial hearing loss and, on examination, the ear drum looks angry and red. Nature will cure this condition either by re-opening the tube to the nose and releasing the infection or through a perforation in the ear drum. As the infection is usually caused by bacteria, antibiotics are given, along with the minor pain-killers, such as paracetamol (Panadol). Most doctors tend to greatly over-diagnose and over-treat ear infections, such is our concern to protect the young child's hearing. Even if the ear drum does perforate, this almost always heals by itself without problems, although, of course, prevention is a better course of action. Even if you don't halt the complaint in time, it is not the end of the world.

Glue ear

Sterile fluid may collect in the middle ear in association with a cold, flu or after an acute ear infection. This is most commonly seen in the early school-age child; a teacher will note that a child's hearing has deteriorated when he starts to talk louder than usual and ignores much of what is said to him. When glue ear is diagnosed, the parents must let the teacher know, so that the child may be brought nearer the front of the class to avoid missing anything that is said.

Pain is usually not a problem with glue ear, and there is no great urgency in treatment. With time, most cases will resolve themselves, although the process can be hurried along by a simple operation in which plastic tubes (grommets) are placed in the ear drum to let the fluid escape. The tubes drop out after a number of months and hopefully do not need reinsertion.

The insertion of these tubes has taken over from the tonsillectomies of earlier days as the most common operation performed in childhood. Studies showing definite long-term benefits are so far inconclusive, and it is uncertain whether this will prove to be a passing fashion or an operation for the future.

With the children I see, I steer a middle road, insisting that a proper hearing test is conducted, which must show definite hearing loss before surgery is contemplated. I also prefer to leave at least six weeks before surgery, since nature has an obliging way of resolving the situation.

Summary

- If a child does not turn towards quiet, unexpected sounds at 6 months, has no word-like babble at 1 year, and is slow to develop speech, a hearing defect must be suspected.

- If infected fluid is trapped in the middle ear (acute otitis media), it causes pain and fever and antibiotic treatment is needed.

- When sterile fluid is trapped in the middle ear it thickens and is referred to as 'glue ear'. This is not an acute condition. It will be cured either by time and nature, or by the insertion of tubes.

Vomiting and diarrhoea

These are both extremely common in the toddler. When vomiting and diarrhoea are present together this often means an infection in the gut (gastroenteritis); if vomiting occurs alone, it is more likely to be due to an infection in the body, possibly a cold, flu or occasionally some more serious problem. If your child is very sick and you have any doubts, medical help should be sought. If the child is not too unwell, however, and vomiting and diarrhoea are a problem, here are a few tips.

Children with acute gut infections need fluids, not solids. If they are going to be harmed, it is not through loss of body 'fat weight', but 'water weight' when too much water and salt have been lost. If vomiting and diarrhoea are caused by gastroenteritis, it is almost always of viral origin. They are not helped by antibiotics, which often have the side-effect of causing the diarrhoea to become worse.

I never cease to be amazed by the stream of odd cures I am confronted with by parents of vomiting toddlers.

'What's the problem?'

'He vomits everything up, doctor.'

'What are you giving him?'

'Oh, not much. A glass of milk with an egg and a little added custard just to keep his strength up.'

After all that, the parents are genuinely surprised when the child throws it all back at them.

Milk is best abandoned altogether, as it is less easily digested, and as every mother knows, it is very much more unpleasant to clean up than second-hand lemonade. The correct treatment for vomiting is to **give *small* amounts of *clear* fluids, frequently**.

Small means no more than one whisky measure of fluid at a time.

Clear means clear, not milk, not solids, not body-building protein, just fluid. It seems silly to force nauseated children to drink fluids that they normally would not like, and you cannot go too far wrong with lemonade. Unfortunately lemonade contains about 10 per cent sugar, which is too concentrated for a child with major gastroenteritis. Nowadays the local chemist will sell mixtures which, when added to water, are designed to replace all the water and chemicals a vomiting child may lose.

If there is a significant amount of diarrhoea I strongly recommend an oral electrolyte solution from your local chemist such as Gastrolyte™, or Repalyte™. Some parents find it easier to present this solution as an ice block.

Life being as it is, unfortunately parents often find they are faced with gastroenteritis in the middle of the night when no access to the local chemist is possible. However, readily available everyday ingredients from the kitchen cupboard are there.

The WHO (World Health Organisation) recommends a solution of:

1 litre cooled boiled water
6 flat teaspoons sugar
$\frac{1}{2}$ teaspoon salt

Frequently means each quarter or half hour during the day. Although this may seem very little fluid, you can in fact administer 1.5 litres a day in this fashion quite effortlessly.

When a young child craves for fluids and the parents give in to his requests on demand, this will probably result in vomiting. A simple way to overcome this excess intake is to set a cooking timer bell to ring every fifteen minutes. This will let the child know when his allotted fluid time arrives and, if treated patiently and not rushed, the vomiting will soon come under control.

Acute infective diarrhoea is almost always of viral origin, and antibiotics should only be used in some rare and very specific cases. If clear fluids are given, the bowel has little to discharge and the diarrhoea will come quickly under control. Chalk medicines to 'slow the bowel' are unnecessary in children and, as anyone who has tried to chew chalk when feeling sick will tell you, are far from pleasant. In the days that follow gastroenteritis, the child usually becomes extremely constipated. This does not need treatment and merely indicates that the bowel is quite empty and has nothing more to get rid of.

Summary

- Vomiting in toddlers is common and may accompany any childhood illness, even the most trivial.

- When the child has considerable vomiting and diarrhoea, the cause is usually viral gastroenteritis, in which case the child does not need calorific foods, milk, chalk medicines, or antibiotics.

- He should be given only clear fluids, in small amounts, frequently.

- If the child looks sick, 'distant', dull-eyed, weak and passes little urine, or if you are at all worried, get medical help at once.

Fevers

When the body is upset by an infection, whether it is a common cold or something more serious, the temperature will rise in response. Some illnesses, such as measles, can cause extremely high fevers, while others, which may in fact be more serious, may have quite low fever levels. The presence of a fever is merely an indication that the child is sick; the height of temperature is not an accurate barometer of the severity of the problem.

High temperature will upset the already unhappy child and make him feel even more miserable. His parents will start to worry since they know that some children with fevers are also prone to fits. For both these reasons, young children with temperatures tend to be treated more vigorously than their adult counterparts.

A feverish child must be dressed sensibly, not wrapped up in extra vests and woollens and put into a bed heaped up with blankets. He should be given one of the commercial children's paracetamol preparations. Children usually find this liquid pleasant to take, and it has few side-effects. Recent international reports have shown that aspirin in young children is dangerous and should not be given.

Plunging the hot child into a bath filled with water straight from the Arctic is not only exceedingly cruel but also counterproductive. When the sizzling body splashes down into the icy water the skin reacts by shutting off its blood supply and diverting the blood to those warmer regions 'inland from the coast'. As a result, little heat is lost by the child, despite the unpleasant experience. Being stripped and sat in front of a gale force fan is another nasty which will only cause the child to shiver and thus, paradoxically, generate more heat.

The proper procedure is to strip the child down to his pants and, if the temperature is still high, sponge him over gently with tepid, rather than cold, water. This gives a gentle, cooling effect and does not precipitate shivering or divert the blood away from the skin.

It seems a jolly unfair world for young children. When I have the flu or a fever I go to bed, turn the electric blanket on to 'summer Sahara' temperature, and sweat it out. But for the poor toddler it is all stripping off and sponging down and general disturbance. Of course the difference is that with the toddler, we have a great fear of 'fever fits'.

Fever fits (febrile convulsions)

In some children, the developing brain seems particularly sensitive to temperature rise, and this causes them to throw a fit. These fits are most common between the ages of 6 months and 3 years, and rarely happen after the age of 5 years. They are not uncommon: 4 per cent of children in this age group will have a fit, usually a febrile convulsion.

For most parents it is a frightening experience, and they can be forgiven for thinking that their small child is about to die. The fit can come on very quickly; many children are only slightly unwell beforehand and give no warning at all. The victims will suddenly go stiff, the eyes roll back, and breathing becomes laboured. They will then start shaking or twitching, before relaxing to lie dazed and confused. After this they become sleepy, and, having slept, will appear fully recovered. Luckily most of these fits last for less than five minutes, although to the watching parent it can seem like an eternity.

If a child has a high fever, the cooling measures and medicines mentioned should prevent many febrile convulsions. If the child does fit, he should be placed gently on his side to prevent choking. Difficult as it may be, try not to panic. Young children do not die, nor do they harm their brains with short fever fits. Stay with him rather than running off for help. Don't force spoons or other objects into his mouth, as the apparently difficult breathing is not due to a blockage in his throat but rather a tightening of his respiratory muscles. If this is a first fit, or if it does not come quickly under control, take the child straight to a doctor.

A child who has a simple febrile convulsion does not have epilepsy, and these fits will not continue through his life. After one febrile episode, however, the child is much more likely to have another before he grows out of the convulsion-prone age group.

Summary

■ The short fever fit does not damage the child, only his parents' nerves.

■ Febrile convulsions do not mean epilepsy.

■ Lie the child on his side.

■ Don't force objects into his mouth.

■ Don't panic. (That's easy for me to say!)

■ Seek medical help when the child comes round or if still fitting at the end of 5 minutes.

Bow legs, knock knees, flat feet

Another area of the body that constantly concerns parents is the legs, including the knees and the feet. In the majority of minor leg and foot problems no treatment is needed. The days of night splints, irons and wedges for self-righting conditions have passed.

When the child first walks, his untried feet can be seen pointing in all manner of interesting directions. They usually right themselves within months, at which point you will notice that the child's legs are extremely bowed and he is walking around in his nappy with the posture of a saddle-sore cowboy. At about 2½ the legs will straighten, although this adjustment may be overdone and the child will then suffer from knock knees. By the age of 5, most legs are relatively straight and the feet point in the right direction. Some children continue walking with their toes turned slightly inwards and, if mild, this is of no great concern. In fact, one specialist colleague of mine sports the theory that these children may make the best footballers, being able to change direction and weave faster than anyone else on the field. There has to be some compensation for having feet that point in two directions at the same time.

All babies and toddlers have flat feet. It often takes until the age of 6 for the ligaments to tighten up and produce a proper arch. This may never happen in some families where there is a history of flat feet. Some believe that the child should walk around without shoes and strengthen his ligaments; others believe that wedges in the shoes produce better arches. I believe that each year more and more are moving towards the 'no treatment' lobby.

Once again these are general observations. If the bends or postures cause any concern, a specialist opinion should be sought.

The sick child: when to panic

When teaching junior doctors I impress upon them that their greatest skill lies not in knowing hundreds of rare medical facts but in being able to reliably spot 'the sick child'. It is difficult and probably dangerous for me to try to express in written form what is essentially a 'gut feeling'. I believe that most of the clues are in the eyes and the child's alertness.

The child who has vomited all day may nevertheless appear alert, have bright eyes, and take a lively and keen interest when you walk into the room. If this is the case, he is probably safe. If the same child were dull-eyed, distant and at all confused, then medical help must be summoned immediately. When a child is pale, sweaty and looks anxious, it is a good idea to get help quickly. This is generally how a child will appear if he is 'shocked' and may have some major surgical or other condition. The child who has sunken eyes, a lack of elasticity in his skin, a dry mouth, and is passing little urine is also a worry. Any child with a stiff neck, which is painful to move or bend, needs medical examination, as does a child with panting, over-breathing or deep, rattling breathing.

When mum is worried, I worry. When mum is worried and grandma is worried, I worry a lot!

Medicines: how to give them

Doctors have no difficulty in writing prescriptions for children. The problem comes when it is time to force the strange substance down the toddler's throat. If an unpleasant-tasting medicine has been prescribed once, it is wise to let the doctor know, as often there is a more palatable alternative for the subsequent occasions. For the child who is a militant drug refuser, sometimes preparations that require fewer doses a day may be prescribed. With antibiotics, this is particularly useful, as often two-dose-a-day drugs can supplant the four-dose-a-day ones. I am all for using the purest and most modern preparation but if the latest no sugar, no preservatives, no artificial colouring product tastes like 'cat's wee', I feel that someone has missed the point.

Most drugs can be given in liquid form to toddlers, preferably slipped into the mouth on a spoon and chased down by a favourite drink. For the reluctant child, sometimes a plastic syringe is more effective. The medicine is squirted through a small opening in the mouth. Watch out for the fine aerosol spray which can blow around the room once the medicine has hit the child's tongue. If capsules or tablets are given, the mouth should be moist before their introduction, or the capsules themselves can be moistened before they are put in the mouth. These measures help to lubricate them on that short, difficult journey from the tongue to the throat. Little tablets toboggan down the throat with the greatest of ease when placed in a little ice-cream. Bigger ones may be crushed, placed on top of a thin layer of ice-cream, with jam or chocolate topping being placed over that, thus making a spoon-sized medicine sandwich.

Bed rest for toddlers

In modern hospitals children who have undergone major surgery will be seen up and about the next day. Meanwhile, not a mile down the road, a child with a red tonsil will be confined to his bed by a worried mother for what may seem to him like an eternity. Bed rest is now an outdated practice reserved for children with pre-paralytic polio and other equally rare conditions. If the child feels well enough to want to be up, good for him. If he leaves his bed to lie on a rug by the fire, that's just as good. If he feels so miserable that all he wants is the peace and comfort of bed, that is when he will get bed rest.

There are no black and white rules. Sense and flexibility are the important things but you will usually find that, in these cases, the child knows best.

Toddler development worries

Books on child care usually list a multitude of clever developmental milestones for the child to attain at any given age. Few of these books, however, distinguish between the important milestones and those that are best termed interesting but useless. Looking at a child's developmental profile, one is interested in his gross motor, fine motor, hearing, vision, communication, social and play skills.

When one has been working for some years in a developmental assessment unit, it soon becomes clear which of these have the most value.

The gross motor area – walking, running and climbing – tends to be of most interest to the parents. In fact, early walking bears little relationship to advanced intelligence and is much more likely to be an inherited family trait. Children who walk early often have a mother who was an early walker. When teaching psychologists, who have a great interest in motor milestones in young children, I cite the case of the greyhound, which is probably one of the most advanced 'gross motor animals' around. Any dog that spends its entire life chasing after a stuffed hare without suspecting it is being fooled is, to my mind at least, not very intelligent.

By far the most valuable skills are those in the area of communication. At 6 months, the child who communicates vigorously with his eyes, takes in everything in his environment, and 'doesn't miss a move' has a good start to life. In the second year, the child with good, appropriate, non-repetitive speech is likely to do well.

If the child has no speech, good comprehension is even more important, and the child should be able to point with accuracy to objects in pictures and books or to things in his environment. I learn much about a child's intelligence, when he is difficult to assess, by watching him play. I look for constructive qualities, where he uses the material provided in an intelligent way. I also look for imagination and pretend play. If these are present in the toddler, it is unlikely he has any major problem of intellectual development.

I worry when a child has little interest in his surroundings, walks around in a purposeless manner, and is slow to respond to sound. I worry when there is little understanding of simple messages and only parrot-like repetitive speech. I worry when there is apparently little understanding; for example, the child may flick through a book in an obsessive manner without displaying any interest or recognition of what is inside it. I worry when a toddler who does not talk to me with his voice does not communicate with his face or eyes either. I worry when the child has no pretend or constructive play and is stuck at the stage of throwing and banging toys together or running around the house aimlessly.

Many books are available on the developmental assessment of

young children. My only aim here is to point out those general patterns that suggest success, and those which cause concern. (See also Appendix I, Meaningful Milestones.)

Now that you've tamed your toddler, a new challenge awaits . . .

- An A to Z of children's behaviours
- Positive discipline and how to put it into practice
- Starting school and developing school skills
- Confident children: beating shyness and making friends
- How to have healthy and active children now – and prevent problems later
- Sole parenting, step families and other family issues
- Talking about sex and death
- TV and the internet

Appendices

APPENDIX I
Meaningful Milestones

Note: There is a wide range of normal development, each child having relative strengths and weaknesses in the profile of abilities presented. If one or two items are delayed it is generally of little significance. If many items are delayed, and there is a lack of comprehension, disinterest in the environment and an absence of quality play, then an expert professional opinion should be sought.

Here is a guide to the general pattern of development at different ages.

At 1 year
- Walks reliably holding onto furniture.
- Some may be walking alone (average age 13 months – range of normal between 9 months and 18 months).
- Picks up small objects between the tip of the thumb and the forefinger.
- Understands the word 'No!' and at this age usually obeys it.
- Knows name and will usually turn when it is used.
- Babbles in a tuneful, foreign-sounding language.
- Understands 'Give it to Mummy', but only if accompanied by gesture.
- Says 'Da da' and sometimes one or two other words with meaning.
- Uses a drinking cup with some assistance.
- Can hold a spoon but unable to load it at the plate and navigate without spillage to the mouth.
- Putting toys and other objects in the mouth is now on the wane.
- Waves 'Bye bye' and enjoys 'Peek-a-boo' games.
- Understands the permanence of objects. If a toy is hidden as they watch, they immediately know where it is.

CONCERNS   Be concerned when:
- No tuneful babble is produced.
- Hearing seems to be a problem.
- No interest is taken in the environment.
- Not yet standing upright beside furniture.
- Not using the finger/thumb grip.
- A child does not 'feel right' in any way or is significantly different to a brother or sister at that age.

At 18 months
- Walks reliably without any support.
- Squats down to pick up a toy.
- Pushes wheeled toys around the floor.
- Loves to put objects in and out of containers.
- Delicate pincer grip allows picking up of crumbs and other small objects.
- Holds a pencil like a dagger and scribbles without purpose.
- Talks tunefully to self in own language.
- Uses between six and 20 appropriate words. (Note: 'appropriate' does not include repeats of what mother has just said.)
- Most start to show preference for one hand.
- Points to shoes, hair, nose, feet, on request.
- Responds to a simple one-part verbal command.
- Points to objects in a picture book, e.g. dog.
- Holds a spoon securely and is reasonably reliable in feeding.

- Manages a feeding cup unaided.
- No longer mouths toys.
- Piles three blocks on top of each other.
- Starts to show discomfort when wet or dirty.
- Starts to go upstairs holding on tight.
- Fluctuates between being very clingy and resisting attention.
- Not the age of reason. Do not know what they want but know they want it immediately.

At 2 years

- Walks well. Runs reliably.
- Walks upstairs placing both feet on each step, holding lightly to a rail. Almost able to come down again upright.
- Enjoys ride on toys, pushing them along.
- Walks backward while dragging a wheeled toy on the end of a string.
- Attempts to kick a ball.
- Piles six blocks on top of each other.
- Removes a wrapper from a lolly.
- Holds a pencil almost correctly.
- Scribbles in a circular manner.
- Can imitate a vertical line.
- Enjoys looking at picture books.
- Turns one page at a time.
- Can usually point out 'Which boy is happy?'
- Hand dominance is established in most.
- Over 50 words in vocabulary and many more understood.
- Puts two and occasionally three words together.
- Refers to self by name.
- Joins in nursery rhymes and songs.
- Delivers simple messages, 'Daddy, come'.
- Chews food well.
- Spoon feeding a success.
- Usually dry by day.
- Usually tells when wants to go to the toilet.
- Imitates mother doing household duties.
- Will help tidy away toys.
- Real help with dressing.
- Demands mum's attention constantly.
- Plays beside, but not directly with, other children.
- Clingy – plays in another room, but checks every couple of minutes to ensure mother is still there.
- Rebellious when does not get own way.
- Possessive of toys and attention.
- Not a time for sharing and seeing another's point of view!

CONCERNS   Be concerned when:

- There is minimal or no speech. (In this case, check hearing, comprehension and other areas of development.)
- Toys are still being mouthed.
- Toys are being thrown in an unthinking way.
- Play is always repetitive – e.g. spinning wheels and banging blocks.
- Interest in environment is not being shown. Should be a real 'sticky-beak' at this age.

- There is a lack of 'body language'.
- There is unusual irritability.

At 2½ years

- Uses 200 or more words.
- Uses pronouns, 'I', 'Me', 'You'.
- Holds pen with a reasonable adult-type grip and imitates a circle and horizontal line.
- Builds a tower of seven blocks.
- Pulls pants down for toiletting but usually unable to get them back up.
- Knows full name.
- May stutter in eagerness to get information out.
- Plays alongside in parallel to other children.
- Little idea of sharing playthings or adults' attention.
- Won't wait, expects everything immediately.

At 3 years

- Walks upstairs using alternate feet on each step and comes down using both feet per step.
- Jumps off bottom step with two feet together.
- Runs around obstacles with speed and accuracy.
- Pedals tricycle.
- Can walk on tip toe.
- Can catch a ball with arms outstretched.
- Threads large beads on a shoelace.
- Copies a circle and imitates a cross.
- Matches three primary colours, but still confuses blue and green.
- Cuts with scissors.
- Speech intelligible even to a stranger.
- Uses most plurals correctly.
- Will volunteer full name and sex.
- Still talks to self at length at play.
- Able to describe an event that has happened, simply but reliably.
- Questions start: 'Why?', 'Why?', 'Why?'.
- Listens eagerly to stories and likes a favourite one repeated and then repeated once more.
- Recites several nursery rhymes.
- Rote counts to ten.
- Counts to ten, but only understands practical counting of two or three items.
- Washes hands but needs supervision to dry.
- Can dress self except for buttons, tight tops and shoes.
- Likes to help adult with home activities.
- Behaviour is less impatient and self centered.
- Able to wait for a short time before getting what wants.
- Understands sharing toys, lollies and attention.
- Plays directly with other children.
- Vivid imagination, loves pretend play.
- Separates reasonably well from mother, but this varies greatly.

CONCERNS   Be concerned when:
- There is an inability to communicate easily through appropriate speech.
- Body language is poor.

- Repetitive play shows little imagination, or richness.
- Behaviour is still like the senseless, sparky and unsharing 18-month-old.

At 4 years

- Walks and probably runs up and down stairs without holding on.
- Throws and catches well; starts to bounce a ball.
- Piles blocks, two to the side and one on top, to copy a bridge.
- Holds a pen like an adult.
- Draws a person with trunk, head, legs and usually arms and fingers.
- Draws a reasonable likeness of a house.
- Names four primary colours.
- Grammar and speech construction is usually correct.
- A few sounds still mispronounced and immature.
- Can describe an occurrence in an accurate and logical way.
- Can state address and age.
- Questioning is at its height. Constantly asks 'Why?', 'When?', 'How?'.
- Listens intently to stories.
- Tells stories, often confusing fact with fiction.
- May have imaginary friends.
- Understands yesterday, today, tomorrow; i.e. past and future.
- Rote counts to 20 and understands meaningful counting up to five objects.
- Enjoys jokes and plays on words.
- Eats with skill and cuts with a knife.
- Rarely uses a knife and fork before age 4.
- Washes and dries own hands.
- Brushes teeth with supervision.
- Blows nose reliably.
- Wipes bottom after toileting.
- Can fully dress and undress except for inaccessible buttons, bows and shoelaces. (Shoelaces are rarely tied before the age of 5 and since the advent of Velcro, for many children it is much later.)
- Plays well with other children.
- Now argues with words rather than blows.
- Verbal impertinence and bickering are developing fast.
- Understands taking turns, sharing and simple rules.
- Starts to believe in justice and everyone keeping to the rules.
- Many like to be the king pin, 'bossy-boots'.
- Shows concern for younger siblings, playmates in distress.
- Usually separates well from mother.

Reference: *Children's Developmental Progress*, Mary Sheridan (N.F.E.R. Publishing Co., UK).

APPENDIX II
Miscellaneous Facts

- At the age of 2 years most toddlers have attained half their adult height.
- From birth till 2½ years every parent can expect to change between 7000 and 8000 dirty nappies.
- A toddler requires 2½ times more food to power each kilogram of body weight as would a mature 20-year-old. This explains why toddlers eat so much to keep their furnaces fired up.
- The average children of today will have witnessed at least 18,000 murders on television by the time they have left school.
- A toddler cannot comprehend the permanence of marriage break-up or death. To them both are reversible states.
- Religion has little meaning for toddlers, who follow without question the beliefs and example of those closest to them. Independent inner faith is first found in late adolescence.
- Home is a very dangerous place. Domestic violence is much more common than street violence.
- About 33 per cent of Australian men and 29 per cent of Australian women smoke. The number of young men smokers is reducing at present, the figure for young women smokers is increasing. Passive smoking is not without its problems. Adults can escape this, but our children are not so fortunate. They have to inhale whatever we put in their environment for 18 years until they are in a position to be able to make up their own minds on whether they wish to smoke or not.
- There is no necessity for routine worming of the average Australian family. Worms are incorrectly believed to cause abdominal pain, pallor and malnutrition. When worms are seen in the motions, or children have an itchy bottom, particularly at night, treatment is needed.
- Sun in excess is extremely damaging to skin, making young adults look prematurely old and wrinkled. Worse than that, there is a strong correlation between UV exposure (especially intermittent) and all types of skin cancer. Now is the time to be sensible in sunshine. Hats, high factor sun screens and covering up are needed from the earliest years.

APPENDIX III
Immunisation

Diphtheria, haemophilus influenza type B (Hib), hepatitis B, measles, polio, tetanus and whooping cough are unpleasant illnesses that can kill. There is no need for this to happen nowadays if we take the trouble to have our children vaccinated.

Before vaccines were available, many thousands of Australian children died from infectious diseases. Babies continue to die from whooping cough because community vaccination levels are still too low. This means very young babies can be infected before they can be vaccinated themselves. Other vaccine-preventable diseases will return, in large numbers, if vaccination rates are not kept up.

Recommended vaccines are effective, though they occasionally have side effects. These are usually no more than a minor inconvenience. Vaccine-related permanent harm or death is very rare, and thousands of times less likely than death from the actual diseases themselves.

Chicken Pox (varicella–zoster)
Chicken pox is an ugly, itchy rash with little fever or feeling of general illness.

This viral complaint takes about two weeks to incubate. It starts with a crop of itchy, raised red spots like flea bites, usually on the trunk. There are often little spots inside the mouth, which is well outside the normal chewing ground of the common flea. The spots enlarge, fill with fluid, and form vesicles (blisters), which eventually burst and are covered by scabs. The child may look awful and feel intensely itchy but he will only have a low fever and feel relatively well in himself. The old-fashioned pink Calamine lotion is probably as good as anything to ease the itching.

A vaccine for varicella is now available. Infants and adolescents require one dose, adults two. At the time of writing it is not yet part of the Immunisation Schedule and is expensive.

Diphtheria
These nasty bacteria set up a focus of infection in the throat which sometimes causes a sudden obstruction to breathing which can be fatal. The infection also releases poisons that can cause paralysis or heart failure. Luckily it has become very rare since immunisation has been widely available. Diphtheria vaccine is given by injection. It is well tried and very safe.

German measles (rubella)
Not as unpleasant or dangerous as ordinary measles, rubella is usually a minor illness. The exception is that when a pregnant woman contracts rubella, the unborn baby is likely to suffer serious, permanent heart, brain or liver disease as well as deafness. The only way to prevent this serious problem is for all children to be immunised against rubella, via the triple vaccine known as MMR (measles, mumps and rubella).

Haemophilus influenzae type B (Hib)
Hib is a bacteria and, despite its name, has nothing to do with 'flu'—which is a short name for viral influenza.

Before use of the Hib vaccine, Hib infection was widespread in the community, most children becoming immune from mild infection. However, Hib was the most common cause of bacterial meningitis, and caused many other serious, often life-threatening infections. Hib will again become a major cause of disease if all infants are not vaccinated.

Hepatitis B

Hep B is a viral infection, which causes inflammation of the liver, it is very infectious, very common and can also be fatal. Most commonly passed through blood contact, open sores and wounds, the sharing of needles between drug addicts, or even normal sexual activity can transmit this infection. It can also be passed from an infected mother to her baby, usually at the time of birth. However, there is reliable immunisation and it is recommended for all infants. Babies born to an infected mother should, in addition, be given hep B immunoglobin within twelve hours of birth.

Measles

This is just about the most infective of all childhood illnesses. Without vaccination almost everyone will catch it. Measles is more than a rash, it causes children to have high fever, be very sick, have a nasty cough, sore eyes and feel very sorry for themselves. In third world countries, where nutrition is poor, it is a much-feared illness. Children who contract measles in this country often become extremely sick but occasionally there are long-term serious complications.

Babies are born with high antibody levels, which have come across the placenta from Mum. These gradually wane in the first year and give sufficient protection for vaccination not to be advised until after the first birthday. Vaccination is by simple injection and usually without side effects. A few children (10 to 15 per cent) will suffer with a slight fever about ten days after the injection when the vaccine takes hold. Some of these may even have a mild measles-like rash. In these instances, it's best to give paracetamol.

Meningococcal infection

Meningococcus is one of the most feared infections of the moment. This has been increased by extensive media coverage. Out of the blue a child can embark on a devastating downhill course that may lead to death or disability. Despite this, it is one of the easiest bacteria to kill, responding to the most basic 1940s brand of penicillin.

The meningococcus bacterium is a relatively common fellow traveller in the community. Why it infects some people and misses the majority is unknown. It is an uncommon infection though cases have doubled in the past ten years. The bacterium enters the body, initially causing a mild illness with fever and often a fine rash. This moves on to septicaemia (blood infection) or meningitis (an infection of the tissue that covers the brain). Most children I have treated had both the septicaemia and meningitis. The presence of septicaemia is suspected in any extremely sick child with an almost-bruised-type skin rash that increases every minute. Meningitis is considered in the child with headache and a stiff neck.

A doctor can easily be caught out, seeing a vaguely sick child in the morning, giving reassurance, and sending them home. But some hours later the infection becomes all-consuming, with the child crashing onto the downhill course.

If any child looks sick and is dropping fast, this is the most urgent of urgent emergencies. The only way to prevent death and disability in meningococcus is a quick diagnosis, immediately followed by that first dose of life-saving antibiotic.

There are a number of different sorts of meningococcus. A vaccine effective against a dangerous strain (Serogroup C) will be included in the routine immunisation schedule in Australia from 2003. Meningococcal B vaccine is currently undergoing trials in New Zealand.

Mumps

For many years there was debate whether to add mumps vaccine to the current immunisation protocol. It was argued that this was a relatively mild condition and not worth the expense of routine vaccination.

Following successful programs in the United States and Canada, it is now believed to be worthwhile and is given at the same time as the measles and rubella vaccination. Also given by injection, it is simple and safe.

Polio

This viral disease often causes permanent paralysis. It is still common in many overseas countries that experience the devastating problems that were seen here before a safe vaccine was available. Polio immunisation is easy. All you do is put two drops of oral vaccine on the tongue. This is safe, painless and gives good protection.

Tetanus

Tetanus, or lockjaw, comes from an organism that is frequently found in the dirt of our streets, paddocks and gardens. It enters the body through a dirty wound, later to release poisons that cause severe spasms and eventual respiratory failure with a high risk of death. Every child should be vaccinated. A booster injection should be given at 15–19 years.

Whooping cough

This illness is very unpleasant although usually not fatal. Those at greatest risk are little babies. About one in 100 of these will die or suffer brain damage from whooping cough. By way of contrast, fewer than one in every 100 000 children given the whooping cough vaccine suffer these symptoms.

The Chinese talk of whooping cough as 'the cough of 100 days'. The child gets into a spasm of coughing, loses breath, whoops as he tries to get air into the lungs, spasms again and often ends up by vomiting. It is all extremely distressing for the child, as well as for the parent watching.

Whooping cough vaccine is the least-liked preparation by doctors. It only gives complete protection to between 80 and 90 per cent of those who are vaccinated. In the past almost 50 per cent would also get a mild reaction that causes fever or a little irritability. This is usually nothing to worry about and will be put right with a small dose of paracetamol. However, since 1997, we have been using a vaccine in Australia that causes far fewer reactions.

The main concern with the whooping cough vaccine debate is the much publicised danger of permanent brain damage. This is *exceptionally rare*, occurring less frequently than one per million children, but it is still of great concern to the medical profession and all childcare workers.

It is important to see the whooping cough vaccine in its proper perspective. If the vaccine is not given, the majority of children will have natural whooping cough. For most this will be a really unpleasant and long illness. For a few there is a risk of residual brain damage or even death. The chances of these serious complications alone are at least 100 times greater than the risk of problems due to the vaccine.

Common questions

Q. What medicine do you give for a child with fever following immunisation?
A. Paracetamol.
Q. If the baby has a cold or flu, with a fever, should he be immunised?
A. No, not until he has recovered.

Q. If you believe there has been a major illness or reaction to a particular vaccine, is further immunisation to be given?

A. Any severe reactions must be reported to your family doctor. If these fit certain criteria, it is possible the doctor may recommend omitting one part of the vaccine.

Q. When do premature babies get their vaccines?

A. If they are healthy, immunisation should start at the same time after birth as it would for any other child.

Q. If I miss one vaccine do I need to start all over again?

A. No! You need no extra shots. Start where you left off and continue at the original spacing.

Q. If the vaccines are commenced at an older age than suggested, do you use the same spacing?

A. Yes.

Q. If a young child has a bad cut or is bitten by a dog, does he need a tetanus shot?

A. Not if he has had a tetanus immunisation in the previous two years. Check with your doctor.

Q. If a child has been sick with measles in his first year of life, does this mean that no measles vaccine should be given?

A. Studies show that most rashes diagnosed as measles in the first year of life are, in fact, misdiagnoses. There is no harm giving the vaccine to a child who has already had measles, so if in doubt, please vaccinate.

Q. What ever happened to smallpox and tuberculosis vaccinations that many of us were given as children?

A. A worldwide vaccination program for smallpox seems to have eradicated the disease and so it is no longer needed. Tuberculosis vaccine is only given in special instances where there is a risk of contracting TB from someone close to your family who is known to have the condition.

Q. If a child is allergic to eggs, should the measles vaccine (which is egg-cultured) be given?

A. Most doctors would now say yes, but with care.

Q. Does MMR (for measles, mumps and rubella) vaccine increase the risk of autism?

A. There was concern that MMR vaccination may increase the risk of autism. This was because the age when autism is usually diagnosed is after the first MMR vaccination is given. There was also an increased incidence of autism but this increase predated the introduction of the MMR vaccine. It is thought that MMR vaccination and diagnosis of autism is purely coincidental.

Immunisation Schedules for Australian children 2000–2002

The Australian Standard Vaccination Schedule (8th edition) shown here is that recommended by the National Health and Medical Research Council (NHMRC). In drawing up its recommendations the NHMRC has sought to reduce the number of injections given at each immunisation session through the use of new combination vaccines, and to limit, as far as possible, the number of vaccine products that a practitioner would need to have available. For the immunisations at two, four, six and twelve months, two options for the use of combination vaccines which meet these criteria are recommended.

Australian standard vaccination schedule 2000–2002*

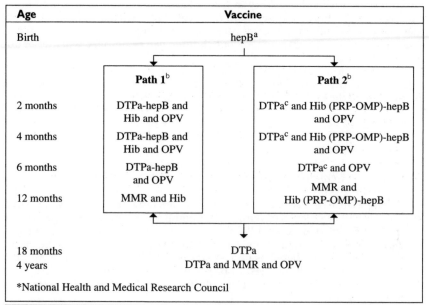

Age	Vaccine
Birth	hepB[a]

Path 1[b]

2 months	DTPa-hepB and Hib and OPV
4 months	DTPa-hepB and Hib and OPV
6 months	DTPa-hepB and OPV
12 months	MMR and Hib

Path 2[b]

2 months	DTPa[c] and Hib (PRP-OMP)-hepB and OPV
4 months	DTPa[c] and Hib (PRP-OMP)-hepB and OPV
6 months	DTPa[c] and OPV
12 months	MMR and Hib (PRP-OMP)-hepB

| 18 months | DTPa |
| 4 years | DTPa and MMR and OPV |

*National Health and Medical Research Council

Disease	Vaccine	Available products
Hepatitis B	hep B	Engerix-B™ or H-B VAxll™
Diphtheria, tetanus, pertussis	DTPa	Infanrix™ or Tripacel™
Diphtheria, tetanus, pertussis, hepatitis B	DTPa-hep B	Infanrix-HepB™
Haemophilus influenzae type B	Hib (PRP-OMP)	PedvaxHIB™
Haemophilus influenzae type B, hepatitis B	Hib (PRP-OMP)-hep B	Comvax™
Poliomyelitis	OPV	Polio Sabin™
Measles, mumps, rubella	MMR	MMRII® or Priorix™

Notes

a Hepatitis B vaccine should be given to all infants at birth and should not be delayed beyond seven days after birth. Infants whose mothers are hepatitis B surface antigen positive (HBsAg+ve) should also be given hepatitis B immunoglobulin (HBIG) within twelve hours of birth.

b When necessary the two paths may be interchanged with regard to their hepatitis B and hib components. For example, when a child moves interstate, she may change from one path to the other.

c Wherever possible the same brand of DTPa should be used at two, four and six months.

Immunisation schedule for New Zealand children 2002

Immunisation is not compulsory in New Zealand, and there is no intention of making it so. Parents of children born from 1995 onwards are requested to show their child's immunisation certificate when starting at an early childhood education centre or primary school, but children can be enrolled whether or not they are vaccinated.

The oral polio vaccine (OPV) has been replaced by the injectable inactivated polio vaccine (IPV) and given as DTaP-IPV. Substituting IPV or OPV can be done at any stage of the immunisation schedule and children can be switched directly to DTaP-IPV.

At 4 years of age a fifth dose of DTaP will now be given to reduce the risk of pertussis being spread through primary school aged children. A second dose of MMR vaccine will also be administered at this time.

Children aged 11 years will continue to receive the Td vaccine (tetanus-diphtheria). For children who have not had four doses of polio vaccine a dose of IPV can be given.

Meningococcal B Vaccine is currently undergoing trials in New Zealand. These trials will be completed during 2003 and if the results are as expected the vaccine will be introduced in 2004. The introductory phase will involve a large-scale campaign, targeting infants, children and young adults, up to the age of 21 years. At this stage there has been no decision about how it will fit into the schedule. Interference trials need to be carried out to establish how best to do this. You can track progress by accessing the Ministry of Health's website at www.moh.govt.nz.

New Zealand Standard Vaccination Schedule from 1 February 2002:

Age	Immunisation given	
6 weeks	DTaP–IPV	Hib–Hepatitis B
3 months	DTaP–IPV	Hib–Hepatitis B
5 months	DTaP–IPV	Hepatitis B
15 months	DTaP/Hib	MMR
4 years	DTaP–IPV	MMR
11 years	Td	(IPV if < 4 doses)

Key
D: diphtheria, T: tetanus, aP: acellular pertussis, IPV: inactivated polio vaccine, Hib: Haemophilus influenzae type b, MMR: measles, mumps and rubella, Td: adult tetanus and diphtheria vaccine.

APPENDIX IV
Heights from 1 year to 4 years

Height in cm – girls (boys)

Age yrs mths		Average height		Lower average 3% will be shorter 97% will be taller		Upper average 3% will be taller 97% will be shorter	
1	0	74.3	(76.1)	69.0	(71.0)	79.6	(81.2)
1	1	75.5	(77.2)	70.1	(72.1)	80.9	(82.4)
1	2	76.7	(78.3)	71.2	(73.1)	82.1	(83.6)
1	3	77.8	(79.4)	72.2	(74.1)	83.3	(84.8)
1	4	78.9	(80.4)	73.2	(75.0)	84.5	(85.9)
1	5	79.9	(81.4)	74.2	(75.9)	85.6	(87.0)
1	6	80.9	(82.4)	75.1	(76.7)	86.7	(88.1)
1	7	81.9	(83.3)	76.1	(77.5)	87.8	(89.2)
1	8	82.9	(84.2)	77.0	(78.3)	88.8	(90.2)
1	9	83.8	(85.1)	77.8	(79.1)	89.8	(91.2)
1	10	84.7	(86.0)	78.7	(79.8)	90.8	(92.2)
1	11	85.6	(86.8)	79.5	(80.6)	91.7	(93.1)
2	0	84.5	(85.6)	78.5	(79.6)	90.5	(91.6)
2	1	85.4	(86.4)	79.2	(80.3)	91.5	(92.5)
2	2	86.2	(87.2)	80.0	(81.0)	92.4	(93.5)
2	3	87.0	(88.1)	80.7	(81.7)	93.4	(94.4)
2	4	87.9	(88.9)	81.4	(82.4)	94.3	(95.3)
2	5	88.7	(89.7)	82.2	(83.1)	95.2	(96.2)
2	6	89.5	(90.4)	82.9	(83.8)	96.0	(97.1)
2	7	90.2	(91.2)	83.6	(84.5)	96.9	(97.9)
2	8	91.0	(92.0)	84.3	(85.2)	97.7	(98.8)
2	9	91.7	(92.7)	84.9	(85.8)	98.6	(99.6)
2	10	92.5	(93.5)	85.6	(86.5)	99.4	(100.5)
2	11	93.2	(94.2)	86.3	(87.1)	100.1	(101.3)
3	0	93.9	(94.9)	86.9	(87.8)	100.9	(102.1)
3	1	94.6	(95.6)	87.6	(88.4)	101.7	(102.9)
3	2	95.3	(96.3)	88.2	(89.0)	102.4	(103.7)
3	3	96.0	(97.0)	88.8	~ (89.6)	103.1	(104.4)
3	4	96.6	(97.7)	89.4	(90.2)	103.9	(105.2)
3	5	97.3	(98.4)	90.0	(90.9)	104.6	(106.0)
3	6	97.9	(99.1)	90.6	(91.5)	105.3	(106.7)
3	7	98.6	(99.7)	91.2	(92.0)	105.9	(107.4)
3	8	99.2	(100.4)	91.8	(92.6)	106.6	(108.2)
3	9	99.8	(101.0)	92.3	(93.2)	107.3	(108.9)
3	10	100.4	(101.7)	92.9	(93.8)	107.9	(109.6)
3	11	101.0	(102.3)	93.5	(94.4)	108.6	(110.3)
4	0	101.6	(102.9)	94.0	(94.9)	109.2	(111.0)

Reference: World Health Organisation Standards.
Note: The ideal relationship of height and weight is to be in proportion (e.g. if the child is of upper average height, his weight should also be upper average).
Note: 1 cm = 0.3937 inches 1 inch = 2.54 cm

APPENDIX V
Weights from 1 year to 4 years

Weight in kg – girls (boys)

Age yrs mths		Average weight		Lower average 3% will be lighter 97% will be heavier		Upper average 3% will be heavier 97% will be lighter	
1	0	9.5	(10.2)	7.6	(8.2)	11.5	(12.2)
1	1	9.8	(10.4)	7.8	(8.5)	11.8	(12.5)
1	2	10.0	(10.7)	8.0	(8.7)	12.0	(12.8)
1	3	10.2	(10.9)	8.1	(8.8)	12.3	(13.1)
1	4	10.4	(11.1)	8.3	(9.0)	12.5	(13.3)
1	5	10.6	(11.3)	8.5	(9.1)	12.7	(13.6)
1	6	10.8	(11.5)	8.6	(9.3)	13.0	(13.8)
1	7	11.0	(11.7)	8.8	(9.4)	13.2	(14.0)
1	8	11.2	(11.8)	8.9	(9.5)	13.4	(14.2)
1	9	11.4	(12.0)	9.1	(9.7)	13.6	(14.4)
1	10	11.5	(12.2)	9.3	(9.8)	13.9	(14.6)
1	11	11.7	(12.4)	9.4	(9.9)	14.1	(14.8)
2	0	11.8	(12.3)	9.6	(10.2)	14.4	(15.5)
2	1	12.0	(12.5)	9.7	(10.3)	14.8	(15.7)
2	2	12.2	(12.7)	9.9	(10.4)	15.1	(15.9)
2	3	12.4	(12.9)	10.1	(10.6)	15.4	(16.1)
2	4	12.6	(13.1)	10.2	(10.7)	15.7	(16.4)
2	5	12.8	(13.3)	10.4	(10.8)	16.0	(16.6)
2	6	13.0	(13.5)	10.5	(10.9)	16.2	(16.8)
2	7	13.2	(13.7)	10.6	(11.0)	16.5	(17.0)
2	8	13.4	(13.9)	10.8	(11.1)	16.8	(17.2)
2	9	13.6	(14.1)	10.9	(11.3)	17.0	(17.4)
2	10	13.8	(14.3)	11.1	(11.4)	17.3	(17.6)
2	11	13.9	(14.4)	11.2	(11.5)	17.5	(17.8)
3	0	14.1	(14.6)	11.3	(11.6)	17.8	(18.0)
3	1	14.3	(14.8)	11.5	(11.7)	18.0	(18.2)
3	2	14.4	(15.0)	11.6	(11.9)	18.3	(18.5)
3	3	14.6	(15.2)	11.7	(12.0)	18.5	(18.7)
3	4	14.8	(15.3)	11.8	(12.1)	18.7	(18.9)
3	5	14.9	(15.5)	12.0	(12.2)	18.9	(19.1)
3	6	15.1	(15.7)	12.1	(12.4)	19.1	(19.3)
3	7	15.2	(15.8)	12.2	(12.5)	19.4	(19.5)
3	8	15.4	(16.0)	12.3	(12.6)	19.6	(19.7)
3	9	15.5	(16.2)	12.4	(12.7)	19.8	(19.9)
3	10	15.7	(16.4)	12.5	(12.9)	20.0	(20.1)
3	11	15.8	(16.5)	12.6	(13.0)	20.2	(20.3)
4	0	16.0	(16.7)	12.8	(13.1)	20.4	(20.5)

Reference: World Health Organisation Standards
Note: The ideal relationship of weight and height is to be in proportion (e.g. if the child is of lower average height, his weight should also be lower average).
Note: 1 kg = 2.2 lbs;   1 lb = 0.45 kg

APPENDIX VI
ADHD: The Essentials in Adults and Children[10]

- Attention Deficit Hyperactivity Disorder (ADHD) is the same as ADD.
- ADHD disadvantages at least 2 per cent of our school-age population.
- ADHD is related to an underfunction in the frontal areas of the brain (the parts that self-regulate behaviour and learning).
- The ADHD child presents with *behaviour* that is out of step with the quality of parenting they receive and *learning* that is out of step with their intellectual abilities.
- Children present with *behaviour* problems of poor self-monitoring and inhibition. (Impulsive, unthinking behaviour, difficulty putting the brakes on behaviour, unaware when to back off, misreads social situations, restless and fidgety.)
- The *learning* problems present with underfunction for intellect. (Self distracts, difficulty working without 1:1 supervision, problems starting, sustaining and finishing work, poor short term memory, disorganisation.)
- Most ADHD children have a mix of behaviour and learning problems. In addition, many have associated comorbid conditions. (Specific learning difficulties, Oppositional Defiant Disorder, Conduct Disorder, coordination difficulties, tics, etc.)
- A number of diagnostic techniques are promoted but no one method is essential or completely reliable in making the diagnosis.
- Some of the most difficult ADHD children will behave relatively well in the quiet of the doctor's or psychologist's office. Ten minutes of good behaviour does not rule out the diagnosis of ADHD. The problems of ADHD may *not* be apparent in all situations.
- Treatment involves accepting the reality of the diagnosis, then using behaviour programs, school support and increasing the child's ability to self monitor with stimulant medication.
- Behaviour techniques work poorly in a child who acts before they think. Parents have most success with routine, avoiding the unimportant and using rewards. Many ADHD children are oppositional and defy on principle. Meeting opposition with force leads to battles. This wrecks relationships.
- Parents need to learn how to side step escalation by keeping calm, active ignoring, counting techniques, Time Out and giving choices.
- The stimulant medications Ritalin and dexamphetamine help the ADHD child self monitor and focus. They do not sedate, they normalise.
- There should be no controversy over this treatment, with over 150 reputable papers supporting the safety and benefits. Stimulants have been used with ADHD for over 40 years.
- Stimulants are used in conjunction with behaviour and learning programs. Stimulants allow you to reach the child and once you reach, you can teach.
- ADHD is a strongly hereditary condition. Many ADHD children have an ADHD parent.
- Adult ADHD affects about 1 per cent of the population. It causes clever adults to underfunction at work for intellect and behave unwisely in their relationships. Psychiatrists who treat adults with ADHD find the greatest problems come from impulsivity (impulsive outbursts, violence in marriage, unwise spending, accident proneness, damaged relationships, work difficulties).

- Many ADHD adults get major improvements with the same treatments we use in children.
- ADHD can damage the relationships of parents with children, children with parents, children with peers and adults with adults. For the reason, early recognition and treatment is of utmost importance.

Appendix VII
Home Safety Checklist
(from the Children's Hospital, Westmead)

Home environment
- Do you have a safety switch to prevent electrocution?
- Can your hot water system be turned down to 50 degrees Celsius to prevent scalds?
- Do you have a smoke detector located outside each bedroom area?
- Are safety plugs fitted in spare power points?
- Do you have a fence that restricts access to your driveway and the street?

Kitchen
- Do your appliances have short cords that do not dangle over the kitchen bench?
- Do you use the back hot plates and turn pot handles around to prevent pots being pulled from the hot plates?
- Are knives and other sharp objects stored out of reach of children?
- Are cleaning products, chemicals and medications stored in a locked cupboard at least 1.5 metres above the ground?
- Do you have a fire blanket within reach of your stove?
- Can you restrict access to the kitchen?

Bathroom
- Does the bath have non-slip mats or hand rails?
- Are medicines and sharp objects kept in a locked cupboard out of reach of children?
- Are any electricals (i.e. hairdryers, electric shavers) stored safely and away from water when not in use?
- Is the bath water temperature always 'tested' before putting the child in the bath?
- Are hot water taps unable to be operated by small children?

Laundry
- Are cleaning products, bleaches and detergents stored out of reach, in a child-resistant cupboard?
- Is the nappy bucket used with a lid on and kept out of reach of children?
- Can you restrict access to the laundry?

Living areas
- Is the furniture located safely? (e.g. away from windows)
- Are sharp edges on tables and furniture covered?
- Are blind and curtain cords out of reach?
- Are glass doors protected by safety film, colourful stickers or made of safety glass?
- Is alcohol stored in a child-resistant cupboard?
- Are toys kept away from the main walkway?
- Are rugs and mats secure to prevent a fall?
- Are there any low-level tables that dangerous items could be placed on? (e.g. watch batteries, tea and coffee, peanuts)

Child's bedroom

- Is the space between vertical cot railings between 50 mm and 85 mm wide?
- Are toys suitable for the child's age?
- Is the furniture located safely? (i.e. not near electrical switches, windows or ceiling fans)

Garden shed/outdoors

- Can your garden shed be locked at all times?
- Are pesticides, paints and other poisons stored in tightly covered, labelled, original containers out of reach of children?
- Check that outdoor play equipment is not damaged or potentially dangerous.
- Does your pool have a fence at least 1.2 m high around all four sides of the pool, that cannot be climbed by children and has a self-closing, self-latching gate?

References

1. Chess, *Temperament and Development*, Brunner Mazel, New York, 1977.
2. Sanson, Oberklaid, Smart and Prior, *The Australian Temperament Study*, Melbourne, 2000.
3. Chamberlin, *Paediatric Clinics of North America*, vol. 21, no. 1, February 1974.
4. Green, *The Journal of Maternal and Child Health*, United Kingdom, February 1980.
5. Anders, *Paediatrics*, vol. 63, 1979, pp. 860-4.
6. Beltramini, et al., *Paediatrics*, vol. 71, no. 2, 1973.
7. The source for this chapter was: Green and Chee, *Understanding ADHD* (revised edition), Doubleday Australia, 2001.
8. Rutter, *Scientific Foundations of Developmental Psychiatry*, Heinemann, 1980.
9. Harvey, *The Journal of Developmental Psychology*, March 1998.
10. *ADHD: Report of the National Health and Medical Research Council of Australia*, Australian Government Printing Service, 1996.

Where to Get Help – Australia

Health and medical

Poisons Information
National Hotline: 131 126 (24 hours)

Child Accident Prevention Foundation of Australia
Kidsafe House, The Children's Hospital
Hawkesbury Road Westmead
Ph: (02) 9845 0890

Help for parents

ACT

Parent Line: (02) 6278 3995

Queen Elizabeth II Family Centre
129 Carruthers Street
Curtin 2605
Ph: (02) 6205 2333 (24 hours)

NSW

Parent Line: 132 055 (9.00 am – 4.30pm Monday to Saturday)

Karitane Mothercraft Society
Corner, The Horsley Drive & Mitchell Street
Carramar 2163
Ph: (02) 9794 1852 (24-hour care line)
Freecall: 1800 677 961 (24 hours)

Tresillian Family Care
2 Shaw St
Petersham 2049

Parent Help Line: (02) 9787 5255 (24 hours); 1800 63 73 57 (Freecall and 24 hours)

NT

Parenting Line: 131 114

Family and Children's Health Services
Ph: (08) 9222 2555

QLD

Parent Line: 1300 301 300

Community Child Health Service
The Riverton Centre
58 Riverton Street
Clayfield 4011

Ph: (07) 3860 7111
Child Health Information and Advisory Service
Ph: (07) 3862 2333 (24 hours)
1800 177 279 (24 hours)

SA

Parent Help Line: 1300 364 100 (24 hours)

Child and Family Health Centres

For your nearest centre, contact:
Child and Youth Health Head Office
Torrens House
295 South Terrace
Adelaide 5000
Ph: (08) 8303 1500

Tas

Parent Information Telephone Assistance (PITAAS): 1800 808 178 (Freecall and 24 hours)

Parentline: 13 22 89 (For deaf, hearing or speech impaired call TTY 13 63 88 – accessible throughout Victoria and Tas for the cost of a local call)

Parenting Centres

HOBART
232 New Town Rd
New Town 7008
Ph: (03) 6233 2700

LAUNCESTON
Walker House
17A Walkers Avenue
Newnham 7248
Ph: (03) 6326 6188

NORTHWEST
35 Mace Street
Montello, Burnie 7320
Ph: (03) 6434 6201

Vic

Parent Line: 132 289 or 136 388

The Maternal and Child Health Service
After Hours Country: 1800 134 883

344

Metropolitan: (03) 9853 0844

O'Connell Family Centre
6 Mont Albert Road
Canterbury 3126
Ph: (03) 9882 2326 (24 hours
  Monday to Friday)

Queen Elizabeth Centre (QEC)
53 Thomas Street
Noble Park 3174
Ph: (03) 9549 2777

Tweddle Child & Family Health Service
53 Adelaide Street
Footscray 3011
Ph: (03) 9689 1577

WA

Parent Help Line: (08) 9272 1466 or
  1800 654 432 (Freecall)
Family Help Line: (08) 9223 1100 or
  1800 643 000 (Freecall)
Child Health Hotline: (08) 9367 3256
  (AH)

Ngala Family Resource Centre
9 George Street
Kensington 6165
Ph: (08) 9368 9368, (08) 9367 3256
  (AH), (08) 9592 3692 (Rockingham)
Freecall: 1800 111 546

Relationships

Relationships Australia
ACT: (02) 02 6281 3600
NSW: (02) 9418 8800; 1800 801 578
NT:
Darwin: (08) 8981 6676
Freecall: 1800 652 404 For Remote
  Areas
Alice Springs (08) 8952 7344
Freecall: 1800 634 405 For Remote
  Areas
Qld: (07) 3217 2900
SA: (08) 8223 4566
Tas: Hobart: (03) 6211 4050
        (Relationship Counselling)
        Launceston: (03) 6336 7000
Vic: (03) 9205 9570
WA: (08) 9489 6363

Single parents

Parents Without Partners Inc
ACT: Southside (02) 6291 9917
        Northside (02) 6258 6026
NSW: (02) 9896 1888
Qld: (07) 3275 3290
SA: (08) 8359 1552
Tas: 03) 6243 9225
Vic: (03) 9836 3211
WA: (08) 9389 8350

Where to Get Help – New Zealand

Health and medical

National Poisons Information Centre
Urgent enquiries: Ph (03) 474 7000
  (24 hours)
Non-urgent enquiries:
  Ph (03) 479 1200
Email: poisons@otago.ac.nz

Plunket Line
Ph: 0800 933922 (24 hours) or (04)
  496 1234
*Health and medical advice supplied by
  trained Plunket nurses.*

Help for parents

Barnardos New Zealand
*Offers a range of family support services
  – branches nationwide.*

Birthright (NZ) Inc.
National office: Ph: (04) 802 5377
*Support services available to children
  and parents in one-parent families.
  Branches nationwide.*

FAIR Family Advocacy and Information Resource Centre
Ph: 0800 222 345

Family Planning Association
*Education and clinical regional offices
  nationwide.*

La Leche League
*Breastfeeding information and support –
  branches nationwide.*

National Network of Stopping
  Violence Services
*Offers group programmes on stopping
  violence for men and their partners.
  Groups operate nationwide.*

New Zealand Multiple Birth Association
*Offers support, assistance, clothing and
  equipment exchange for parents of
  multiple births. Branches nationwide.*

Parents as First Teachers (PAFT)
*12 centres nationwide – check your local
  telephone directory.*

Parent Help/CAPS New Zealand
Ph: 0800 568 856
*Phone and couselling service for families
  with parenting and family problems.*

Parent to Parent
*Provides information and groups for
  parents of children with special needs.
  Branches nationwide.*

Plunket Society
*Trained Plunket nurses monitor the
  growth and development of babies to
  five years old. Volunteers join local
  Plunket committees to provide parenting
  courses and information on support
  groups in the community. Branches
  nationwide.*

Index

347

Beyond
Toddlerdom

Beyond Toddlerdom

Keeping five to twelve year olds on the rails

Dr Christopher Green

Illustrated by Roger Roberts

DOUBLEDAY

SYDNEY•AUCKLAND•TORONTO•NEW YORK•LONDON

Contents

Acknowledgements

Thanks to my wife, Hilary – without her this book would have been impossible. She supports and encourages and sees the humour in life.

Thanks are also due to Lorraine Partington, a secretary with the ability to bring order to my chaos, and a loyal friend; Dr John Coveney of the Department of Public Health, Flinders University – friend and dietitian who helped with *Toddler Taming* and brought the same good sense to this book; and Dr Kit Chee, who has worked with me and is now development and behavioural paediatrician at The Sydney Learning Clinic. I have learned much from parents, especially Glyn Patrick.

And finally to colleagues and friends at the New Children's Hospital, Westmead for their sound advice, especially Dr Ted Beckenham, Professor Margaret Burgess, Dr Frank Martin, Professor Kim Oates, Dr Maureen Rogers and Professor Richard Widmer.

ACKNOWLEDGMENTS

Introduction

I once wrote a book about toddlers, which sold a million copies around the world. *Toddler Taming* was practical, reassuring and based on reality. What's more, it could make mums laugh. After all, you can smile about toddlers because you know that most of their odd little behaviours will disappear when their brain discovers sense at the age of three years.

But five- to twelve-year-olds are much more complicated, which made this book a lot harder to write. These children are influenced by school, their friends, their families and their abilities, and their problems can easily deepen rather than disappear.

Beyond Toddlerdom looks at how primary school-age children feel, think and behave. The emphasis is on behaviour, with the aim of keeping parents close and in love with their children, so homes need never become a war zone.

I learnt the ideas you will read in this book from the thousands of parents and children I have attempted to help every day in my work. But I don't pretend to have all the answers: even after twenty-five years I still struggle to find ways to help some families I meet.

Hopefully, though, you will find lots of useful advice here. To help you find what you're looking for easily and quickly, *Beyond Toddlerdom* contains a clear index and plenty of tables that set out the main points.

Once I asked a mum how things were going. She said, 'It's like this, Doctor. Before we met you we were riding on a roller coaster completely out of control. Now we're still on a roller coaster but it's finally on the rails.'

This book is about keeping relationships between parents and children strong and happy. It's also about keeping children on the rails. I can't promise a smooth ride, but I hope I can help you avoid some of the bumps.

Christopher Green
2002

The secret of successful parenting: treat children the way you would like to be treated

This book is cram-packed with the latest child care information. But it is not a book about 'taming', 'compliance' and 'perfect behaviours'. Instead, *Beyond Toddlerdom* is about relationships: the art of keeping parents close and in love with their children. If we can achieve this, the rest usually falls into place.

Now, the key to a good relationship, whether it's between two adults or a parent and a child, is to treat the other person the way you would like to be treated. And that's what this book is all about: treat your children the way you like to be treated and your relationship with them won't go far wrong.

As you skim through the chapters, you'll find that the same messages keep reappearing. These messages are the secret of successful parenting, but they could apply to any relationship. Here they are:

- Children need you to be available to admire, encourage and marvel.

- Children like routine, consistency and clear communication, but they also need flexibility and choice.

- Discipline is not about pain and punishment. In this new millennium we mould good behaviours through encouragement and reward.

- Confrontation, force and heavy discipline wreck many relationships. You may appear to win but at the cost of resentment, anger and hate.

- When things have gone badly, quickly forgive and restart with a clean slate. There is no place for grudges in a good relationship.

- Let unimportant behaviour pass. Take a step back and ask, 'Is this getting me anywhere?' If you are up a cul-de-sac, back off.

- Children do strange things and muck often hits the fan. Don't over-analyse. I have been at this for more than a quarter of a century and I still watch in wonderment.

Be available

Christopher Green is a busy man, but if I was always so busy that my wife never saw me, and when she did I told her I was way too busy to stop and talk, she might, quite rightly, start to feel as if she must be the least important person in my life.

Children don't need 'quality time'; they need a parent who is available to sit, listen, do things together and marvel at what they see.

Point 1: More than anything, children need you to be available.

3

Routine and structure

Everyone loves surprises, but if every day when you woke up you had no idea what was going to happen it would be very unsettling. Chaos makes us all feel as if we've got no control over the situation. Like adults, children are happiest when they know what's coming next.

Point 2: Children are happiest when they have a structured routine.

Consistent limits and rules

As I drive to the hospital I pass through three speed zones (60 kph, 80 kph and 90 kph). I know each legal limit and the level of tolerance before I am booked. Right or wrong, Sydney drivers go at 66 in a 60 zone, 88 in an 80 zone and 99 in a 90 zone. I cope because I know the stated limits and levels of tolerance. I would be very confused if either of these changed from day to day. Children may protest our limits but at least they know we care enough to care what they do. Unpredictability causes confusion, anger and emotional insecurity.

Point 3: Children are at their most secure when they know the rules and how far they can push these limits.

Flexibility and compromise

I don't cope well with rigid-minded people who insist that everything is done by the book. They quote council by-laws, can't compromise and never shift an inch.

I come up against schools who will only allow important medication to be given at 12.45pm because this is the one and only time they hand out tablets. But the child I care for falls apart without their 11am dose.

Here is another example. The rules state that the bus is designed to carry six people and the operator sees no difference between six sumos or six child-gymnasts. Adults with an almost autistic-like inflexibility need their rules, but a successful relationship won't work without compromise.

Parents need to adjust the rules to fit the individual situation: children sleep in their own beds, but during a thunderstorm everyone can sleep together; children must tidy away the dinner dishes, but tonight there is so much homework they can be excused.

Point 4: Rules and consistency are important for children, but there must be room for flexibility and compromise.

Choice and freedom

I wake up in the morning and am about to get dressed. 'Just wait a minute,' says my wife. 'Today you will wear a blue shirt, cream trousers and a red tie. For lunch you will have a gherkin and ham roll with a skim-milk cappuccino.'

'Hey, you wait a minute,' I think. 'Don't I have some say in my own life?'

A two-year-old can't cope with choice but a school-age child needs some freedom to decide their own destiny. Controlling parents create unhappy children who can't make a decision.

Point 5: School-age children respond best to choice.

Communicate clearly

Sometimes I enter a shop where the assistant doesn't bother to look up before asking coldly what I want. It seems as if my presence is an annoyance and they have no interest in me, the customer. Rude adults are immensely annoying; I like to be greeted with eye contact, interest and civility.

If you wish a child to respond, address them with interest and enthusiasm.

Point 6: To gain a child's attention, look them directly in the eye, talk simply and speak as though you mean it. Show them you're interested.

Ask, don't nag

Christopher Green hates being nagged. 'Have you done that yet? Why not? When will you do it? What's keeping you?' The more I am nagged, the more obstinate and angry I become.

If you want compliant children tell them what you wish them to do, encourage action, monitor results, then get off their backs.

Point 7: Children switch off and go deaf when parents nag.

Reward good behaviour

The rock concert has been spectacular and you wish it would never end. As the last note fades the audience springs to their feet and shrieks their appreciation. The band responds to this show of enthusiasm and plays two more numbers.

The audience rewarded the band for their good playing. The band rewarded the audience for their enthusiasm. This was a win–win situation. If we had wanted the band to pack up and go home, we would have kept quiet.

With our children we mould their behaviour by ensuring the right (not the wrong) actions pay off.

Point 8: Encourage good behaviour by rewarding the good. Discourage bad behaviour by preventing any pay-off for the bad.

Subtle rewards are the best

How do you know that things are going well in your adult relationship? Does your partner give you a dollar or a smiley stamp? Of course not. We know that things are on track because we sense the positive vibrations between us. This subtle feedback is the main way we mould human beings of all ages.

Children know they are doing well by the way we look at them, the twinkle in our eyes, our tone of voice, our level of interest and the gentle reassuring touch as we brush by.

Point 9: Soft, subtle encouragement is the most powerful way to boost behaviour.

Notice the good

In my wish to be a domesticated dad, I go out to get the shopping. But when I return home it's all complaints: 'Could you not have got a larger loaf? Didn't they have redder apples? Why choose the dented can of dog food? Were there no straight bananas?' I busted myself but it seems everything is wrong. Soon I think, 'What's the point bothering?'

Children often get this treatment from their parents. They set the table with great care: 'You've got the knives and forks the wrong way around.' They clean the dishes: 'There's egg on that plate.' They vacuum the lounge room: 'You missed a bit.' When humans work hard and others only notice their faults and not the effort, it's a sure way to discourage and dishearten.

Point 10: Let children know when you are pleased. Change the focus from only seeing the bad. Catch them being good.

Confrontation causes resentment

When the first officer of the *Titanic* sees an iceberg ahead it is no time to ask nicely, 'I'd appreciate it if you could turn a little to the left.' He must issue a firm order. But when we are steaming in clear waters, humans are more receptive when asked rather than told.

We don't like being steamrollered and bullied: 'Just shut up and do it'; 'Do it or I'll hit you!' This heavy form of discipline would bring out the worst in any of us. I would resent this confrontation and feel angry, drag my feet and wonder how I could get even.

As parents hammer their child into shape the young one thinks, 'Damn you, Dad! I'll make it harder for you next time.' Force and confrontation may get action, but often at a price.

Point 11: Confrontation and bullying lead to opposition and resentment.

Calm, not escalation

Let's imagine you are flying from Melbourne to Sydney when the engine falls off the plane. The confident pilot would transmit calm: 'This is Captain Smith speaking. I have to inform you that the port engine has just become disengaged. Don't worry, the crew will soon be through the cabin serving complimentary drinks followed by a hot meal, then we'll attempt a crash landing in Sydney.' The example has a bit of author's licence, but the message is clear: a calm attitude spreads calm.

Even the sweetest child can be intensely irritating, but successful parents don't escalate by adding heat to an already overheated situation. They communicate in a calm voice, repeat their request like a broken gramophone record and move away before they lose their cool.

Point 12: If parents can keep calm, children are easier to control.

Cool off and regain control

Your German shepherd guard dog has an attitude problem. In the park he starts a skirmish with a psychopathic sheepdog. As the hair flies, do you issue polite instructions such as 'Sit, Fritz', or 'Lassie, heel'?

When we are in the midst of a dogfight, the first priority is to separate and reduce the heat. Once calm is re-established, rules and discipline can return.

Point 13: When a child's behaviour has escalated over the top, this is not a time for rational reasoning. The first priority is to cool down the situation and regain control.

Forgive and move on

I do something really foolish. I know I have been silly and I apologise. But my words are not accepted. I apologise again and I ask what I can do to make up, but the door is slammed in my face. Now

I feel intensely angry and am damned if I will say sorry again. Communication is now blocked and we have moved poles apart in our relationship.

Children don't want to be at war with their parents, but often they are left with no other option. Be a peace maker. If at first your efforts are not accepted, keep offering the olive branch. Children eventually grasp the leaves and come back in close.

Point 14: After anger or punishment, forgive fast and start afresh with a clean slate.

Don't stir up the animals

Life is full of frustrations, but we will go mad if we rise to every annoyance. When working in the lions' cage do you take a stick and poke them in the backside or do you tread gently and avoid trouble?

Some parents nitpick and escalate every trivial event. They are incapable of letting an unimportant behaviour pass. I spend hours every week trying to encourage parents to back off, but often I am wasting my breath. We don't want to let our children get away with murder, but it isn't clever to stir up the animals over every imperfection.

Point 15: Let the unimportant things pass.

Treating children the way you like to be treated

1. More than anything, children need parents to be available to admire, encourage and marvel.
2. Children behave best when they have a structured routine.
3. Children are at their most secure when they know the rules and how far they can push these limits.
4. Rules and consistency are important for children, but there must be room for flexibility and compromise.

5. School-age children respond best to choice.
6. To gain their attention, look a child directly in the eye, talk simply and speak as though you mean it.
7. Children switch off and go deaf when parents nag.
8. Encourage good behaviour by rewarding the good. Discourage bad behaviour by preventing any pay-off for the bad.
9. Soft, subtle encouragement is the most powerful way to boost behaviour.
10. Let children know when you are pleased. Change the focus from only seeing the bad. Catch them being good.
11. Confrontation and bullying leads to opposition and resentment.
12. If parents can keep calm, children are easier to control.
13. When a child's behaviour has escalated over the top, this is not a time for rational reasoning. The first priority is to cool down the situation and regain control.
14. After anger or punishment, forgive fast and start afresh with a clean slate.
15. Let the unimportant things pass.

TWO

Age five to twelve: how they think, feel and behave

You may be wondering why I didn't write this book years ago. The answer is simple: the way five-year-olds to twelve-year-olds think, feel and behave is far too complicated.

Writing about toddlers was easy. They only have one problem – a serious lack of sense. But school-age children are much more complex little humans, who regularly make parents wonder if they are the ones who lack the sense.

Luckily, you need not feel that you are losing your marbles permanently. Because school-age children are easier to understand once you realise that they go through not one but two very different stages of development during these years: the dependent and innocent stage between the years five and eight and the much more independent and grown-up stage between eight and twelve.

This chapter looks at how children of the two age groups think, feel and behave, so you can gain a better understanding of what makes your child tick.

The two stages: an overview

Five- to eight-year-olds

These little people still carry much of the unspoiled innocence of the preschool years. They remain close and immensely dependent on their mum and dad. They are cuddly, uncomplicated and usually keen to please. They skip, effervesce and believe in ghosts and monsters.

Eight- to twelve-year-olds

At eight years children stand on the first rung of the ladder that leads towards adulthood. Dependence on Mum and Dad starts to weaken. They are increasingly influenced by teachers, school friends, the media and their environment, and they start to question their parents' values and wisdom.

Children of this age compare their looks, school performance, social acceptance and sporting abilities, then become worried when they don't match up. Skipping and cuddles become rare, and now only babies believe in monsters.

Between eight years and twelve years they also lose that wonderful openness that young children have, and they start to be more secretive and to hold hidden agendas.

The five- to eight-year-old

Our story starts when they are five years of age. They seem so grown up as they stride off in their new school uniform. They can sit, concentrate, mix, communicate clearly and write and read some words. But don't be fooled by this superficial show of maturity, because the five-year-old is still a baby in many ways.

Total dependence

Little children can treat Mum and Dad like lesser beings, but behind the show they are still immensely influenced and dependent on us. The degree of dependence or independence varies greatly from child to child, but young children need us much more than we realise.

They may appear to ignore what we say, but behind this pretence they watch what we do and tune into our beliefs and values. If Dad believes that Elvis is alive and pumping gas on the Gold Coast, they believe the King still lives. If you think the greenhouse effect is caused by cattle passing wind, there's no debate, it's cows farting that does it. Other children and teachers may seed some ideas in their minds, but we parents are still the main source of wisdom.

Even your words get recycled. As you hear them talk to their friends, they might sound like you on a bad day: 'I'm tired of having to tell you'; 'I don't think I can play. I feel a headache coming on.'

At this age, children have few independent thoughts, and you are the main policy maker. For these few years you are seen as infallible. Enjoy this brief moment of power, because it passes all too quickly!

A magic mind

Six-year-olds are fitted with a technicolour imagination. They don't really believe in ghosts and monsters, but when the night is very dark, they worry that something might be out there. The idea of reindeer, chimneys and the North Pole may seem far-fetched, but as it gets close to Christmas, Santa becomes very real.

This blur between fact and fiction can add technicolour to the truth. So a passing car braking hard while the kindergarten class plays outside may become, over the course of the day, a multiple car accident involving the police rescue squad and a fleet of ambulances.

It's important to be aware of this imaginative exaggeration. Behind every exaggeration lies a seed of truth, but sometimes the story is bigger than the seed. If your six-year-old makes claims about his teacher, the story you hear may not be the complete truth. It is wise to first check the facts before you round up a posse of neighbours for a shoot-out with the principal.

Skipping and cuddling

This is a wonderfully unspoiled age of innocence. It is a time when children don't just walk: they skip, wave their arms and bounce with enthusiasm. They are like little lambs that frolic just for the joy of being alive.

It is a magic time when children sit on your knee and snuggle up close. If it's cuddles you are after, this is the age to get your share.

Also, young children are unfazed by nudity. A six-year-old will race around the house wearing nothing more than a whoop of joy. At this age they do what feels right and their minds are unpolluted by adult shame and modesty. Six-year-olds know nothing of apples, serpents and Original Sin.

Open and helpful

Seven-year-olds are remarkably up front, and if you listen you will hear most of what's on their minds. Such is their openness they can't keep a secret, so when they buy your birthday present they have to drop hints – they can't wait until the big day. Make the most of this forthrightness to establish clear lines of communication at this time because, as they get older, they will be less open.

Children of this age work well beside their parents and are usually happy to help. Obviously some requests are more attractive than others: 'Would you like to turn off the television and go to McDonald's?' gets more response than 'Would you like to turn off the television and tidy your bedroom?' This is hardly surprising – they're not stupid.

Too honest

Under-eights know nothing of political correctness. They call things as they see them, and have not yet mastered the almost-honesty of adults. So when a five-year-old spots a fat lady or a one-legged man, they will announce it to the world. They get confused when we tell Grandma her cooking was a cordon bleu extravaganza, because they know Dad thought it was boring mush. They are surprised when we tell Uncle Bill he looks good, because to them he's looking close to expiry. Even when they pass wind, they apologise politely rather than disown the noise.

Likes rules and tells tales

The six-year-old is a miniature bureaucrat who loves rules and regulations. Most six-year-olds enjoy the clear structure of school, where they work quietly and raise a hand before they speak. At this young age classroom regulations are like commandments delivered on tablets from the mount. Even at home they may quote these rules to brothers, sisters and babes in arms.

They are not only interested in rules, but also in their obeyance: 'Please Miss, Jack took Sarah's pencil'; 'Please Miss, Kate's talking again.' But this time of informing on others is short-lived, and by the age of seven or eight it's already uncool to tell on your mates.

Property is a fuzzy notion

The under-eight has little idea about money or value. They can quote the price of a Paddle Pop and jingle coins, but that is the limit of their financial wizardry. If the ball they kick shatters a priceless vase, it is Mum's anger, not the monetary value, that catches their attention.

The idea of ownership is another fuzzy notion. Though most children are reasonably honest, the under eight-year-old is often fitted with remarkably light fingers. Some infants teachers joke that their pupils could do with a strip search at going-home time, as pencils, toys and trinkets seem to slip into pockets.

This immaturity with money and ownership is all part of growing up. Our response to petty pocketing at this age should be low key: just state what you believe happened, register your disapproval and watch out for repetitions.

Lives for the present

A five-year-old has no appreciation of the long-term future. The world they understand is happening now. Once I asked a little boy, 'What do you want to do when you grow up?'

'I don't want to grow up,' he said. 'I would have to drive a car and might not be able to stop it.'

This was a relevant answer for a five-year-old, but by eight years he will see beyond the present and by twelve he'll probably understand the advantage of four-wheel discs with an anti-locking option.

We might explain a complex idea to our under-eights but they won't really understand: 'Grandma got sick, developed pneumonia, went to hospital, died and is now in heaven.'

They can repeat this, but have no understanding of pneumonia, heaven or death and can't grasp the permanent nature of this event. To them Grandma is on a long holiday and may well come back.

Unspoken worries

As a young child, I was always warned about the dangers of germs. At that time we lived near a large hospital for infectious diseases that was bounded on its front by a high wall. Every time my parents drove along the road outside I crouched low in the back of the car and held my breath to protect myself from any germ that might vault over the wall and land on me. It was very real in my mind, and I believed my parents were negligent in subjecting me to such risk. But they never knew that this was troubling me: they just wondered why I was blue and breathless.

Psychiatrists are continually amazed at how five- to eight-year-olds can grasp the wrong end of the stick then worry themselves silly over unimportant things. If Mum and Dad have a major tiff their six-year-old may anticipate a break-up. If Dad is late to pick them up, they may fear abandonment. If Mum is admitted to hospital, they may worry she might die. If their sister develops leukemia, they might believe they are in some way to blame. It can be a confusing time for children, and little minds may worry more than we think.

Similarity of boys and girls

In the early school years, the size, strength and sporting ability of boys and girls are almost the same. While girls are generally more verbal and boys may have more behaviour and learning problems, at this age boys and girls are more similar than they ever will be again.

Both boys and girls wonder about their anatomical differences, but this is an innocent interest without any sexual overtones. At this age boys more often play with boys and girls with girls, but it's okay to mix any way you want.

However, after the age of eight years, growth, development and maturity race ahead, and with this comes a definite segregation of the sexes.

The eight- to twelve-year-old

It's now their eighth birthday and, as the last candle flickers out, they stand at a crossroad in life. Behind them is all the openness, innocence and unspoiled imagination of the young. Ahead lies a more serious world where they must compete and make the grade.

As parents, the years ahead will test both our patience and stamina.

Parents out of power

The under-eights know all about disobedience, but they still see our proclamations as the one and only truth. Sadly, all good things come to an end, and our divine power starts to ebb at seven years. By the time our child is eight, all our words and actions come into question.

Before, you could just lay down the law: 'Because I say so.' Now, you will get poor compliance without some explanation and good reason. In the past, you could tell them El Niño was caused by the French bombs in the Pacific. Now they laugh at your ignorance as they quote their teacher. Teachers are never wrong; mothers often are!

This shift of power takes many parents by surprise. It was never mentioned in the owner's manual: you had always believed that parents were in charge! Now you're not so sure.

The influence of others

The under-eights will spend the majority of their time at home. But after this age you may only see them at the pit stops, as they fuel up ready to hit the circuit again.

Parents lose their monopoly position as other people exert their influence. The soccer coach talks about the dangers of smoking, and now John confronts his puffing dad about fitness, heart attacks and toes dropping off. We have spent eight years teaching politeness, manners and healthy eating, and now the influence of their mates dismantles much of our hard work.

They are now affected by the attitudes of the herd. They watch the 'in' TV programs, wear the right sort of clothes and buy certain brands.

This can be a strange time for parents, where we see less of our children and know they are being influenced by others.

A long-term view of life

The five- to eight-year-old's view of life is strictly in the here and now. But after eight they look into the distance and can see the permanent nature of events. If Grandma were to die, they know she has gone forever and they now grieve like their parents. If a marriage breaks up they realise Mum and Dad have split for life. They can see how they will grow into an adult, and by twelve years some have started to develop major goals.

The silly worries of the younger child have disappeared, but they are replaced by the usual insecurities, fears and paranoia that trouble most people between the age of eight and eighty years.

Competes and compares

The young child will breeze along, not too concerned by their differences and difficulties. But at eight, they start to worry about how others see them. They develop an awareness of looks, learning abilities, body shape, strength, mixing skills and social acceptance.

We can tell our children they are bright, good-looking and wonderful, but they still match themselves against the group. They feel inadequate when they don't make the grade, and with this can come problems of esteem and even depression.

A loss of innocence

Before the age of eight they skipped, cuddled and believed in Santa. Now Santa is silly and skipping is for babies. The only time you will get a cuddle may be when they are almost asleep, ninety-eight per cent unconscious and unable to resist.

If you open the door on a naked nine-year-old they cover everything and protest. Now there is no talk of ghosts, monsters and pretend people: the imagination moved out along with the magic. The once uncomplicated mind has matured to a more adult plane, and with this, the age of innocence has gone.

The school-age smart arse

Beware! You are entering an age where children can verbally out-point you. From now on it's best to avoid arguments, as grown-ups will rarely win.

Children can make a nonsense out of our attempts to be serious:
'Don't bounce on the new lounge suite.'
'I'm not bouncing, just bobbing up and down.'
'Don't annoy your sister.'
'I'm not. She's annoying me.'
One friend opened her washing machine to find it white with tissues. 'Who left these in their pockets?' she asked.

Her nine-year-old looked her in the eyes and replied, 'It couldn't have been me. You know I only use my sleeve.'

They are also perfecting the art of put-downs. You make some earth-shattering observation to which they respond, with a yawn, '*Fascinating*, Dad.' Soon you are told your jokes aren't funny, then your taste in music is geriatric – and that's just the start. It gets worse in adolescence.

School learning and language

There is a big difference between the mothering and spoon-feeding of the infants classes and what happens after the age of eight. From now on the successful students will need to self-motivate, organise and keep on task.

Learning takes a giant leap forward during the years between eight and twelve. The average six-year-old can read single words; by twelve, they can manage simple newspapers and almost this book. For eight- to twelve-year-olds, school is so important that those who have a learning weakness or who can't stick at a task are hurt by failure and suffer in esteem.

The use and understanding of language increases with age. At six years they can cope with a simple concept, for example, 'Why does the sign on the petrol pump say "No Smoking"?' By eight years they understand more complex questions and by twelve years they are fully versed in innuendo, double meaning and the subtle differences that come with a change in tone.

This is also the start of abstract thought, where they take pre-programmed information and use it to create something new outside the program.

Segregation of the sexes

When little boys and little girls start school they enjoy one another's company and are pleased to play together. But after eight, boys tend to play with boys and girls with girls.

The boys often hunt in packs and don't welcome children who are different or out of step. Girls usually play two or three together and are generally more accepting of those who are shy or less popular.

The segregation that starts around eight remains an uneasy part of life until, in adolescence, boys and girls reunite in a more individual way.

Girls in general are easier-going and more mature. Boys have a higher incidence of learning difficulties and over-the-top behaviour. The pubertal growth spurt hits girls before boys, but once growth sets in, boys become physically stronger and more solid.

The five- to eight-year-old: the age of magic and innocence

1. Total dependence
   - totally dependent on parents
   - accepts parents' beliefs without question
   - parents remain the one source of true wisdom
2. A magic mind
   - believes in ghosts, monsters and Santa
   - has a technicolour imagination
   - truth and pretend get blurred
3. Skipping and cuddling
   - skips and frolics like a lamb
   - cuddles, sits on your knee
   - baths together, no worry about nudity

4. Open and helpful
   - communicates openly
   - can't keep a secret
   - likes to help and work with parents
5. Too honest
   - reports things as they see them
6. Likes rules and tell-tales
   - likes to have rules
   - likes to dob in rule breakers
7. Property is a fuzzy notion
   - has little idea about the value of property
   - has no idea about the value of money
   - some innocent petty theft
8. Lives for the present
   - their world is happening today
   - has no understanding of the long-term future
   - cannot understand the permanent nature of death
9. Unspoken worries
   - may get the wrong end of the stick
   - can worry greatly over non-worries
10. True equality of boys and girls
    - size, strength and sporting ability are equal
    - boys and girls play together

The eight- to twelve-year-old: life starts to get serious

1. Parents out of power
   - questions their parents' opinions and values
   - parents are no longer infallible
2. The influence of others
   - influenced by others outside the home
   - starts to follow the herd
3. A long-term view of life
   - starts to plan for the future
   - death and divorce are permanent
   - can now see their life as an adult

4. Competes and compares
   - starts to compare and worry over differences
   - worries over school work, abilities, looks, social skills
   - gets upset if don't match up
5. A loss of innocence
   - locks doors, covers up nudity
   - rations cuddles, stops sitting on your knee
   - stops skipping, stops believing in ghosts and Santa
6. The school-age smart arse
   - verbally too clever for their own good
   - verbally puts down parents
7. School learning and language
   - starts to self motivate and plan school work
   - language and reading become almost adult
8. Segregation of the sexes
   - boys play with boys and girls play with girls
   - girls hit puberty spurt before boys

THREE

Why children behave badly

In my early years of training I was taught that children were created equal and that bad behaviour came from bad parenting. This confused me, particularly when I came across some spaced-out punk couple who had been blessed with an angelic child, then the local vicar, who had an entire terrorist cell operating from his crypt. I finally realised that any parent who had more than one child would know what my teachers had missed: children are not created equal in their behaviour and temperament.

Once it was fashionable to regard differences between children as being a consequence of birth order: there was the dispossessed first child and the competitive middle child. But a child can be easy or difficult, regardless of birth position. I see first children who are so extreme, they set their parents on a life-long course of contraception. In this case no one is dispossessed or competing: the child is just plain impossible.

We have moved a long way from the guilt trips and parent blaming of the past. Instead, in this new millennium a child's behaviour is believed to be a mix of four influences:

1. temperament

2. parenting style

3. reaction to stress and uncertainty

4. the pursuit of attention and power.

Each child starts with a very individual genetic temperament, part of which arrives out of the blue and part of which comes from Mum and Dad. This unique package of temperament is then uplifted or depressed by the actions of us, their parents. It is further altered by security or stress in the child's living environment. Finally, behaviour is driven by the wish for attention and the pursuit of power.

Temperament

Variations in children's temperaments are immense. Children can be easy-going, intense, focused, fidgety, dreamy, distractable, demanding, oppositional, compliant, clingy, fearless, whingeing, dissatisfied, obsessive, disorganised, volatile. Often you get a mix of these qualities, which makes each parent's lot different.

The seeds of temperament are pre-programmed at birth. Look at a tiny infant of three months of age and, even at this early stage, you can start to see what joys lie ahead.

Temperament is the foundation on which we parents build our eighteen-year-long construction project. Some children have movable foundations while other children's foundations are dug so deep in the bedrock they are almost impossible to budge.

Difficult temperaments: the statistics

In the preschool years it is estimated that about 40 per cent of children have a relatively easy temperament, 35 per cent are on middle ground, 15 per cent are quite difficult and 10 per cent are going to be a challenge.

Follow-up studies suggest that the temperament of the preschool years carries through school age with reasonable consistency. If this is true we can expect that about one-third of children will be a breeze, one-third will be manageable and one-tenth will visibly age their parents.

Let's be honest here: there are some extremely challenging children out there. When I asked one mother, 'When did you first know you had a problem?' she answered, 'At birth. He was born by Caesarean section under epidural. When the obstetrician opened me up the little fellow was looking out wide-eyed at him. The obstetrician passed me the baby and said, "This one's going to be interesting." He was right.'

Another mum told me, 'We only once used a baby sitter. When we arrived home she was standing in the hall. "I don't want any money," she said. "I just want out of this house."'

This sounds bad, but it can get even more serious. I have had extreme children who crashed the family car, sold their parents' valuables at a street stall and accidentally burnt down the family home. And you thought you had problems!

Who creates temperament?

I often look at a child and wonder where they got their temperament from. The gentlest of parents can be devastated when they unexpectedly land an out-of-step child. But the difficult child does not always drop out of the blue: they may be very like their mum or dad. Temperament is God-given, but God often has a lot of help from us, the parents.

Mothers ask me with wide-eyed innocence, 'How did I get such an active, non-stop child?' As she talks I watch Dad rock, fidget, jiggle and become distracted by what's outside the window. Others complain their child is impulsive, explosive and has no patience. I ask, 'Is he like anybody you know?' Suddenly the penny drops as they realise he is a mini version of the person they chose to marry! An out-of-step child can arrive out of the blue, but often you don't need to look far to see where they came from.

Troublesome temperaments

There are three temperamental types of children that cause particular pain to parents:

1. oppositional

2. demanding

3. explosive.

When the **oppositional** child is asked to do something, they will look you in the eye and say, 'Make me.' You set a limit and they step over the line as if to say, 'Come on, make my day.' If you say hurry, they go slow. Chores may get done, but everything is an effort. For more information on oppositional behaviour see Chapter 8, page 105.

The **demander** interrogates, invades your space and is at you like a mosquito. 'Can we go now? . . . Is it time to go? . . . When will we go? . . . Let's go.' On a long car trip it's 'When will be get there? . . . Is it much further? . . . Are we there yet?' Demanders never realise how close they come to being put up for adoption or understand why their parents are getting so upset all the time.

The **explosive** child is fitted with a very short fuse. Their sister innocently sits on their Game Boy and the detonation is felt three blocks down the street. These children are like a stick of unstable gelignite: any sudden movement and you get your head blown off. They don't know when to back off or turn the other cheek.

I mention these difficult temperaments not to depress parents but to explain the differences. Even if you have scored an easy, compliant child, don't get too smug, because your luck may not hold out forever. If you have a child with a difficult temperament, don't take it personally: this is when the parenting techniques of this book will be put to the test.

Parenting style

Attention, temperament and environment are all part of the equa-tion, but without a positive parent, nothing will work well. I don't tame children, I change parents, who then get the best out of their individual child.

As I get older, the toddlers I once treated are now adolescents or even adults. Most have done extremely well, but a few still live in the same war zone they occupied when we first met. Many of them started with a challenging temperament that their parents attacked head on. The parents' position was uncompromising: they were going to win this war and take no prisoners. As the battle got bogged down, both sides brought in ever-bigger artillery, until everyone was angry, resentful and oppositional. As I tried to move things along, the parents would say it was the child who had to change – not them. In cases like these, hostility feeds from both sides, and when no one will compromise, soon you are standing in a war-torn country where relationships are wrecked for a generation.

I can't overestimate the importance of getting attitudes right at the start. When children are treated nicely, they treat you nicely. When children know they are loved, they let you know they love you. When children set out on the rails, they generally stay on the rails.

As I observe parents and children interact, some seem so close, natural and in tune, while others are more angular and remote in their relationship. You can sense whether parents have a nurturing style or a negative style, but it's not so easy to put into words what the differences are. There are some things that stand out, though:

- Positive parents communicate warmly with and without words. Words are important but they make close communication with their eyes, tone of voice and body language.

- Positive parents listen, take time, and enjoy doing things with their children. Any human being knows when they are only afforded half of our attention. There is a difference between spending time as an act of penance and *savouring* time together.

- Positive parents use positive discipline. Discipline is not about waiting for a child to misbehave then dumping heavily on them. It is the moulding of behaviour through encouragement and reward. Positive parents establish good patterns, set limits, remain consistent, then catch their children being good.

- Positive parents forgive quickly and restart with a clean slate. It's easy to get angry and stay angry. A child may not openly apologise: they circle the perimeter, hoping we will extend an olive branch. Positive parents quickly pull their children back in close, end the issue and hold no grudges.

- Positive parents instruct with expectation. They transmit instructions with the expectation that things will happen.

- Positive parents see past the problem. Even the most angelic child will get into some pretty silly situations. It is important for parents to look past the end behaviour to see the preceding events and recognise innocence of intent.

- Positive parents watch with interest, pride and wonderment. This is what you see in the eyes of a besotted parent.

- Positive parents see the humour. One day later, you can look back on some of the things your children got up to and laugh. Positive parents keep their humour and their perspective.

On the other hand:

- Negative parents use hostile, critical communication. I would not like to be addressed the way some parents talk to their children. The tone is hostile and there is an expectation that instructions are not going to be obeyed. This confronting, trouble-seeking style creates opposition in a child.

- Negative parents can only see the worst in their children. Most of us see our children better than they are in reality. A negative parent sees nothing but fault and trouble.

- Negative parents show disappointment and resentment. Some parents transmit a feeling that parenting has not lived up to expectation. It's almost as if their children were sent to disturb and intrude upon their enjoyment of life.

- Negative parents focus overly on the bad. Even the worst-behaved child is good for ninety per cent of the time. Negative parents only see the bad ten per cent, which they reinforce with the full focus of their attention.

- Negative parents believe that the child has the problem. It takes two parties to fight and two parties to come to a resolution, but negative parents see the child as causing all the problems. They are reluctant to be part of the process of change themselves.

Reaction to stress and uncertainty

A child's behaviour is intimately entwined with the stress and difficulties of their living environment. The child may not always understand what is going on around them, but they are acutely aware of any tension.

However, parents are often blind to the link between problems at home and their child's poor behaviour. They tell me, 'Our relationship is a mess, but our children know nothing about it'; or 'My husband is about to be retrenched, but our children don't realise how stressed we are'; or 'I'm being treated for major depression, but I pretend I am happy when the kids are around'; or 'We moved across the country to a new job. We have a nice house with lots of space, but for some reason the children seem unsettled'; and 'Grandpa is dying from cancer, but we haven't told the children.'

I have two cocker spaniel pups. These dogs have never attended a university course in counselling but they are totally in tune with feelings. If I am about to leave on a lecture tour they act strangely, hiding behind curtains and becoming extremely unsettled. They are like little children: they don't know what is happening, but they *feel*. Never underestimate the effect of stress, change or parental unhappiness on a child.

How children react

Young children have super-sensitive antennae which pick up on upset and translate it back as a change in behaviour. Most commonly, a child will react to tension by becoming unsettled and ill at ease: they have a vague restlessness, seem unavailable, have upset sleep or their performance at school suffers.

Another reaction they have to stress is anger. Parents start by being upset with each other and the child tunes in to their feelings. The child doesn't know what is going on between Mum and Dad but they don't like what they feel. They react to this stress by digging in their heels, being difficult or dumping on Mum.

This reaction can easily escalate. The parents are struggling with their own emotions; the child picks up on their upset and gives them a blast. The stressed parent reacts to this with anger, and then the child becomes doubly confused. This problem is common where there is relationship stress, family illness, relocation or money worries.

The under-six-year-old may react with clingyness and regression. They pick up on the uncertainty in their environment and grasp tightly to that life belt, their mum. In a family break-up a child knows they have lost one parent and are quite determined they will not lose the other. So they may be reluctant to separate from Mum when she drops them off at school, or they may come to her bed at night.

A few children show their stress by withdrawal. The child feels ill at ease, becomes solitary and quiet and loses enthusiasm for their usual activities. This is most common in the over-eight-year-old. As they withdraw away from us, it is hard to know at which point a normal reaction to stress becomes serious depression. For more information on depression see Chapter 8, page 92.

Whatever the reaction, whether it is restlessness, anger, clinging or withdrawal, these children are shouting at the top of their voices, 'I don't know what you are doing but it hurts.'

What hurts children

For children under the age of eight years parent problems cause most pain. After this children react to troubles at school, problems mixing, learning difficulties and worries about the world. As parents, we can't protect our children from everything, but if we get our own emotional baggage in control we've won half the battle. Unfortunately, there are some hassles that we can't always avoid.

Break-ups

When I was seven I believed in happy-ever-after stories, but now I realise that Cinderella was a fairy tale. Many of today's children live in a war zone: there are no guns or bombs, because the hostilities are taking place within the home.

About one-third of today's relationships will have broken up by the time our children leave school. It's not the break-up that damages the child but the stress before, and the antics that can continue after, the event. These break-ups are going to happen no matter what I do. All I ask is that parents think of the children and handle the inevitable as amicably as is possible.

There is a story of two families who 'lose' a father. In one, a child loses a father to a bitter break-up, following which the parents are full of hate and hurt for years. In the other Dad is killed in a car accident. Psychiatrists looking at this scenario see that a child suffers much more emotional damage from the painful split than they do from the accident. As parents, we can cause much greater harm to our children through our deliberate actions than life's unavoidable accidents can cause. For more information on break-ups and sole parenting, see Chapter 20.

Employment, moves and money

These days employment is less certain, and for many families redundancy is a reality. A change of fortune caused by unemployment can alter the equilibrium in a family, affect everybody's esteem and stress children.

To improve opportunities many couples choose to cut the family ties and move away to a better area of employment. But, like animals, human beings can be destabilised by new surroundings. To make matters worse, in the new environment parents may be feeling emotionally vulnerable, support might be limited and children will feel uneasy.

Even without unemployment or moving, money problems are a major cause of stress for all the family, including children.

Learning and social difficulties

If life were fair all children would be created with equal learning and social abilities. But life is not fair, and not all children do well in or out of the classroom.

Children who aren't doing so well are often acutely aware of the fact. You can tell a child with reading difficulties that they don't have a problem, but they know otherwise. If this child were just slow, they might not feel so bad, but clever children who struggle feel pain and paranoia. No matter how positive we are, children with major learning weaknesses get stressed and may behave badly. For more information on learning difficulties see Chapter 11.

Attention Deficit Hyperactivity Disorder (ADHD) disadvantages about two per cent of our school-age population and upsets many good parents. These children underfunction for intellect and are out of step behaviourally. Their behaviour can be many times more difficult than any parent or teacher deserves. For more information on ADHD, see Chapter 12.

Some of the stroppiest young children I see have language problems. When children can't express or understand what is going on in their lives they can show immense frustration. Some stoics try twice as hard, others withdraw, some to the edge of autism, and some get angry and kick heads. It's not our fault, but it's often we who end up with the headache. For more information on language problems, see Chapter 11.

It is cool to be an out-of-step extrovert at school, but it's uncool to be shy, socially uncomfortable, obsessive, odd or clumsy. Shy children feel stressed, kids that appear odd are teased or treated like outcasts and clumsy children are excluded from games.

Some children with these difficulties keep going without complaint, while others act out their frustrations with bad behaviour. Stressed children clown in the classroom and take their upset home to dump on those they love. Such behaviour is not the fault of the parent but it still lands on them.

Attention and power

Whatever a child's temperament, the parenting style or the living environment, annoying behaviour is always to do with gaining attention and power. The main way parents and teachers mould behaviour is through the giving and withdrawing of attention. For some children, power is an important motivator, but not for all.

Attention

Every child loves to receive good attention, but when this is not on offer, they will try to attract any sort of attention that's going. Say Mum and Dad are having an important discussion. John feels excluded from their attention and tries to get in on the act. He asks a question but this is ignored. He interrupts and is pushed aside. Now he turns on the TV, torments the dog and imitates fart sounds. Mum and Dad close the conversation, become intensely irritated and John is rewarded with 100 per cent attention. This is poor-quality attention, but it's better than being ignored.

We shape our children's behaviour by boosting the good patterns with attention and reward while discouraging the bad by pulling back on our attention. This giving and taking of attention is the basic principle of effective discipline.

Every day we see how attention affects behaviour. A second-rate author wants to get their book mentioned in the media. They create a bogus beat-up, the media respond and sales increase. The behaviour is rewarded and more books will follow. Or a rock star dyes his hair orange, applies lipstick and wears fishnet stockings: with his new image he now fills the stadium. He gets so much attention, he keeps on cross-dressing. For rock stars, authors and children, attention is a powerful motivator.

In children it is the most powerful way to steer both good and bad behaviour.

Power

Some children are heavily into power politics, while others are much more easy going. Power play involves testing limits, dragging feet, arguing and opposition.

You draw the line; they see how far they can push you before you respond. You ask if they will do a simple chore; they respond with provisos and conditions. You say it's black; they say it's white. This power play involves having the last word, wanting more, acting the smart arse and just being difficult with non-compliance.

Attention and power are major factors in difficult behaviour. And that's what the next six chapters are all about.

34

A final word

The foundation of behaviour is in the genes, which is moulded by stress in a child's environment and the need for attention and power.

And then there is parenting. Since Spock's day it has been wrong to be a permissive parent, but research does not agree. Ideally, every child should have clear, consistent limits and discipline. But many times more important is the influence of warm, caring parents who enjoy being with their children. An upbringing which is warm, clear and consistent is the first choice but warm and permissive parents come a very close second.

Why children behave badly

1. Temperament
   - the volatile temperament – 'the stick of gelignite'
   - the demanding temperament – 'the KGB interrogator'
   - the oppositional temperament – 'Come on, make my day.'
   - the introvert temperament
   - the obsessive temperament
   - the disorganised temperament
   - the fearful temperament
   - the fearless temperament
2. Parenting style
   - nurturing, encouraging, positive
   - hostile, critical, negative
3. Reaction to stress and uncertainty
   - little children may not understand; they react to what they feel
   - older children understand and feel
   - common stresses
     - marriage conflict and break-ups
     - employment, moves, money
     - illness, parent depression

  – school stress, bullying
  – learning and social difficulties
  – worries about the world
4. Attention and power
  ■ the giving of attention encourages a behaviour
  ■ the withholding of attention discourages a behaviour
  ■ power play involves limit testing, foot dragging, smart-arse behaviour, opposition

The positive side of discipline

A n eight-year-old has a rush of blood to the head and tidies her bedroom. We inspect her handiwork and reward her with enthusiasm and some extra privilege. With this pay-off, a clean bedroom will happen again tomorrow (and pigs might fly, I hear you say).

There is one important principle that steers our children's behaviour: *a behaviour that pays off for the child will usually be repeated; a behaviour that does not pay off will disappear.* This is the basic rule that allows parents to increase the good and decrease the bad. All it takes is a wise choice as to the behaviours that pay off.

The pay-offs we use are:

- soft rewards (enthusiasm, encouragement, noticing, words, body language)

- hard rewards (time, privileges, food or other treats, money)

- cumulative rewards (star charts, tokens, points).

Soft rewards

Recently I dined at a top Sydney restaurant. The food and service were so good I called the head waiter over to give specific praise to the chef and waiting staff. Later, with an expectant smile, the waiter approached and handed me the bill. My wife suggested I should leave a large tip, so at this point I took the opportunity to explain to her about soft and hard rewards. She listened graciously, then summed it up quite simply: 'An interesting theory, but you are still cheap and mean.'

On that occasion, my wife was probably right, but never underestimate the power of soft and subtle pay-offs, especially when it comes to children. Though these are of most importance to the under-fives, their influence is immense right through life.

Catch them being good

If humans are to continue doing good, their good needs to be noticed and reinforced. One of the greatest traps for parents is to become so negative that we see nothing but the bad: 'Don't annoy your sister'; 'Leave the dog alone'; 'You were such a pain at the shops'; 'What a mess'; 'You're so rude.'

Positive parents turn this around and use their words to boost the good: 'I like it when you both play so well', 'Rover thinks that's fun'; 'Gosh, you were such a help at the supermarket'; 'Have the cleaners been here?'; 'I like it when we talk together like this.'

The power of body language

Every day I am asked 100 times, 'How are you?' Those who enquire have no interest in my health, happiness or emotional wellbeing; their greeting is as empty as a pre-programmed tape recording. Words can be meaningless but we sense genuine interest by attitude and body language.

Children know we are pleased by the tone of our voice, the way we look, the twinkle in our eye and the things we whisper. This subtle form of encouragement is one of the most powerful tools of discipline.

Be specific

School-age children are unmoved by unfocused, over-used encouragement. We blandly say, 'Good girl', 'Well done', 'Clever boy', which is about as genuine as the parrot who announces, 'Who's the pretty boy?' Older children may even react badly to these unfocused comments and turn our words back on us: we say, 'That's good' and they reply, 'No, it sucks'; 'You're looking great' – 'No, I'm not'; 'I like your story' – 'No, it's boring.'

I sympathise with this response. Often I bust myself to put on some special fundraising talk. I know it has gone well but a week later an impersonal letter arrives that might have been written by a computer before the talk. I know when people are genuinely appreciative – it's when the thank you is personal, specific and picks up on some part of my message. 'Dr Green, I like your ideas about refocusing on the good and being specific in what we say.'

Children also need our encouragement to be specific. 'Gosh, this room is not only tidy, you've even polished your desk'; 'In your story, I like the boy character who saved the ship'; 'I really like the way the sun lights up this side of your painting.'

Hard rewards

Now we are entering the real world where humans encourage action through gifts, favours, privileges, money and bribes. Hard rewards are particularly useful for the older child, adults and Olympic officials.

Some experts get their underwear in a knot debating the difference between rewards and bribes. A reward consolidates a good behaviour, coming almost as a bonus after the event. A bribe is arranged beforehand and if there is no performance there is no payout. We all prefer to use rewards rather than bribes, but sometimes the difference is academic. If what you are doing works, just call it a reward and we'll all be happy.

Choosing the right hard reward

This author might be motivated by money, a meal or some exotic, coronary-clogging ice cream. But I wouldn't move a muscle for the latest Spice Girl CD or a front-row seat at a boxing match. All humans are motivated by different means, and as parents we must find the magic motivator for our child.

When I set up a behaviour program with parents, we first list the rewards that are likely to grab their child's interest. If we don't tailor our program to that one child, what follows will always fall flat.

The most effective rewards for eight- to twelve-year-olds are

■ time

■ privileges

- little gifts

- food

- money.

Time

We often forget that time is one of our most valuable possessions and is also one of our most appreciated rewards. Your son has stuck at his homework and done it well: 'Would you like me to help fix your bike?'; 'Fancy going for a splash down in the pool?'; 'Would you like me to run you over to Steve's house?'

Privileges

These are great motivators for the six- to eighteen-year-old. When things have gone well, they are allowed some extra bit of the action. This may be time on the telephone, more television, a later bed time, access to the computer, being excused from doing a usual chore, choosing dinner, having a friend to stay, picking where you go for a meal out.

Food

It may come as a disappointment to the animal admirers, but sea lions don't do tricks because they like to impress humans. They perform because each action is rewarded with a mouthful of raw fish. Purists dislike the idea of bribing children with stuff that rots teeth, but this technique has been popular since it was first invented by grandmothers. People may object, but if food works for all other animal trainers, it must be worth a try with children.

Of course, we can reward with the healthiest of health foods, but children tend to value these less than foods high in sugar, preservatives, additives, colours and flavours, especially if they come with the latest in movie merchandise.

Food is mostly a motivator with the under eights, but it can focus interest at any age. I for one can always be bought by the offer of

a good meal. With your children, don't go over the top but if some mouth-watering snack tunes in the obedience antennae, it can't be all that bad.

Money

This may be the root of all evil, but it sure grabs the attention of some children. Young Australians are created in two sorts: the emerging entrepreneurs who are heavily into the cash economy and the philanthropists who function on some higher plane.

Money becomes of increasing interest after the age of eight years, and if your child is a dollar lover, you may use the filthy stuff to reward compliance.

By ten years a small sum can be given for each completed task or you may add a productivity bonus to their pocket money. With the bonus, you give the base salary and this can be doubled in reward for extra effort without complaint. For a more immediate reward, a silver coin can be put in a jar to register completion.

There is one major drawback when you reward with money: it leaves you open to extortion. A task that was worth twenty cents this week may be worth thirty cents the next, and soon there is out-of-control inflation. So a productivity bonus should be capped at an appropriate level. Small cash payments can be varied and mixed with other rewards to prevent them becoming a God-given right.

Cumulative rewards

As children get older they can appreciate rewards that are more abstract and less immediate. Now they can visualise the payout from stars, points or tokens.

Star charts

Stars allow us to focus a child's attention on specific behaviours that need to be changed. The chart is a simple piece of paper, ruled into rows across the page and columns down. The column on the left-hand margin lists the days of the week and the row across the top the behaviours we wish to target.

Each time the behaviour is achieved we stick a star in the appropriate square. If there is compliance, soon a galaxy of stars illuminates the page and this is rewarded with some prearranged payout. The chart is put in a place of prominence, usually stuck to the fridge door. As fridges are opened continually, the average child can monitor their progress throughout the day.

Stars only work with children who are old enough to recognise what they represent. They have no meaning for the under-four-year-old.

You also need to remember that stars create maximum interest in the first week, less in the second and soon the star burns out, leaving a black hole.

Stars: the behaviours to target
The targets we star must be clear-cut and easily achievable. It's pointless expecting a child to 'be good all day', or to 'not annoy

your sister'. A turnaround of this magnitude is reserved for faith healers, miracle workers and saints.

I use stars to highlight two or more simple behaviours; for example, brushes teeth, makes bed, does dishes, ready for school on time.

Stars can also be used when there are problems of bladder training. A dreamy five-year-old leaves things too late, which results in little leaks. Using the chart we focus all attention on short periods of dryness. If dry from the moment they wake until breakfast time, they get a star. From breakfast to mid morning break – a star. From break to lunch, to mid afternoon, to dinner, to bedtime – the stars continue.

Some use stars to motivate bed wetters, but this has little success. When children are asleep they are not thinking of stars.

We can also use the star system to treat children who still soil their pants (see Chapter 8, page 114). First you must ensure your child is not constipated, then use stars in a step-by-step way.

The first goal is to get them to sit for five minutes after breakfast, after school and after dinner. Each sit is recognised with a star. Once sitting is established the focus now moves to using the toilet. If on any occasion a pooh pops out we give great praise and the appropriate square is coloured in. Finally, the focus moves to being clean from dawn to dusk with four gold stars for a soil-free day.

The token system

This is a popular technique that takes an impossibly big task and divides it into small manageable units. It is based on the same principle as my Frequent Flyer points. My favourite airline wishes to encourage a certain behaviour (loyalty to Qantas) so I receive 700 points each time I fly from Sydney to Brisbane. These points have no value but I know that if I keep producing the desired behaviour (flying Qantas) the individual points will eventually be rewarded with a free flight. After a year of this correct behaviour I get a special treat, like a holiday in Alice Springs.

Tokens in the classroom
A child with Attention Deficit Hyperactivity Disorder (ADHD) has great difficulty sustaining attention in the busy classroom. They can

be motivated by a promise of time on the computer, for example, but even with this carrot they can't concentrate long enough to earn the reward. Our goal is to increase that child's time on task by focusing on small, achievable periods of good concentration.

The teacher breaks the day into ten-minute periods, and each period on task is acknowledged with a token. These are simply a bead, button or piece of chalk that is placed in a glass. When ten tokens have been earned, this is rewarded by time on the computer.

Tokens and car travel

Many parents dread the drama of long-distance car travel:

'He hit me.'

'She's looking out my window.'

'He's taking all the space.'

'Are we there yet?'

You buy books and games and even place a large barricade of well-secured luggage between the combatants but the pain continues. Now try a token system. For every fifteen minutes of peace a token is dropped in a cup and this adds up to a payout of money or a special treat at the next fuel stop. Tokens won't turn a terrorist into an angel, but they are more appropriate than deep sedation or a straitjacket. See also Chapter 8.

Points and money

Good behaviour can be encouraged by a simple system of points or money. Feeding the dog gets one point or ten cents. Bedtime without complaint, two points or twenty cents. A tidy room at 6pm gets three points or thirty cents.

When the points reach a certain number, this represents a special treat. When the money gets to a certain total it can be used to buy some much-wanted piece of junk.

Purists dislike the thought of buying good behaviour, but if it works and gets you off your Valium, I won't object.

Every child has their price

Parents often tell me that none of my suggestions will motivate their child. But I believe every human has their price. I expect if you placed a big enough sheaf of crisp new bank notes in the hand of a twelve-year-old, they might listen. I expect if a tip-truck were to dump 1000 Mars Bars in your front drive, most five-year-olds might show some interest.

It's up to us to work out what we can afford and sustain. Fortunately, for most children the major motivator is the subtle system of attention, noticing, time, interest and specific appreciation.

A final word

Start with the basic rule: a behaviour that pays off for the child will be repeated. Then it's up to us to find the pay-off that suits the individual. The secret of positive discipline is to tailor-make the reward to the individual child. But never underestimate the importance of soft, subtle encouragement. To put this into practice see Chapter 8.

This chapter was about the positive side of discipline. However, we can encourage all we like, but there are times we need to take a stand. Punishment also has its place, and that's what you will find in Chapter 5.

The positive side of discipline

1. Soft rewards
   - tone of voice
   - appropriate words
   - eye contact
   - touch
   - enthusiasm
   - noticing
   - genuine interest
   - be specific with praise

2. Hard rewards
   - time
     - working together
     - playing together
     - taking them somewhere
   - privileges
     - telephone
     - computer
     - television
     - later bed time
     - excused a chore
     - a friend to stay over
   - food
     - a treat
     - dessert
     - choose from a menu
     - choose take away
     - choose a meal out
   - money
     - coins put in a jar
     - saving for a purchase
     - productivity bonus
     - costed system for chores
3. Cumulative rewards
   - star charts
     - for target behaviours
     - for daytime wetting
     - for school-age soiling
   - the token system
     - to increase attention
     - to soothe car travel
   - points and money
     - to focus on specific behaviour

Punishment without pain

B y this point in the book it will be clear that discipline is based on encouragement and reward. There is, however, a small place for punishment, but it is punishment without pain. We don't hit or hurt children. Instead we punish using things like

- our tone of voice
- switching off attention
- active ignoring
- time out
- withdrawing privileges
- grounding.

You might also want to try setting up a system of penalties, but these can backfire.

The tone of disapproval

If your poodle piddles on the carpet or your basset barks all night, who arc you going to call? Barkbusters! And these dog trainers will start by telling you, 'Use fewer words, but more tone.' You don't explain to your barking dog that your neighbour is on Prozac for a nervous disorder and it would be good if he kept quiet. You look him in the eye and sternly say, 'Bah!'

Now, I am not suggesting we get Barkbusters to sort out our children, but tone transmits more message than a chapter of carefully chosen words.

Switching off attention

Children thrive when they live in a home filled with interest and interaction, where they get plenty of positive attention. We know that giving attention is the greatest reward, so it follows that cutting attention is a potent punishment.

A six-year-old is being tickled and bounced on Mum's knee. In a burst of innocent enthusiasm he headbutts Mum in the mouth.

As the pain rises you could explode or explain the dangers of horseplay. But it is more effective to briefly register your hurt then walk away. The child feels the cool change from full attention to total ignoring. This registers your disapproval and will encourage more care the next time.

A showing-off ten-year-old calls Mum an idiot.

You could give a lecture full of biblical quotes about respect for one's parents. You could go psycho, or you could simply state, 'It upsets me when you talk like that,' then walk away, cutting all attention for a short period.

Active ignoring

When a defiant child is hell-bent on confrontation, it's a hard call to ignore. Active ignoring allows us to take a step sideways yet remain in control. With this technique, you stay calm, make your point, disengage and then return.

The ten-year-old stands nose to nose, daring Mum to discipline. You quietly repeat your request, walk away, straighten the curtains, pour yourself a cup of coffee, then return to restate your position in a matter-of-fact way. Active ignoring sidesteps a stand-off, gives space and signals that we are not going to be manipulated.

Time out

This is one of the most useful weapons in our armoury. Time out has a double impact: first it punishes by withdrawing the child from positive attention, then it provides the space to cool off an over-heated situation. Time out is effective from age one to eleven years. It allows us to put a lid on escalation and to sidestep a stand-off.

The young child is moved calmly to a bedroom or a time-out chair. The older child is expected to take themselves. It is useful to have a trial run in a time of peace, to prepare for when the technique is used in earnest. The period of exclusion is calculated as approximately one minute for each year of age, but parents have to find the time that best suits their child.

Time out is signalled by a statement, a sign or taking the five-year-old by the hand. If they refuse we move to plan B and use techniques such as counting to three, active ignoring or giving a choice.

If they call out, this is ignored. If they ask whether the time is up, don't rise to the bait – set a cooking timer and let it be the adjudicator. If they come out early, the clock goes back to the start.

At the end of time out, briefly restate your case but don't heap guilt or demand an apology. Then forgive fully and start afresh with a clean slate.

Time out for toys

Another use of time out is to withhold toys, television and computers from feuding children who won't share.

Jack wants 'Heartbreak High', Jill wants 'Home and Away', and as they squabble no one sees anything. Mum issues a warning, then the television is put in time out. Switch off the set, start the cooking timer and, when fifteen minutes is up, start again.

The boys Arnold and Sylvester both want GI Joe and they are prepared to go through a bloody military campaign to gain possession. Here Mum intervenes, puts the plastic marine in time out, and starts the timer. Ten minutes later the battlefield is quiet, GI returns to the front line and hopefully there is some compromise.

Withdrawing privileges

Good behaviour is rewarded with privileges and older children can be punished by the removal of privileges. Removing privileges can make children angry, so don't remove too much, and keep the sentence short.

Your eight-year-old annoys Grandma, and in the heat of the moment you say, 'No television for a month!' The child gasps at the harshness of the sentence and thinks, 'Let's find the old lady and get my money's worth.' Then over the next four weeks they nag, promise to be good and interrogate every day, leaving Mum the one who has been severely punished.

When removing privileges keep it fair and keep it short. They might miss the first half of a TV program, have no television or telephone that night, no dessert or bedtime comes half an hour earlier.

Removing privileges is effective, but never issue a threat you are not prepared to carry through. It's pointless saying, 'I'll cancel your party,' when the cake is bought, friends are being scrubbed up ready to attend and you have no intention of pulling the plug.

Grounding

In American sitcoms, parents often ground their troublesome teens. Hank is late home from the ball game and misses the Thanksgiving turkey; Dad looks perplexed and declares him grounded for a month.

This is mostly a discipline for older children, but at any age we can put on our American accents and ban sleepovers, keep them in at night, or prevent them from attending some entertainment.

A more flexible technique moves from the fixed period of punishment and ties the grounding to the completion of some work. They are still grounded but this will be lifted once the bedroom is cleaned, the weeds removed from the front flowerbed or reparations made to the one they have wronged. This gives children the option of paying their dues quickly or dragging their feet. If they refuse to deliver the goods they remain on the ground.

Penalties

Every day my life is a minefield of consequences and penalties. I don't put petrol in my car – I have to walk to work. I drive too fast – I get a speeding ticket. I annoy the butcher – I get tough meat. I don't pay the electricity bill – the lights go out.

By school age, children are members of this same world and need to feel the consequences and penalties that go with membership. You don't wear your bike helmet – the bike is locked up for two weeks. You don't brush your teeth – lollies are banned and water is your drink. You stick chewing gum on the dog – no gum in the house for one month.

Consequences are part of life, and school-age children need to understand them. Penalties are slightly different: they usually involve removing possessions or money. And here you can hit a lot of trouble – human beings get mighty stroppy when you start taking their stuff.

You set up a point or money system that rewards good behaviour. They have tried so hard they have almost enough to buy a much-wanted CD. Now, on the last day, the exuberant one bounces off the settee and lands softly on the family cat. The cat and Mum scream, and then half the promised points are removed. Now you have a very angry child, mother and cat.

Most of our star, token and money systems should give for the good but don't subtract for the bad. Penalties are possible, but it's usually not worth the aftershock.

One penalty technique that encourages the positive is to start with ten points, then add two for the good and deduct one for the bad. With this it's hard to hit a negative balance.

Some parents discourage bad language by penalising with fines. When a colourful word slips out, twenty cents is docked from the next pocket money. This works well when the cash reserves are high, but when close to losing all, you may hear words that no amount of money could buy.

The three-strike system is used by some schools. A disruptive child starts each class with three lives. These can be shown as three cardboard stars sitting on the desk, a tally on the edge of the blackboard or three strokes on a sheet of paper. For each indiscretion, one life is quietly removed. If there are none at the end of the lesson, they must sit for five minutes before release.

Hitting, smacking, beating

These days, only outcasts would suggest a smack as suitable punishment for children. International organisations, local dignitaries and most professionals are united in making child care a hit-free zone.

While this is a worthy viewpoint, it has more credibility with library-bound academics than stressed parents at the battle front of child care. From my experience every parent has resorted to hitting at some time. But there is a great difference between the occasional limit-registering tap and the violence of a hostile, disturbed home.

Does smacking work anyway? In easy kids, smacking may get some response, but so do all the other techniques, so it is unnecessary. In difficult, defiant children, smacking doesn't work and it can be downright dangerous because it can lead to escalation. You smack, they defy you. You hit harder, they say, 'Damn you.' You wallop, and soon there is anger, resentment, hate and a wrecked relationship.

Besides, when do you stop smacking? Do you wait until they are bigger, quicker or more violent than you? And then what's the alternative?

I always ask parents why they smack, to which dads often say, 'It's the way my father brought me up and it did me no harm.'

I then ask, 'Is your dad still alive?'

'Yes,' they reply.

'Do you see much of him?'

'Well, not exactly.'

'Why not?'

To which they often answer, 'We have nothing in common.'

Wars start with a show of force that escalates into bloodshed. The United Nations may keep the peace but the force has resolved nothing. It takes generations for damaged relationships to repair.

I don't support the groups who wish to imprison parents and teachers who smack, but it does not mean I encourage violence. School-age children should not be smacked. There are much better ways to discipline and force leads to greater problems.

A final word

Punishment is not about smacking, locking in a bedroom or grounding for a month. We register our disapproval by the use of tone, switching off our attention, time out and withdrawing privileges. Our children may dislike punishment but they enjoy knowing where they stand and that we care enough to care what they do.

For advice on putting these punishments into practice see Chapter 8.

Punishment without pain

1. Tone
    - few words, more tone
2. Switching off attention
    - ignore
    - walk away
    - switch off
3. Active ignoring
    - disengage, move away, then re-engage
    - exerts control without escalation

4. Time out
   - to punish
   - to cool off
   - for TV, or toys
5. Withdrawing privileges
   - television
   - early bedtime
   - no dessert
   - no friends to sleep over
6. Grounding
   - for a fixed period
   - until a chore is completed
7. Penalties
   - point system
   - money system
   - three strikes
8. Hitting and smacking
   - with easy children there are much better techniques
   - with difficult children it doesn't work and is dangerous

The dos and don'ts of discipline

Now it's time to move on from general principles and get specific. This chapter will repeat much of the information already covered. The aim is to condense the techniques of the previous chapters into a useable form.

If you have had enough of basic theories, skip this and move straight to Chapter 8. There you will find how these ideas work with the common everyday behaviours of school age.

Children need routine, structure and consistency

Human beings are happiest with structure and when we know where we stand. Even in adulthood much of our behaviour is conditioned and quite automatic, a bit like Pavlov's technique of conditioning dogs to dribble at dinner time. Whether we call it conditioning, doggie discipline or the importance of routine, children behave best with consistent structure.

In the morning our children get two wake-up calls, they rise, wash, make their bed, dress, have breakfast, feed the canary, pack their bags and board the bus.

In the evening, after the meal is finished, they take the dishes to the sink, put the jam in the fridge, then think about homework. Then they shower, get into pyjamas, drink their Milo, brush their teeth, choose a book and go to bed.

We are not promoting bureaucratic rigidity, but routine, structure and consistency are the first steps to successful discipline.

Children need rules

We don't want to run our homes like the army, with every action governed by 100 regulations, but we need a sensible framework of rules. These should be drawn up in advance when the situation is calm – not in the heat of battle.

Rules should be simple, fair, few in number and clearly understood: 'There will be no eating snacks just before your evening meal. You may bounce on the trampoline, not on our new lounge suite. You don't interrupt your sister while she is doing her homework.'

When a rule is challenged, it should be clearly restated and then enforced. Parents must allow some flexibility, but no amount of a child's nagging can change the referee's decision. A rule is made, a child is reminded, action follows.

Communication: get their attention

Whether you are training dolphins at Marine World, lions at the circus or children in your home, nothing will happen until you get their attention. Turn off the television, wait until the dog stops barking then transmit your message.

Look them in the eye and give instructions, clearly, simply and step by step. Mumbling, nagging, shouting and burying the message in words will get you nowhere. If your child is not one of the stubborn members of the species ask for feedback to ensure the message has been taken on board.

Try to make positive statements, not negative instructions. Instead of saying, 'Don't forget to wash your hands,' say, 'Wash your hands so they will be clean for tea.' Otherwise, life becomes a constant barrage of don'ts and negatives. The secret to communication is eye contact, simple positive words, enthusiasm and step-by-step instruction.

Ignore the unimportant

As parents we can't help ourselves – our child waves a fragment of red rag and we charge like a wounded bull. If the plan is to maintain your blood pressure at a life-preserving level, please try to ignore unimportant irritations. If they blow a raspberry, slurp their drink or a pea falls to the floor, ask yourself, 'Does this really matter?' Successful parents take a step back and only engage in the big battles.

Know what triggers behaviour

There are certain events that are dynamite to discipline: parties, tiredness, living with in-laws, visits from school friends, sickness, long car journeys and changes of routine. We can't always avoid these, but it is easier to cope when we are prepared for problems before they hit.

Make good behaviours pay off

The basic law of behaviour modification states, 'A behaviour that pays off for the child will be repeated; a behaviour that brings no advantage to the child will disappear.' If we reward the right behaviour it should happen more frequently, and by ignoring what's undesired, it should go away.

Unfortunately, it is just as easy to encourage the bad behaviour as the good. A five-year-old says, 'Bum.' We make a fuss and soon it's 'Bum, bum, bum, pooh!' Parents must take a step back and be sure it is the good we are encouraging, not the bad.

Use encouragement and rewards

Good behaviour is encouraged with soft rewards (praise, enthusiasm, interest, parental pride), hard rewards (money, food, special privileges) and cumulative rewards (stars, points, tokens). Though privileges, tokens (and even bribes) have a place, the most effective way to mould behaviour is through our voice, eyes and interest. Never underestimate the power of encouragement through these soft, subtle rewards.

Democracy without debate

When it comes to democracy, the under-fives can be told what they will do, the five- to eight-year-olds should be given some explanation and the eight to twelves need some say in their own destiny. Democracy is commendable but it can be abused by these over-verbal mini lawyers. Be respectful but don't be manipulated with arguments and debates. In these, parents never come out on top; it just shortens our lives. Make your point, state the limit, act – don't argue.

Avoid escalation

When we get irritated with our children it is easy to lose the plot and escalate every unimportant behaviour. Try to stay calm, use a matter-of-fact voice and repeat your instructions like a broken gramophone record. Children generate enough heat without us adding fuel to the fire.

Avoid last-straw explosions

It's a miserable, wet day, the children are stuck inside and they are at their most irritating. After a long series of annoying events, one final straw drops and snaps the camel's back. You blow a gasket and your child looks surprised.

I might ask them what happened, and they'd reply, 'Mum went ballistic and I was grounded for a week.'

Try to avoid last-straw explosions like this. Good mums and dads keep a check on behaviour throughout the day and give good warning before the straw hits the humpy bit.

Look at the start, not the end

Recently there was a crisis with one of my Attention Deficit Hyperactivity Disorder (ADHD) children who was referred with a request for an urgent brain scan. His school principal reported that the child had taken to beating his head against a wall, and in this man's twenty years of teaching, this suggested a psychiatric disturbance or brain damage.

On face value this was bizarre behaviour, but nobody had looked at the events that led to the incident. My patient was playing happily when he was deliberately taunted by the school bully. With the over-reaction that is part of ADHD, he rose to the bait and soon was out of control. A teacher who came to the rescue threatened and blamed our innocent boy, which sent him over the top. The principal was summoned and further fanned the flames, the boy became hysterical and, in total exasperation, he hit his head against a wall.

This head banging was not a sign of severe disturbance or brain damage. It was the end point of an avoidable sequence of events. Those who needed treatment were the bully who started it, the teacher who blamed and the principal who lacked the insight to back off.

When analysing behaviour, always look at the beginning, not the end. A gentle puppy would never want to hurt its owner, but if frightened or teased, it may bite. The puppy is not to blame; it is those who upset and mishandle that deserve the punishment.

Use 'I' statements, not 'you' statements

It is possible to say the same thing in two ways, and each will get a different response. If I use an 'I' statement, it transmits how I feel. If I use a 'you' statement, it implies that you are being criticised.

When a child annoys us it is the behaviour we dislike, not the child. It may seem trivial but where possible change 'you' to 'I'.

'You are always hurting your sister' becomes 'I get upset when there's so much fighting.'

'You've ruined the outing for all of us' becomes 'I am upset when we have to come home early.'

'You are such a rude boy' becomes 'It makes me unhappy when I hear that talk.'

'I' statements are valuable when you wish to register upset but do not want to get into an argument. The aim is to make a brief statement of how you feel and quickly move away from the battle front.

Punishment has a place

Though the predominant part of discipline comes through boosting good behaviour, there is also a place for punishment. If you have laid down the rules, clearly stated the limits and given a warning, it's now time to act. The most effective punishments are described in Chapter 5.

When possible, warn before you punish and explain your action. Punishment should be of short duration, have a clear end and be followed by forgiveness.

The danger of confrontation

I sometimes see such hostility, hate and resentment in families that I can do little to help. Often a difficult, defiant child clashes with confronting, forceful parents and this starts a war where there are no winners.

Parents are strong, clever people and there is no doubt that we sail in a battleship with bigger guns than those of our children. If we choose to use all our fire power, we can blast them out of the water, but this settles nothing.

Parents are under pressure to be tough. When they have a difficult child they may feel they are being criticised due to the common attitude that firmer parenting is the only solution. In the street, people mumble under their breath, 'That child needs nothing more than a good boot up the backside.' Many families have given that boot, only to find themselves in a conflict of immense proportion.

The history of the world consists of wars, power struggles, wars and more wars. Someone fires a bullet, a hundred come back. They shoot off a shell and a thousand are returned. They drop a bomb and bigger bombs come back. Now you are standing in Bosnia and it will take generations before families can relate closely again. Parents do have the fire power, but for the sake of relationships I urge you to sidestep rather than to confront.

Sidestepping confrontation

When locked in a nose-to-nose confrontation our instinct is to increase the force. This produces a battle of wills, two angry parties, opposition, resentment and damage to relationships. All parents, particularly those with a defiant child, need to learn how to sidestep a stand-off. There are eight well-tried techniques:

1. keep calm

2. state the rule

3. count to three

4. active ignoring

5. time out

6. give a choice

7. use 'I' statements

8. use humour or diversion.

Keep calm

It is difficult to stay cool when a defiant school-ager is daring you to discipline. But if you increase the heat, things will escalate out of control.

One of the best methods to prevent a boil-over is called 'the broken gramophone record' approach. You tell the ten-year-old to get in their bath.

'No way.'

Normally you would respond with all guns blazing, but today you stay cool and be a calm, persistent gramophone record. 'It's bath time ... Bath time now ... It must be almost bath time ... Time for a bath.'

Politicians, talk-show hosts and parents must all appear to be in control. We cease to have credibility when we lose control.

State the rule

Quoting a rule helps to depersonalise an argument. My local council places a large pole just outside my window.

I am fuming with anger as I meet the chief surveyor. 'This is ridiculous,' I say.

'But Dr Green, under council by-law 21, subsection D . . .'

I explode, but all I hear is, 'Sorry, Dr Green, under council by-law 21, subsection D . . .'

With children rules must be fair and fully understood before the event.

'John, it's 8pm and 8pm is bath time.'

'But Mum!'

'Bath and bed are 8pm. You know the rule!'

Count to three

When you were a six-year-old your granny would ask you once, ask you again, then count slowly to three. Usually by two there was instant obedience. Counting may be an old technique, but it's a wonderful way to defuse a situation and allow time to back off.

'John, it's time for your bath.'

. . .

'It's eight o'clock. You know the rule.'

. . .

'One,' wait five seconds, 'Two,' wait five seconds, etc.

Counting can be used from about three years to twelve years. At eighteen it might look a bit out of place: 'John, bring in the keys of the Volvo . . . One, two, three!'

Active ignoring

This is one of the simplest ways to sidestep in a stand-off. John still refuses to go to his bath. Mum has counted and stayed cool but he stands firm and dares her to make the next move. Active ignoring will stop you being beaten by deliberate defiance and challenge. Calmly disengage, go to the kitchen, pour yourself a drink, take some deep breaths and return as if nothing had happened.

'Now where are we – yes, it's time for your bath.'

This gives a moment for reflection and space. John sees that Mum is in the driving seat, able to steer, accelerate and brake as she wishes. It gives an opportunity to save face, start again and compromise.

Time out: separating the warring parties

You can be calm, have your rules and your counting techniques, but there comes a time when things are heading seriously out of control. Once behaviour gets past a certain point, there is no place for reason. This is where we need to back off and get some space. Now we use time out.

Time out allows a deteriorating situation to be defused by briefly removing the child from all attention and audience. You can use a quiet corner, a time-out chair, sitting on a step or a period of isolation in the bedroom.

'Don't annoy your sister when she is doing her homework.'

'I'm not annoying her.'

'You know the rule.'

'One,' wait five seconds.

'Two,' wait five seconds.

'Three,' wait five seconds.

'John, go to time out now!'

Some parents don't put the child in time out, they take themselves to the back yard, or even lock themselves in their bedroom. Once time has been served, even though they are not openly repentant, the child restarts with a completely clean slate. See also Chapter 5, page 49.

Give a choice

In theory calmness, rules, counting and time out give sure-fire success, but you may still be stuck in a stand-off. Remember that forcing is not the answer. You've aimed for calm, you've got space, it's now time to give a choice.

'I want you to go to time out.'

'No!'

'John, if you go now, you can come out and we will watch "The Simpsons" together. If you choose not to go, there is no television tonight.'

A choice allows some room to manoeuvre and lessens the risk of reflex refusal. Humans don't like being pushed into a corner. A choice will sidestep confrontation.

'I' statements

When you can take no more, make a statement and move away (see earlier this chapter). 'It makes me unhappy when we are at each other like this.' Then go.

Forgive: hold no grudges

If you listen to some families discuss their relatives, you hear of uncles and aunts who have fallen permanently from favour. It started years ago with some small incident, but no one has been prepared to back down and make an effort to heal the wounds. With time the rift has become impossibly deep and there is no chance of resolution. You would think that blood relatives would try to resolve the differences, but often no one is prepared to make the first move.

I see the same situation with many parents and children in my care. They get angry and resentful with each other until they are poles apart. It's very easy to get a relationship into this situation; it's much more difficult to get it out again.

As peace-loving parents we must get rid of grudges, resolve differences and bring our children back to us. Your efforts at reconciliation will not always be accepted, but when the olive branch is genuinely offered, it is usually grasped.

Some time ago I was speaking on talk-back radio when one mother phoned with an interesting story. She and her six-year-old were constantly at war, to the point she despaired of what had happened to their relationship.

She said that one night her husband was away from home, the other kids had gone to bed, and she and the six-year-old were watching the telly, seated at opposite ends of a long settee. He moved up a little. She moved up a little. They moved more. He leant against her arm. She rubbed her hand over his back and held him close. With emotion in her voice she then said, 'Things changed that night.'

Children don't want to be at war with their parents. After they have annoyed us they may not make a formal apology but they circle the perimeter, hoping we will show them the olive branch. Be quick to put an end to hostility and pull them back in close.

The dos and don'ts of discipline

1. Most discipline comes from subtle feedback, where children sense when they are doing well or doing badly. They pick this up through the tone of our voice, the twinkle in our eyes and our level of interest.

2. If you want a child to respond, first gain their attention, look them in the eye, speak warmly and mean what you say.

3. Argument and anger inflame and we lose control. Let unimportant happenings pass, keep calm and repeat requests like a broken gramophone record.

4. Nagging causes irritation and deliberate deafness. Say what you want done, encourage action, monitor progress and get off their backs.

5. Wound up humans are irrational and do foolish things. When a child is over the top, the priority is a cool-down period, not a lecture or discipline.

6. A hostile, heavy, confronting style of parenting leads to opposition and resentment. Children need to feel they are respected and have some choice.

7. Humans are happiest with structure and self-discipline in their lives. Children need rules and structure that lets them know where they stand.

8. Rules are important but they must be interpreted with sense and appropriate flexibility.

9. Children don't want to be at war with their parents, but often we hold grudges and refuse peace. After anger or punishment, forgive and pull them back in close.

10. Reward good intent and effort, even if the result falls flat. Change from seeing problems and bad behaviour, refocus and catch them being good.

11. A behaviour that is rewarded will usually be repeated. Make sure it is the good, not the bad, you are rewarding.

12. It's easy to squabble with children. Sensible parents take a step back and ask, 'Is this really worth it? Is this getting me anywhere?' Let the unimportant things pass.

SEVEN

Ways to approach a behaviour problem

W hen parents come to me many are in a state of numb confusion. They are quite clear that they don't like what is going on, but they can't see why it's happening. When I ask parents about the behaviour, they tend to become bogged down on some unimportant part, they over-interpret or they get entirely off-beam.

My first priority is to find the true nature of the problem. How much of the difficulty is in the child? How much of the difficulty is in the parenting? What stresses are stirring the environment? What brings calm and what triggers a blow-up? Then I need to know what techniques are being tried and which bring the best chance of success. There are a number of simple methods to cut through the confusion.

The magic wand

When parents are asked, 'What's the problem?' they often are so stressed they answer, 'Everything.' Only a miracle worker can sort out 'everything'. I can only deal in specifics.

To help narrow the focus I ask, 'If I had a magic wand and could only change one bit of behaviour, what would that be?' When I get that answer, I then ask, 'If you had a second wish, what is the next most troublesome behaviour?'

The magic wand helps parents think more clearly and shows me where I must target my treatment. Mums often see things differently to dads, but both know what is causing them pain. If you think your child has a behaviour problem first try the magic wand to pinpoint what's bothering you.

Describe a day

Children can be irritating and obnoxious at home, then act like angels in my office. Parents worry that I won't believe their story and secretly hope the child will be abusive and trash my room. Even the worst-behaved child can make you look a liar in a non-confronting interview situation. To get around this I get the parents to take me through the typical day.

What time does she wake? Is she usually in good form? What happens between getting up and breakfast time? I then go through the day, getting a technicolour picture of every moment. I want to hear about the usual day, not the worst-case scenario. Armed with this information I then know how to help.

Keep a behaviour diary

A good psychologist will usually start by asking parents to keep a behaviour diary. This measures the frequency, severity and duration of all behaviour, good and bad. From this baseline the psychologist documents the reality of what is happening and can then see when the techniques they suggest are creating change. It is useful to write down what is going on as our perception can be very unreliable.

Don't over-analyse

I meet some parents who are so analytical they would make Sigmund appear an amateur. Every action is interpreted as having some deep significance. An ornament gets bumped by an exuberant child and this is analysed as a deliberate act of destruction. An impulsive outburst is seen as premeditated aggression. Even teasing their sister is labelled spiteful jealousy.

Parents who over-interpret may blame incorrectly, become paranoid and miss the point. The more I work with children the less I understand about their behaviour. My job is to help parents change to a happy relationship, not to over-analyse their children.

The ABC approach

ABC is a simple way to sort out behaviour. Each problem is looked at in three parts:

A. the antecedent (what triggered it off)

B. the behaviour (what the child did)

C. the consequence (how we reacted and what were the pay-offs).

Putting ABC into action

A mother complains that her daughter is obstinate, abusive and never does what she is told. I ask for a specific example.

'Last night was a disaster. I called Lisa to come for dinner, she refused, got angry and ruined the night for both of us.'

I now approach this with the ABC technique.

The antecedent
What was happening before the blow-up?

'Lisa was in the lounge room watching a TV soap. I told her to switch off the set, to tidy away her toys, wash her hands and come to the table immediately. She ignored me. I turned off the television, she shouted at me and I lost it.'

The behaviour
Lisa dragged her feet, came to the table, grumbled throughout the meal, fiddled with her food and provoked all the way until bedtime.

The consequence
Mum had a spoiled and an unhappy night. She felt resentful at what her daughter had done. Lisa felt angry with her mum, but secretly believed she had won the battle.

How the disaster could have been handled, using ABC

Now we have got the picture, let's see how things might have been handled differently.

The antecedent
Lisa's television program had only eight minutes to run. Could she have waited until the next commercial or the end? Mum might have given a five-minute warning: 'Lisa, dinner is almost ready, can you start to tidy up please?' Was it important to tidy the toys before dinnertime, or could that have happened later? Was it helpful to turn off the television or was this an unnecessary act of provocation? Would Mum have treated one of her adult friends with such hostility? If Lisa didn't eat her dinner, who was going to miss out?

The behaviour
It takes two people to keep a battle on the boil. Was Mum committed to forgive or was she spoiling for a fight? Was this a time for a simple statement: 'I love you, but it makes me feel unhappy when we annoy each other?' Should Mum and her daughter have moved apart for a short time or even used time out?

The consequence

What was the pay-off for Mum? She showed she was tough, uncompromising and not going to give in to a child. What was the loss for Mum? Three hours of anger, a spoiled meal, disturbed sleep and damage to a relationship. What was the pay-off for Lisa? She proved she was a powerful person who could call the shots. She watched her mother lose control and credibility. She was given endless attention. What was the loss for Lisa? She missed five minutes of her favourite program, she had a stressed mealtime and an uncomfortable evening. She upset the relationship with someone she loved.

Was it worth it? There were no winners, just losers. Things might have been different if there had been a warning, if Mum had waited until a commercial break, if Mum had resorted to less confrontation and had tried to stay calm, instead of stirring the conflict.

Finding the best behaviour technique

Life must be easy for those who write advice books but don't work with difficult children. By the time I meet parents, most have tried all the usual techniques and are still in trouble. I often look at the difficulties and wonder what more I can suggest. When faced with this I go back to basics. I review every possible method to see what brings some success, what is of little value and what is a total failure.

As a rule, shouting, smacking, nitpicking, confronting, arguing and escalating all make things worse. Rules, rewards, letting the unimportant pass, time out, keeping calm, 'I' statements and forgiveness give the best chance.

I ask parents to drop the techniques that don't work. But old habits die hard.

'Do you smack him?'

'Yes' they reply.

'Does it help?'

'No, it makes him angry and impossible.'

'Why do you keep doing it?'

'You don't suggest we let him get away with bad behaviour?'

'But is it working?'

'No'

'Then you should stop it.'
'But that's letting him get away with bad behaviour.'
'READ MY LIPS!'

A final word

Now you can clearly focus on the main problem behaviour. You know the triggers that set it off. You have listed the techniques that work and have discarded those that don't. In the next chapter we'll look at how this works with the everyday behaviour problems of school age.

Focusing in on a behaviour problem

1. Deal in specifics
   - 'If I had a magic wand . . .'
   - What is the most major behaviour?
   - What is the next major behaviour?
2. Describe a day
   - take an average day – not a disaster day
   - the extent of the problem
   - the triggers
   - see the pattern of behaviour
   - the techniques that work
   - the techniques that fail
3. Don't over-analyse
   - don't get bogged in academic theories
   - resolution is more useful than analysis
4. The ABC approach
   - A (antecedent) – the trigger
   - B (behaviour) – what happened
   - C (consequence) – the result
5. Find the best behaviour technique
   - What usually helps?
   - What occasionally helps?
   - What makes things worse?

EIGHT

An A to Z of children's behaviour

I have little patience with child care experts who have a quick fix for every behaviour problem. Quick fixes sound impressive, but life is not so simple in the real world.

When the late Benjamin Spock was asked to write his first child care book, he initially declined. Spock told the publisher he had too many failures in his day-to-day practice, and to write a book would imply he had all the answers. I can relate to Spock's honesty: I have a head full of clever theories, but I still struggle with children in my care.

As parents read through my suggestions some will think, 'This man is crazy. Some of his techniques are off the beam.' So a word of warning. What I present is a long list of ideas for every problem. Some are sure-fire, others are way down the pile. What you use will depend on the age and temperament of your child and, of course, the extent of the problem. The final decision will be based on only one thing – getting the right result.

Contents

Topics covered in other chapters

Accident prone

Insurance companies know all about how different people pose different risks. Sometimes, they will refuse cover for drivers under twenty-five, especially if they are male, aggressive and impulsive. Girls of this age are always a safer bet, but in both sexes there are a few high-risk individuals with an accident-prone temperament.

Research into accident proneness has often looked at bus drivers, comparing those who arrive safely with those who bump things along the way. As always it is the impulsive temperament that causes most trouble. The fast-moving drivers are useful when running late, but for safe arrival the calm, reflective temperament is the winner.

Meanwhile, away from the bus depot, an impulsive temperament leaves some children an accident waiting to happen. I see impulsive children with repeated fractures or following several near-death experiences. One mother wrote about her son: 'Our son has just had his seventeenth birthday. I never thought he would live this long. At two years he climbed to the top of a tall wardrobe and took his grandfather's heart tablets. He was rushed to hospital.

'At three years he released the hand brake on our car. This careered down our steep drive. The car overturned. Our son had one small bruise; the car was less lucky.

'At four years he hit our neighbour's beehive with a large stick. He thought they were blowflies. He only had two stings; the neighbour who went to his aid was not so fortunate.'

The list of disasters covered several more pages and it appeared that he had attained Gold Frequent Flyer status at the local casualty department. The letter ended on a note of panic: 'Today he is reading the Highway Code – he wants to learn to drive!'

So how can we help the impulsive child who shoots from the hip?

- An impulsive temperament is often inherited from an impulsive dad or mum (usually dad). Clever children should choose their parents with great care.

- Child safety must always be the first priority. Take special care with the crossing of roads, supervise closely and have strict rules about bike riding.

- Teach the traffic light technique of 'Stop. Think. Go.' (slow the pace, then encourage them to reflect for a moment, then act). It sounds very simple but it is a challenge when children are all go and no stop.

- Accident proneness is a classic symptom of Attention Deficit Hyperactivity Disorder (ADHD). If the child is found to be suffering from ADHD and is successfully treated, they will be much safer.

Arguing and backchat

Such is the talent of some children, they could start an argument in an empty room. In fact, one of my patients argues with his computer, complaining that it cheats when he is playing card games. Of course, you need two people to argue and talking to a computer is about as useful as squabbling with your mother-in-law. Life's too short for lost causes.

Children argue in order to hijack attention, look smart or push a power struggle. If attention is the goal, the arguing should be ignored. If it's to show off in front of visiting mates, give a warning then send the friends home.

A power struggle is much more complex, as the child is looking for a victim, and when this happens we must remain unruffled to avoid falling into that role (see also this chapter, oppositional behaviour, page 105).

Here are some ways to handle a keen arguer.

■ Improve communication. If a child is addressed with heavy, abrasive, sarcastic tones, these will bounce back at you in their reply.

■ If possible, ask, don't tell.

■ Be enthusiastic, show interest, be positive.

■ Be matter-of-fact and use humour.

■ Change tack with a different intonation or a whisper.

■ When arguing and the child uses smart comments to wind you up, don't rise to their bait but let the water roll off the duck's back. 'That's fine.' 'I hear you.' 'Now I'm just going outside for a moment.'

■ Don't let protest change the referee's decision. If young McEnroe disputes a line call, don't bend to his bullying.

■ Be a courteous listener, but at a certain point, state your position and close down that channel of reception.

■ If they feel you are being unreasonable, give two minutes to put their case, after which 'It's finished.'

- Keep asking yourself, 'Is this getting me anywhere?' If the answer is no, it's time to start thinking with your brain.

- When they show off in front of friends, give fair warning (preferably in private), then send their mates home. If their friends cannot go home, put the show-off in time out. Before the next visit give a quiet reminder of the rules.

- When stuck for ideas, use an 'I' statement: 'I feel embarrassed when addressed like that'; 'I feel sad when we argue'; 'I would feel happy if we got on together.'

- Give feedback for good times: 'Gosh, you are such good company'; 'I so much enjoyed being with you.'

- Arguing can be part of the power politics of the oppositional child. With these difficult young people the aim is to sidestep confrontation, give choices and let them feel they have a say in the outcome. (For more information on oppositional behaviour see this chapter, page 105).

- Most children do what they are told but there is a lot of argument and complaint along the way. They have to get ready for school, do homework, bathe, brush teeth and go to bed. All you are asking for is action without excuses. Use a star chart to encourage compliance without complaint or add a bonus to the pocket money for a grumble-free life.

- Some older children can be bought with a significant cash payment. One extremely difficult child in my care gets a dollar for each hassle-free day. This sounds like extortion but nothing else worked and it was a small price to pay for his mum's sanity.

Bad language

Even royalty use rude words, but only in private. Our children get the same royal flush, but the words appear at inopportune moments. The reason for bad language is ignorance of the meaning, releasing tension, attention seeking and acting 'cool'.

In the early school years children use a lot of silly language where even the word 'bottom' is seen to be as entertaining as an entire season of 'Seinfeld'. This language has no malice; it's part of the fun and nonsense of being young. At this age children repeat words they have heard at school, but they have no knowledge of their meaning. Words may also be used to wind up Mum and Dad.

Silliness can be stopped with a simple comment, our tone of voice or the way we look. Handle innocent but inappropriate language with an explanation of its meaning. Where words are used to stir up parents, it is important to avoid rising to the bait.

By late primary school, bad language is normal behaviour for the herd. Some children use the f-word to register their position in the group, much like a dog might pee around a perimeter to stake his claim. At this age it is important to make it clear what we will and will not accept.

Primary-age children often have words and secret sayings that are part of the common language that bonds the group together. When my boys were at school, the in word was 'skills'. I don't know where it came from or what it meant, but it was like some special hand-shake of a secret group. The word lost favour when my older son bluffed the class: 'You shouldn't say "skills", it's a rude word.' The others looked surprised. 'It's a nasty disease of the bum. I know, because my father is a doctor.'

The words we use have a different significance in different cultures and countries. As I miss my serve at tennis it sounds so trendy to say, 'Merde!' but to a Frenchman it is still 'Shit!'

One ex-Australian prime minister was well known for his intolerance of groups that were all talk and no action. When working on a high-powered UN committee, he was forever baffling the interpreters. One day, exasperated by the lack of progress, he stood up and said, 'It's about time we stopped playing silly buggers.' With this, the interpreters flicked through their dictionaries and over the headphones came a confused statement about sport and feeble-minded homosexuals.

My list of suggestions gives a number of approaches, but what you use will depend on the age of the child, the extent of the problem and the reason for the bad language. In my experience, any young child with an extreme, abusive foul mouth, has acquired this from someone in their dysfunctional living environment. If language is a symptom of home disharmony or a rift in the parent–child relationship, the language is not the main priority for treatment.

- State clearly what you will not accept: 'John, that is not a word we use.'

- Use 'I' statements: 'I feel upset when I hear that sort of language.'

- In young children explain the meaning of rude words and show the silliness of describing reproductive anatomy in public.

- Notice and reinforce when they talk, and relate in an appropriate way.

- When language is used to bait parents, where possible, let it pass. When ignored, the baiting may initially increase then, with no pay-off, it will lessen.

- Older children enjoy shocking their parents. They think that their generation know words that we old timers can't use. We can capitalise on the surprise value of remaining completely unfazed and reply using their word. 'John, it's not very clever to say f—.' When response is laid-back it removes the shock from shock tactics.

- Some parents still wash out mouths with soap and water. This is old-fashioned, dangerous and creates children who resent their parents.

- Swearing helps release tension. Teach children how to let off steam in other ways: count to ten, punch a pillow or have a quick run around the block.

- Allow the use of almost rude words: 'Shoot!' or 'Fruit cake!'

- Put limits on swearing. 'You can use those words, but not here.'

- A lot of rude words involve religious figures and begatting, but they are not recommended in church.

- Give a warning and follow with removal of privileges: 'Bed fifteen minutes earlier.'

- Give a warning and follow with time out.

- Make good language pay off. Convert the weekly pocket money to twenty-cent coins and place these in a glass jar. For each blasphemy deduct one piece of silver.

- If they are acting smart to impress a friend, warn them that their mate will be sent home if they continue. After fair warning, act.

- Children parrot the speech, abusive attitudes and bad language of those they are close to. In the early years this comes from us, the parents.

- When parenting has been hostile, negative and verbally abusive since the early years, it is normal for children to treat their parents in the same way.

Bike riding

When I was young everyone either walked or rode their bike to school. The handful who were driven by car were seen as feeble, spoiled children. Today things have changed: it is the riders to school who are risk takers and the odd ones out.

Bikes can give children a great release for pent-up energy as well as freedom and mobility. We usually remove trainer wheels when the child is about five years old, but children continue to need close supervision until eight or nine years. It's important to have rules in place right from the start. Before purchasing a bike have a strict set of rules that everyone agrees on. 'No rules – no bike.'

- Have clear rules about helmets, stopping at intersections, crossing main roads and areas that are off limits.

- Have rules about care of the bike, locking and putting it away at night.

- Notice and reinforce safe riding.

- Teach about safe braking and keep brakes serviced.

- Teach about the dangers of bags carried on the handlebars that can catch in the front wheel.

- Supervise when children are challenging their friends on jumps, ramps and riding through the air.

- When rules are disregarded, lock up the bicycle for a week and don't debate or argue your actions.

- Bike ride as a family. This is good for children and helps unfit adults avoid heart attacks.

- If you worry about bicycles, wait until they start driving your car!

Birthday parties

Younger children are full of bubble and bounce. Parents tell me that sugar in the party food is the cause of this over-the-top behaviour. I'm not so sure: this age group would be airborne even if we fed them on the purest of sugar-free food and natural spring water.

When planning a party for the under-eights, make an invitation list then divide it by two-thirds, which is all you can manage.

The over-eights will want a more sophisticated party: a live performance from a famous pop group or the guest appearance of Manchester United would be popular but not essential.

- For timid partygoers, talk it through before they go. Role-play introductions and thank yous.

- With an over-rowdy raver, arrive a little late and pick up a little early.

- When organising your own child's party, ensure you have enough adult minders on hand.

- Consider inviting a favourite teacher from school. They can wander around and provide a form of police presence.

- Check all toilets are capable of quick throughput and full flush.

- Consider using an outside party centre. It may not be more expensive and it has the advantage that others tidy up.

- A trick candle (that won't blow out) never fails to impress.

Bragging and boasting

We recognise bragging as a suitable talent for the politician who wishes re-election. Yet despite the example of our leaders, we teach our children that it's vain and offensive to blow your own trumpet.

The under-seven-year-olds live in a world where everything is larger and more spectacular than life. Listen at bath time as five-year-olds discuss their most private parts:

'My dad's is bigger than your dad's.'

'No, my dad's is huge! It's like this!'

Maybe it isn't an exaggeration but it's still part of their quaint, uncomplicated world.

After eight years of age, boasting is either an adult-type behaviour or a sign of emotional insecurity. When my boys were at school, the taller stories came from friends with the most convoluted, much-married backgrounds. Certainly I couldn't work out how all the relatives fitted together, and the children must have been equally confused where they belonged.

How you handle a boast depends on the child's age, the extent of the problem and the state of their esteem.

- For minor bragging, ignore it altogether.

- Explain how boasting can make you look stupid. Illustrate with a play on your own brilliance: 'My spaghetti bolognaise is the best in this street. It's better than anyone's in this city, in fact, aliens from far off planets may land on our lawn, knock at the door and ask for the recipe.'

- Put the brakes on bragging. 'You have talked all morning about your goal. We know you are a top player, but this is bragging.'

- With tall stories, listen and then state, 'I hear what you are saying but this is not quite true.'

- Ask the ten-year-old how they feel when others brag. Does it impress them or not?

- Notice non-bragging days or weeks. 'Today you played a blinder of a game, you were brilliant, yet not a brag or a boast!'

■ Don't be too tough. Life would be pretty boring if we didn't stretch the realms of credibility. Every successful author knows that you can't let truth get in the way of a good story.

Breaks in unthinking rage

When children have a short fuse they may overreact and even destroy their own treasures. After the event they see the stupidity of their behaviour, which makes them twice as stroppy.

■ The angriest human beings are those who are angry at their own silliness.

■ Don't nag or say, 'Told you so', as this adds insult to injury.

■ If they break something important to them, for example, an almost-completed model aeroplane, support, don't criticise.

■ Don't rub salt in the wound. Even if they say they don't care, they hurt deeply.

Breaks their sibling's property

Some children have fiddly fingers. They have to touch and things get broken. Here's what you can do.

■ Have a small number of rules about what can and what cannot be touched.

■ Notice when care and respect is shown for other people's property.

■ Distinguish between the occasional unthinking act and damage that follows the deliberate disregard of a warning.

■ Instruct siblings to keep their treasures secure and make their personal space a no-go area.

■ Breakages can be replaced via a small levy on the pocket money.

■ Don't set up an impossibly harsh repayment system, as this causes resentment and hostility.

Car travel

One mother with three extreme ADHD boys told me of her trips to and from school. 'Car seating is run on a strict roster. On week one John sits in the front seat, Tom in the back right, and Jack in the back left. Week two, Jack moves to the front, John moves to back right, and Tom to back left. On leaving school the occupant of the front seat can talk for five minutes, then the back right, then the left.' Finally, the mother said, 'And we never allow the car to stop. Even if the fuel needle is on empty, we speed past service stations.'

It doesn't need to be this bad but some children make cars a moving hell:

'It's not fair, she's looking out my window.'

'Mum, he's making that noise again.'

'Are we there yet?'

Just because adults like long-distance driving, it doesn't necessarily follow that this suits their children. If your child fights, squabbles and protests on the trip to the corner store, a 500-kilometre car trip could be a challenge. When long-distance travel ages parents and is a hazard to mental health, consider a quick air flight, a seat on a train or a holiday at home.

In case you have to take that trip, though, here's some ideas:

■ Before you start, set down the ground rules about teasing, poking and annoying.

■ Plan regular breaks and keep the passengers informed of the time to touchdown.

■ If the car tape player is to be used for everybody, allocate tape time in advance.

■ Borrow some talking books from your local library.

■ A Walkman may help.

■ Construct a token system where short periods of peaceful travel are rewarded with a small token (a tick, star, bead, etc.). These all add up to a worthwhile reward (such as spending money) at the next fuel stop.

- Secure a large piece of luggage between the occupants of the back seat.

Chores

Child care experts are divided into two groups: the philosophers who expect children to work for the common good of the family; and the pragmatists who buy and bribe. I would like all children to help, just for love, but I can accept anything that keeps the peace and achieves results.

Children are genetically created with different attitudes to help. Some have an unquestioning wish to tidy, wash, clean and cook, while others expect room service from the age of five to fifty years. Of course, example is important. I see teenage boys who treat Mum like an inferior-intellect housemaid. Often their father is equally arrogant and insensitive.

With my own family, I always hoped that our adult sharing and working together would rub off on the children. But with both boys now in their twenties, the jury is still out on the verdict.

It is important to introduce chores at a young age, as this capitalises on the under-fives' wish to be helpful. Give a few responsibilities, then build on this with age. Start with a small number of important tasks that should be completed with minimal reminding and zero complaint. Here's what to do:

- Start young and give a few basic chores.

- Clearly communicate what you expect from your children.

- Draw up a list of duties together.

- Set a time for completion and inspection.

- Work together where possible, as this gets jobs done and helps relationships.

- Give one reminder, but don't nag.

- Divide chores equally between boys and girls.

- Don't be a nitpicker, but don't pay for substandard work.

- Appreciate effort, and notice when tasks are done without asking.

- Stand back and share the satisfaction of the completed job.

- Use a star chart to highlight specific tasks, for example, making their bed, washing dishes, tidying their room.

- Pay a basic level of pocket money then add a bonus for work completed without complaint.

- Use an immediate reward system where coins are placed in a jar.

- With older children, consider suspending payment for all those incidentals, for example, cinema tickets, drinks and treats. Cost out each chore then pay real money for a real week's work.

- Set an example. Parents who work together have children who we hope will become helpful husbands and wives.

- The ultimate aim is to encourage children to see what needs to be done and get on with it without being asked.

Clingyness

One- and two-year-old children are clingy by nature but this eases with age, and most will separate confidently by three or four.

However, there are a few who still cling right into the early school years. If friends visit or when addressed by a stranger they hide their face and hold onto Mum. Relatives become the expert psychiatrist: 'That child has an emotional problem. It's about time you toughened them up.' But the child's fears are real to them and forcing makes things worse.

A few children cling because they are stressed. This is common following a marriage split where the child knows they have lost fifty per cent of those they trust, and they are determined to stay close to the remaining half.

- If the environment is in equilibrium I encourage parents to steer gently and go with the flow. Little people vary in their ability to separate and they have another seventy-five years to sort things out.

- Let them know about visitors before they arrive. Role-play eye contact, greetings and small talk.

■ Notice, praise and reinforce appropriate behaviour.

■ Encourage small group friendships, then build to bigger numbers at more distant venues.

■ Don't push. They know how they feel and don't need railroading by some insensitive adult.

■ When reacting to family change, tread softly. They need all their supports at this time.

Conflict cycle

This negative spiral is one of the most damaging situations I see. The parent gets angry, the child returns fire, no one backs down and the relationship turns to resentment. Soon parents see every action as a deliberate attempt to provoke them. Now they address their child with a negative, antagonistic tone that presumes non-compliance. The child responds with anger and foot dragging, insolence and opposition.

I encourage parents to get off their high horse but I am often told that the child has the problem and must change, not the parent. They return again and again over the years but nothing changes and I am powerless to help.

Some of this conflict starts with an irritable infant who is impossible to settle, or with a relationship damaged by post-natal depression. Many of these children are born with an oppositional temperament. Whatever the cause, the only remedy is to get in early, then teach parents to use an olive branch rather than a stick.

■ This is not a holy war. Forget about who is right or wrong. Without compromise and change everyone will end up in the wrong.

■ Avoid cold, condescending tones, quiet anger and passive aggression.

■ Be positive and transmit the message that you expect action.

- Avoid 'you' statements like 'You expect everything'; 'You give nothing'; 'You are never satisfied.'

- Use 'I' statements: 'I feel sad that we annoy each other this way.'

- Notice and appreciate any small gesture of compliance and closeness.

- Have a round-table conference. Discuss how you annoy them and they annoy you. Each side can then try to change two of their specific irritating behaviours. Review progress one week later.

- Use the techniques suggested for oppositional behaviour (see also this chapter, page 105).

Dawdling and won't get dressed

I am told there are children who jump with enthusiasm out of bed, get dressed and are ready for school hours ahead of time. But this endangered species is outnumbered by whole divisions of dawdlers.

Dawdlers come in two sorts: those created with a dreamy, slow-moving brain, and the ones who go slow to damage their parents' health. You send the dreamer off to get dressed; half an hour later they're stuck in a catatonic trance, blankly staring at a sock. This is different to the wind-up child who is deaf to all warnings until Mum is close to seizure. Then they grab their belongings and jump on the bus.

Dreamers need to be woken early and reminded many times. Their clothes should be laid out and ready the night before. They get rewarded for the little steps they make: 'He's got his pants on! . . . Wow, now he's got his singlet on too!'

The secret is to nudge gently yet be immensely patient. In reality nothing short of a faith healer will transform this temperament. Often their dreamy style is quite like someone you chose to marry.

The deliberate dawdler also needs an early start, but after this, only allow a limited number of reminders. After two or three prompts, set the kitchen timer to announce ten minutes before departure. If the child is running late, that's their problem and they must sort this out with the school.

It takes an exceptional parent to watch as their child leaves home hungry and partly dressed. But change can only come when a child takes responsibility and is allowed to feel the repercussions of their actions.

Daydreaming

Some children are created with a dreamy temperament. Teachers despair as the child glazes over and their thoughts slip out the window. Schools may dramatise daydreaming, diagnosing this spaced-out boredom as 'petit mal epilepsy' (see Chapter 21, page 262).

A few of these dreamers have the predominantly inattentive form of ADHD. Here they lose attention and drift off target and this is often associated with moments of unreliable impulse control.

Some children switch off to escape from the difficulties in their life. We often see this with family breakdowns and other unhappiness. If a previously sparky, alert child becomes detached and disinterested, suspect an emotional trigger or even depression (see over page).

After the age of eleven years children develop the ability to use abstract thinking. Some of these older children become dreamers as the potential Einstein tries to think through a new theory of relativity.

Here are some tips for dealing with dreamers:

- Dreamers need structure, encouragement and reminders of time.

- Work beside the child to keep the focus on the task at hand.

- Use a kitchen timer to add some urgency to homework completion or eating dinner.

- Consider the possibility of predominantly inattentive ADHD (inattentive, slightly impulsive, disorganised, poor short-term memory).

- Exclude specific learning disabilities (such as dyslexia) where attention drifts as they lose interest in that one area of difficulty.

- Daydreaming may be in the genes. The child may be just like Mum or Dad!

- Sometimes we can't change the daydreamer; we can only change our expectations.

Depression

Though our greatest worry is the depressed teenager, children of all ages can be depressed. Depression is more than the kind of short-term sadness we all experience. True depression immobilises, dulls interest and turns out the light at the end of the tunnel.

The depressed five-year-old becomes unhappy, quiet and less animated, usually in response to an upsetting life event. Depression in a ten-year-old may be less obvious, with the main symptom a change from their usual outgoing state. School grades slip, attention fades, they retreat inward and lose friends and interests.

Depression tends to draw adults and children into their own claustrophobic company. Now everything is an effort, and with this can come open or hidden feelings of hopelessness.

Though I am supposed to be skilled in my understanding of children, I rarely diagnose depression in this age and know I must be missing some. The main warning signal is a change in behaviour, particularly when related to some disruption or loss in life.

- Be alert to a change where the child withdraws from friends and interests.

- The child's feelings are real. It's pointless to suggest they pull themselves together. They would do this if they could.

- Try to keep the child busy. Encourage them to get up at weekends, get out and look neat.

- Encourage them to talk about, write down or draw how they feel.

- Try to distinguish the common martyr statements like 'I'm ugly' or 'No one would care if I die' from a true call for help. There are a thousand martyrs for each crisis call but it's this one cry we can't afford to miss. Words alone are probably unimportant;

words accompanied by isolation and a change in behaviour are of greater concern.

■ Opposition and anger often accompany depression. This makes the child extremely difficult and it is our instinct to retaliate with hostility. Tread gently as it is easy to deepen the depression.

■ Depression has some hereditary link. If you have personal experience of this problem, be more alert to the possibility in those around you.

■ When a child has severe learning problems this causes stress at school and blocks many avenues of success in life. These children are more vulnerable to depression and it is hard to show them the achievement they so much need.

■ Encourage outside interests and looking forward to something.

■ Professional psychological or psychiatric help is recommended for all depressed children and is a matter of urgency when self-harm is a possibility.

■ The old-fashioned anti-depressants like Tofranil (imipramine) have little effect in depressed children, though there is some evidence that the newer selective seratonin re-uptake inhibitor (SSRI) drugs like Zoloft and Prozac may bring some gains.

Diet and behaviour

A horse trainer knows that the right diet gives speed on the final furlong, but it doesn't make a horse behave badly. A good diet prepares our children for the long run of life but, for most youngsters, it has no effect on behaviour.

In about five per cent of all children diet affects their behaviour, and their most common symptom is irritability or restlessness. There is a myth that diet only affects ADHD children but any child, whether ADHD or not, can show a behavioural change. A second myth suggests that the only food offenders are artificial colourings, preservatives and additives, but the evidence shows that organically grown oranges, tomatoes and pure honey can sometimes be just as troublesome.

There are four common groups of chemicals that cause food intolerance: salicylates, amines, monosodium glutamate and food additives.

The salicylates are natural chemicals found in many fruits, vegetables, nuts, herbs, spices and jams. Salicylates are highest in unripe fruits and there is more near the skin than inside.

The amines occur in high levels in cheese, chocolate, yeast extract and fruits such as bananas (especially when overripe).

Monosodium glutamate (MSG) occurs naturally in strong flavoured foods like tomatoes and cheeses and is also sometimes used as an additive in stock cubes, yeast extracts and some styles of cooking.

Food additives are either preservatives used to keep foods fresh or colourings to make them look more attractive. Hundreds of these are used but only a few are likely to cause trouble. A code number on the product label indicates which chemicals have been added, for example, sulphites are numbered between 220 and 228, while antioxidants are numbered 310 to 321.

In my experience, when there is a sensitivity, parents are usually aware of the offending drink, food or fruit and give this a miss. But the situation can be much more complex where the effects of food chemicals are cumulative. For example, the natural preservative salicylate can come from a variety of sources. A child who is sensitive to it may eat first tomato paste, then some raisins, then peppermint and finally a glass of orange juice. In the cumulative child any two or three of these would have been no problem, but the total intake creates an overload. Parents are now confused as orange juice previously caused no reaction but today it has tipped the balance.

It takes a clever dietitian to untangle all this. If they suspect a natural or artificial product is affecting behaviour they will withdraw it and then reintroduce it at a later time to see what happens.

Diet has a lesser effect on behaviour than popular belief might suggest. Sugar is the target of much criticism but this has not been shown to cause behavioural problems. I rarely suggest the diet approach to behaviour, but I support parents who want to give it a fair go. For them I recommend that the diet be supervised by a knowledgeable dietitian. For more information on this issue see the excellent publication *Friendly Food* by Swain, Soutter and Loblay, Murdoch Books, Sydney, 1991.

Fears

We all have secret fears, which may seem silly to others but are very real to us. The adult who fears flying can be shown safety statistics, but at 10 000 metres they remain terrified by the slightest change in engine sound. Everyone is allowed their fears – it's only when they become major phobias that damage our day-to-day lives that we need help.

Children have different worries at different ages. A three-year-old might be terrified of loud noises, electric hand dryers, ambulance sirens and dogs. By six years they may fear the dark, falling, losing their mum, wind, thunder, ghosts and monsters. At ten years they worry about school failure, speaking in front of the class, looking foolish, how they appear and possible friction in their parents' marriage.

Most school-age fears are fed into our children by what they see in the world or hear from their parents. Our necessary warnings about road safety, stranger danger and home security may cause our children to fear injury, abduction and burglars.

Miscommunication also raises fears. When Grandma is rushed to hospital it is often easier to say she has a severe cold than explain heart failure. But if Grandma dies in hospital, the child's next cold may be seen as a serious event.

I remember family gatherings when adult relatives talked in whispers about the sadness of senile decay. It seemed an entire generation of my blood relatives were suffering from this incurable illness. It must have been very serious or people wouldn't whisper and pray about it.

To make things worse, 'senile' sounded like an important male personal part. The thought that this might decay or drop off filled me with fear. If the adults in my life had said straight, 'Your relatives are getting old,' I would have understood.

I often see school-age children who have a fear of walking around the house alone at night. We can support them through this fear by holding their hand as they walk through a dark room then standing near the door as they go alone. If dark is the problem, keep lights on dim and reduce the power until confidence starts to grow.

It seems crazy that a nine year old can't go from the family room to the toilet without an escort, but for some reason it's important to them. They gradually get better with help from an accepting, reassuring parent. I do not psychoanalyse these children; I aim to support and use gradual desensitisation.

Forgetfulness

In the brain, the bit that imparts intelligence is not always attached to the centre of organisation and reliable memory. This causes some children to leave their belongings on the bus, have the wrong books for homework and forget the tutor after school. Parents look on in disbelief. You are not asking much: they have to deliver a note to their teacher, not the Gettysburg address.

With the disorganised and forgetful you can't work miracles, but memory jogs help reliability. For more information on teaching children to be organised see Chapter 10, page 139.

Teach children to stop for a minute before they leave home, to think through the day's program and check they are carrying the right gear. They can stop again on leaving the swimming pool and when they finish school for the day.

- Write notes and 'To do' lists.

- Write a reminder word on their hand.

- Tie a knot in their handkerchief.

- Put a rubber band on one wrist to remind them.

- Set a watch alarm.

- Wear the watch on the wrong wrist to jog their memory.

- Have a chart on the fridge door that lists all important activities throughout the week, and encourage them to refer to it regularly.

Gratitude

'It's not fair,' Dad unloads to me. 'I took him to the zoo, we had a fantastic day of father–son togetherness then, on leaving, he saw a Mr Whippy van, created a scene and grizzled all the way home. I bust myself for him – so where's the gratitude?'

I have news for you. Don't expect gratitude in this world. Your reward will come in the hereafter! You are in this parenting because you love them, not for thanks and reward.

Many children are full of thanks and appreciation, but for others it's all take and no give. If it makes you feel better, deliver them a lecture about the injustice of it all, but it won't change anything. Enjoy it when you receive it – even if it's a once-a-year event.

Grazing

There are some children who nibble all day like sheep. Grazing is not unhealthy as long as the pasture is of reasonable quality.

For some, grazing is their favourite way to feed. Others graze out of restless boredom. In school holidays these are the children who pace around, opening and closing doors until the fridge is unable to keep food cool.

The solution to boredom is to steer children towards more structured activity. When scavengers are on the prowl lock away the goodies and avoid buying treat snacks.

Bored or not, grazers need easy access to healthy affordable snacks. A chilled jug of tap water, unflavoured milk, bread, fruit and plain biscuits are a start.

Hair and eyebrow plucking

I don't know what pleasure children get from pulling out and nibbling their hair, but it's probably similar to the pleasure they get out of nail biting and finger picking. I have seen school-age children with no eyebrows or eyelashes and others with thin hair or even a patch of baldness.

If there is some obvious cause of tension this must be addressed, otherwise adopt the gentle redirection, minimum-fuss approach. Children usually pull and chew when they are bored, falling asleep or watching television. At these times consider getting something more appropriate to twiddle, like a worry ball. Give a gentle nudge but don't ridicule them as this increases the tension and they will become an underground plucker.

Have fancy hairstyles and focus on attractive eyebrows and lashes. Be quick to notice any improvement or any area of regeneration.

Occasionally a patch of hair drops out for no good reason (alopecia areata). This may be associated with stress but more often it just falls out for no good reason. Time will tidy up the alopecia, but you may want to pay a visit to the paediatrician or skin specialist for reassurance.

Interrupting

Children who are impulsive or forgetful may interrupt. The impulsive have no patience and can't wait. The forgetful will lose their words if they don't get them out immediately. We want to keep the lines of communication open and also encourage them to wait.

■ Give a gentle reminder: 'Your turn in a minute, John.'

■ Keep repeating the rules of conversation, without becoming a nag.

■ Allow the forgetful child to interrupt with a cue word that you pick up later. As you are talking they say 'New teacher,' and when appropriate you ask, 'What's this about a new teacher?'

■ Teach through role-play how to interpret body language. Show when you are receptive and when your eyes are telling them to back off.

Lying and bending the truth

When the children of this impeachment generation hear of young George Washington they think, 'What a dork.' Fancy standing in front of your dad and saying, 'I cannot tell a lie.' George's father was probably more worried about annoying the environmentalists than his horizontal tree.

Every adult knows that lying is a sin, while bending the truth is a talent much cherished by lawyers. Children under the age of eight years tend to be open with their parents and are quite transparent in their dishonesty. But by ten years their deceit is much more subtle and some events in their lives are guarded with secrecy. The aim is to establish honesty in the early years and to ensure that openness gets more reward than hiding the truth.

- With the four- to six-year-old, don't overreact. Calmly say, 'I don't think this is true.'

- Don't debate; quietly state your opinion.

- Make sure that honesty pays off. There must be less punishment for owning up than denying fault.

- Notice their honesty and appreciate their openness.

- Before the age of eight children are immensely open. If we encourage this when they are young, they will confide more in their tempestuous teens.

- It is unfair to expect our children to be more truthful than the adults they live with. See also Chapter 10, page 134, and this chapter, Shoplifting, page 109).

Martyrdom

Through the ages, martyrs have shown great talent at grabbing attention. It may seem a bit extreme to be stoned or burned but it sure puts you on centre stage. Martyrdom is still alive and well and being practised by many six- to twelve-year-olds. They approach their Mum, look pathetic and state, 'I'm dumb. I'm ugly. You don't love me. I've got no friends.' Occasionally some of this may be true, but for most, martyrdom is used to get an avalanche of attention.

We don't want to be insensitive to genuine concerns but when playing for attention, remember that martyrs get nowhere without an audience. Avoid getting dragged into debates about intellect, good looks and their number of friends. Make a brief statement: 'You are clever and brilliant at swimming'; 'I think you are a real good looker'; 'I love you all'; 'You have good mates.' Then give a reassuring cuddle and move on.

Meal-time behaviour

When a foreign dignitary lands in our country they are welcomed with a state banquet. Leaders since prehistoric times have known that sharing a meal boosts relationships and increases communication.

As the president chats, his emphasis is on communication, not manners. There is no chief of protocol saying, 'Sit up straight, sir . . . Stop slurping . . . Don't talk with your mouth full . . . You can't leave until you eat your broccoli.'

Every night the evening meal provides time when families can sit, listen and relate. It is essential that the television is switched off and we turn a relatively blind eye to mess and imperfect manners. Initially there may not be deep conversation, but with time the guttural grunts may become words.

- Food is about nutrition and meal times are for families to get together and communicate.

- Don't let squabbles and nitpicking cause stress. We want peace, not perfection.

- Establish basic rules about leaving the table, rushing and dawdling.

- Rushers must stay for a certain time and when they depart, they should leave the room.

- Dawdlers are given time, then left to sit by themselves.

- If dawdling is extreme set a cooking timer and when it rings, clear the table.

- Have some non-negotiable rules: 'You can touch or kick anything you want, as long as that "thing" is not your sister!'

- Give feedback for good manners and fun times.

- Clear the table together and establish good habits through example.

Nail biting and finger picking

There is a very simple reason why children bite and pick their nails – they enjoy it. When parents see the raw sores they wonder about pleasure, but humans do many things we don't understand. Grown-ups light their first morning cigarette, convulse with coughing and say, 'Gosh, that was good.' Though I can't understand this, it must give pleasure or they wouldn't do it.

Nail biting is probably an extension of the preschooler's thumb sucking or twiddling the tag on a security blanket. It is unusual under the age of five years. It occurs in about one in three eight-year-olds, one in two fifteen-year-olds and one in four at the age of twenty.

Biting is worse when tense, bored or watching television. There are many recommended remedies, though none are very successful. Whatever happens, don't nag, nitpick and create a battle. The best results come with gentle reminders and noting the good.

- Find the peak times for biting and picking. Keep better occupied during these times.

- Let them hold a little toy, a smooth comfort stone or a stress ball.

- When tempted to bite, they could try clenching both hands super tight for fifteen seconds, then relax and move on.

- Give a simple sign or gentle touch to alert them to biting.

- Compare their nails against other unbitten nails.

- Let them bite their fingers while in front of the mirror. This is not a pretty sight.

- When enough nail appears, manicure and make this special.

- With girls, use nail polish to draw attention to intact nails.

- With the older child encourage them to preserve one nail, then build on this quota.

- Use skin softeners and encourage hand care.

- Prepare a star chart to focus on each two hours without a pick or bite.

- Consider your chemist's best anti-bite nail paint. This may tip the balance but only when there is motivation.

Nightmares

All children have dreams, but not all of these have happy endings. A nightmare is an unsettling dream that leaves a child upset and semi-awake. They respond to our comfort, drift back to sleep and are aware of what happened the next day. Children have their most disturbed dreams when sick and almost hallucinating with fever.

Dreams were once seen as the window to our inner emotional state, but nowadays dreams are seen as nothing more than a normal part of sleep. Though daytime stress, heavy television and scary stories will upset children, there is uncertainty that these cause a child's nightmares.

What we do know is that children sleep best when we put them to bed calm and relaxed. There is no place for stress, arguments and heavy exercise before their head hits the pillow.

Distressed children need cuddles and comfort, but there is one trap for parents. Young children may pretend they are frightened just to attract an audience. Bad dreams occur occasionally, while regular call outs are probably an attention-seeking hoax.

- Come to the child, hold, stroke, comfort, soothe.

- Emphasise that this was a dream and the bad people won't come back.

- Turn over the pillow. The cool side has special properties that prevent bad dreams!

- Place a dim light in the room.

- When ghosts and monsters cause fear, explain they have gone; even do a joint search behind the curtains and under the bed.

- One boy said he couldn't sleep as his bed was full of insects. His mother got the dust buster and after a whirr of vacuuming he was assured they were all gone.

- Creative parents use ghost repellent spray. This is a simple water spray with glitter particles in the bottom. Spray around doors and windows for guaranteed security.

- Talk about dreams by day to emphasise what is real and what is pretend.

- When distressed with fever give paracetamol.

- Allow frightened children to come to your bed.

- Beware the child who repeatedly cries wolf, using fear as a way to attract attention. When attention seeking is the aim, gradually lengthen the response time until the reward is not worth the effort.

Night terrors

Night terrors are different from nightmares. They are not a dream, just an uncomfortable move through the deepest part of sleep. The child cries out apparently frightened, yet totally switched off, open-eyed and unaware. Nothing seems to soothe; all we can do is to stay close, talk gently and wait until they settle. In the morning they have no recollection of any disturbance.

Night terrors are more common in the preschool and younger school ages. They occur in the early part of the night and, if regular, can be avoided by waking the child half an hour before the usual time of terror.

Obsessive behaviour

It is cute when your child hops down the footpath, avoids the lines and steps only in the squares. It's impressive when they can name and draw every dinosaur. But there comes an extreme point when this is neither cute nor impressive – it is obsessive and odd.

There are thousands of children out there who are normal yet very unusual. Most are boys and most have a preoccupation with order, routine and an area of over-interest.

One eight-year-old I work with has an obsessive bath routine. Only he can insert the plug and the bath water can only rise to a certain level. The bath cannot end until he has lifted out his toys and placed them in an exact spot. Then he removes the plug and some normality returns.

Another seven-year-old insists that only he turn off the television set. If others interfere, it must be turned on, run for a minute, and then only he can switch it off. On leaving for school he must close the front door and can only enter the car through the back left-hand door.

We see others who will only eat at a certain spot at the dining table, insist on wearing specific clothes despite the temperature or hold tight to a favourite object.

Some parents who read this will think, 'Stop pandering to the brat. Just knock him into shape.' But those who have tried this find the explosive aftershock is not worth the effort. We often try to desensitise and remove the obsessions, only to find they are replaced by a new area of over-interest.

Many of these children are fixated on some part of learning. They may have an immense knowledge of animals, cars, planes, football, video titles or events in history. Their conversation is often inappropriate, turning into a lecture on their special topic. At school some are branded 'weird', while others are accepted as an eccentric professor.

Sometimes there is a worrying over-interest in wars, guns and death. Though this is no more sinister than an over-interest in football or dinosaurs, it usually results in psychiatric referral.

As I work with these children I must decide when this is a normal odd temperament and when it is a pathological problem like Asperger syndrome, autism spectrum disorder, semantic pragmatic language disorder (see Chapter 11, page 153) or obsessive compulsive disorder.

My decision is based on the depth of the fixation, how it interferes with life, the child's social skills and the quality of both verbal and non-verbal communication. When in any doubt, children who may have obsessive behaviour should be referred to a paediatrician, child psychiatrist or specialist in child development.

Only children

The only child is often said to be lonely, spoiled and over-influenced by adults. There is a seed of truth in this, but there is more to the story. On average, the only child gets more stimulation, education and individual attention at home. This shows as a slight increase in academic ability, and they are more in tune with adult thinking.

The downside for the child is the lack of company and absence of a playmate. They may be weaker in the skills they need to mix with other children. Their attitudes may be too adult and their talk can be inappropriate for a child.

There are more only children born to older or sole parents. One of these groups is disadvantaged by lack of energy, the other by lack of cash. But when you add it all up it's a case of swings and round-abouts. If we use a good preschool and arrange for extra mixing with other children, everyone is a winner.

I believe that an extended family upbringing is of more impor-tance than having a brother or sister. This lets children see their roots and gives them experience with babies and family relation-ships and a respect for the elders of the tribe. There is a saying, 'It takes a village to raise a child.' I think a village full of people is more important than a brother or sister in an empty city.

Oppositional behaviour

One of the most common and difficult problems I see is the child with entrenched opposition. When this problem is in its most minor form the child is reluctant to comply with any request. When it is major, home life becomes deadlocked and parents feel they have lost control.

You ask politely, 'Would you please do this?'

They reply, 'Try and make me!'

You draw a line in the sand, they jump over the limit and ask, 'What are you going to make of it?'

Parents with compliant children have no understanding of how difficult this can be. Opposition generates immense hostility, which ruins relationships.

When I am told, 'My eleven-year-old refuses to do anything she is asked,' I know this is not a new behaviour. Opposition usually starts at about the age of three years and gets deeper as parent and child become more entrenched. Opposition hits its peak in teenage, by which time it is almost impossible to move.

The amount of opposition in a child depends on their individual style of temperament and how this has been managed. Many children are created with an obliging temperament, and whatever we do they generally remain compliant. But most children have the potential to some opposition. If they are nurtured and encouraged, this rarely poses much problem, but if they are parented with force, confrontation and hostility, this seed may sprout into considerable trouble.

A few children are created with a large potential for opposition. Even with the best parents, behaviour will be a battle, and when pushed heavily these children become defiant, angry and totally immovable. Some of this extreme group are spiteful and paranoid, blaming all the other ratbags for their problems.

There is good and bad news about opposition. The bad is the damage it does to families where mums and dads may get no pleasure from parenting. The good news is that most turn into well-adjusted, normal adults. Many will later feel remorse and wish they had done things differently, but this is often at their parents' funeral, and by then it's too late.

Opposition is extremely hard to treat. Be realistic in your expectations. A twenty per cent change in six months is an appropriate goal.

- Go gently with the difficult three- and four-year-old. This is the best age to nip opposition in the bud. At three and four years be positive, encourage the good, let the unimportant pass and steer around confrontation.

- With the oppositional school-age child avoid debate as this escalates and places parents on the back foot.

- Don't rely on reason. This does not impress the oppositional child.

- Avoid hostile, cold, passive-aggressive or sarcastic comments.

- Avoid ultimatums and rigid limits. These provide a clear line to challenge.

- Avoid backing the child into a corner. Allow them to feel they have some choice and power over the outcome: 'You can choose not to do your homework now but you will be choosing not to watch "The Simpsons". It's your choice.'

- Communicate in a way that transmits an expectation of compliance.

- Talk in a calm, matter-of-fact way. Use the broken gramophone technique, quietly repeating the message.

- Use the technique of active ignoring. Briefly move to another room, or water the garden, then return and re-engage.

- Use an 'I' statement. 'I feel sad when we are angry with each other.'

- Make your statement and move on. Don't hang around waiting for retaliation.

- Immediately grasp any good behaviour and appreciate the positives.

- Work as a team: 'We managed that well together.'

- Calmly give a choice: 'You can do this now or I can wake you early and you can do it before school.'

- With older children consider a trade-off: 'You can choose not to do your chores and I can choose whether to drive you to soccer training.'

- Withdrawal of privileges may be of benefit, though it can back-fire. 'No television tonight'; 'To bed half an hour early'; 'No telephone'; 'No friend to stay over'; 'It's your choice.'

Pocket money

Little children have no need for pocket money before they start school. A six-year-old gets a small allowance that is usually squandered or lent to their sister, the con-artist. But by the age of eight years the potential Bonds and Bransons have realised that money talks. These short-pants entrepreneurs can be motivated by the sight of a silver coin, but by teenage it takes crisp notes, gold bars or share-option certificates to have the same effect.

The amount of pocket money depends on how much you can afford, what extras the child must buy and your neighbourhood norm. After this you have three choices:

1. Pay a fixed weekly sum that is reviewed each year, with adjustments based on inflation, the world economy and how you are feeling on that day.

2. Provide a base salary, then pay double for each day that work is completed without reminders or complaint.

3. With older children you can draw up a carefully costed contract. List what purchases will come from consolidated revenue and those they must fund themselves. Agree on a fee-for-service scheme where you are charged a small levy for every chore. This provides a basic wage with extra pay for productivity.

Pretend friends

At my age, if I start talking to imaginary people you would probably call for an ambulance. But normal young children are allowed to talk and play with pretend people.

This occurs in about one in ten children, usually starting at about the age of three years, an age of technicolour imagination. The friend is usually of the same sex as the child and always has a name. To the outsider there is an air of reality, but the child is actually quite aware of what is fact and fiction. Imaginary friends are not a sign of disturbance, loneliness or emotional stress. They are more common in girls and may signify a more creative style of temperament.

If your child prattles on to some pretend person, just relax and enjoy this brief window of undisturbed innocence. These friends have usually evaporated by the age of six years. Some children befriend an animal. One little boy used to bring a dinosaur on a rope when he visited me in my office.

Some families chat to objects as a bit of fun. One well-known Australian told how his daughter loved the Sydney Harbour Bridge. Every time they drove across she talked to the bridge and her dad joined in to keep her company. 'Recently,' he said, 'my daughter and I were driving across with my mother-in-law. I talked to the bridge as usual, at which point Grandma asked, "What's your father up to?" My daughter looked blank and replied, "Beats me if I know." '

Shoplifting

Petty shoplifting is probably more common than any parent wishes to acknowledge. It is more likely when children are allowed to loiter around shops or they associate with friends who set the wrong example.

With shoplifting, it is easier to pretend it never happened, but parents and child must front up to the shop. It's tough, but unless the child faces up to their actions no lesson is learnt. Goods must be returned and if this is not possible, repayment comes from future pocket money. Don't set impossible reparation demands: this is how the Second World War started.

In my experience, children from functional families will usually respond to a firm, friendly, non-critical approach. Some parents introduce the offending child to the local constable who gives some fatherly advice, but this is further than most need to go.

If stealing ever becomes a major problem, you may need to seek help from a psychologist or community clinic.

Short fuse

There are a lot of sparky children, some with the stability of out-of-date gelignite. Parents handle these with the greatest of care, knowing that the slightest bump may blow their head off. Poor impulse control is predominantly a boy problem, though girls, including mothers, are not exempt. This style of temperament has a strong hereditary link, and many of these children are like a parent or grandparent.

This is often part of the spectrum of ADHD, a condition caused by inadequate function of the frontal parts of the brain. These parts affect the self-monitoring of learning and behaviour. The biggest problem of ADHD comes from the child's unthinking actions and impulsive behaviour. For more information on ADHD see Chapter 12.

Short-fuse ADHD behaviours are more common in sole-parent situations. This may be because ADHD can be inherited from a parent, and in these cases conception may have been somewhat impulsive and ongoing impulsivity has destabilised the relationship. I work with many mums who are left with the difficult child of a difficult man.

Explosiveness is at its most extreme in the three- and four-year-old. With age, the fuse gradually lengthens. One of the most memorable children of recent times was a boy aged three years. After a consultation punctuated by tantrums and flying toys, I asked the mum, 'Is it always as bad as this?'

She calmly replied, 'Yes. I can't cope, my husband can't cope, the grandparents can't cope, even our German shepherd guard dog is terrified of him.'

This story did have a happy ending. Tim had extreme ADHD, which responded well to treatment. Three months later I asked his mum, 'How are things?'

'The difference?' she said. 'Now I love him.'

The main problem at school age is volatility and unpredictability. The smallest unimportant event can trigger the most unexpected explosion. Parents gasp in disbelief: 'How so little can result in so much!' Outside the home other parents look over as if to say, 'Is that child mentally all right?' At school the sparky child is sought out by bullies who know they are easy to stir. When upset they may go berserk and hit out, and many may be suspended from school.

A parent who has not experienced this short-fuse type of temperament has no idea how it affects discipline. Mums and dads are in a dilemma about whether to stand firm and treat the child the same way they treat their other children or to back off and preserve the peace. The more I work with these children, the more often I promote the path of peace.

- With young children anticipate, avoid triggers, divert, keep calm.

- With older children get them to think how the behaviour appears to others and teach self-control techniques.

- Avoid debate and argument; this inflames and escalates.

- Try to maintain a calm, matter-of-fact appearance.

- Avoid actions and words that inflame. One mum said, 'We get on much better if I avoid the word "no".' There are better ways to say it without using that word.

- Move yourself away from the scene.

- Put the child in time out. This is a good idea but often it's impossible.

- Do not interpret the hysterical actions of a child as premeditated or malicious. The gentlest, most good-natured puppy may bite when stressed and frightened.

- With older children talk about the behaviour when they are calm. Get them to realise how stupid they appear in front of their friends.

- Try the stress-control techniques of taking deep breaths, counting to five, punching a pillow, getting outside.

- Notice and encourage when they turn the other cheek and let irritation pass.

- Try the 'traffic light' technique, where they stop, think and then go.

- When impulsivity is part of ADHD, its treatment will dramatically improve this behaviour.

Sleep problems

By school age most children sleep through the night. The main sleep problem they have is a difficulty getting off to sleep. This comes from one of three reasons:

1. a poorly disciplined sleep routine

2. a temperament that needs less sleep or

3. a busy mind.

A disciplined sleep routine is essential for all children and adults. Every night we should go through the same sequence of preparation at the same time. Don't accept procrastination in six- and seven-year-olds; get them horizontal and hope the eyes glaze and shut. Only allow slight modification of routine at weekends, as late nights and long sleep-ins disrupt the week-day pattern.

The need for sleep is similar in most children at a given age. But there are extremes, where some children need much more sleep and others run happily on less. If a child settles late, yet is fresh and well-rested in the morning, they may be designed for a later bedtime. Often the child with low sleep needs will have a late-to-bed, early-riser parent.

A busy mind stops some children from settling at night. They go to bed with their brains racing and they can't let go. We see this in busy or anxious children as well as some with ADHD.

With these circling minds we need to help them unwind and establish a routine that prepares for bed. Stories seem to relax, particularly when a child is old enough to read to themselves. Video games and television in the bedroom tend to stir. Relaxation tapes and gentle music are said to be of benefit, but despite all this I still have great difficulty helping this group.

In recent years I have reluctantly sedated some extreme four- to six-year-olds who had never been able to settle before 11pm.

A few five-year-olds still come to their parents' bed each night. If everyone is happy with this situation there is no need to act. Children soon get fed up sleeping with their parents in the same way that we get fed up sleeping with them. If you have had enough of this intrusion, give advance warning and then evict. You can accommodate the occasional visit by placing a mattress on your floor, but they must lie down low and not rise to a higher altitude.

Sleep walking

This is not a rare condition – about ten per cent of all children have an occasional walk and two per cent are quite regular. It's more common in boys and usually occurs in the early part of the night.

Sleep walking is not a dream state – these children are in the deepest part of sleep. They sit up and start to move in a stiff, robotic manner. Their eyes are glazed, yet they can navigate around obstacles, open doors and perform simple tasks. If addressed, they respond but the words are like computer speech or unintelligible. If woken, they are unaware, and in the morning they remember nothing. Each walk lasts a few minutes, though some can continue for up to an hour.

There is no need to wake the sleepwalker. This can be extremely difficult and causes nothing but confusion. Instead, bring them back to bed and protect them from danger. One of my earliest experiences as a junior in paediatric emergency was treating a seriously injured girl who had walked through an upstairs window. Parents can't stop sleep walking but they must keep their children safe. This is done with security locks, alarm bells or saucepans balanced on door handles. Sleep walking lessens with age, though some are still on the move as adolescents or adults.

Socially out of tune

Most children are out and out charmers, but a few are socially clumsy. They play poorly, mix with difficulty and don't see how their behaviour irritates others. If you feel that your child may be socially out of tune there are some things you can do to help:

■ Reinforce when they play well and interact appropriately.

■ Give a brief reminder when their actions are upsetting others.

- Don't become negative or constantly criticise.

- Discreetly ask them how it would feel if they were in the other person's place.

- Social skills training programs are sometimes suggested but these are often more successful in the therapy room than the outside world.

- The development of social skills comes gradually with age and maturity.
  See also Chapter 14.

Soiling, or encopresis

Almost two out of every 100 children at the age of seven years will still pooh in their pants. Over half of these have never been bowel trained, while the others have slipped from the straight and narrow. There are more boy soilers than girls. The literature suggests that most of these are chronically constipated, but this is not my experience.

Soiling rarely occurs during the night, is unusual in the morning session of school and is most common between 2pm and bedtime. Analytically minded psychiatrists interpret this timing as a symbolic landing of manure on your mum.

But I believe these children are created with a soil-prone gut, which is tipped over the edge by some known or unknown trigger. This may result from the pain of constipation, the birth of a sibling, admission to hospital or stress in the family. But most commonly there is no obvious triggering event.

Some parents believe the child has control and the problem is deliberate. But this is not true: the children I see would like nothing better than to stop soiling. I see parallels with adults who smoke – the majority would love to quit, if only they had the strength. The adult only changes when one night they attend an inspirational session with the Dalai Lama. They leave the hall uplifted and never smoke again.

Often it takes an outside force like this to change entrenched human behaviour. When soiling has gone on for years parents are defeated, and children can't do it alone. Often the change comes with the enthusiasm and inspiration of a talented psychologist or paediatrician (the outside force).

The first step in treatment is to exclude constipation. This is not always straightforward as some children are badly blocked yet present with the confusing symptom of diarrhoea. This happens when a large ball of constipation grossly distends the gut and allows looseness to seep around the edges. This block can be excluded if the child is able to regularly pass sausage-shaped motions. When in doubt we trial a laxative such as liquid paraffin in its more palatable form of Parachoc.

Behavioural change comes with an encouraging attitude and a simple star chart (see Chapter 4, page 42). We initially put all the focus on sitting three times a day: before school, following school and following dinner. After this we direct the attention from sitting to encourage one moment of success. Then we concentrate on regular usage and clean days. About one-third respond to this rapidly, one-third take six months or more and the remainder are extremely hard to shift.

Suicide talk

Youth suicide is a great concern and any child who talks of self-harm must be taken seriously. Though teens and young adults are at greatest risk, the child of ten years or younger can occasionally suicide.

In the five- to twelve-year age group talk of self-harm is a common means of hijacking attention. Children will often say, 'I'm dumb. I'm bad. I've got no friends. What's the point in living? What would you do if I killed myself?' The dilemma for parents is to separate these martyr statements from a genuine cry for help.

Though cautious, I generally underplay such comments in these younger ages, but only if all else is on track. The alarm bells ring when there is a change in personality, loss of interest, withdrawal from friends, major sadness or an over-focus on the means of self-injury. Children are also at greater risk following the suicide of some major public figure or someone in their close community.

At this young age most of the talk of self-harm has the sole purpose of stirring up mums and dads. But nothing in this world is completely certain, so when in the slightest doubt be quick to ask for help. See also this chapter, Depression, page 92.

Suspension from school

Most suspensions follow unthinking outbursts where a child hits, hurts, insults or gets so angry they refuse to comply. This is usually associated with the short-fuse temperament described in this chapter on page 109.

In my experience most of these children are kind, sensitive kids with no malice in their make-up. For them, they have a vulnerable Achilles heel in their volatile temperament. When pushed too far they snap and hit trouble.

With many school suspensions the wrong person has been blamed. One child in my care was suspended for abusing a teacher and kicking the principal. It all started when he was peacefully eating his lunch. A well-known bully pushed over his drink and called him a retard. This ignited the fuse and he went wild. A passing teacher misread the situation and abused him further. The principal intervened clumsily and got a kick for his ineptitude. The boy was banished for a week, the parents, who worked, were disadvantaged and the thug who started it all was never cautioned.

Recently, a seven-year-old was suspended and referred to me for psychiatric assessment. He was seen as severely disturbed as he had tried to hang himself in the school yard. Everyone was so busy psychoanalysing the child they failed to think back to the previous day's teaching on the outlaw Ned Kelly and his death by hanging. This ADHD boy, with mild intellectual disability, was playing out a story. His problem was imagination and lack of sense, not a death wish.

When a child is suspended from school, always look past the reported crime to see why it happened. It may not change the decision, but the true culprits should be brought to justice. When suspension results from the impulsivity of ADHD, this is the priority for treatment.

Parents will be annoyed but they must not get too heavy and bully the school. Even in suspension the parent–teacher relationship must be guarded at all costs (see Chapter 9, page 126).

Thumb sucking

This is an innocent habit, not a sign of emotional insecurity. It gives pleasure to one-third of young children; the other two-thirds never suck their thumbs. The average age that children stop is three and a half years, though many continue until they're five and two per cent are still sucking at thirteen years.

The main reason that parents discourage thumb sucking is the criticism they get from passers by and well-meaning relatives: 'That child has an emotional problem. He's behaving like a baby.' Dentists become worried once the second teeth are about to appear, because heavy sucking increases the risk of protruding front teeth, which may need wiring to realign. Bank managers are not unhappy with thumb sucking and are quick to provide a large loan to fund the wires.

At school age most thumb sucking is in times of boredom, tiredness and especially when settling to sleep. A little gentle comfort is never a problem, but hours of heavy tooth bending could prove expensive.

The old-fashioned psychoanalysts had no interests in tooth alignment. To them this was full of the sexual symbolism of large upstanding lighthouses, trains and tunnels. Treatments used to involve elbow splints, sleeping in gloves and covering thumbs in foul-tasting paint. Nowadays there is no such interpretation: we just let the child know we worry what other people think and we explain the risks of sticking-out teeth.

It's okay to allow gentle sucking while settling to sleep, but on other occasions distract or give a low-key reminder. Never nag or become too heavy as this causes stress, which increases sucking and then drives it underground. When in doubt, talk to your dentist. They will advise and tell you if damage is occurring.

Tics and twitches

A tic is caused by an involuntary twitch of a small muscle. Usually this involves the head and neck, the most common being a blink or twitch of the eyelid. Tics may show as movement of the lip, nose, neck or shoulder or a clearing of the throat.

When a child twitches they have no direct control of this movement. Stress makes things worse, while the tic totally disappears in sleep. Tics can be there most of the time, but they are usually intermittent. They tend to wax and wane and many, if not most, resolve spontaneously. The peak starting age is around seven years, but tics can appear at any time from four years to twelve years.

Tics cause frustration to parents and teachers, but are usually of less concern to the child. By themselves they are benign, though they are often not alone, being associated with ADHD difficulties with learning and behaviour. In this combination it is ADHD that causes most of the problem and is the main priority for treatment.

The best management is to remain calm and make a minimum of fuss. Give gentle reminders but don't over-focus, as this makes things worse. Counselling to reduce tension, relaxation and reward techniques are sometimes recommended, but the results are fairly unimpressive. Very occasionally we treat children with tic-reducing medication but this is only in extreme cases. A severe case may be termed Tourette syndrome, which involves major movements of the neck and shoulder and noises in the throat.

Tidying the bedroom

I often wonder if there is a tidiness gene. If there is, some children are born with this vital bit missing. With untidy children we must accept there will be some shambles and hope a good spouse will fix them in the future.

There are other children who have reasonable tidiness, but their over-tidy parents have the problem. I know one family where the son is average-messy, but his mother has an overdose of organisation. On her return from the fruit market she can't relax until the apples are polished and the carrots lined accurately in the veggie drawer.

Everything at home is in its place and it is no surprise that she fights with her son over his untidiness. For most of us parenthood brings new meaning to the word 'mess', but it's a concept this mother has not grasped. Her ordered brain is better suited to the obsessive administration of the contraceptive pill than children.

The secret of tidiness is to start early. Children between the age of one and four years like to be helpful, so build on this while it is there. After the age of five there are a selection of suggestions:

- Provide easy access to storage and hanging space.

- Get stackable plastic boxes and label what goes where.

- Regularly cull all junk and outgrown clothes.

- Sort through toys, removing stuff that doesn't work and small items that constipate the vacuum cleaner.

- Remove glass marbles from the toy box. When they hit the Hoover the beaters go berserk.

- With a young child, tidy together.

- Before complaining, make sure your children know what you expect of them.

- Ask them to tidy, and make it clear that you will follow up with an inspection.

- Use a kitchen timer to count down to inspection.

- Use the 'carrot' incentive: 'You tidy this, I'll get your drink ready.'

- Have a preset inspection time each day.

- A star chart can help focus attention on the clean room at inspection time.

- For each day of relative tidiness add a small productivity bonus to the pocket money.

- Be quick to notice effort and tidiness: 'Gosh, have the cleaners been here?'

- After giving adequate warning, place all untidied items in a large polythene bag. Lock this away for several days.

- Go one step further and gather all you see at a fixed time each evening. Lock away for one week. At an agreed time, empty the week's collection in a pile and reimpound anything that is not put away.

- Don't expect children to be more organised and tidy than their parents. Children who live with pigs learn to grunt.

- If you don't have this sorted out by teenage, take a step back and ask, 'Is it worth driving my children from home for the sake of a clean bedroom?'

Tooth grinding

When teeth are noisily ground by day, this is usually associated with severe intellectual disability. But tooth grinding at night is extremely common in normal, well-adjusted children.

Dentists worry that the repeated grinding can cause long-term tooth damage, while parents are more concerned by the noise. Some people believe that tooth grinding can cause malocclusion of the jaw, while others suggest that malocclusion can be the reason why they grind. Whatever is going on, discuss it with your dentist. If your child's teeth are becoming worn your dentist will provide a small night splint to give protection.

In your great grandmother's day tooth grinding was a sure sign of worm infestation. But she got her ends mixed up: any worm that is out and about at night is at the bottom, not the top end.

Whingeing

Some children are born with an amazing talent for whingeing. When smacked by the midwife at birth, they don't cry, they just start whingeing. The grumbles go on through childhood, and presumably, as adults they complain about everything then join a protest group.

At the other end of the spectrum there is a remarkable breed of children who are totally whinge-free. They take life as it comes and never complain. As adults they can cope with all the major disasters such as flood, fire, earthquake, even bad hair cuts, wet Saturdays and tickets from the parking police.

Finally, there are those children who don't start out as complainers but learn to whinge because it gets them what they want.

If you have a whinge-free child, light candles and give thanks for your good fortune. If whingeing is a learned habit used to change our decision, we must stand by our guns and prevent paying off.

- Give maximum attention for no whinge and, when possible, withhold attention for whingeing.

- When addressed, recognise the child is speaking, even if you can't answer their question immediately.

- If you ignore a child's attempts to talk politely they may replace this with whingeing.

- If you can't address their problem now, state clearly when you will answer their question. Say, 'I hear you – I will be with you in thirty seconds.'

- When you make an unwise decision, be quick to say, 'I got it wrong.' A quick turnaround removes the need to whinge.

- When you have got it right, don't let whingeing change the referee's decision.

- Label whingeing for what it is: 'That's whingeing. I don't answer whingeing.'

- Set some rules: 'If you are quiet for two minutes and ask again properly.'

- With a child who is a born whinger, anticipate, divert, ignore, occupy, put in another room, go outside, play music, use time out.

NINE

Starting school: the first weeks

School has an immense impact on our children. It's their seat of learning, their place of employment, their office and their social hub. Here they compete with others and develop the skills they need to achieve in the world.

School is supposed to be the happiest time of our lives, and this will be true for those who are academically and socially strong. There are some children, however, who tolerate but don't enjoy school, and others who hate it with a passion.

We feel the ups and downs of school as children bring their stresses home and dump on their mums and dads. Parents of star students walk with confidence and are prominent on school committees. Those with children who struggle or disrupt keep their heads down and react with an adult form of school refusal.

In the years between five and twelve there is a massive explosion of knowledge. At the start a child can barely hold a pen, write their name, count past twenty or read a word. By their thirteenth birthday most write with style, perform complex calculation and read like an adult. All this comes from hours of effort by teachers, parents and children.

This chapter takes a look at starting and settling into school.

To start early or hold back?

Modern parents suffer from a speedy condition called hurry sickness. Life is lived at such a pace there is no time to savour the present. From the moment of birth they are pushing their children on the fast track to independence. If the local law allows their child to start education at four years and seven months, that's when they will begin.

But there is no need for such a rush: school enrolment is usually not compulsory until the age of six years. Young children vary greatly in their social and emotional maturity. Some are ripe for an early start, but others need more months to develop.

Children must be socially ready, and preferably academically ready, at the start. The necessary **social skills** include mixing, sharing, playing together, working in a group, the ability to sit and listen, independent toiletting, good behaviour control and the ability to separate from Mum. The preferred **academic skills** are holding a pen, writing your first name, recognising some letters, knowing numbers, counting objects and good receptive and spoken language. Parents will often push their young child into school on the strength of their academic abilities without recognising the greater importance of appropriate social maturity.

It is possible to enrol early and, if things go badly, to repeat next year. This sounds reasonable, but schools rarely repeat the starting class, and by the time the child has struggled for two years it is getting to be too late to fix the damage. Those who encourage late enrolments note that mature starters have stronger self-esteem and more impressive leadership skills in later years. Some children who start before they are ready remain on the outer edge and never make it to centre stage.

If your child is eligible to start young, look carefully at their social readiness. Discuss next year with their preschool director. They know how your child compares with the others who are preparing for school. When the director says no, take it seriously.

Many parents have no choice as, for them, school provides the only affordable form of child care. But if you have concerns and finances will support it, take the safe option and hold back. A late start will never do harm, but starting too soon can cause problems that don't go away.

The first day

The start of school for a child is like arriving to take up a new job for an adult. There are strange faces, names to learn and uncertain expectations, and unease hides behind every smile. This out-of-depth feeling is different from the tears and clingyness of the first day in preschool, which had all the dampness of a Kleenex advert.

It takes two months for an adult to feel comfortable in a new situation, so do allow equal time for a child to settle.

Preparation is important. Talk about the school, try on the uniform, visit the class and participate in the orientation program. Be positive but be realistic – school is for education, not entertainment. School may cater for a lot of children but it's not Santa's cave or Disneyland.

Find out whether a child from preschool or the neighbourhood will be in your child's class and, if possible, ask them over during the holidays. Plan the food for little lunch and big lunch, but don't overcompensate with treats that rot their teeth and clog the coronaries.

On the first day allow yourself plenty of time to avoid the pressure of a rush. Ensure there are no clashing appointments so that you can have as much time as it takes. Walk in with a positive stride, make your number with the class teacher, locate the toilets, put down the school bag and find a friend. Let them know what is going to happen, when you are going to leave and the time you will be back. If there are any problems the teacher will tell you what to do. When they are settled, depart decisively.

Home behaviour: up and down

As learning and playing consumes so much energy, excessive tiredness is almost universal among children starting school. Whether they want to discuss their day with you is much more variable. Some children arrive home with their heads full of adventures and a wish to talk non-stop. Others would divulge nothing, even if the KGB were providing a prompt.

For many, school becomes so important they talk, think and play it all the time. Infant sisters, dogs, cats and anything that can sit will be commandeered to become part of their teacher–pupil games.

Some children behave well at school but bring home their stresses and dump these on Mum. A few become nasty and spiteful to younger siblings, for a reason unclear to anyone but themselves. Occasionally they call on the sympathy vote and become the martyr: 'I'm dumb. No one likes me. I have no friends.'

Starting school is a major disruption to the stability of life, and behaviour that is normally good can slip off the straight and narrow. It's quite common for children just starting school to suddenly have unreliable bladders, unexpected clingyness, be defiant, or experience disturbed sleep and start coming to their parents' bed.

Some children start off well but after the second or third weekend they think, 'Home isn't all that bad after all.' This can produce temporary school refusal which resolves quickly if we are supportive but completely firm about attendance.

School behaviour: up and down

Teachers never have it easy, but the main problems for teachers of infants classes are holding attention, curbing call-outs and keeping bottoms on seats.

Sometimes I see a child who is emotionally or intellectually unsuited to start school. They may opt out, won't comply, crawl under desks or run off. These children may need the school counsellors to pinpoint their general or specific area of weakness.

At the start of school, children who suffer from Attention Deficit Hyperactivity Disorder (ADHD – which affects two per cent of school-age children) may be disruptive, distractable and out of step with others. A few of these children are immensely volatile, with explosive outbursts that occasionally put other children at risk. For more information about ADHD see Chapter 12.

Teachers in general are tolerant people who allow time for all but the most extreme behaviours to come good. For this reason it is unusual for parents to hear much negative feedback in the first month.

However, occasionally it is almost instantaneous that the muck hits the fan. With major problems I always ask the parents when they got that call. For a long time the record stood at twenty minutes on day one, but another mum trumped this: 'My son was suspended on orientation day.'

Good parent–teacher communication

At the start of school make a commitment to keep in touch with the class teacher. It's unfair to ambush a tired teacher every day and expect an in-depth consultation, but a lack of involvement may be interpreted as a lack of interest. It's best to take a mid-position: not too pushy but make sure you know what's happening. Aim to touch base every two weeks. Just ask, 'Is everything okay? Is there anything I can do to help?'

If you hear rumours, worry about any part of learning or are just concerned, be quick to talk to the class teacher. If there is a major problem, make an appointment to meet, so that the school can be prepared and allocate ample time to address your questions.

Over the years I have dealt with a lot of unreasonable, aggressive parents who have more interest in kicking heads than supporting their child's education. Don't front up with anger, accusations and heavy confrontation. Teachers are human and, like anyone else, they will become defensive, official and distant when aggressively challenged. So if you intend to keep your child at the school, establish close and respectful parent–teacher communication from the start.

Worries about learning

At least one child in ten has some weakness in learning (see Chapter 11). The most common problems include specific learning problems with reading and spelling (dyslexia), problems with attention, memory and work output (ADHD), problems with expression and understanding (language delay disorder), or a general slowness in learning (borderline or mild intellectual disability). The specific learning weaknesses are strongly hereditary, which means that a parent who struggled at school may have a child with the same difficulty. If your child seems to be following in your footsteps, be quick to ask for help.

Most early concerns are just a lag in maturity that will come good with short-term help. For others, the difficulties will cause pain throughout the school years and into adulthood. Be aware that learning problems can pass unnoticed and may only be looked into when a child opts out or expresses their frustration via bad behaviour.

As schools tend to give children the benefit of the doubt and allow time to settle, it is often the parents who will make the first move in asking for help. If you have the slightest concern talk to the class teacher. Ask direct questions about your child's abilities in general learning, reading, maths, independent work output, mixing and playground behaviour. Ask if they are middle of the class, above average or below average in each one of these specifics.

Ask if these concerns should be taken further. When specialist assessment is required, all state schools can arrange direct access to their counsellor and private schools can arrange this through their own channels. The help is out there, but it's often you, the parent, who needs to make the first move.

Starting school

1. Are they ready?
   - emotional readiness (most important)
   - can mix, share, has the ability to sit and listen, able to play together and work in a group, independent toiletting, has the ability to separate from Mum, has good behaviour control
   - academic readiness (less important)
   - can hold pen, write name, recognise some letters, count objects, has good expressive and receptive language, can tell news
   - does your preschool director say they are ready?
2. Preparation
   - attend orientation day
   - talk about school
   - find a friend who is starting
   - prepare for independent feeding and toiletting
3. The first day
   - allow plenty of time
   - let them know what's going to happen
   - let them know when they are going to be picked up
   - if there is any trouble, talk to the teacher
4. Home behaviour
   - tiredness is universal
   - some dump on Mum or a sibling
   - some become unreliable in sleep or night wetting
   - some refuse to go to school after two weeks (this is temporary)
5. School behaviour
   - attention drifts
   - callouts
   - walkabout
   - behaviour may be a sign of a learning problem
6. Good parent–teacher communication
   - make this a priority
   - show interest but don't be too pushy

- ask how you can help
- don't overreact or get too heavy
- when parents are aggressive, teachers become defensive and communication stops

7. Worries about learning
   - one in ten have some learning difficulty
   - specific difficulties, especially reading, language and attention, can run in families
   - first talk to the teacher
   - then talk to the school counsellor

TEN

The early school years: behaviours and concerns

E ach morning parents face an uphill challenge: how to steer that slow-moving body towards school. Mission accomplished, the child's day is filled with periods of listening, learning, mixing, acting smart and getting annoyed. In the afternoon they return home to do homework and to unload on their parents. Let's look at the behavioural hurdles that concern parents as they try to make a success of school.

Wriggling and walkabouts

At the start of school most little children sit, listen intently and marvel at the words of their teacher. A few are much more noisy, wriggly and disruptive. They are not naughty, it's just that they haven't located the switch to control impulse. Every infants teacher will regularly restate the rules of the class: 'Stay in your seat. Keep hands and feet to yourself. Speak only when you're asked. Hand up if you need help or need to go to the toilet.'

Compliance is reinforced with positive statements: 'Good sitting'; 'Good attending'; 'Good work'; 'Good manners.' When the rules are broken the teacher registers this with a sign, a single word or the shortest of short statements.

As children get older, the most inattentive can be refocused using a token system. For every ten minutes they stay on task, a bead is popped in a container. When the total reaches ten, there is a payout with a privilege such as a special book, delivering a message, or possibly computer time. Privileges motivate but are tough on the silent majority, who wonder why the 'bad boys' get all the good stuff.

Teasing and taunts

When my children started school I taught them to sidestep taunts. My wife, who is more practical, suggested they turn the other cheek then aim carefully and hit hard.

The child who is most teased is usually the one who overreacts to the smallest annoyance. Bullies target the impulsive, short-fuse child because they provide a jackpot every time. The teased child is usually innocent, but because they throw the last punch they are labelled aggressive.

I see children suspended from school following their justified overreaction to an annoying bully. They are put out for a week while the aggressor who caused the problem gets off scot-free.

When a five- or six-year-old is victimised at school parents should discuss the problem with the teacher or principal. Don't get too heavy: just state the facts as you see them and ask for advice. Teachers can deal with the problem by extra supervision or through a general instruction to the class about the treatment of fellow humans. In some schools a buddy is attached to those who are vulnerable for extra support.

When children are eight years or older parents can discreetly discuss the problem with the teacher, then use role-play to show how to sidestep conflict. Act things out in the calm of your home: get them to count quietly to five, walk away or respond with a set piece – 'That's interesting'; 'You seem to be having a bad day.' You would probably like to teach them a cleverer response like 'Did someone talk or did a dog pass wind?' but this might get them flattened.

Our aim is to teach children to fight with their brains rather than their bodies. But it is much easier to talk about turning the other cheek than it is to put it into practice. Ignoring annoyance is hard enough for an adult – it's almost impossible for a young child.

Bullies

We teach our children that bullying is bad, but bullies are often the ones that make it big in our adult world. Children may bully because they have low self-esteem and feel uplifted by dragging others down. Some have poor social skills and are slow to realise they have overstepped the mark. A lot bully because that's what they see at home.

Bullying takes many forms: intimidation, physical force, stand-over tactics and the emotional cruelty of isolation and exclusion.

As parents, our first aim is to protect our children; the next is to promote assertiveness. Giving in to bullying all the time can bring peace, but it has its own dangers. Children who always give in may never develop assertiveness, or may begin to enjoy being the victim because it attracts adult attention: 'Why does everybody treat me so badly?' (see also Chapter 8, Martyrdom, page 99).

With a five- or six-year-old, take your worries straight to the class teacher. With older children help them to develop assertiveness. Teach them to use words instead of retaliating physically or just surrendering: 'I don't like you pushing me'; 'I don't want to be held or touched'; 'I'm not going to chase you'; 'That's my property.'

A good school accepts that bullying does happen but makes it clear that it will not be accepted at any level. The class teacher can intervene directly or talk to the class about the feelings of others. If the school develops a herd resistance to teasing and bullying, the problem will diminish.

School refusal

It is quite common for a child to start school with great enthusiasm then, after several weeks, have a change of heart. Absence makes them see home as a pretty special place and they decide to opt for early graduation. The child has a point: if we make home life so good, why should they want to go to school? This temporary reluctance can be easily overcome if parents are gentle but firm and work closely with the teacher.

At older ages school refusal is a more serious problem. Sometimes it is due to learning difficulty or the child is socially uncomfortable. If you see it from their point of view, why should they go to a place that causes such pain? The remedy is to address the primary problem and try to create areas of success that will make school worthwhile.

School refusal can be a psychological symptom where a child is frightened to leave their mum or dad. Sometimes these worries are without foundation, but often, where there is smoke there is a fire. I recently saw a ten-year-old boy who refused to go to school. Two months previously his mother had been diagnosed with early breast cancer. Though no one had said much in words, he picked up on his parents' fears and upset. This boy didn't want to let his mum out of sight as he was frightened he might lose her.

Sometimes it is a parent who secretly clings to their child and generates separation anxiety. This can be hard to unravel and solve because the parent's manipulation is often subtle or subconscious. Here we need to address the parent's unresolved problems of emotion with psychiatric intervention.

The first step in managing school refusal is to return the child to the classroom. Missing school is like falling off a horse: if you don't get in the saddle now it becomes much more difficult in the future. If decisive returns and quick exits have not worked, the parents and class teacher need to meet and work out a joint plan.

There can be concessions but also firm limits. Dad will drive the child to school and walk in the gate with them, but then they are in the hands of the class teacher and they must stay. When the situation is stuck in deadlock the school counsellor will provide more specialised support. Where a child or parent's emotional baggage is causing the block, it's time for expert psychological or psychiatric intervention.

Tall stories

The mind of a six-year-old still bubbles with magic and innocence. They have the ability of a Fleet Street editor to blur truth and fiction. If your little one still believes in Santa and the Easter Bunny, their account of what happened at school may be pretty unreliable. If they come home to report that they are being beaten because they can't read, this may not be fact. Start by finding the truth – 'The truth is out there.'

When stories are over-colourful or untrue, it's best to listen, then simply state, 'I hear what you say, but I don't think it's quite like that.' Don't get too heavy; this magic age ends all too quickly. After eight we have a more secretive little person with many of the hang-ups and strange ideas of an adult.

Telling tales

A five-year-old is not only fascinated by rules, they believe they have a duty to inform on their mates. 'Miss, Jenny isn't listening'; 'Jack made a rude noise'; 'He can't go to the toilet without asking.' Though no one has published the research, it is possible that the fairer the sex, the more frequent the dobbing.

This is a quaint behaviour that only lasts for a very short time. It's best to be deaf to dobs or to make a brief comment: 'That's dobbing. I don't want to hear that.' Telling tales hits a peak between five years and six years, but by the age of seven it's on the fade. After eight there is a code of silence where it becomes uncool to tell on your friends.

Petty theft

Young children are not adults: they don't understand our attitude towards possessions, ownership, money and the finer print of contractual law. At infants school, if a piece of property is left within reach, it may end up in a pocket. This small-time stealing is quite common and relatively innocent.

Unfortunately, however, there are always other parents who think the worst: 'That child has home problems'; 'They are a deprived child who is stealing love'; 'It's a throwback to her convict or bush-ranger relatives.'

I often see parents create a major drama. A child lifts another's pencil or some piece of valueless plastic junk. The parents feel their child has been violated, and they almost dial 000 to summon a team of detectives to interrogate the kindergarten kleptomaniac.

In the early school years children should be discouraged from bringing small stealable items to school. When an offence happens, make the minimum fuss, just state that the property is not theirs and return it to the owner.

With age we need to be far firmer. A few, apparently well-adjusted children continue to steal belongings or money from their mates. In general it is overcome by a firm but low-key response, followed by close supervision (see also Chapter 8, Shoplifting, page 109).

Acting smart

After the age of eight years every class has its prize smart arse. These children are masters of the art of taunting teachers. They clown, answer back and generate strange bodily sounds. Boys cause the greatest bother and the problem gets worse right through to the end of high school. Many of those who clown are weak in some area of education and their performance allows a few moments of recognition.

The skilled teacher has a nose for stirrers and will seat them apart while keeping them well in view. They anticipate times of trouble, hold attention and keep minds occupied. But it is hard to handle these intrusions. To turn a blind eye gives a message of acceptance; to make a fuss takes the bait and keeps them fishing.

With a class clown, it is essential to lay down some ground rules in a time of peace, after which the teacher will give a pre-discussed sign and follow through. Some use a three-strike system. The child starts each lesson with three 'lives', and for each intrusion, one life is lost. Zero at the end results in a five-minute wait before release.

Acting smart is often a sign that the child's ability to learn or the teacher's method is inadequate. Unfortunately for teachers, some children are unsuited to school. They think of it as worse than a prison sentence, except that at least when you're sent to prison you usually score less than thirteen years.

Hard-working, achieving class mates sense the injustice when the worst-behaved child gets the most attention, earns extra rewards and receives merit certificates. At this early age children are discovering a well-known fact of life: 'He who makes the greatest fuss gets the most.'

Homework

Most children see homework as a necessary evil that has to be done, but for some it's about procrastination, foot dragging and excuses. In the early years homework plays a small part in learning but by teenage the ability to organise, stick at a task and study independently is vital for tertiary success.

The foundation for good study is to start early and for parents to be actively involved. Parents can provide structure, encouragement and a means of quality control, but it's not about spoon feeding or doing it yourself (one father recently complained that his highly researched project on the environment had scored a worse mark than the multi-page thesis written by another class parent). The ways to encourage homework are:

- Establish the importance of home study right from the start.

- Have knowledge and interest in the syllabus, check that work is completed and be enthusiastic about marks for effort.

- Have a regular homework time and keep strictly to this every day.

- After school give twenty minutes to change, snack and prepare.

- Give a ten-minute, five-minute and one-minute warning – then start.

- Work in a special place that is always associated with homework.

- Get them started, go through the instructions, give structure and set time limits.

- If attention span is weak, expect twenty minutes full output, a ten-minute break, then twenty minutes more. Use a timer to act as a referee.

- When the work is completed, check but don't dishearten or snoop. Sign it off if necessary.

- Some children manage better when homework is done before arrival home. The school may have a homework class or they might use a room at Auntie's work.

- Some children are morning people. An hour before breakfast may be worth two hours in the afternoon.

- Don't let homework destroy your parent–child relationship. If it gets too heated, discuss the options with the class teacher. Sometimes we have to let the school police their own problems.

To hot-house or not?

Recent research suggests that preschoolers carry a large number of unused brain cells just waiting to learn new skills. Then between two years and twelve years of age they shed the unused neurones, leaving a more trim, focused brain.

These cells may have nothing to do with important learning. For all we know, at twelve, children may discard the throwbacks from our ape ancestry, perhaps the pathways needed to swing from trees and scratch our bottoms. But it is possible that our children are losing a reservoir of untapped talent that is only available at this young age.

Certainly little children show great abilities to learn. I see new migrant children, without a word of English, yet six months of preschool has them chatting like native Australians. I am also impressed by the fact that many sports people, singers, movie stars and musicians have children with similar talent to their parents. Part of this may be in the genes, but early teaching must also make a difference.

We live in times when academic attainment seems all-important and an early education must have a value. But life education may be of more importance in the long run. In life, a child learns as an apprentice to their parents as they watch and work together.

The question on every parent's lips is, 'How much pushing is enough pushing?' The answer from this expert is, 'I don't know.' My heart favours the path of apprenticeship, example and time together, but I can't escape the evidence for teaching new skills early. Until we understand more clearly, there must be some sort of compromise. Not hot-housing; just a warm, nourishing home environment with some extra stimulation.

Tutors

When your children are learning to drive, you employ an outside instructor because, not only are they willing to risk their life, but they are usually more patient and effective than a parent. Tutors are in the same league: they can impart more knowledge than Mum or Dad and with a lot less stress.

Tutoring can lift a child who is weak and maintain their enthusiasm to learn. The down side is that any remedial work naturally focuses attention on the child's areas of difficulty and failure. Parents misunderstand the pain children feel and will tell me, 'He's lazy, he won't do his extra reading.' Of course, the child is not lazy; they are telling you it is hard and, in fact, it sucks!

Think of it from an adult point of view. If my wife had me tutored in line dancing and synchronised swimming, you'd see one mighty stroppy Christopher Green. For me, root canal therapy would be preferable – at least that's done under anaesthetic.

When arranging a tutor, try to get a personal recommendation and don't continue if the individual does not suit your child.

Never replace all play, sport or even television, with tutoring. There must be a balance: if school is stressful a child doesn't need to be further traumatised in their relaxation time.

Time and 'quality time'

I am a sailor who loves to escape to the blue sparkle off Sydney. If I have a few hours and the wind is fair, that is the time to get out there. I have various friends who crew, but not all are prepared to sail at the moment when the weather is just right. Some make so many conditions before they give of their time, it seems that Venus must be in line with Mars and the moon in its first quarter. Then there are the flexible enthusiasts who enjoy life and seize the moment. And they're the ones who get the benefit.

Parents can be like my sailing friends: they can either seize the moment and enjoy their children now, or forever put it off. And I'm not talking 'quality time', a trendy term that I hate with a passion. 'Quality time' implies small allocations from a parent's busy diary that is almost like a weekly appointment with a therapist. In fact, there is no such thing as quality time unless it is time that tunes in to a child's needs.

As I look back on the time I have spent with my own children, I have some regrets. I gave quality time but, as a busy paediatrician, it was usually on my terms. My youngest son had a fabulous stunt kite, which we loved to fly together. He often asked, but usually on occasions when I was too busy. When I had time, there was no wind. The kite has long since disintegrated; an opportunity was lost that will not return.

Organisation: teaching children to lower the wheels before landing

I have had some memorable landings in Sydney, watching from the flight deck of an in-bound Jumbo. The bridge and the harbour are spectacular but more impressive is the organised attitude of the pilots. They have landed thousands of times before but they still check, double check and talk through every step.

I don't know when a person first has that ability to stop, think ahead and move on. I doubt if there is much planning before the age of eight years, and in some humans, organisation is never a strong suit.

When I was at school I blocked valuable brain space learning Latin, algebra and a smattering of Greek. I might have been a genius if they had taught me instead the art of setting priorities, managing

time, thinking ahead, jogging memory and giving the impression that I was in control.

As a child leaves the swimming pool we want them to stop for a second and ask, 'Have I got my towel? My cossie? My goggles? My bus pass?' At the end of the school day: 'What is my homework? Do I have the right books? Are there any notes for Mum? Is there anything else?' (see also Chapter 8, Forgetfulness, page 96).

Organisation starts with the tiniest baby who establishes a routine where they sleep, interact, feed, play and sleep. The toddler has a routine that leads to their bedtime, a bath, dinner, a story and then sleep.

At school age our goal is to get children to stop, think and plan. We can help this by asking at bedtime, 'What day is tomorrow? What's your first lesson? What do you need to bring to school? Any forms, money or messages for the teacher? Any sport or swimming?' Before leaving for school ask them to stop for a minute and run through the pre take-off checklist. Some parents act like the entertainment officer on a cruise ship: each morning they post the day's program on the fridge door.

As children get older we should encourage notes and 'To do' lists, and we direct the focus onto priorities. We might attach written reminders to important objects like the bus pass, the lunch box or to prevent early entry to the mid-morning drink.

When a child rambles when they are talking we can give some structure: 'You saw a dog – which dog? . . . What did the dog do? . . . What happened after Jack was bitten? . . . What then?' With written work we introduce order: 'You went on a school excursion – where did you go? . . . What did you do? . . . What did you learn? . . . How did it end?'

As exam success is so essential we need to teach children to be organised in tests: 'Read the question carefully. Stick to the instructions. There are six questions and there's one hour. That's ten minutes for each question.'

At home we can teach forgetful children to do things at once or to use a memory jog. They can write on a hand, tie a knot in a handkerchief or move their watch to the wrong wrist. Help them remember things with simple rhymes: 'Thirty days hath September, April, June and November'; 'i before e, except after c'; 'It's your **pal**, the school princi**pal**'; 'The **car** is station**ar**y.' When children have a poor memory for names they can learn the technique of association. When they are introduced to Francis, Elizabeth and Monica, they think, 'Francis – he's the Saint'; 'Elizabeth – she's the queen'; 'Monica **was** the President's friend.'

All this sounds so unnecessary when a child has an organised brain. But many children have been created with all the forgetfulness of an absent-minded professor and need all the memory jogs we can give.

Maintaining the magic

As I was writing this chapter I received an unusual letter. The first two pages described a five-year-old boy who was pure perfection. Then the letter continued: 'You can see that Matthew is a well-adjusted, happy little person. So what's the reason for writing to you? I'd like to keep him that way!'

Most mums can relate to this. You spend five years getting close and supporting, nurturing and immersing your child in the values of your family. Then, at the start of school, the innocent Christian is cast to the lions.

There is no doubt that they will meet teasing, spite, drag-downs and bad language, but the home foundation will always remain the strongest influence. Even the twelve-year-old who treats their mum as if she's mentally impaired is far more influenced by the family circle than those outside.

It would be cosy to maintain this age of trust. These eternal Peter Pans could fight pirates, believe in fairies and know they will always come out on top. But living is about leaving the past and moving on. If we prepare our children properly and keep the family foundations strong, no Darth Vader will turn them to the dark side.

The early school years: behaviours

1. Wriggling and walkabouts
   - remind of rules
   - reinforce good sitting
   - wriggling may be caused by ADHD
2. Teasing and taunts
   - the short-fuse child is the one most teased
   - with five- and six-year-olds tell the teacher
   - with older children, role-play a better response
   - teach to fight with the brain, not the body
3. Bullying
   - can be physical or emotional
   - use assertiveness techniques
   - consider the buddy system
4. School refusal
   - often happens in week two but is temporary
   - may be due to a learning or social problem
   - may be due to worry about the family
   - may be due to a parent's problem
   - don't let refusal get entrenched
   - talk to teacher and school psychologist

5. Tall stories
   - part of the magic mind of the under-eight-year-old
   - get the facts straight before you overreact
6. Telling tales
   - a common behaviour of five- and six-year-olds
   - label this as telling tales
   - discourage dobbing
7. Petty theft
   - under-eights have little idea of ownership
   - maintain a low-key response
   - with children older than eight years supervise closely and seek help if needed
8. Acting smart
   - often a symptom of learning problems
   - lay down ground rules and give a sign
   - use the three strikes technique
9. Homework
   - start early and be involved
   - set aside a time each day
   - don't spoon feed
   - don't let it spoil your relationship: refer the problem to the school if necessary
10: Hot-housing
   - we need to compromise between keeping children stimulated but not over-pushing them
11. Tutors
   - tutors can be more effective than a parent
   - tutoring can maintain a child's enthusiasm to learn
   - don't overly focus on the child's weakness
   - make sure the tutor suits your child
   - don't replace all relaxation and leisure time with tutoring
12. Time and 'quality time'
   - children need you to be available to tune in to their needs
13. Organisation
   - help your child to stop, think and plan

- when they are talking help them avoid rambling by giving structure
- help them to be organised and prepared for tests
- help them to remember things using rhymes and sayings

14. Maintaining the magic
    - children are influenced by others as they get older, but they remain most influenced by their family

ELEVEN

Help for learning difficulties

For some children, school is a time of stress and struggle. At least one in ten in each classroom will have a weakness in some area of learning. If a parent had a problem at school, such as weak reading or attention deficit, the risks that their child will have difficulties are many times higher. With major learning difficulties we cannot move mountains, but smaller hills can be levelled off a little.

Dyslexia, or developmental reading disorder

Dyslexia refers to a specific weakness in the area of reading and spelling. Purists prefer the term developmental reading disorder, but

I like dyslexia. This old label comes from the Greek (dys – bad + lexis – speech), and indicates a difficulty with language. This is more appropriate than ever, because modern research sees dyslexia as a problem of decoding words into language. This emphasis on language has attracted the interest of speech pathologists, who are now some of the leaders in the treatment of reading difficulties.

Strongly hereditary

When I diagnose a child with major dyslexia, I usually find a father or mother (or a close relative) with the same problem. The parents often deny any problem but when you ask them specifically about their spelling and their enjoyment of more solid literature, it often becomes apparent that the residue of childhood dyslexia is still there. This is an extremely common condition that disadvantages at least five per cent of the population. Figures as high as fifteen per cent are often quoted.

It is often said that parents who read to their children will prevent dyslexia. Certainly, parents who love books and read avidly are likely to be strong readers who will probably pass on strong reading genes to their children. On the other hand, parents who find reading stressful and read less to their children may tend to have more children with dyslexia. (I talk of the reading gene as though it were identified and sitting in a jar. Such a gene has not yet been located but I guarantee we will have it within the next decade.)

Dyslexia, learning disabilities and ADHD are much more common in children who are adopted or in foster care. When you think about it, there are sensible reasons why this might be the case. These conditions have the potential to affect adversely a child's education and their esteem. If we're right that problems like ADHD and dyslexia can be inherited, then the poor planning and impulsivity of ADHD may increase an adult's risk of ill-considered conception, and the child may inherit their parent's problem. Or, learning problems may increase an adult's risk of bottoming out and being unable to cope, so their children may end up in care.

Temperament, learning, language and behaviour are intimately entwined in our genes. It comes as a surprise to parents when I point to the origin of their children's problems. If the parent was a racehorse breeder, they would research more carefully before conception, but with humans it's done in the name of love.

Identifying a reading weakness

Reading requires a number of skills. We must scan and quickly recognise the shape of a known word, or break down the parts of one we have not met before. Then there are all the rules and exceptions. After this we learn to anticipate through groups of words that go together and by the flow of meaning. Finally we must take the decoded words and turn them into meaning.

The simplest way to assess reading is to look at a child's skill in recognising known words (sight word reading) and their ability to break unknown words into their various sounds (phonemic awareness). We can test sight words by asking a child to read irregularly spelt words that are not able to be sounded out, for example, yacht or duchess. We can test a child's ability to sound out using non words, for example, oripandom, which is easy to break down, but as we haven't met it before, it cannot be recognised by its shape.

A weak reader may initially use their visual recognition ability and may seem quite talented at reading. But problems appear when they have to break down the words and learn the rules, or some children seem to read quite well but such is the effort it involves, they miss the meaning.

The slow starter

All children develop at different rates. John may be slow to ride a bike or learn to swim, but he may eventually star in the Tour de France or get a medal in Olympic freestyle. A late start at reading does not necessarily mean a long-term problem. Many children fully recover with maturity and tutoring. However, despite the good outlook, it is important to call for help when worried.

Encouraging reading

Before rushing to get outside help, remember that there is much you can do yourself. Whether you have a child who is a strong or weak reader, read to them as much as possible. When they are slow and struggling, you read a bit, they read a bit, and this keeps the story moving. Choose books that are interesting yet written in a simple style. Before turning the page, stop for a moment and ask what is about to happen next. Read, read again, and then read some more.

Older children with a major reading problem are eligible to borrow the talking books from the local library.

Our aim is for all children to develop an interest in what's written, rather than what is spoon-fed through television and videos. A good book allows a child's mind to create colours, tones and characters, which is much more exciting than the work of any film director.

Help for the weak reader

If you are worried about any part of your child's learning ability, be quick to discuss this with the class teacher. If they are also unhappy they will call on the services of the school counsellor. The basic assessment will check general learning, measure the degree of reading delay, then pinpoint the area of maximum weakness, for example, whether it is phonemic awareness, visual recognition, comprehension or speed. Then your child can receive remedial teaching through the path of learning that is strongest.

The school may recommend a tutor who works in their local area, or you can approach one of the parent support groups, for example, SPELD or the local LD Coalition, for their suggestions. As most dyslexia comes from a difficulty turning visual symbols into language, some of the most effective remediators are language therapists. Private speech therapy is not cheap and may be long-term, but parents report that programs such as Lindamood Bell, the Spalding Method and others get good results.

Whatever therapy you use, don't go overboard. Remember you are focusing on the child's area of weakness and that can cause stress and unhappiness. I see many parents who attack remediation with great gusto and expect that the problem will be resolved in a matter of months. But, in reality, there is no quick fix for a major weakness in reading. Unrealistic expectations lead to immense frustration.

Also, when traditional methods seem so slow, it's easy to become seduced by alternative claims. Eye exercises, tinted lenses, stimulation of the balance centres, sensory motor integration, Vitamin B6, primrose and fish oils. Most of these sound quite spectacular as presented on the Internet, but there are few scientific studies to support their claims. A minor sub-group of children may be helped by tinted lenses, but they are very small in number. The best treatment for a language-based learning problem is a language-based approach. This is usually provided by a remedial teacher or a speech pathologist.

Dyslexia, or developmental reading disorder

1. General facts
    - the most common specific learning weakness
    - more common in males
    - often hereditary
    - often associated with ADHD or language delay
    - severe dyslexia is present for life
    - some children are late starters, but eventually read well
2. Problem areas
    - sight word recognition
    - ability to sound out a word (phonemic awareness)
    - a mix of both
    - difficulty with reading comprehension
    - difficulty with reading speed
3. Testing the weakness
    - sight word ability: whether they can recognise an irregular word such as 'yacht'
    - sounding out ability: whether they can sound out a non-word such as 'oripandom'
4. Other indications of a weakness
    - avoids reading
    - weak spelling (often continues through life)
    - does not read for pleasure
    - loses attention, daydreams
    - poor writing abilities
    - difficulties looking up information

5. Helping weak readers
   - parents read to, and read with, all children
   - a private tutor
   - a speech pathologist
   - schools can provide reading help by using a special teacher or parent volunteer
   - advice from a support group such as SPELD or LD Coalition
   - major dyslexia is painfully slow to help
   - reward creativity ahead of punctuation, spelling and setting out

Mathematics: a mystery

There are clever children with a specific learning weakness in reading (dyslexia); there are also children with a specific deficit in mathematics (dyscalculia). Some never get a grip of the basics, others can't cope with tables, and many drown with complex calculations. Dyscalculia is less common than dyslexia and is often associated with problems of coordination and writing. These children are probably helped more by a good tutor than is a child with the same degree of dyslexia. Tutoring gives children confidence and helps them to catch up.

Problems of speech and language

Language is the vital link that lets us communicate and enjoy the company of each other. It's no surprise, then, that language delays and disorders are a common cause of stress in children and concern in parents.

Speech is made up of what you say (expressive language) and what you understand (receptive language). Children may be slow to develop language (language delay) or children may develop the right words but they may be oddly expressed or only partly understood (language disorder). Or the words may be there but the child's pronunciation is poor (an articulation problem).

Expressive delay

Einstein did not talk until he was four years of age, yet he was quite smart. Einstein must have had a pure expressive language delay that often appears in isolation. This is sometimes a hereditary problem and I often find brothers and sisters are similarly delayed.

However, as a specialist in child development, I am always on my guard for the sinister side of expressive delay: deafness, global intellectual disability or autism spectrum disorder. But if a child has normal hearing, understanding, awareness, interaction and general development I will then diagnose pure specific expressive language delay.

Parents can encourage early language skills by talking, listening and enrolling their children in a good preschool. Speech therapy is helpful, though often hard to gain access to or afford. But it is always possible for a speech therapist to assess a child then give them a program that can be followed at home.

Receptive delay

Receptive delay is when a child continues to have difficulty understanding language. It is usually associated with expressive language delay and often with global developmental delay or autism spectrum disorder. However, some children can suffer from receptive delay alone and this puts them at great disadvantage. For these children it is as if they are living in a foreign country where they don't understand the language. They may smile and seem to comprehend, but they are out of their depth. If you are worried that your child is having difficulty understanding what is said, have them assessed by a paediatrician, a community health team or a speech pathologist.

Language disorder

Some of the most puzzled parents I see have children with lots of words but they don't quite make sense. These language-disordered children may sound like a tape recorder, and use smart-sounding phrases that aren't quite appropriate. They find it hard to describe their day's activities or to have a rich, two-way conversation. Questions are answered off tangent. I might ask, 'Where do you go to school?'

They respond, 'I'm in First Class. Mrs Smith is my teacher.'

Some children get stuck and either repeat one word (echoing) or keep on at one topic (perseveration). Echoing is strongly associated with, but is not exclusive to, autism spectrum disorder (see this chapter, page 156).

I see other children who mix meaningful speech with unintelligible nonsense (jargon). Sometimes there are new migrants who are thought to be speaking a mix of English and, say, Russian, but when we get a Russian interpreter they don't understand either.

Language disorder is often hereditary. I regularly find myself struggling to communicate with apparently normal parents who have immense difficulty giving a clear history of their child's problem. That's because they have the same problem as their child: they can't quite answer the question that has been asked.

Articulation problem

Some children continue to pronounce words in a way that is immature and like a child who is much younger. They miss ends or mispronounce bits of words, so 'dooce' means juice, for example. This sounds cute, and usually it will resolve with time.

But other children have a more serious pronunciation problem that makes speech quite unintelligible. I sometimes see children whose mums understand eighty per cent of what they say, while I pick up only about forty per cent. This is often (but not always) associated with problems of swallowing, tongue movement and dribbling. This combination is called oral dyspraxia, and it can be quite disabling and slow to remediate.

Stuttering

An under-four-year-old may stutter when they are excited and tired. But by school age, stuttering is not usual and must be taken seriously, especially when there is a family history. Children are allowed the occasional jumble in their expression but if they have an impediment that continues whether they are tense or calm they need to be referred to a speech therapist.

Problems with concepts, subtleties, semantics and pragmatics

Some children hit great difficulties when they move from concrete language to concepts. I might ask, 'If you had a can of Coke, a box of tissues and a Mars Bar, which would you drink?'

The child with difficulties might answer, 'The water.'

They don't understand the full question; they just react to the one word 'drink'.

A child who is weak in concepts will tend to be literal rather than lateral in their thought processes. They might repeat the rhyme about three blind mice, yet not know the number of tails that were axed. If asked, 'Why does it say "No Smoking" on the petrol pump?' they answer in a concrete way, 'Smoking is bad for your health.'

Some of these children can't generalise. They look blank when I ask, 'Where do you live?' or 'Where is your home?' They can only understand if I ask in the specific way they have been taught: 'What is your address?'

Semantics involve the subtleties of understanding, and children who have problems with subtleties and semantics may have difficulty understanding humour, for example, which plays on double meanings. Many of these children can't tell the difference between a joke and a wind-up, making them a target for teasing.

This literal language amazes parents. One mother told her son, 'Run off to the toilet before we go home.'

He looked at her seriously and replied, 'Mum, we are not allowed to run in the school yard.'

Another child was told, 'Put a sock in it,' and he wondered what to do with his sock.

With problems of pragmatics the child is unable to play the tennis match of good, two-way communication. You open, I respond, you return, and I answer in tune. Pragmatics refers to the appropriate focus, picking up on cues, intonation, eye contact and body language.

Children with this language disorder may feel the stress of not being able to fully express and understand. Some try hard, but others withdraw and become detached and almost autistic. This subtle area of language disorder has a grey edge of overlap with autism spectrum disorder and the current fashionable diagnosis of Asperger syndrome. I'm a specialist in this area and it confuses me. No wonder parents get totally bewildered!

Language problems

1. Problems involve:
   - expressive language (what we say)
   - receptive language (what we understand)
   - language delay (slow to develop)
   - language disorder (the words are not spoken or understood in a normal way)
   - articulation (words are not pronounced in the normal way)
   - stuttering
   - concepts, subtleties, semantics and pragmatics.
2. Expressive language problems
   - language delay
   - slow to develop expressive language
   - usually an isolated problem
   - often runs in families
   - can be associated with receptive delay
   - occasionally caused by deafness, intellectual disability or autism
   - check hearing, understanding, relating to the environment and general development
3. Receptive language problems
   - language delay
   - slow to develop receptive language
   - usually associated with expressive delay
   - when expressive and receptive are both delayed, there may be other problems

- can be a sign of global delay (intellectual disability)
- can be due to autism spectrum disorder
- check hearing, expressive language, general development and the relationship with the environment

4. Language disorder
   - echoes what has been said
   - perseverates – goes on and on
   - uses jargon – talks in 'Russian'
   - responds in a rote, preprogrammed way
   - has difficulty describing a new experience
   - has difficulty with two-way conversation
   - response is almost appropriate

5. Articulation problem
   - young children often mispronounce (immature articulation)
   - immaturity usually resolves with, time, school and possibly speech therapy
   - major articulation problems can cause speech to be unintelligible
   - oral dyspraxia is a major problem often associated with feeding difficulties, unusual tongue movement and dribbling
   - major problems can be very slow to resolve
   - rhythm problem (dysfluency)

6. Stuttering
   - a family history of stuttering is of concern
   - persistent stuttering in a school-age child needs immediate speech therapy referral

7. Problems with concepts, subtleties, semantics and pragmatics
   - misses concepts
   - responds to one word, not the group meaning
   - misses a sequence of instructions
   - has difficulty generalising
   - has problem with double meaning, innuendo, humour; takes things literally

- teased as can't see past the words
- may withdraw and appear autistic
- a grey area between pure language disorder and the language disorder that is part of autism

Autism spectrum disorder and Asperger syndrome

Autism spectrum disorder varies greatly in its severity and presentation. It covers the widest spectrum from the totally detached institutionalised child to the university professor who is brilliant at maths but quite disabled in social skills. It refers to a child who communicates poorly in both verbal and body language. One who is inflexible, somewhat obsessive and repetitive and works to their own agenda. These children may be distant and detached and may relate inappropriately. Most autism spectrum children have areas of relative brilliance, particularly in visual memory (for example, sight reading) and rote learning (for example, knowing every dinosaur). The majority of children with autism (seventy per cent) have associated intellectual disability.

The high functioning edge of autism is sometimes called Asperger syndrome. This has a great overlap with some of the more withdrawn temperaments we see in children with the pure language delay disorder just described.

Children with a major degree of autism are aloof and most unusual. Those with less severe autism are slightly detached, socially unaware language-disorder children. This milder group cause great confusion as they may simply present as square pegs in round holes. Many of these children show the obsessive behaviour described in Chapter 8.

If you are concerned that your child may suffer from autism spectrum disorder, Asperger syndrome or a language disorder, get expert assessment from a paediatrician, speech pathologist or specialist developmental clinic.

Autism spectrum disorder and Asperger syndrome

1. A biological condition – in the child's make-up
2. Not related to environment or poor parenting
3. About seventy per cent have associated intellectual disability
4. A much more common problem than ten years ago
5. A wide spectrum that ranges from the severely disabled person to a socially inept professor
6. The milder, high-functioning edge of the spectrum is termed Asperger syndrome
7. There is a grey area where Asperger syndrome joins language disorder
8. Autism and language problems are both more common in boys
9. The mildly affected child presents as a square peg in a round hole
10. The autistic child has a problem with communication
    - language
        - delay or disorder
        - literal not lateral
        - echoes
        - rote replies
        - speaks like a tape recorder
        - not a flowing two-way conversation
    - body language
        - lack of facial expression
        - poor eye contact
        - doesn't talk with their eyes
11. The autistic child is inflexible
    - obsessive, over-interest
    - likes routines and sameness
    - over-focuses, repetitive play
    - overreacts when obsession is disturbed
    - fixed and works to own agenda
    - plays for hours with one interest

12. The autistic child is hard to steer; like a train running on tracks
13. The autistic child is detached and distant
    - unusual relationship with their environment
    - aloof, looks past you
    - more interested in objects than people
14. The autistic child has areas of talent, such as
    - strong visual recognition (photographic memory)
    - reads
    - recognises change
    - knows the layout of places
    - remembers street names after one look
    - strong rote memory
    - repeats detailed information
    - repeats stories, rhymes, advertisements
15. The autistic child has areas of weakness, such as
    - communication
    - picking up on unspoken messages
    - picking up on emotion
    - the ability to generalise
    - reading comprehension weaker than their expressive reading
    - working out problems that have not been directly taught before

Fine motor and gross motor problems

Some children are created with the fine motor coordination of a world-class watchmaker. Some have the gross motor skills of a gold medal gymnast. But for many, their fingers fumble and they have two left feet.

Some children are truly clumsy and others appear clumsy due to their bull-in-a-china-shop temperament. Others move well but have problems planning.

Gross motor clumsiness affects a child's self-esteem. When their mates are choosing the sports team they always select the potential Olympian ahead of the stumbler.

Motor planning is a more subtle problem where a child appears in tune until they try to coordinate three actions at the one time. These children have difficulty tying shoelaces, swimming with style and following the flow in aerobics. Fortunately Velcro laces have replaced knots, swimming does not need style and aerobic exercise can be left to the high-stepping hyperactives.

However, many of these children may underachieve in written work because their handwriting is illegible. While some have a difficulty with letter formation, others have problems planning work, or may rush without checking. The clumsies, motor planners, awkward movers and poor writers need help from an occupational therapist (or see Appendices IV and V, pages 299–302). The rushers may need treatment for ADHD (see Chapter 12).

TWELVE

Understanding ADHD

A ttention deficit hyperactivity disorder (ADHD) refers to a cluster of learning and behaviour problems that cause a child to underfunction for intellect and underbehave for the quality of parenting they receive. These behaviour and learning problems are caused by a subtle difference in the fine-tuning of the normal brain. This difference seems to be related to a slight imbalance in the brain's message-transmitting chemicals, the neurotransmitters. This mostly affects those parts of the brain that self-monitor learning and put the brakes on ill-considered behaviour (the frontal lobes and their close connections).

ADHD affects at least two per cent of the school-age population, and some quote figures as high as five per cent. Boys are more affected than girls. The first signs of ADHD are usually apparent before three years of age, but few children require treatment before they start school.

ADHD is a chronic condition and it is now believed that approximately sixty per cent of children who suffer from it will take some of their symptoms with them into adulthood. Happily, adults with ADHD can now be successfully treated.

A modern view of ADHD

When parents describe their ADHD child they talk about four separate parts, but only two of them correctly fit the ADHD diagnosis. The two parts of true ADHD are

■ ADHD hyperactive impulsive behaviours

■ ADHD attention deficit learning weakness.

Most ADHD children have a mix of both the first behaviour part and the second inattention learning part. But some have one of these in isolation (when they are termed ADHD predominantly inattentive). This is probably more common than we realise and is often not picked up because these children underachieve but do not underbehave. A small group have an even purer presentation of ADHD inattentive only, which makes them like dreamy, drifty 'space cadets'.

These two ADHD parts are then affected by the presence or absence of a third part, the comorbid conditions. Comorbid conditions are associated problems that are not caused by ADHD but coexist in over half of the children who have true ADHD. They may be problems like dyslexia, oppositional defiant disorder or conduct disorder.

And finally, this mix of ADHD and comorbid conditions is greatly influenced by a fourth element – parenting and the child's living environment.

ADHD: the four parts

1. ADHD hyperactive impulsive behaviour: poor self-control of behaviour
   - Impulsiveness: speaks and acts without thinking, interrupts, calls out in class, has low frustration tolerance, can't walk away from trouble, may appear aggressive, has difficulty putting the brakes on behaviour, rushes carelessly through work, accident prone, volatile
   - Demanding: unaware of when to let a matter drop, intrudes, generates tension, has difficulty backing off
   - Social clumsiness: misreads social cues, overpowers, bosses, wants to do things their way, acts silly in a crowd, makes inappropriate comments, intrudes into others' space
   - Overactivity: restless, fidgety, taps, fiddles, has to touch, overcharged, has an overwound spring
2. ADHD attention deficit and learning weakness: problems of output
   - Inattention: works poorly without one-on-one supervision, has difficulty regrouping after distraction, has a busy, circling brain, self-distracts, daydreams, flits from task to task, has inconsistent work output, gets over-focused on one part and misses the big picture
   - Poor short-term memory: forgets instructions, loses focus, reads but does not remember, has difficulty with mental arithmetic, learns a spelling list but has forgotten it by test time
   - Disorganisation: forgets homework books, misjudges time, procrastinates, has poor prioritisation, variable performance, poor planning, loses things like uniform items, lunch boxes, swimming costumes, bus passes, has difficulty starting, sustaining and completing work
3. Comorbid conditions
   - Over half of those with ADHD have at least one associated comorbid condition.

- Between forty and sixty per cent have oppositional defiant disorder where they say no on principle.
- Approximately fifty per cent have a specific learning disability such as dyslexia, language delay disorder, weakness in mathematics etc.
- Other comorbidities are conduct disorder, tic disorder, poor coordination, motor planning problems, depression, anxiety, obsessive compulsive disorder and bipolar disorder.

4. The child's living environment
   - Supportive, nurturing parenting versus hostile, critical parenting
   - Supportive schooling versus unaccepting, punitive schooling
   - An extended stable family versus an isolated, unstable, rejecting family

Typical symptoms of ADHD

When a child with ADHD has predominantly hyperactive-impulsive behaviours they may be out of step with brothers, sisters and other children. Often these children were easy babies, but once they started to walk many were active and into everything. At preschool some were more restless and found it hard to sit at story time, while others had low frustration tolerance and caused great trouble through their unthinking aggression to other children. Despite some difficulties, most manage reasonably well until the start of school.

At home, the hyperactive-impulsive child is demanding, intrudes into others' space and generates tension. These children stir, wind up their siblings and don't know when to let a matter drop. Many have a short fuse, act without thinking, interrupt and are accident prone. Some are messy, disorganised, forgetful, restless and constantly fiddling. They may unintentionally break things: 'It just fell apart in my hands.'

In the playground some are socially out of tune, come on too strong, annoy other children and may not get asked to birthday parties.

Many children are taken for treatment at the start of school, when they have been said to be distractable (due to attention deficit) and disruptive (due to hyperactive-impulsive behaviours).

Children with ADHD do best when stood over or encouraged enthusiastically. Otherwise they don't complete work. Teachers are confused that such an apparently intelligent child is so erratic and underachieving. Some may have been tested by the school psychologist, who often finds a surprisingly good concentration in the one on one of the quiet test room.

Children who have the predominantly inattentive type of ADHD may experience problems of learning, memory and underachievement at school.

When is a child normal and when do they have ADHD?

There is no clear cut-off between those children who have a normally active, impulsive and inattentive temperament and those who suffer ADHD. If these behaviours are not causing anyone any trouble, they can be ignored. If these behaviours are causing a child to significantly underfunction at school and underbehave at home, they must be taken seriously.

If we use the American Psychiatric Association's criteria for the diagnosis of ADHD (called the DSM-IV guidelines), six out of a list of nine difficult behaviours must be present. But life isn't as simple as this. If one child has these six behaviours yet has a saint for a mother and the best teacher in the country, we may not consider diagnosing or treating them. If they have only five behaviours but home and school are hanging by a thread, the child may be diagnosed and treated for ADHD. If a child has only four of the listed behaviours, they are not said to suffer from ADHD, but they will still be difficult for parents and teachers. Academics deal in pure black and white situations; but when you're operating in the real world you see life in much more flexible terms.

The cause of ADHD

Until relatively recently, professionals blamed parents' attachment or relationships for causing ADHD in children. Others said that ADHD was due to additives in the food. Now we know that neither of these is the cause of ADHD, though, of course, the standard of parenting and some food substances may influence already existing ADHD.

Two things are for certain: first, ADHD is strongly hereditary, and second, it is a biological condition.

Heredity is obvious, as so many families have a parent or close relative who has similar problems. If one identical twin has ADHD, there is about a 90 per cent chance the other will also have the condition. If one sibling has ADHD there is about a 30 per cent chance another child will also be affected. The majority of children in my care have a parent or close relative who has experienced many of the same difficulties.

And now it has been shown that ADHD is a biological condition. For years it was presumed, but not proven, that ADHD was caused by a minor difference in brain function. Now this can be shown by the most modern research scans (PET, SPECT and special MRI). In ADHD these scans show a slight difference of function and anatomy in the behaviour-inhibition areas of the brain (the frontal lobes and their close connections). This underfunction seems due to an imbalance of the brain chemicals that transmit impulses between certain nerves (the neurotransmitters – noradrenaline and dopamine). So the stimulant medications that are used to treat ADHD work to normalise the imbalance of these natural chemicals. One researcher has shown a normalisation of the SPECT scan of an ADHD sufferer after such stimulant medication had been administered.

Diagnosing ADHD

Many professionals claim that their method is the only way to diagnose ADHD, and this can be confusing for parents. In fact, there is no one conclusive test, and such is the greyness of the cut-off point no two professionals will have exactly the same limits regarding diagnosis.

In fact, there is no clear and simple dividing line we can pinpoint that separates the two per cent of children that we believe have a major degree of ADHD from children with an active, inattentive temperament. The cut-off is blurred by other factors such as the calmness and consistency of home, the tolerance of the parents and the skills of the class teacher. Diagnosis sometimes remains a matter of trial and error. I believe that if a child responds well to medication treatment it confirms the diagnosis, but many see the suggestion that diagnosis should be made by means of treatment as politically incorrect.

In general, though, diagnosis can be approached in four steps:

I. Be alert to the alarm signals

Alarm bells ring when a child underfunctions at school for intellect and underbehaves at home for the quality of parenting. In other words, they are significantly out of step with brothers, sisters and peers who have the same background and level of development.

2. Exclude ADHD lookalikes

Exclude major developmental delay, the normal spiritedness of a preschooler, or parenting or family problems.

3. Use pointers to help with diagnosis

There may be some other pointers that could help with diagnosis, like parent and teacher questionnaires, test profiles, brain tests or a continuous performance test (CPT). The CPT, such as the Conners or TOVA CPT, is of particular help when a child has predominantly a learning problem or the picture is clouded by comorbid conditions.

4. Take a careful history and observe the child

'When she walked she was into everything'; 'He would never hold my hand but was always running ten steps ahead of me'; 'At the start of school he was disruptive and distractable'; 'She only works well when stood over'; 'He goes on and on, intrudes and causes tension'; 'He's impulsive, short fused, and socially out of tune'; 'He breaks nearly everything he plays with'; 'Discipline and management are many times more difficult'; 'She's disorganised and has a poor short-term memory'; 'School reports say he could do better if only he could focus.'

Treatment

Managing ADHD involves:

- helping school and the classroom teacher
- structuring home for peace
- boosting self-esteem and developing outside interests
- medication
- considering other therapies.

At school

At school teachers need to accept that an ADHD child's behaviour isn't simply naughtiness – it is part of their make-up and they can't help it. As well, ADHD children at school need:

- a structured class run by a teacher who will be there every school day, all year
- a firm but encouraging teacher who knows when it is best to back off
- seating near the front, away from distracting influences
- clear step-by-step instructions and constant feedback
- special supervision at times of change, such as coming in from a break or when they are on a school excursion
- trying methods like token reward systems to help increase time on task.

At home

At home all members of the family need to accept that this is the way your child has been made and no amount of force will beat it out of them. Be patient and have realistic expectations.

But remember that while poor parenting can cause bad behaviour, with ADHD, the child's bad behaviour causes good parents to appear poor. Normal techniques for coping with behaviour work poorly with an ADHD child, because they have a biological difference in their ability to inhibit behaviour (they act before they have thought of the consequences). For this reason, disregard anyone who believes that a standard behavioural program or parent effectiveness course will easily change your ADHD child. But it is possible to change behaviours using small, well-planned steps and there are things you can do to help your ADHD child:

- Routine is essential.

- Rewards should be frequent and constantly repeated.

- Think before you act and learn to ignore all but the important misbehaviours.

- Don't lock horns with an ADHD child then increase the pressure. This produces a battle of wills, two angry parties, opposition, resentment and damage to relationships.

- Don't argue. Don't get heated. Don't escalate. Use a matter-of-fact, unemotional, controlled voice.

- Give yourself room to manoeuvre:
    - state the rule
    - count to three
    - use time out
    - give choices
    - don't force the situation into a cul-de-sac.

- When it's all over, be quick to forgive. Don't hold grudges.

Remember, even the worst-behaved child is good ninety per cent of the time. Reward this positive side – catch them being good!

Esteem

Try to avoid being too negative or always using negative words, because this can affect a child's self-esteem. Listen, value what they say and give them a reasonable amount of responsibility.

Encourage them to try out a variety of sports, hobbies and interests, in the hope they may savour success at something. Swimming, bike riding, bush walking, fishing, cooking, judo or computers may all be useful. Team sports and scouts suit some ADHD children but not all. ADHD children may have poor coordination making some sports difficult to master. For ways to help with coordination, see Appendix IV, page 299. When they are successful at sport, ADHD children get an immense boost.

To help with school work, out-of-school tutoring may be useful, but don't overdo it. Tutoring puts all the focus on your child's areas of failure. Some ADHD children have poor handwriting. For ways to help with handwriting see Appendix V, page 301.

ADHD children often have trouble building friendships. Encourage them in this area by inviting school mates over or taking one of your child's friends on outings.

Medication

Stimulants
The main medications used to treat ADHD are the stimulants dexamphetamine and Ritalin (methylphenidate). These have been shown to be effective in over eighty per cent of ADHD children in the short to medium term, but there is still a lack of data on the long-term benefits.

Ritalin is similar but not identical to dexamphetamine. I would recommend that both preparations be trialed to ensure that a child receives the most effective medicine with the fewest side effects.

Stimulant medication has now been extremely well researched and proven and was first used to treat ADHD in 1937. The drug Ritalin has been used since 1958. See full details and research references in Green and Chee, *Understanding ADHD*, Doubleday, 1997.

However, there are still people who say that stimulants are new, controversial, addictive, dangerous and unproven. Be extremely suspicious of anyone who voices such out-of-date ideas, as the rest of what they say may be equally unreliable.

Stimulants act by normalising the imbalance in the brain's natural neurotransmitter chemicals, that is, they increase noradrenaline and dopamine. Stimulants are not sedatives. Instead, they enhance normal brain function. While stimulants may work to a minute degree in a child without ADHD, when they are effective in treating a child with ADHD the benefits are usually quite miraculous in both behaviour and learning.

Stimulants help focus attention, keep the mind on task and allow a child to consider the possible repercussions before they act. Successfully medicated children become more organised, less impulsive and are easier to reach.

Stimulants are short acting, starting about half an hour after the child takes them, and the effect has largely passed three to five hours later. But while their effect is short lived, about half of the medicine is still in the blood after four hours and one quarter after eight hours. For this reason we tend to give children larger doses early in the day, which are then topped up by subsequent smaller doses, for example, one and a half tablets at 8am, one tablet at 12 noon, and three-quarters of a tablet at 3:30pm.

Usually children take the medication in three doses during the day (although this may vary for different children from two doses to five doses). But not all ADHD children take the medication every day. When there are only problems with schoolwork, medication may only be given to the child on school days; while when there are problems with behaviour, socialisation, and stress to parent–child relationships, medication may be given every day, including weekends and holidays.

There is no evidence to suggest that a correctly diagnosed ADHD child will become addicted to their medication. Stimulants help a child focus and bring them into reality. You don't get addicted to reality.

Side effects are remarkably rare and can usually be avoided if your doctor trials both preparations and fine tunes carefully. The most common side effect when starting medication is for a child to become withdrawn, teary and irritable. This usually only happens at the time of commencing the medication or raising the dose. If it does happen it can be solved by introducing medication gradually or by trying the other medication.

Also, many children report that they have less appetite and a few find it is more difficult to settle to sleep. These and most other problems can be avoided by careful fine tuning of the dosage.

Non-stimulants

ADHD is also treated using other, non-stimulant drugs like Catapres (clonidine) and Tofranil (imipramine), either alone or in combination. Catapres is particularly useful when stimulants alone are unable to adequately control a child's impulsivity and overactivity. It is also used when they have trouble settling to sleep. Tofranil is the second-line drug that helps behaviour and attention when stimulants are shown to be ineffective.

But these non-stimulants are not without their risks, and they must be used cautiously. In particular, there is the danger of accidental overdose, so tablets must be given correctly and stored securely.

Other therapies

Be sensible when it comes to finding treatments for your ADHD child. Use the well-researched therapies that are known to be safe and successful ahead of those that are controversial and unlikely to bring big benefits.

However, there are a range of therapies that parents try. When you are looking for alternatives, the things you need to know are:

■ Diet does not cause ADHD and too much or too little sugar doesn't influence ADHD behaviour. Most current research suggests that less than ten per cent of ADHD children are affected by natural or artificial preservatives, additives and colourings. Where diet is incriminated, most parents have pinpointed one or two foods, which they now avoid. Irritability and overactivity seem to be the most diet-sensitive behaviours, but these are not the main problems of the true ADHD child.

■ Occupational therapy can help ADHD children to improve their handwriting if it is poor (see Appendix V for ways to help with handwriting).

- Speech therapy, with emphasis on phonics, may help when a child has spelling and reading difficulties.

- Many researchers view brainwave-modifying techniques of bio-feedback as controversial.

- Multivitamins and natural products are unproven treatments (even those promoted on top-rating television shows).

- Eye exercises, tinted lenses and sensory integration are all of questionable benefit in the treatment of learning and attentional difficulties.

Long-term effects of treatment

While the long-term side effects of medication are not a concern, the benefits of long-term therapy are still to be conclusively proven. One study has shown that ADHD children who are treated with stimulants are less likely to drop out of high school or engage in substance abuse than those left untreated.

In my experience, ADHD children become closer and relate better to their friends and families when given medication. And relationships are of vital importance for long-term happiness and esteem.

Medication can continue for as long as a child's parents and teachers see significant benefits. But if you are ever in doubt, stop for a week and see what happens.

Remember, parents, not doctors, are in charge. Doctors can recommend these medications, but it is always the parents who have ultimate control. Stop the medication if you think it is not working or is causing any unwanted side effect. If you are worried, call for help.

The hazards of not treating ADHD

Many untreated children are at war with their parents and get to adolescence with destroyed family relationships and a second-rate education. Some are accident prone, and a number may be seriously injured or even killed. While there is no completely safe drug, the dangers of medication are much less than the emotional and physical dangers of untreated ADHD.

A final word

ADHD is a real condition which has only recently started to be understood in Australia. When misdiagnosed and mistreated, it can cause amazing stress and long-term damage to esteem and family relationships. At school, these clever children underfunction and start to believe they are stupid.

We cannot cure ADHD with medication and other treatments. But we can keep a child's enthusiasm to learn, keep families at peace and help a child maintain self-esteem until, hopefully, adolescence brings some academic acceleration and a more reflective style of behaviour.

In the past most ADHD children remained undiagnosed, and arrived at adulthood with a belief that they were inferior and dumb. This may have been acceptable in the past, but we are not going to let it happen today (see Appendix V, page 301).

ADHD: the essentials

1. Attention Deficit Hyperactivity Disorder (ADHD) is the same as ADD.
2. ADHD disadvantages at least two per cent of our school-age population.
3. ADHD is related to an underfunction in the frontal areas of the brain (the parts that self-regulate behaviour and learning).
4. The ADHD child has behaviour that is out of step with the quality of parenting they receive and learning problems that are out of step with their intellectual abilities.
5. ADHD children have behaviour problems of poor

self-monitoring and inhibition (impulsive, unthinking behaviour, difficulty putting the brakes on behaviour, unaware when to back off, misreads social situations, restless and fidgety).

6. The learning problems involve an underfunctioning for intellect (self-distracts, difficulty working without one-on-one supervision, problems starting, sustaining and finishing work, poor short-term memory, disorganisation).

7. Most ADHD children have a mix of behaviour and learning problems. In addition, many have associated comorbid conditions (specific learning difficulties, oppositional defiant disorder, conduct disorder, coordination difficulties, tics etc.).

8. Family doctors find it hard to access quality care for their ADHD children. Help comes from paediatricians, psychiatrists, community health centres, private psychologists and the specialised ADHD clinics.

9. A number of diagnostic techniques are promoted but no one method is essential or completely reliable in making the diagnosis.

10. Some of the most difficult ADHD children will behave relatively well in the quiet of the doctor's or psychologist's office. But ten minutes of good behaviour does not rule out the diagnosis of ADHD.

11. Treatment involves accepting the reality of the diagnosis, then using behaviour programs, school support and increasing the child's ability to self-monitor with stimulant medication.

12. Behaviour techniques work poorly in a child who acts before they think. Parents have most success with routine, avoiding the unimportant and using rewards. Many ADHD children are oppositional and defy on principle. Meeting opposition with force leads to battles of Bosnian proportion. This wrecks relationships.

13. Parents need to learn how to sidestep escalation by

keeping calm, active ignoring, counting techniques, time out and giving choices.

14. The stimulant medications Ritalin and dexamphetamine help the ADHD child to self-monitor and focus. They do not sedate; they normalise.

15. There is no controversy over this treatment, with over 150 reputable papers supporting the safety and benefits. Stimulants have been used with ADHD for over forty years.

16. Stimulants are used in conjunction with behaviour and learning programs. Stimulants allow you to reach the child and, once you reach, you can teach.

17. ADHD is a strongly hereditary condition. Many ADHD children have an ADHD parent.

18. Adult ADHD affects about one per cent of the population. It causes clever adults to underfunction at work for intellect and behave unwisely in their relationships. Psychiatrists who treat adults with ADHD find the greatest problems come from impulsivity (impulsive outburst, violence in marriage, unwise spending, accident prone, damaged relationships, work difficulties).

19. Many ADHD adults get big improvements with the same treatments we use in children.

20. ADHD can damage the relationships of parents with children, children with parents, children with peers and adults with adults. For this reason, early recognition and treatment is of utmost importance.

THIRTEEN

Sibling squabbles and competition

One day I was watching nature enthusiast David Attenborough, and he unlocked one of the great mysteries of life. In his hesitant tones I heard the answer to why brothers and sisters squabble:

> 'It seems that all little animals (with the exception of hedgehogs) love to trip, roll and fight. This quickens their reflexes, tones up their bodies and prepares them for life in the wild. A little lion that fights with his brother or sister is more likely to survive in the hostile adult world.'

Now, I am not suggesting we encourage teasing and squabbles, but it probably has some residual benefit. Athletic strength is built on all those taunts, tumbles and fights. Verbal sparring tunes woolly words into a razor-sharp response. Sisters who cope with an annoying brother will be better prepared for an irritating man in their later life.

Why siblings fight

Related but not identical

My brother always wanted to be an only child. It's not that I am particularly painful; we are just very different people. As he sat with his head in a book, I wanted to be out inhaling fresh air. My school achievements were average, despite hours of study and homework. He worked for ten minutes each night then won every prize and scholarship. We have always been emotionally close, but we are very different people.

Parents fall into the trap where they believe all brothers and sisters will have identical personalities and interests. For their convenience the parents encourage different children to do the same activities, which may not suit.

Age gap also makes a difference: children of similar age generally play better but compete more, and when ages are close, children often can't get on when they're together, but they can't bear being apart. The message for parents is to use no one program, or no fixed expectation for all. Even identical twins are not identical.

Attention and boredom

Analysists interpret skirmishing as an unresolved power struggle, but most squabbles are due to boredom. Life slips into a quiet patch and a taunt generates a power surge of attention.

Sister is engrossed in her favourite TV soap, her brother walks over and 'inadvertently' blocks the screen. She hurls abuse, cries foul and protests to the referee. In the commotion the channel is changed and the power mysteriously unplugged.

Later, as he struggles with his homework, she brushes past, knocking a book to the floor. 'I never touched it,' she says. 'It just fell.

Maybe it was the wind.' 'It was shaken by a distant earthquake!' Behind this protest of innocence, that twinkle in her eye registers the pleasure of victory.

After the age of twelve years, words become the main weapon. 'Gosh, that's a big zit'; 'Is that a dress or a tent?'; 'Have you ever wondered if you were adopted?'

It is tempting for parents to rush in like the United Nations at the first sign of trouble. They ask who started the fight and each child points at the other. Intervening may bring peace in the short term, but by rewarding with attention it encourages further fights. Parents must realise that a fight includes two combatants, and it's often hard to separate the good from the bad guys. Also, with the perversity of human nature, the one who complains loudest is usually the most guilty.

Life's not fair

The early school years are a time of competition, complaints and that constant cry, 'It's not fair, Mum.' Avoid being intimidated by comparative justice: 'When Jan was eight, you bought her a new bike'; 'When John got on the tennis team, he got a new racquet'; 'Jack does fewer chores but gets the same pocket money as me'; 'You're always doing things with Jane and do nothing with me.'

Equality is a worthy but impractical goal. You may love your children equally, but they will not end up with the same amount of attention.

The demanding, dissatisfied, intrusive child always insists on more of our time. In life it is always the one who shouts loudest who gets most. The sensible parents go for peace before equality.

Don't get into debates about justice – you never win. When told, 'It's not fair, she got more,' acknowledge the statement but don't enter into the argument. I was in my twenties before I fully appreciated the unfairness of life. If your child gets this message at the age of eight, they will be advanced in their education. If they are really unhappy, suggest they take the matter to the Anti-discrimination Tribunal.

How to cope with sibling fights

The ways to cope with sibling fights involve:

- establishing limits

- encouraging conflict resolution

- learning to take the peaceful path.

Establish limits

Setting limits won't stop squabbles, but they let the combatants know where they stand. Rules should cover ownership, the use of joint property, personal space and acceptable behaviour. Join the Marquis of Queensberry and set down your rules for the ring, such as:

- This belongs to your brother. It cannot be touched without his permission.

- This shelf is for your sister's treasures. It is totally out of bounds.

- This bedroom is personal space. It cannot be entered without an invitation.

- Jointly owned toys, games and computers must be shared. If you are not currently playing with the computer, you cannot reserve it for your use.

- If you don't share, the toy will be put in time out for fifteen minutes.

- No disturbances are ever permitted during homework time.

- Broken belongings will be paid for from pocket money or one of your good toys will be offered in exchange.

- At dinner time there will be no touching, insulting or kicking your brother.

Encouraging conflict resolution

It's easy to become a referee in our children's battles but it is better they develop the basics of conflict resolution. Here's how to help them:

- When hit with complaints, don't adjudicate. Ask, 'How can we resolve this problem?'

- Suggest some options.

- Say you will come back in one minute to hear their solution.

- Use a three strike system –
  1. 'How can you both resolve this problem?'
  2. 'I expect resolution in one minute or you will both be sent to time out.'
  3. 'Both go to your rooms.'

Take the peaceful path

When siblings fight, parents have two options: to take the confronting path or the peaceful path. Some cynics suggest the complete ignoring approach: no parental intervention unless there is blood on the carpet. It doesn't have to be this extreme, but I still support the laid-back approach.

A final word

- Ignore minor squabbles.

- Keep bored bodies busy.

- Encourage cooperation by interesting the squabblers in a joint project.

- Suggest they move their battle outside or to another room.

- Remind all parties of the house rules.

- Ask them, 'Is this a real fight or just horse play?'

- Give feedback for good cooperation: 'I love to see you two playing so well together.'

- Give stars and tokens for squabble-free hours.

- Put the disputed toy, computer or television in time out.

- The child who complains about getting hurt should be advised to keep clear of trouble.

- Don't interpret and apportion blame; just describe what you see and say what you will not accept.

- When nothing works punish both with time out in different rooms.

Occasionally one child is unacceptably vindictive or resentful to a sibling. This is more than normal sibling rivalry, and needs professional intervention.

Sibling squabbles

1. Siblings fight for a variety of reasons:
    - they may be related, but they're not identical – they are of different ages and have different personalities and interests
    - they are bored or want attention
    - by continually intervening parents are rewarding with attention
2. How to cope with sibling fights
    - set limits and rules so children know where they stand
    - encourage them to resolve the conflict themselves by asking them to suggest resolutions
    - use time out if the conflict isn't resolved
    - take the peaceful path of minimum intervention where possible

FOURTEEN

Shyness, making friends and strengthening social skills

The joy of belonging to the human race comes from meeting and relating. So parents are sad when they see their children as loners. They watch other youngsters gather friends around them like a Lotto winner at the bar, yet their child remains on the edge.

I am often asked if I can turn an introvert into a thick-skinned extrovert. There is no way to work this miracle but I can teach skills that help a shy child appear more outgoing.

Introverts and extroverts

Some years ago I was promoting my book *Toddler Taming* on the North American authors' circuit. Between studios I shared a limo with a Manhattan psychoanalyst who had written a book on the interpretation of dreams. We were chatting about unrealistic expectations and how they caused so many emotional problems. With this she came out with a wonderfully wise statement: 'The world is divided into two sorts of people: extroverts and introverts. But there are very few true extroverts – just introverts pretending they are extroverts.'

Parents who were shy when young hope for a more extrovert lifestyle for their own children. But the parents' temperament may have passed through the genes, and their children's introversion is then increased by living with introvert adults.

We should respect our child's temperament and not try to change it. Look at it this way. The majority of adults have an intense fear of speaking before a large audience. You could push them on stage but they would be apoplectic and even more fearful in the future. In the same way, shy children do not need to be belittled, forced or hassled. For them socialisation comes gradually with time.

When your child hides their face and won't communicate, it's best to make a matter-of-fact comment: 'John is a bit overwhelmed. He will come and chat to us when he is ready.' If you say 'John won't speak. He's shy,' the chances are John will fill the role you've set out for him.

Building friendships

There are two problems children have building friendship: some have difficulty making friends and others have difficulty keeping them. The first group are timid about asking people to play and get swept aside by the pushy hordes. The others boss and always want things their own way, or when a child comes to play they ignore their guest and go off to do their own thing. I see children who never get asked to a birthday party, and at school they are known by all but liked by none.

We can teach the timid how to approach others and ask them to play. Or we can resort to schemes that create opportunities for socialisation. For example, when we go to the beach, the zoo or out to eat we might invite another child. One parent told me how they built a swimming pool in their backyard just to attract the neighbourhood kids. It was an extreme effort to attract friends but it worked.

Changing the socially blind is much more difficult. Communication is like tennis; we read the other player's game and carefully direct our returns. As a doctor, when I talk to parents I watch their eyes, listen to the tone of voice and pick up on what they don't quite tell me. By tuning into their verbal language and body language, I know when to keep talking, when to slow down, and when to change direction.

Some children seem unaware of these subtle cues: they misread the game, hit too hard, return out of court and miss the point. In the past children learnt through the school of hard knocks, but nowadays we can teach some of the basics needed for social skills.

Teaching social skills

When social skills programs were first promoted in the early 1980s, they seemed an exciting new way to help shy, inappropriate and ADHD children. Unfortunately, the follow-up studies were disappointing. It seemed that much of the success in the therapy room was not carried into the outside world.

Social skills training is neither easy nor particularly effective, but it is a move in the right direction. The formal programs I have watched as an observer gave immediate feedback for good communication, pulled the child up for inappropriate communication and tried to get them to see how their actions affected others.

At home we can attempt something much simpler. We can:

- practise through role-play

- teach the basics of communication

- help children enter a conversation

- show them how to tune in to social cues

- show them how to finish a conversation

- show them how to join in play

- show them how to ask a friend home

- show them the tricks of negotiation

■ show them how to use a common interest to help communication.

Practice through role-play

Role-play is useful but only in that small proportion of children who are prepared to play along. Role-play allows us to run through common situations, acting out the different ways we can respond. This provides a flight simulator to try out different approaches without crashing out when we get it wrong.

The basics of communication

Children don't need the painful handshake and trust-me eyes of a used-car salesman. But they must be able to greet and communicate. We can help them by showing them the basics. Good eye contact and a friendly smile show we wish to communicate. A slouching posture suggests we are disinterested while a slight lean forward shows we intend to engage. Heads nod and bodies move when communication is in harmony. Standing far apart signals a lack of confidence, while too close is an invasion of space.

Conversation openers

Even at my age I feel overwhelmed when I enter a room packed with strangers. As I struggle to start a conversation I find myself resorting to three well-tried techniques:

1. I ask a question – 'Is this your first time at this venue?'

2. I make a pleasantry – 'It's remarkably hot for this time of year.'

3. I comment on something of joint interest – 'What did you think of that speaker?'

Children can also be shown how to open up with a question: 'What are you playing?'; 'Do you live around here?' Or they can use a pleasantry: 'Gosh, it's windy today.' Or they can open with a common interest: 'That maths class was pretty boring'; 'Did you hear Jones call teacher a butthead?'; 'What did you think of last night's episode of "Neighbours"?'

These pleasantries are bland and boring, but they are just an opener. Once communicating, they can then get into something more meaningful.

Reading the cues

On returning home in the evening, a switched-on husband is quick to suss out the situation. They have something important to say, but as they see their wife's tired, tense eyes, they hold back for a more opportune moment. Some children have no idea about the right moment, while others can read their parents to perfection and know the exact second when the request for money or new clothes will score the greatest payout.

Reading the cues can be helped along through role-play. We demonstrate how the enthusiasm in another's eyes signals interest in our conversation. When bodies fidget and eyes glaze over our audience have had enough. Restlessness, rapid head nodding, throat clearing and flitting eyes signal a crisis in boredom and it's time to back off.

Conversation closers

It's sometimes easier to get into a conversation than close one without appearing awkward. But children can be taught the techniques used by us adults: 'I'd better get going'; 'See you later'; 'I should say hello to John'; 'I've some work to do.' Then, with a twinkle of the eye and a friendly smile, they move on.

Joining in play

Some children stand enviously on the side lines but can't pluck up the courage to ask, while others barge in, disrupt and act inappropriately. It's easier for us to help the standers than the bargers. The bargers continue to barge, whatever we say.

We can teach them that it's best to wait for an appropriate gap in the game then to try out some openers: 'This looks cool. May I join in?'; 'I'm Jane. Can I play?'; 'Do you need a hand?'; 'Can I join the next game?'

Unfortunately, children are capable of being extremely mean and may exclude all but the favoured few. When this happens the timid child has only three options: to get into a rival team, to play alone or start their own league.

Asking a friend home

You would think there should be no difficulty getting a friend over to play, but for some children this poses an insurmountable hurdle. To help, start by working out the basics. What day? What time? What to do? How to get here? Then ask! When procrastination and shyness prevent a child from asking, parents may need to deal directly with the other child's parent.

Negotiation

In life nothing ever goes quite to plan and to survive we must be able to roll with the punches and negotiate. Children who are socially smart learn this through life experience, but others struggle and need some help.

It may be possible to teach this through role-play: 'You can't join in our game now.'

'Well, could I play with you in the next break?'

Or, 'I'm not able to come to your house on Saturday.'
'Could you come on Sunday or the Saturday after?'

Or, 'You must finish your homework now.'
'I am so tired. Could I get up early and do it before school?'

A common interest

One of the best ways to ease communication and help mixing is to be with people of similar interest. The boy may be a poor communicator, but he will talk continuously with fellow footy fans. The horse-loving girl is mostly mute, but chats non-stop with other horsy types. The computer buff can talk megabytes to those with a silicone chip on their shoulder. The bike rider chats, rides a bit, chats more and feels close to their fellow bikers. When general mixing is poor, a common interest will encourage socialisation.

Strengthening social skills

1. Sensible expectations
   - the world is full of introverts trying to pretend they are extroverts
2. Conversation openers
   - ask a question
   - make a pleasantry
   - comment on a joint interest
3. Reading the cues
   - a welcoming smile
   - enthusiastic eyes
   - body movement
   - restless boredom
   - respect space
4. Conversation closers
   - 'I'd better be going.'
   - 'See you later.'
5. Asking to play
   - pick the right moment
   - know what you want
   - have a back-up plan
6. Negotiation
   - be flexible
   - regroup and try Plan B
7. Common interest
   - footy fans
   - computer addicts
   - sports or clubs

FIFTEEN

Increasing self-esteem

S elf-esteem is how a child feels about themselves. When self-esteem is high, they are likely to be confident, positive, sociable, kind to others and more willing to attempt new tasks. When it is low, children may be negative, withdrawn, socially insecure and can even be quite paranoid.

Most writing on self-esteem places all the emphasis on the positive interaction between parents, teachers and children. But it's not that simple: children are also uplifted and put down by things like their academic abilities, social abilities and physical attributes and their temperament and resilience. Then all these elements form a picture that can be distorted by the child's perception, especially when they compare themselves to their or society's role models.

While there is no easy way of boosting a child's self-esteem, there are things we can do to help.

Factors that affect self-esteem

Learning, physical and social abilities and attributes

A child who has advanced intellect, ease in relating, strong work output, good looks and is talented at sport will start from a favoured position. On the other side there are many clever children with problems of attention, learning, language or mixing, who bust themselves and get nowhere.

In theory we live on a level playing field, but in reality, some children will always play uphill and against the wind. Our aim is to help them savour success, but despite our best efforts many will experience more than their fair share of pain and self-doubt.

Temperament and resilience

Each of us has been dealt an individual hand in the cards of life, but not all will react equally to the same hand. Some who are attractive, influential and intelligent still carry a monumental chip on their shoulder, while others with far fewer winning attributes plod on unperturbed.

How tough a child's temperament is will affect their resilience, which is then boosted or lowered by outside events. Resilience rises with stability, close support, a trusted confidant and the feeling of belonging. Children are better able to cope with adversity when they have an extended network of people who believe in them. This includes aunts and uncles, family friends and others in their close community.

A child's self-perception

Children have no direct measure of their performance, and they gauge this through feedback from those around them. This reaction from other people provides the mirror through which they see themselves. Unfortunately the mirror of life is fitted with side-show glass that distorts the image.

Even the most successful, clever and attractive children may have a poor perception of themselves. So a child may have an attractive, well-proportioned figure, but to them the reflection appears fat and droopy. Or the reliable, much-respected child may feel they are a social bore with no small talk. Those who are shy may believe they live in a world of extroverts, when in fact most of their friends are introverts pretending to be extroverts.

It's bad enough worrying about non-problems, but when there are genuine concerns about ability, appearance, body size or social skills, a child may distort these way out of all proportion.

Role models

As parents we would like our children to be as talented as a film star, as popular as a princess and as impressive as a much-admired public figure. These role models shine out from the pages of today's glossy mags, but when they are dead and gone their biographers reveal most of them to have been crippled with self-doubt, personal problems and an inability to maintain relationships.

It's important to set our sights and our children's on realistic goals. Our children are doing much better than they realise, if only they could see past the play-acting.

Encouraging self-esteem

There is no magic bullet to boost esteem, but here are some simple suggestions. Children do best when we listen, respect their feelings, appreciate effort and accept their mistakes. We can also boost their self-esteem by avoiding using words that wound, giving them some responsibility and helping them succeed at something. Teachers also can help boost esteem in the classroom. But it is important to start all this early.

Start early

Esteem is not something that develops at the age of six. Its foundation is laid in the toddler years. Young children are intensely dependent on their parents, and if we treat them as special, they feel special. But it takes more than having us around to boost esteem – we also need to be available. Littlies need a listener, a comforter, a responder, an encourager, an audience and a safety net.

An unhurried grandparent has special powers that boost esteem. They listen in wonderment as their tongue-tied granddaughter rambles on, making the little person feel like a wit, a raconteur and a legend in their own lifetime. This early feeling of security and importance sets the foundation for better esteem.

Notice and listen

School-agers can ramble, lose the plot or wallow in such trivia your brain starts to ache. They talk of non-topics such as teenage pop groups or some program that would be better taken off the telly. But listening is important. If a child is to feel valuable, what they say should be valued. Show interest in their friends, work, hobbies, sports and words. Give feedback that lets them know you are with them.

Avoid the bland emptiness of 'Well done', 'That's good', 'You're clever.' Pick up on specific bits, as this lets them know you have a genuine interest. If we tune in to what our children do and say, obviously they must be worth noticing.

Respect their fears and feelings

All of us have our problems and worries: some are quite genuine, others are largely in our head. You can comfort the anxious air traveller with safety statistics, but five miles up in turbulence you might as well be telling Leonardo the *Titanic* is unsinkable.

Whether our worries are real or perceived, our bodies feel the same adrenalin upset and nothing others say will make much difference. School-age children may fear child abductors, germs, bullies, dirty toilets, the dark, spelling tests, talking in front of the class or being alone. It's not for us to reason why; our goal is to acknowledge, desensitise and give support to help them get on top. If we trivialise how a child feels, this affects their feeling of esteem.

Children should be accepted along with their fears, feelings and frustrations. When hurt, acknowledge how they feel, then see how you can help. When they are upset with their results, let them know that they worked hard, then together work towards a better outcome next time.

It's okay to be wrong

The only people who don't do anything wrong are those who don't do anything. Children need to know that we all make mistakes. When a child makes a mistake or fears failure the problems appear bigger than they are and this eats away at their self-esteem. Children need to be encouraged to try, accepted when they fail and supported to try again. Explain that by making mistakes we learn from the process. Let them hear you say, 'I was wrong. I made a mistake. Next time I'll do it differently.'

Avoid words that wound

Children can be stubborn, defiant and intensely annoying. As parents we can accept this with a turn of the other cheek or give it back with all guns blazing. When parents are driven to the edge of mental destruction, it's easy to drop the nice talk and use words that wound: 'You've ruined it for all of us'; 'What's the point, you've destroyed the day'; 'Grow up'; 'Just go away'; 'Don't be so stupid'; 'Don't talk to me'; 'You know it all'; 'You just don't bother.'

Remember it is the behaviour, not the child, that we dislike. Even when they are merciless in their assault try to avoid using only negative words.

Use 'I' statements, not 'you' statements

Humans feel less criticised when they hear a statement about how *you* feel rather than how *they* annoy. So turn things around and say,

'I feel upset when we fight with each other'; 'I feel embarrassed when this happens in front of my friends'; 'I feel sad when I hear words like that'; 'I feel upset when my friends see this behaviour.' Also avoid the chill of passive-aggression, where the words are okay but the intonation is laced with poison.

Give them responsibility within reason

If I am to trust myself, I must feel I am trusted by others. Children need to experience independence, but they must also be kept safe. This balance between trust and safety is a tightrope we all tread.

Children can be slow, messy, unreliable and wasteful, but if we don't let them do real tasks, they will never learn. We also need to avoid constantly using negative words: 'Don't slice the bread, you'll cut your finger'; 'Don't run, you'll trip'; 'Don't touch it, you'll make a mess'; 'Don't climb, you'll fall.' Instead, turn the sentence around: 'Hold the railing so you're safe.'

The aim is to let our children hold the controls and fly as co-pilots with the captain sitting close by. Children need to feel trusted if they are going to trust themselves.

Help them savour success

Every human is made up of a mix of strengths and weaknesses. As adults we keep confident by promoting our attributes and camouflaging the rest. Many of the most impressive actors, artists and entrepreneurs of the moment are dyslexic, disorganised people, some with the attention span of a gnat. Yet they have risen to the top by moving the focus from weakness to strength. They may not read or attend but they are worshipped for their wit, creativity or humanity.

Every child needs to feel they have talent. Some get a great boost from team sports, while the lone spirits enjoy running, cycling, swimming or ascending some far-off peak. Craft, music, computers, drama and clubs are useful outlets. The aim is to move away from what our children cannot do to what they can do. For children to gain confidence they need to savour success at something, and it's up to us to find what that something is.

Aim for confidence in the classroom

The child who is strong socially and advanced academically will usually be confident at school, but those who underachieve find it hard to stay positive. Teachers boost esteem by making each child feel they are important and belong. So the child who struggles gets the same responsibilities and privileges as the potential Rhodes Scholar.

For example, a child who is weak in one area or socially insecure can be asked to tutor other children in their area of strength. Many schools have a 'buddy system', where a mature older child guides and supports one less able. With schoolwork, attempts are appreciated, mistakes are accepted and effort is acknowledged.

If homework is causing pain, set a fixed period during which they put in a full effort, then the books close and home life returns.

A final word

Over the years I have attended day-long seminars and read volumes on the subject of self-esteem. But much of the material was impressive-sounding fluff. I have no miracle methods, just these commonsense suggestions: start early, notice, listen, show genuine interest, recognise effort, be specific in praise, watch your words, accept feelings, give responsibility, show trust, accept screw-ups and allow each child to savour success at something.

Factors that affect esteem

1. Learning, physical and social abilities and attributes
    - held down by learning problems
    - held down by attention problems
    - social or mixing problems
    - physical problems – short, thin, fat, clumsy
2. Temperament and resilience
    - some are created more resilient than others
    - boosted by 'belonging'

- boosted by a close family
- boosted by a mentor or confidant

3. Self-perception
    - you think you are the only one
    - you see problems bigger than they are
    - you worry over non-problems
    - you believe that your role models are perfect

Encouraging self-esteem

1. Start early
    - they need structure, stability, to know where they stand
    - they need a close parent who is available
    - they need grandparents who marvel at their cleverness
2. Notice and listen
    - show genuine interest
    - give specific feedback
    - let them know they are worth listening to
3. Respect their fears and feelings
    - fears are real – don't trivialise
    - accept, support and help through
4. It's okay to be wrong
    - accept mistakes, help them regroup, then try again
5. Watch your words
    - avoid words that wound: 'You ruin', 'pest', 'stupid', 'get lost'
6. 'I' statements and 'you' statements
    - state how you feel, not how they annoy
7. Responsibility and trust
    - give responsibility within reason
    - if we have trust in them, they have trust in themselves
8. Savouring success
    - move the focus from failure to areas of talent
    - seek out fun activities they can succeed at
    - if school causes stress, build a fortress of outside activities

9. Classroom confidence
   - to feel wanted and to belong
   - responsibility and privileges
   - tutor others in their area of strength
   - the buddy system
   - homework with a focus on effort
   - outside activities

SIXTEEN

Diet, weight and exercise

Until recently the word 'diet' meant a brief, painful period of deprivation. Weight was something you lost before your high school reunion and exercise was pounding the pavements or a six-month subscription to the gym.

Now the secret is to establish a sensible diet, maintain appropriate weight and adopt a more active, fitter lifestyle from an early age. And to do it at a level that can be easily sustained over the next eighty years.

We can help set up our children for a healthy life by establishing a sensible and sustainable balance of diet, exercise and lifestyle at the earliest age. And that is what this chapter is all about.

A balanced diet

The energy that powers our children comes from the carbohydrates, fat and protein in food. Of these, fat is by far the most potent provider of energy. Such is the metabolism of young children, they need all the zip they can get, and quite a bit must come from fat. After the age of six years, however, they need to gradually change to the low-fat, high-carbohydrate diet of the health-conscious adult.

Children also need iron, calcium and a range of vitamins.

A balanced diet of a small amount of meat, a substantial amount of dairy products and a variety of fruit, vegetables and cereal foods (such as breakfast cereals, bread and pasta) will give children everything they need to stay healthy and strong and to grow.

Children don't need lots of fizzy drinks or litres and litres of fruit juice. Good old tap water is a much better option.

Carbohydrates: quite complex

Carbohydrate is the main source of energy for parents, footy players, athletes and children. It comes as simple, quickly digested sugars or the slower-released complex carbohydrate found in bread, breakfast cereals, pasta, rice and vegetables.

Complex carbohydrate foods contain varying amounts of dietary fibre. While fibre is not digested, it is vital to the long-term health of body and bowel.

Within reason, children can eat unlimited amounts of complex carbohydrate without increasing the risk of obesity. However, highly refined sugars do require some restriction as they are easy to take in excess, which can easily turn to body fat. Sugars also damage teeth. In an ideal diet at least two-thirds of the carbohydrate should be in the complex form.

Fats

If you were carrying all your provisions for a long Himalayan trek, fat would provide the most efficient source of energy. Children under six years need a high level of fat in their diet, but as they get older we should move them towards a diet that is lower in fat and high in complex carbohydrate.

Fat has over twice the kilojoules of carbohydrate so, while useful on a mountain climb, in normal life it tends to increase the risk of obesity and heart attack.

Today's new breed of cardiologist believes that the time to start preventing adult heart disease is not at the age of forty but at the age of six years. This is because studies have found that the earliest signs of coronary artery narrowing are commonly found in both young adults and adolescents. These fatty deposits in artery walls are laying down the foundation for future trouble.

The fat in our diet is intimately involved with the body's production of cholesterol. And cholesterol can cause the damage to arteries that causes heart disease.

A high total cholesterol is not necessarily a problem – it's the *type* of cholesterol that makes the difference. When fats are broken down they may produce 'good' cholesterol – high-density cholesterol (HDL), which reduces the risk of artery damage. But they can also produce 'bad' cholesterol – low-density cholesterol (LDL), which greatly raises the risk of heart attack and stroke. Those with the best chance of maintaining healthy arteries either have a low level of LDL cholesterol or an average LDL cholesterol, which is protected by a high HDL cholesterol.

Now this is where the fat intake and more specifically the type of fat eaten becomes important. Fat comes as saturated, polyunsaturated and monounsaturated fat. Fatty meat, butter, cream, many frying oils, cake shortenings and coconut milk have particularly high levels of saturated fat. When saturated fat is ingested it greatly increases LDL, the bad cholesterol, and lowers HDL, the good cholesterol. This raises the long-term risk of heart attack and stroke.

Until recently polyunsaturated fats were heavily promoted because they reduced the level of LDL cholesterol. Unfortunately, we now realise they also lowered the good, HDL level as well. This means they are better than saturated fats but they are still a problem. Monounsaturated fats are now promoted as the healthiest form of fat. They are found in olive oil, peanut oil and canola oil, including spreads and 'butters' made from these. Monounsaturated fats raise HDL, the good cholesterol, and lower LDL, the bad cholesterol.

In practical terms you don't need to buy the most expensive forms of olive oil (extra virgin, first pressed, lurid green etc.). Switching to canola or peanut oil is fine. Also use spreads which boast they are 'high in monounsaturates'. Remember:

- saturated fat increases LDL (the 'bad' cholesterol)

- polyunsaturated fat decreases LDL but also HDL (the 'good' cholesterol)

- monounsaturated fats decrease 'bad' cholesterol but tend not to affect 'good' cholesterol.

The ability to lay down fat in the arteries has a strong hereditary link: certain families seem relatively immune despite their diet while others who take great care may still develop heart disease. We can't change our genes but we can improve our children's chances if we lower the LDL and raise the HDL levels of cholesterol.

Protein, iron, calcium and vitamins

In this country the majority of children will consume more protein than they really need. If the majority of their protein supply is coming from meat, it will bring with it an ample amount of the best quality of absorbable iron. Iron is needed to make haemoglobin, which carries oxygen in the blood.

Milk and dairy products provide most of our children's intake of calcium. Establishing a good calcium habit is essential, as the mineral we set down in the first half of our lives helps protects us against brittle bones in older years. Statistics suggest that two-thirds of older women and one-third of older men suffer from osteoporosis, which is a lack of calcium and strength in the bones.

Where a family is strictly no meat and no dairy, they can easily run low on calcium and iron. If there is ever any doubt about the balance of a special food regime, discuss it with a dietitian.

Iron does not have to come from meat, and calcium does not need to come from a cow. There are alternatives, but sometimes it takes a mountain of other food to attain the correct levels of nutrition. The average ten-year-old requires 30 grams of quality protein, 7 milligrams of haem-type iron, 800 milligrams of calcium (girls need 900 milligrams) and 30 milligrams of vitamin C.

Vitamins can come as packs of pills, or through nature, by eating a wide variety of fruit and vegetables. The natural way has the added advantage of providing trace elements, antioxidants and other essential micronutrients.

In general, a child will have the right nutritional balance if they regularly eat small portions of meat, have a substantial dairy intake and enjoy a wide variety of fruit and vegetables.

Fruits and vegetables: the forgotten food group

While there has been much made of fats in recent years we seem to have overlooked fruits and vegetables. Survey after survey has shown that children are seriously short-changed in this department. And yet it is becoming clear that these foods are not only brimful of vitamins and fibre but also umpteen other ingredients, such as antioxidants, which are now believed to play an important role in preventing degenerative diseases (heart disease, cancer, even diabetes) in later life.

Since this is a book on health, not chemistry, I will spare you the finer technical details. The main point is that children between six and twelve years need to get interested in fruit and vegetables and the wider the variety the better. While all this might sound like 'grandma knows best', it is worth taking seriously. Of course, most parents would give up their superannuation to get their kids to salivate over vegetables. But there are some tricks and, like superannuation, a small, early, regular investment gives good long-term results. Exposure is the key. Here are a few dos and don'ts.

Do

- Offer fruit morning, noon and night – and as snacks.

- Buy small amounts of many different kinds of fresh fruits and vegetables. Variety and freshness really help.

- Offer vegetables at every main meal – even in small amounts.

- Zip up the flavour by adding a little dressing to salads or a little margarine to cooked vegies.

- Remember: fruit with a little ice-cream is better than no fruit at all!

Don't

- Fuss, cajole or bribe children to eat vegetables.

- Despair if they say 'no thanks' with monotonous regularity; exposure is all-important here.

- Sneer at frozen or tinned vegetables.

- Expect children to eat vegetables that you would find tasteless.

- Give up. Fruit and veg are important for children.

Water: the ultimate health drink

The advertisement says, 'Diet Coke – less than one calorie.' But according to my research Diet Water has even less calories than Diet Coke. Water is a readily available, competitively priced drink. It should be introduced to our children early so as to establish brand loyalty.

Water is at its most boring when it splashes straight from the tap, but when chilled and served with ice or lemon it is much more appealing. For the ultimate presentation, put an empty glass in the freezer, then bring to the table frosted, as if ready for the best French champagne.

Parents often overlook water and see fruit juice or milk as the main health drinks. The problem with juice is that it can be taken in excess. If one serve of OJ contains over three oranges, after three drinks ten oranges are gurgling round, which can cause diarrhoea. While milk is the best source of calcium, when weight is a problem, it's wise to go for the low-fat varieties.

Some foods are better than others

'Health' foods

When your child goes to school with an all-natural health bar, while your neighbour's child has a slice of cake or a chocolate biscuit, you may not be providing any great health advantage. Some foods claim a healthy status due to the addition of yoghurt, carob, glucose or honey. But many, especially snack bars, may also contain too much fat and sugar. A muesli, carob or fruit bar may have half the fat content of chocolate, but that is still too much. Also, they are sticky, which glues sugar to the teeth and increases the risk of cavities. These bars certainly contain fibre, but only half what you would get from a Queensland banana.

Sugar is still sugar, whether it's called glucose, honey or molasses. Fat is always fat, whether it's called a health bar or not. Before you part with your money, read the label. The best health products for children are fruits, yoghurt, milk, bread, sandwiches and a wide variety of inexpensive, everyday foods.

'Cholesterol-free' food

Other snack foods that parents believe must be healthy are those labelled 'cholesterol free'. Yet, despite what is implied in advertisements, almost none of the cholesterol that damages our hearts comes from cholesterol we eat. The cholesterol that blocks arteries is mostly produced by the metabolism of fats in our diet.

You may buy a packet of chips that is advertised as 'cholesterol free', but the chips can still contain twenty-five per cent of an unhealthy sort of fat. Don't be fooled by misleading claims about cholesterol: read the label and establish the fat content before purchase. If you believe the manufacturer is trying to deceive, boycott their product.

Snacks: approximate fat and kilojoule levels

Note: Fat, especially saturated fat, is our greatest concern, not kilojoules.

Food	Fat content	Kilojoules
Anzac biscuit	4.5 g	370 kJ
apple, large	0 g	400 kJ
banana, large	0.5 g	585 kJ
baked-bean sandwich	3 g	930 kJ

banana smoothie (full-cream milk), 250 ml	10 g	1100 kJ
banana smoothie (half-fat milk), 250 ml	4 g	850 kJ
banana smoothie (low-fat milk), 250 ml	1 g	800 kJ
cheese, 30 g	10 g	505 kJ
cheese cake (baked), average slice	55 g	3280 kJ
chocolate (fruit and nut), 6 squares	9 g	640 kJ
chocolate-chip cookie	3 g	225 kJ
carrot cake, average slice	42 g	2740 kJ
cup cake	6 g	760 kJ
doughnut (iced)	19.5 g	1425 kJ
Mars Bar, 63 g	11 g	1090 kJ
muesli bar	4.5 g	495 kJ
muffin (cake-bran)	8 g	530 kJ
lamington cake	9 g	980 kJ
potato crisps, 50 g packet	16 g	1050 kJ
quiche Lorraine, average slice	44 g	2400 kJ
Tim Tam	5.5 g	400 kJ
Twisties, 50 g packet	13.5 g	1065 kJ
Violet Crumble, 50 grams	8 g	885 kJ
yoghurt (fruit), 200 ml	4 g	740 kJ
yoghurt (low-fat), 200 ml	0.5 g	630 kJ

Fast food

The problem with fast food is not its speed but its fat content. What's more, it is usually the saturated, less healthy fats that predominate. A Big Mac and chips, half a Super Supreme pizza or a normal serve of Thai red curry would deliver more than a day's fat intake in one hit.

I don't wish to be a killjoy and ban these foods, but there must be sense in the servings. A Big Mac, eaten alone, has less than half the fat of a Big Mac, thickshake and medium fries. A Junior Burger and small fries has less fat than one Big Mac. One slice of pizza has half the fat of two slices. A half serve of that wonderful Thai curry has fifty per cent the saturated fat of a whole serve.

If weight is on target and the general diet is healthy, there is no problem in having one, or even two of these meals each week. Where weight is a problem or exercise limited, go slow on fast food.

Fast foods: approximate fat and kilojoule levels*

Food	Fat content	Kilojoules
Big Mac	24.6 g	2113 kJ
baked beans, one cup	1.5 g	715 kJ
bread slice	1 g	290 kJ
bread fried	12 g	840 kJ
chicken breast (baked, no skin), 90 g	3.5 g	470 kJ
chicken (deep-fried), 1 average piece	15 g	900 kJ
chicken nuggets, 6 pieces	17.7 g	1265 kJ
croissant	16.5 g	1150 kJ
fries (medium)	22 g	1702 kJ
ice-cream Cornetto	12 g	775 kJ
Junior Burger	8 g	1118 kJ
pasta bolognaise	20 g	1800 kJ
pasta carbonara	44 g	2750 kJ
pepper steak	36 g	2250 kJ
pizza Super Supreme, one quarter	22 g	2140 kJ
rice (boiled)	0.5 g	915 kJ
rice (fried)	13.5 g	1490 kJ
sundae (hot fudge)	10.6 g	1318 kJ
sundae, no topping	6 g	772 kJ
sweet and sour pork	23.5 g	1925 kJ
Thai thick red curry	44 g	2220 kJ
thick chocolate shake, regular	9.5 g	1508 kJ

* *Nutritional Values of Australian Foods*, Australian Government Publishing Co, 1991; Leaflet, McDonalds Family Restaurants, 1998; Rosemary Stanton, *Fat and Fibre Counter*, 1993 (available in Australian and New Zealand bookshops or fax 03 96505261).

Weight and losing weight

It seems seriously unfair that some people eat enormously yet remain thin, while others go plump on the thought of a chip. In the past, it was thought to be quite simple: overweight was caused by overeating. But now we realise that fatness or thinness is greatly determined by genetic predisposition, which is then modified by the type of food consumed and the energy that is expended.

Studies suggest that if both parents are lean there is only a one in ten chance their children will be obese. When one parent is genetically overweight, the risk rises to forty per cent, and where both have this problem, it rises to eighty per cent. Putting on the pounds is not all bad news: those people who do are effective metabolisers who are making the maximum use of what they take aboard. They're the family sedans with a fuel-efficient engine. So when the famine hits the land it is the plump ones who will survive, and the skinny super-models will fade as quickly as you can say, 'Fabulous, daahling.'

The overweight baby or toddler will usually tone up and grow into an adult of normal size. But weight is much more serious at school-age, because the fat child tends to become a fat adult. For this reason, if a child is an efficient metaboliser they will gain weight on an average diet, and will need to be committed to weight control all their life.

Adults find it relatively easy to maintain weight, but losing weight is many times more difficult. Fortunately, growing young children have an advantage: it is usually sufficient for them to maintain but not lose weight. So as an overweight child grows in height their steady weight will gradually slip into a body of perfect proportion.

Losing weight for any child or adult must be approached as a long-term project. It is achieved by changing the balance of food intake and increasing exercise. So while we can't change our genes, we can change diet and exercise. As weight increases the ability to exercise reduces and that makes sensible food intake even more important.

The main target for weight reduction is to reduce fat. Get rid of fried foods, chips, sausage, pizza and fatty meat. Reduce the amount of butter, cream and the fat you add to bread, vegetables and pasta. Watch for the hidden fat in cakes, chocolate, biscuits and adding oil, butter or fat to normal cooking. Move from full-cream to half-cream milk and low-fat yoghurt.

Once fat intake is in control, target sweets, soft drinks and excessive amounts of fruit juice. The aim is to move from an over-sweetened, fatty diet to one that is high in the complex carbohydrate of bread, vegetables, cereal, rice, pasta and fruit. These by themselves need little restriction, but if they are greased up with butter and fatty spreads, the diet becomes a waste of time.

As well as diet there must be an increase in exercise. This starts by limiting television and computer time and getting children up and out. Increase the baseline level of activity by walking to school, going to the pool or getting on their bike.

Replacing fatty foods with low-fat foods

A child with a weight problem can be encouraged to cut down on fatty foods and to try some lower-fat alternatives. Here's a list of some popular fatty foods and some alternatives:

Cut down on these	Try more of these
fatty meat, sausages, salami, Devon and other smallgoods	lean meat, chicken, fish (canned or fresh)
cakes, biscuits, snack foods (chips, etc) pastries, croissants	bread, rolls, plain buns, plain crackers, pasta, rice
full-cream: milk, yoghurt, cheese, cream, ice cream	skim or semi-skimmed milk, low-fat yoghurt, low-fat cheeses, low-fat ice cream, frozen yoghurt
fruit juices, fizzy drinks, sports drinks	fruit, vegetables, water, diluted fruit juices
fried foods	grilled or baked food with little fat
butter, margarine, oil	low-fat spreads or butter substitutes that are light on kJs

Remember, the point here is emphasis and stealth. Few chubby nine-year-olds are going to relish an overnight abolition of their favourite foods, so gradually replace things in the left-hand column with those in the right. Even if you are only able to do this some of the time it will help.

Common drinks: approximate fat and kilojoule levels

Drink	Fat content	Kilojoules
milk, 250 ml	9.5 g	675 kJ
milk (low fat), 250 ml	3.5 g	550 kJ
milk (flavoured), 250 ml	9.5 g	820 kJ
milk (soya fortified), 250 ml	8.5 g	800 kJ
milk (Shape), 250 ml	1 g	500 kJ
orange juice, 250 ml	0 g	380 kJ
apple juice, 250 ml	0 g	440 kJ
cola, 250 ml	0 g	430 kJ
fruit cordial 250ml	0 g	350 kJ

Exercise

Don't expect that by attending school an unenthusiastic child will suddenly begin to enjoy exercise. The lead has to come from home. As parents we must set the right example by increasing, if necessary, the amount of exercise we do. The aim is to start them young and to develop patterns that we hope will last a lifetime.

With today's technology it is easy to be quite sedentary; in fact, you don't even have to move a buttock to adjust the telly. Previous generations had more fat and kilojoules in their diet, but they burnt them off with extra activity. As adults, we should try to walk instead of drive, use stairs instead of lifts and be more mobile in every part of our day. As for our children, we should walk with them to the shops, ride bikes and swim together. Television and computers should be limited and replaced with play. We should encourage them to play sport by being interested and supportive.

Regular exercise keeps muscles strong, helps mental state and improves sleep. It controls weight and seems to lower the levels of the dangerous LDL cholesterol in the blood.

A final word

Good health in children comes from inheriting the right genes, having the right diet, watching weight, if necessary, and doing appropriate exercise. After the age of six children need a balanced diet that is relatively low in fat but high in complex carbohydrate. While we can't do anything about our genes, we can help a child keep their weight in check by eating well and doing exercise. Finally, the key to good health that lasts a lifetime is to *start early*.

Diet, weight and exercise

1. Diet
   - Up until the age of six, children need a diet high in fat. From the age of six, their diet should gradually change to one lower in fat and higher in carbohydrates.
   - A balanced diet consists of a small amount of meat, a substantial amount of dairy products and a variety of fruit, vegetables and cereals.
   - Water is the best thirst quencher.
   - Children also need iron, calcium and a variety of vitamins. The best sources for these are foods, not vitamin pills.
   - Children should be encouraged to eat a wide variety of fruit and vegetables.
   - Like snack foods and fast food, some 'health' foods are high in fats and sugar.
2. Weight
   - Fatness or thinness is greatly determined by our genes.

- Overweight school-age children tend to grow up into overweight adults.
- The best way to help a child lose weight is to reduce their fat intake by replacing fatty foods with low-fat alternatives.

3. Exercise
   - Good exercise habits start at home: encourage your child to play sport, ride bikes or swim, and do some exercise yourself.
   - Limit television and computer time.
   - Regular exercise keeps muscles strong and improves sleep.

SEVENTEEN

A child's view of death, divorce and religion

A death or divorce in the family destabilises a child's world and reduces the emotional availability of those they depend on. The child's reaction to this situation will depend on their age and how well their custodians can come to terms with their own upset.

Religion brings support and values to many families. At the age of six, children will follow faithfully; by ten years they may start to question; and by adolescence they are beginning to plan their own destiny. This chapter looks at death, divorce and religion to see how they impact on today's children.

Children and death

Children learn about death through hearing their parents talk, watching the news and when Rover goes to the doggie pound in the sky. Where a death is within the family, how the child responds will depend on how close they were to the person who died and how the death disrupts the equilibrium of their life. Also, a child's reaction to death varies greatly with age.

The under-six-year-old

At this age a child has no grasp of the concept of death. They respond to the disruption and perceived abandonment in their life but have no understanding of death and dying. When asked what happened, they repeat what they have been told, but they don't know what it means. To them there is no finality in death – the person might as well be on a long holiday.

This is an egocentric age where children are concerned about their own immediate needs, and don't grieve directly for the one who

has died. They may feel angry that this relative has walked out as well as unsettled by the fears and tension that have overtaken the home.

The reaction of young children to the effect of death in their home can be intense and immediate. They become restless, clingy, difficult or they may regress. I am often asked to arrange counselling for an upset child following a family loss. But with these under-six-year-olds, it is usually the parent, not the child, who needs counselling. Once the adults find their equilibrium again, the child miraculously returns to normal.

When it is the closest and most important attachment figure who has died, it has an immense impact on a young child. Now it is an urgent priority to surround them with as much alternative and consistent support as possible.

The six- to eight-year-old

Though children aged six to eight are more mature, they are still predominantly influenced by the emotional state of their parents. They now have some slight understanding of death, but to them it may not really be permanent and their grandma may still be alive if they visit her home.

At this age a child may carry hidden worries and sometimes think they are to blame. For example, their brother may have died of leukaemia, and they worry they may have caused the death through resentment or jealousy. These secret agendas are at their most severe when parents retreat inwardly, bottle up their feelings and don't keep children informed.

The under-eight-year-old will ask copious questions. What they are after is reassurance, not a detailed answer. Their unsettled behaviour will resolve once stability and warm communication return.

The eight- to twelve-year-old

After the age of eight years a child starts to develop an almost-adult understanding of death. They see life far into the future and they realise that death is permanent.

Children will always be influenced to some extent by the stability or distress of their parents, but their grief is now their own. A nine- or ten-year-old will show the adult emotions of tears, preoccupation and periods of sadness. Some withdraw and become hard to reach. Occasionally their behaviour may be difficult, but this is more a sign of irritation with the world than a deliberate challenge to their parents.

To visit or not?

When a close relative becomes terminally ill, do we encourage a visit or preserve a happier memory? If the event is sudden, catastrophic and short term, there is little benefit in a visit. Where there is more time and the relative is still mentally alert, there is good reason to keep contact.

For children under the age of six years a visit brings no great benefit to their understanding, acceptance or adjustment. If they go, this is for the needs of their parents and the relative, not their own. After six years and particularly after the age of eight, a visit will allow the family to share together, gives a major life experience and provides a point for the older child to start their grief.

There is no right or wrong answer – just some guidelines. For me, I would not involve under-six-year-olds. However, I would take a child over eight for all but the most major or short-term situations.

To view the body or not?

Viewing the dead is favoured by some families, and when it is the norm, adults and children should observe this practice together. It has no emotional advantage for the under-six-year-old, who will probably just ask endless, awkward questions. However, for the older child it is a moment they will appreciate being a grown-up and part of their family.

For me, the lid will be nailed and glued tightly shut. I want to be remembered as warm, enthusiastic and alive.

Children and funerals

A funeral is an occasion when adults can say their last goodbyes and start the process of resolution. A child eight years or older has the same need to grieve as their parents, and should be encouraged to attend. The six- to eight-year-old has less to gain, but while not essential, it's best to include them in the family group. The three-, four- and five-year-old has little understanding of death and gets no benefit from a funeral. At this young age it is parents and the expectation of others that influences whether a preschooler attends or not.

The need for open communication

Young children ask endless questions but don't have much interest in the answers. Adults often cope with these queries by hiding behind the jargon of death: 'We have just lost your grandma'; 'She is sleeping in wonderful peace'; 'She is happy up with the angels.' With explanations like these children may wonder where it was you lost Grandma or may see sleep as a dangerous occupation.

Adults also make the mistake of believing that the under-eight-year-old needs deep and detailed answers. But when a five-year-old asks an innocent question they will be happy with a few words of general reassurance. It is your availability and unflustered attention they want because this lets them know they are safe and secure.

The over-eight-year-old wants more information, and it's best to be honest and open. When Grandma is ill, tell the truth: 'Yes, we are very worried. She may die, but we are doing all we can to help.' If parents become stoic and non-communicative, children may bottle up their feelings, generate strange fears and get stuck in their resolution. But of course, it is hard for parents to talk openly and clearly when they are drowning in their own grief.

Divorce and separation

There are many similarities between a child's reaction to death and their reaction to divorce. Their understanding of the event depends on their age, and all children are immensely influenced by the stability and emotional wellbeing of their parents.

It is believed that the children of a hostile break-up suffer more deeply than a together family that loses their dad through a tragic accident. When a parent dies friends flock around, there is a funeral, then life slowly starts to get back on track. In a messy divorce friends have confused loyalties, there is no turn-around point and hostility can go on for years.

How children react

The under-six-year-old is all feeling and no understanding. They resent what has happened and react by clinging closely or responding with bad behaviour. They don't know what is going on but they hate the tension and disruption.

The six- to eight-year-old is also confused and disturbed by the disruption. They have a limited understanding, and are more unsettled than disruptive in their reaction.

The over-eights are more aware and they know that this event is forever. They may be confused in their loyalties. They often react with preoccupation, withdrawal and a reduction in academic grades.

Whatever the age, children do best when parents act amicably and maintain the maximum environmental stability. For more information on separation see Chapter 20.

Religion

Humans are at their emotional best when they see a future, a purpose and a meaning to life. Religious faith provides this for many families. Religion at its best brings values, a common goal, family strength and a supportive community network. At its worst, it can create fear and guilt and can legitimise inequality.

With my interest in the emotional welfare of children, I see the family strength and togetherness of religion as an immense advantage. And as one who studies child development, I wonder how much of a child's faith is the blind acceptance that is a normal stage in the young child and what part comes from a deep, personal commitment.

The development of true belief

The under-eight-year-old will totally accept the sayings, values and beliefs of their close family. At this age their parents are the most important source of learning, and they will repeat word for word what they have been told, without question.

The child over eight years ceases to take things at face-value and may start to question their parents' beliefs. Though most will follow their family's beliefs and practices, they may start to have inner doubts and unspoken worries.

Eight years is an important milestone. At eight, children become less selfish and tune in to the needs of others in the group. They start to compare, compete and worry that they are not as good or as giving as others. This new-found conscience and self-criticism bring the first feelings of genuine guilt. This kind of guilt is different from the pseudo guilt of the four-year-old who eats Mum's chocolates and looks guilty. The four-year-old's response is conditioned by the memory of the sore bottom they got the last time. But an eight-year-old's feelings of guilt come from conscience.

Guilt can be a catalyst that inspires humans to strive for self-betterment. On the other hand, feelings of negative self-worth have kept a generation of adult psychiatrists in business. But guilt does play an important part in some of the world's religions: it drives the wish to reach a higher plane and seek forgiveness. With extreme fringe groups fear and guilt hold the flock together, because to falter leads to perpetual damnation.

In **adolescence**, religion comes of age. These almost-adults challenge everybody and everything, especially the values of their parents. But this is the dawn of the development of abstract thought, when we work out our own values, causes and convictions. It is here, in the late teens, that true personal belief has its foundation. Now it is faith that comes direct from the heart.

Children and death, divorce and religion

1. Death
    - the under-six-year-old has no grasp of the finality of death
    - the six- to eight-year-old may have hidden worries, which can be made worse if parents don't keep them informed
    - the eight- to twelve-year-old is developing an understanding of death and needs to be allowed to grieve
    - visiting terminally ill relatives can be a positive experience for older children but the under sixes will benefit little
    - viewing the body, if favoured, should be done as a family
    - children over six can benefit from attending the funeral with their family

- children need to be kept informed, but don't give overly detailed answers to questions
2. Divorce and separation
   - under six years, children don't understand but will hate the disruption
   - between six and eight, children have some understanding and can be confused and disturbed
   - over eight years, children understand the finality of separation and may be confused about where their loyalties lie
3. Religion
   - religion can bring families together, providing values, a common goal and a supportive community network
   - religion can create fear and guilt in children
   - the under-eight-year-old accepts without question the beliefs of their close family
   - the eight- to twelve-year-old may start to question their parents' beliefs

EIGHTEEN

Sex education, sexual development and other sex-related issues

C hildren are created in two sorts: little girls and little boys. At the age of six years, their size and physical strength are very similar. Then, somewhere between the age of ten and fourteen years, the pubertal growth spurt will start. Girls are first to take off, and for a brief time are taller and more physically strong than the male of the species. After this there are considerable differences between the sexes, the male becoming larger and stronger, the female probably more mature and sensible.

Though adolescence is the age that causes most sexual concern for parents, the attitudes to sex that are important are laid down very much earlier.

Sex education

It's simple: start early, be open and address questions as they arise. Gone are the days when you waited until sixteen years to say, 'John, there is something I have to tell you.' Now, many sixteen-year-olds could educate their parents.

From the youngest age, address genuine questions when asked. If you sidestep and look flustered this suggests that sex is nasty, rude or taboo. Sometimes questions are asked to gain attention. I remember my boys asking their grandma, 'What's that word that begins with f and ends with k?' This got her full attention after which they continued, 'Ah yes. "Fire truck." '

The biggest mistake parents make is being evasive or giving more information than is wanted. The under-tens need the simplest of answers, not the surgical details of breast augmentation, research findings on feromones or a summary of the Kinsey Report.

For the over tens, if I were clever enough to get through to them, my sex education message would include the following:

- sex is appropriate, but creating children without a stable relationship is rarely wise

- sole parenthood for the majority means poverty and loneliness

- trusting in luck is not an effective form of contraception

- both sexes are responsible for making children, and both sexes are responsible for contraception.

As for AIDS, I would quote a wise but politically incorrect Australian, the late Professor Fred Hollows: 'Currently in Australia almost all cases of AIDS result from two things: anal receptive sex and the misuse of dirty needles. If you're going to get serious about AIDS education, these must be the main areas to address.'

Sexual development

The first sign of approaching puberty is a sudden acceleration in height. For girls the average age that this happens is eleven and a half years (this ranges from ten to thirteen years). Boys get moving slightly later, with the average age being thirteen and a half years (the usual range is ten and a half to fifteen years).

As this growth spurt gets going, pubic hair appears and girls see the first sign of breast development. The breasts are fully formed by about fifteen years (this ranges from twelve to eighteen years). The first period occurs at about thirteen years, but with great variation – somewhere between eleven and sixteen years.

Sexual development often follows a family pattern. A mother who started to develop early or late may have daughters that follow the same pattern. But there is a considerable variation between children, which means there can be great differences in the height and maturity of children around this eleven to fourteen age group. If you are in any way concerned that puberty has arrived too early, too late or is unusual in any way, it's best to discuss this with your paediatrician. When they are undecided, they will ask the advice of a specialist in growth and endocrinology.

Other sex-related issues

Sexual interest and exploration

The under-eights have little worry about nudity, and at this young age there is no problem with communal changing. Five- and six-year-old boys and girls can bath together as can seven-year-olds with some supervision. But after the age of eight years our society expects us to segregate the sexes.

Children vary greatly in their maturity and wish for modesty, and we must be sensitive to their wishes. For parents it doesn't much matter what society expects – our aim is to protect innocent little people from hurt and exploitation.

Young children are fascinated by anatomical difference. It is quite common to find a four-year-old boy and girl, stark naked, checking out each other's assets. This is an innocent part of life education, which we calmly accept but firmly discourage. Six- and seven-year-olds are still inquisitive, and it's not uncommon for some superficial investigation and touching. At this age, and to some extent in the following years, our response should remain low-key, but rules must be clearly stated and the opportunity for repetition avoided.

Interest in the opposite sex is not unhealthy, and nudity, viewing and superficial touching are usually harmless. However, this depends on there being a mutual interest, no force and the children being of similar age. A ten-year-old investigating a six-year-old may be part of an isolated episode of innocent curiosity, but the inequality of age is potentially dangerous and should be guarded against in the future. Where one child demonstrates overtly sexual behaviour that is significantly out of keeping with their developmental age, this is of great concern, as it can be a sign of sexual abuse (see this chapter, page 226).

Using the correct words

Preschoolers can have pet names for private parts, but by schoolage it's best to stick to the correct terminology. Whether we like it or not, our children will be exposed to 'improper' words, because these are used in the real world.

One infants principal told me of his campaign to clean up the language in his school. There were no rude words allowed, and private parts were to be labelled appropriately. Then one boy was brought to his office after having called his mate a 'dickhead'. The principal decided to set an example, telling the boy, 'John, you are not allowed to use the word "dick". What is the proper name for what you have between your legs?' John seemed puzzled, then looked down and immediately saw the answer: 'It's the carpet, sir.'

Masturbation

Both boys and girls play with their private parts because it gives them pleasure. This was once considered an evil perversion, but now it is accepted as a normal, healthy part of life. Parents feel distress when a child self-stimulates, but our disquiet must not cause our child to feel guilty about this normal activity.

Little boys can get erections from the first day of life, and obviously this has no sexual relevance. Once their nappies are removed, boys and girls (predominantly boys), will frequently hold or touch. This continues to some extent throughout childhood but, with age, they do it with more discretion or in private.

The incidence of masturbation varies considerably from child to child. Occasionally we see early school-age children who rub against objects or are quite open in this activity. This is usually a sign of boredom or stress, and though it is extremely upsetting for parents and teachers, it is usually an innocent behaviour. If the child is persistent and does it in public state the social rules, suggest they move to another room, give a subtle signal of disapproval and use a behavioural approach that turns the focus to fiddle-free days. Occasionally major masturbation can be a sign of sexual abuse.

Homosexual or heterosexual

It's amazing how attitudes change. In my medical student training homosexuality was seen as a psychiatric disorder. Homosexual men came seeking desensitisation therapy. Treatment involved the viewing of compromising pictures and when incorrectly aroused viewers were rewarded with an electric shock. But we have moved a million miles from that position, and homosexuality is now accepted as a common and unchangeable difference.

With such publicity and 'outness' from the gay lobby, parents may wonder whether their children might start to march to a different drum. In fact, most modern researchers believe that homosexuality and bisexuality are, to a large extent, in the biological make-up of the individual. They are certainly not caused by parenting style, homosexual assaults or mixing with the wrong sort of company. But how homosexuality might be recognised in the five- to twelve-year-old is much less certain.

Many normal ten- to eighteen-year-old heterosexuals have periods of attraction to those of their own sex, but their main interest will remain heterosexual. However, retrospective studies of adult homosexuals often report a more predominantly homosexual preference in childhood. While the majority of effeminate boys and tomboy girls are destined to be heavily heterosexual, retrospective studies again suggest more homosexuals come from these beginnings.

Though some homosexual boys are firmly oriented by the age of fourteen years, for most this realisation comes after some trial and error close to the age of twenty. For homosexual girls the realisation can often be somewhat later, even in the thirties, after marriage and children.

But gone are the days of shock therapy: you don't drive homosexuality out of the brain and body. And while it's common, it's probably less frequent than has been recently promoted.

Cross-dressing and gender dissatisfaction

Adults may cross-dress through their wish to be of a different gender (transsexual), their desire to attract a homosexual partner (effeminate homosexual) or as a fetish that gives sexual pleasure (transvestite). But these preoccupations are not in the minds of young children, and ninety-nine per cent of all cross-dressing and gender confusion in children is harmless, normal childhood play and of no concern.

Young children will often dress in their mum's or dad's clothes. This is quaint, normal and not a sign of perversion. It is best managed without undue comment or fuss. But where there is persistence and preoccupation rather than it being an occasional fun activity, it is wise to seek reassurance from a child psychologist.

It is quite common for a boy under the age of ten years to say they want to be a girl, and vice versa. This is usually entirely innocent and irrelevant. However, when a child overstates it and is persistent for over a year or more it's best to check what's happening by arranging a referral to a professional. Occasionally a psychiatrist may believe that some uncertainty in the home environment is the cause of gender confusion.

Parents: how intimate is too intimate?

Families who are open in communication and free from sexual hang-ups produce children who will develop the most appropriate adult attitudes. These parents are comfortable about nakedness, but they have boundaries between appropriate intimacy and overstepping the mark. The current emphasis on abuse has led many good parents to question the instincts they once trusted.

There is no problem with young children bathing, showering and sleeping with parents. There will be times when even a seven- or eight-year-old will ask about or even touch adult parts. This is common and best managed in a matter-of-fact way: state that there are social rules and that this is not appropriate.

With the tens to teens it's fine to be intimate, but quickly move away when anything happens that might arouse or lead to mis-interpretation. Fathers can relate closely to older daughters and can be even closer when two parents are present.

We have to be particularly careful after a marriage break-up, however. When hostility continues after the break-up we need to exercise extreme caution, because the smallest incident can be mis-represented to the maximum malice. Take extra care when new companions, partners or potential step-parents are involved.

Concerns of sexual abuse

The statistics vary from study to study but, at the most conservative estimate, one in ten adult women and one in twenty adult men have suffered sexual abuse in childhood. The extent of this varies from an incident of touching to major repeated sexual activity.

The worst part of sexual abuse is that the perpetrator is usually a trusted adult or adolescent who is well known to the child. They can be a relative, family friend, stepfather or even father. In sexual abuse, power is inappropriately misused and children are made to feel guilty and frightened to speak out.

As a paediatrician, I find this an extremely difficult diagnosis to make. In its most clear-cut presentation, abuse shows as obvious physical damage or there is an unmistakable history. More commonly, the only sign is a change in behaviour. The child may withdraw into themselves, become angry or display inappropriately explicit sexual behaviour. When an astute parent sees this change they may pick up clues of the assault, but often the child is so guilty and confused they maintain a code of silence.

I often see another side to this when parents are incorrectly reported and investigated as abusers. In my experience this usually happens with children who have a major developmental problem that results in some disinhibited, inappropriate sexual behaviour. There is no evidence of abuse, just out-of-step behaviour that prompts the diligent child care worker to make the report. Often the families are already struggling to stay afloat, and while this assault on parents may be legally necessary, it is extremely destructive. Abuse damages children, but false claims of abuse can pull apart stressed families.

The main message for parents is to educate but not terrify children about the possibility of abuse, stranger danger and the importance of saying no. We need to know the whereabouts of our children and thus lessen the opportunity for misuse. We must listen carefully, especially when a girl becomes withdrawn or a boy becomes unexpectedly aggressive. We must be on our guard when there is any unexplained, inappropriately explicit sexual behaviour.

One of the saddest aspects of abuse is that the child can no longer trust the adults who are supposed to protect them. The sad part for me is that I probably diagnose only a small proportion of the children in my care who are abused.

Sex education, sexual development, and other sex-related issues

1. Sex education
   - start early
   - answer genuine questions clearly and simply
2. Sexual development
   - girls reach puberty between ten and thirteen years
   - boys reach puberty between ten and a half and fifteen years
   - how early or late a child develops may follow a family pattern
   - if you have any concerns about your child's sexual development, talk to your paediatrician

3. Other sex-related issues
    - masturbation is normal, healthy and usually innocent in children
    - homosexuality is probably part of an individual's biological make-up
    - homosexuals may not be sure of their sexual orientation until their twenties or even thirties, but they may show a preference in childhood
    - cross-dressing in children is normal and should be managed with minimum fuss, unless the child overstates it or is persistent for a year or more, in which case, see your paediatrician
    - families who are open in communication and free from sexual hang-ups produce children who develop the most appropriate adult attitudes
    - sexual abuse is most often committed by a known and trusted adult or adolescent

Television, computers and the Internet

I worry about the current assault by television on both children and adults. I dislike the way it impedes conversation, reading, physical exercise and creative play. I resent the beaming of so much cruelty, horror, unhappiness and anger into my home. I don't wish to be a hermit or a Luddite, but there must be more control over this intrusive invention.

Computers and the Internet provide another screen. When they are used appropriately they can bring valuable skills and knowledge, but when they are misused, they can promote isolation, poor social-isation and glazed-eyed solitude.

The main thing to remember, whether it's television, computer time or access to the Internet, is that parents have control – they are not controlled by other people's transmissions.

Television

Today's television is so influential, parents need to take their children's choice of programs as seriously as they would their diet or education.

We can't act like the KGB and jam all unwanted radio signals, but parents must take charge of the tube. However, this can be extremely difficult, because marketing forces have raised some shows to the status of essential viewing. At school, the previous night's episode is the hot topic of conversation and those who missed out look like oddballs from a distant galaxy. Maybe it's time to join with other parents from your children's class and lay down some limits to resist these pressures.

Parents setting limits

At home you can start by establishing a rule that the television is turned on for specific programs, but when the show's over, the plug is pulled. Parents need to set a good example: watch what is important to you and switch off the rest. Check program guides and plan in advance what your children will and will not watch.

Television should be off during family meals in the hope that parents and children can rediscover conversation. Discuss the content of programs and the tricks of advertising with your children. Children can learn that commercials rarely advertise what is essential or healthy: we can point out that there are few adverts for tap water, fresh fruit, or warnings against the fat content of fast foods or confectionery.

If you're watching the news clarify the stories for your children. They need to be reassured that most of what they see is happening at the other end of the earth and should not cause fear or concern in their own community. Unfortunately, young children under eight years don't always understand: to them, horror footage from central Bolivia might as well be happening at the end of their street.

I recognise there is a definite place for television and videos, but in overdose they desensitise and destabilise and may replace other useful activities like exercise, conversation, hobbies or even homework.

Television violence and fear

Studies of North American seventeen-year-olds find they have spent more time at the television than in face-to-face education at school. While this is going on, they will have been exposed to multiple murders, countless acts of violence, role models of dubious character and a stream of sadness and cruelty.

There are over 1000 reviews and studies that point to a link between TV violence and aggression in children, adolescents and adults. Organisations now exist in most countries that draw attention to this effect on our children (such as Young Media Australia (E-mail info@youngmedia.org.au; Fax 08 82321571)). These organisations are concerned that cartoon violence and the mistreating of others on television distort the views of the very young child. They can show evidence that the stream of attractive, violent heroes we see on our screens influences the ideals of children and encourages aggression. They note that even violence mixed with humour can lead to desensitisation, so children fail to notice the hurt or suffering of others. They are especially unhappy with the current presentation of the news, which, through unnecessary images, leaves children and adults suspicious, frightened and with a scary view of their world.

I agree with these views and have special concern about news programming. To be high rating a story must promote controversy, discord, wallow in the suffering of others and be accompanied by graphic visual footage. News is driven by these criteria – not the relevance of the information.

In Australia I have to endure images of an irrelevant murder–suicide in California, a spectacular car accident in Ohio, or a helicopter hitting power lines in Luxembourg. This arrives in my home just because a Sydney TV channel has secured some explicit footage. It is no wonder that adults and children are afraid to walk the streets or see the world as hostile and without compassion.

Television viewing and violence

1. With current viewing habits, at the age of seventy years each of us will have spent a total of seven years in front of the television.
2. In their first eighteen years of life, the average North American child will see 18,000 murders, observe 200,000 sexual remarks or acts and be exposed to 360,000 commercials.
3. Reports from the US National Institute of Mental Health acknowledge a strong link between long-term exposure to television violence and aggressive, insensitive behaviour.
4. Children and adults can become numb and less compassionate with an overfocus on cruelty, injustice, discord and violence by watching too much negative television. This leaves people demoralised and fearful of a world that in reality contains much gentleness and good.
5. Even violence associated with humour disturbs, desensitises and increases aggressive behaviour.

Computers

Computers are a fact of life. We live in a world where knowledge of computers and how to use them is becoming more and more important. When today's children reach adulthood, many if not most of them will work with computers in their jobs. Most schools provide access to computers but, understandably, many parents feel that a computer at home will be of educational value to their child.

Supervision is the key

The trick with computers and children is supervision. Keep a close eye on your child's computer use. One way to do this is to limit their access to it. If you haven't already invested in a computer, before you do, decide how it will be used, for what and when, and make sure your child understands these 'rules of use'. Start your child on software that is 'beneficial', such as educational software. Most of these are now sufficiently game-like to grab the attention of the uninitiated for hours. Or, at first, you could insist that the computer only be used for school projects.

Computer games

Once children have been exposed to 'real' games, they are less interested in other types of software, and you'll probably be fighting a losing battle if you try to insist that the computer is only to be used for educational purposes. The best way to manage this is to limit access time and, as always, supervision is the key.

When you're buying a new computer, ask the hardware provider not to load games onto the hard drive. If games are offered as part of the purchase package, ask for the discs to be supplied separately. In this way, you have more control over what games your child can play.

Computer games do have their uses: they are a powerful source of behavioural modification and can be used as incentives or rewards. However, they have this power only if the child doesn't have free access to them at all times. By keeping the discs safely out of reach, you retain command.

Delete any 'adult' or violent games from your hard drive, even if you don't possess the disc for it and will lose it forever. Of course, your child may have access to unsuitable games at friends' homes. If you know that computer games are on the agenda during a visit, a quiet chat with the parents usually helps.

When supervised, computer games have their share of benefits. They can act as a tutor: word processing or a fun typing program sometimes help even the most unmotivated with pencil and paper to become productive on screen. As well, computer games can help the disorganised to plan. Eye–hand coordination and speed of reflexes can be honed. High quality graphics can incite creativity.

So the news isn't all bad: some experts believe that playing computer games excessively is unlikely to do most children harm, any more than playing other games. The key with computers is to retain control: you decide what the computer will be used for and when.

It will probably be impossible to prevent your child from playing computer games. Instead, set limits and stick by them.

The Internet

Once you have a computer, you (or your child) will probably be keen to get online to discover the 'wonders' of the Internet. And the Internet can be wonderful: there are countless informative, educational and fascinating sites that can provide an excellent resource for homework and school projects (the Encyclopaedia Britannica site is one such site). But the Internet can also be incredibly time consuming, time wasting and sometimes inaccurate, and because anyone can set up a site about anything, a lot of sites are unsuitable for children.

The key, again, is supervision. Children should never have access to the Internet unsupervised, even if supervision is just out of the corner of your eye. Cyberspace can broaden general knowledge, help with assignments and homework, build self-esteem and provide opportunities to practise social interactions. But unfortunately it is also the gateway to online 'child predators' and unsound advice.

Before you decide to hook up to the Net there are some other things you will need to consider.

Cost

The Internet can be very expensive, so make sure you are connected by a low-cost phone call and that the Internet provider offers good value. Of course, the cheapest provider may not be the best if you spend longer on the phone line downloading pages.

Rules of access

As with the computer, you'll need to set out some firm rules of use. Perhaps your child is allowed on the Internet on only certain days or evenings. When there are two or more children jostling for access, you will need to set strict time limits for each child. When children are surfing the Net or zapping aliens in some computer game an hour seems to them like five minutes, so if there are any disputes, set up a timer.

Internet access can also be used as a reward, and loss of access as a punishment.

Where to go in cyberspace

If you are unsure of where your child should go, there are guidebooks to Internet addresses suitable for children, such as *Web Sites for Primary Kids* by Karina Bray. A hazard of even a harmless Internet address is that children may be able to access other tempting sites via advertisements placed by shrewd advertisers. These temptations are hard to ignore and are distracting to even the most tunnel-visioned adults. Agree beforehand that clicking on advertisements is taboo.

Remember too that not all the information available on the Internet is reliable or even true. It may not be evil, malicious or unsuitable for children but they may have to learn early that not everything that grown-ups tell them is correct and to check more than one source.

Avoiding unwanted sites

Recently a young boy in the United States bought a medical practice in Florida with his parent's credit card over the Internet. Even if you think your child is a budding doctor, you're probably not ready to invest in their first practice just yet. Shopping over the Internet is just one of a list of 'services' to which you'd probably prefer your child had no access. Luckily, there are sites on the Internet that provide programs to screen out dangerous or unwanted information. For example, anything with a sex theme, drugs, gambling, alcohol, shopping (unless you want to lose a lot of money quickly!), cults, firearms, explosives and so on can be blocked off. There are also programs to block online advertisements. However, be aware that blocking is not foolproof, as some unwanted Internet sites have innocuous names that belie their true nature. Also, bright children will always find a way around Internet 'walls' – or their friends will tell them. Again, supervision is the answer.

What are the don'ts?

Children should not give out personal information on the Internet. This blanket rule includes not only their or their family's real names, address and phone number but also credit card details. (In fact, children of this age should not have access to any lines of credit at all.)

A final word

Television is here to stay. But TV can become a negative presence in our homes when we are overexposed to it, leaving us no time for other enjoyable things (a chat around the dinner table, for example). As well, studies have found a link between exposure to violence on television and aggression in children and adults. The answer is to set limits: limit your child's viewing to one or two hours a day and certain programs only.

There is no reason for parents to shy away from computers and the Internet. If we don't master them, we will be their slaves. Ignorance of computers or the Internet may be considered akin to illiteracy before long, so there is every reason for parents to take the first step.

Your children will spend most of their lives working with a keyboard and computers and should learn good practices early, such as typing skills and the importance of backing up homework. Learning keyboard skills now might prevent RSI in twenty years.

If children have learned to troubleshoot computer problems, how to save their work and housekeep discs, how to run a new program from first principles without the manual and how to search the Internet, then time spent zapping aliens will not have been wasted.

Television, computers and the Internet

1. Television
   - Set limits: read the television guide ahead of time and allocate appropriate viewing.
   - When a chosen program is finished, turn off the set.
   - Restrict viewing to one hour per day, with an absolute maximum of two hours per day.
   - Recognise the effect of excessive television viewing on fitness and obesity.
   - Don't watch television during family meals. Reintroduce talk and relating.
   - Many studies have shown a direct link between violence on television and aggression in children and adults.
   - Discuss the content of programs to provide a reality check.
   - Limit news watching by both adults and children.
   - Discuss news stories to differentiate between what is happening in our local community and events far across the globe.
   - Television channels beam a signal; parents control the power supply.
   - The most important goal is to switch from constant bombardment to the watching of specific programs.

2. Computers
   - Agree on limits of use in advance.
   - Supervision is the key.
   - Start children off with fun educational software.
   - Avoid exposing your child to adult or violent games.
   - Games can develop your child's learning and motor skills.

3. The Internet
   - Agree on limits of use in advance.
   - Supervise children's access to the Internet.
   - The Internet can be educational but teach children that not everything on the Net is 'true'.
   - Invest in an Internet screening program.
   - Teach children that personal information must not be given out.

TWENTY

Separation, sole parenthood and step situations: protecting our children

I t is estimated that between one-quarter and one-third of today's children will be living with just one parent at some time before they have left school. No matter how positively we approach sole parenthood, it can make life immensely difficult. Even with the most amicable settlement there is usually a major change to the stability and living standard of the family. This chapter is not about the rights of parents; it's about children who are being hurt and how we can protect their welfare.

Though the Family Law Reform Act of Australia 1996 replaced the term 'custody' with 'residence' and the term 'access' with 'contact', I use the outdated words in this chapter because I believe they are still the labels that most parents understand.

The games people play

Woody Allen fans are fascinated by the emotional tangles of the characters in his films, but these are nothing compared with the tangles of his own life. The Allen–Farrow break-up was fought with such bitterness that even at this distance I felt the anger. If I could sense it fifteen thousand kilometres away, what were the children feeling?

But their case is not unique. I frequently see children who have been used as a weapon in their parents' battle. Some couples spend thousands of dollars arguing in court what less angry people could settle in ten minutes over a cup of tea. I see access used to cause the maximum amount of hurt and disruption. Over the years I have come across abductions, bogus claims of sexual abuse, unjustified attempts to block access and countless demands for children to be kept away from a new partner. I have seen intelligent mums try to change the child's name to their maiden name, just to punish the father.

Some fathers feel they have been given an amazingly raw deal, and it leaves them disheartened and sometimes quite dangerous. Other self-employed fathers hide their true income and, after the settlement, they live in under-the-counter affluence while their family sinks into poverty.

Many custodial mums come out of the break-up confused, isolated and depleted in self-confidence. When they start a new relationship, they're caught between the needs of the children and their need to make the relationship work. These two demands often conflict, especially when the new partner has an emotional inadequacy that motivates them to be over-possessive and jealous.

Frequently I see relationships like this, where a new partner cannot cope with any competition. They are intensely jealous if the children show any affection towards their natural father or mother, their grandparents or to people they have known for years. They cannot accept that children always have enough love to share. Sometimes the new couple will move to a far-off location. While this may be for genuine reasons, it is often to help the insecure adult avoid competition. But in the process, the children are deprived of much-needed support and love.

It's not fair

After breaking up, many parents feel they have been treated unfairly. Often this was a split they never wanted and it has been made worse by adverse decisions about property, custody and maintenance. But this is just the start.

Over ninety per cent of children will live with their mother. In the months following the break-up both partners' living standard may drop, but a year later there is usually a marked discrepancy in available money between the sole mum and the non-custodial dad. Fathers generally lead a relatively free life, while the expense of child minding, the limited opportunity for part-time work and the restrictions on social life are more confining for the custodial mum.

Most custodial parents get the worst end of access. After a day of spoiling, the tired child is returned, accompanied by a pile of dirty washing. To add to the injustice, the child is unsettled and takes out their anger on the parent who gives most time and love.

The damage

It is not the break-up but hostility and ongoing instability that affects children badly. With **hostility** there can be so much tension before separation that the split comes as a relief. After this, there may be fights over property, possessions, custody and access. So children sometimes spend years in a chronic war zone, and it can leave deep emotional scars.

The impact of **instability** is usually underestimated. Most children live with their mother, and the majority of solo mums experience a dramatic drop in living standard. The problem is not just available cash, but a lack of funds can often result in frequent moves of home. This disrupts a child's life, with unnecessary changes of school and friends and the loss of a sense of belonging to a community. Plus there may be new partners who come and go, adding further confusion for the children.

Our young ones are damaged by this mix of hostility, instability, frequent moves, and people coming in and out of their life. We counter this by aiming for an amicable settlement and the minimum of change and being particularly careful with new partners.

Divorce and sole parenthood: the damage

1. Unresolved hostility – ongoing anger, especially concerning access
2. Disruption and instability – move of home and school; move away from friends and local community
3. Lack of support – isolated from friends and extended family
4. Economic hardship – child poverty is commonly associated with sole parenthood; poverty affects the stability of housing and life
5. Unavailability – the parent may have to work unreasonable hours or is so stressed they are emotionally unavailable
6. New relationships – step situations cause difficulties, especially with older children

How children hurt

The under-six-year-old will usually be quite open in their reaction, with an immediate and often intense response to the break. They don't know what it means but they dislike how it feels. However, children of this young age recover quickly once the adults get their act together.

The six- to eight-year-old is in the middle ground where they almost, but don't quite, understand. They know this is a major event but may not realise that it is permanent. Children of this age may worry that they are in some way responsible for the split. They also worry about being abandoned and replaced. Their reaction and the depth of their hurt still depends on the stability and emotional resilience of the caring parent.

The eight- to twelve-year-old understands the implications of the split and understands it is forever. Often they will take sides and have confused loyalties. They may show bravado and a false disinterest, but behind this can be intense anger at what their parents have done. Most of their upset is open, but at this age they may bottle up emotions that can smoulder for years.

The adolescent: in the past it was thought that children of this age remained relatively unscathed by divorce but now it is believed they carry the greatest hurt. This is a point in life when children are fighting to make sense of their own personal relationships. Their confidence is shot when their role models screw up so spectacularly. Many worry that they may follow their parents' example.

How children react

There are three ways that a school-age child may react to major upset. They

■ cling close

■ act out and

■ take it to heart.

Clinging close

Clinging is most common in children under the age of six years. They don't understand our adult antics, but they feel they have been abandoned by fifty per cent of those they trust. Clingy children hold tight to the remaining parent. They shadow their mum around the house and they're reluctant to separate at the school gate for fear that Mum may not return at pick-up time. At night they procrastinate about bed and many insist on sleeping with their mother.

The child's action makes good sense, but some parents are blind to what is happening. One mother told me how she split up with her boyfriend in the middle of the night so as not to upset their child. She then sounded surprised as she told me: 'I can't understand why her behaviour has become so odd since that night.' Of course, the little girl was now terrified to close her eyes in case she lost another parent.

Acting out

When a child feels stress they may transmit it back as bad behaviour. Younger children don't understand what is going on – they just react. Older children can be more vindictive and may single out one parent to abuse. Unfortunately, it is the parent who gives most love and care who usually gets the hardest kick.

Acting out is a particular problem when parents are emotionally fragile and intolerant of irritation. The child picks up on the stress in their home and reacts with irritating behaviour. The parent retaliates with anger, the child gets more distressed and their behaviour worsens. This starts a vicious circle, which, if not nipped in the bud, can escalate.

Taking it to heart

Though most children transmit their hurt outwards in the form of difficult behaviour, some older children bottle up their feelings and withdraw. Now the once-outgoing child appears distant, moody and lacking spark. School grades may slip, although occasionally a child may escape their unhappiness by overfocusing on study. Often they lose interest in friends and activities that used to give pleasure.

These children need to be able to talk about their feelings, but often their parents are so overwhelmed by their own problems they are emotionally unavailable when their children try to open up. Withdrawal is often the least recognised of a child's reactions and probably the most serious. It starts as grief but can slip into full depression.

Protecting our children

Amicable access

Visits are going to happen whether we accept the inevitable or create trouble. If you are interested in your own, and your children's mental health, make access as peaceful as possible.

Arrange the times in advance so that everyone knows where they stand. Don't send the child with a list of petty conditions that dictate what they must wear, where they may go and who they may meet. Accept that things will not always be done as you would like, but with joint custody, you cannot make unrealistic demands.

Stay in control of what you say. Children become confused when those they love are belittled and scandalised. And don't ask too many questions – your children are on an access visit, not a spying mission.

Where a dispute threatens to destabilise a visit, try to sidestep trouble and address the problem at a time when the children are not present. If tension is running too high, arrange pick-up and set-down from a neutral place, or allow a friend to be an intermediary.

As children become older, they have sport and other commitments. These can interfere with a fixed pattern of access, but we need to be flexible to fit in with the needs of an eleven-year-old.

Unfortunately, even amicable access can confuse children. When Mum and Dad appear so civil the youngsters may wonder why their parents don't stop the nonsense and get back together. But civil it has to be – when access is used to cause pain, children become acutely anxious or physically sick before the visit and it takes days for them to recover.

If separated by distance try to maintain communication by visit, letter, tape, photo and phone. Absence is said to make the heart grow fonder, but lack of communication dilutes the closeness between the non-custodial parent and their child.

Don't divorce the grandparents

At the wedding celebration there were guests on the bride's side and guests on the groom's side. At the divorce the relatives are still seen as being aligned. But little children don't understand the dynamics of a break-up; they have no interest in branding people as good guys or bad guys. They are unsettled by the change in their parents' life, and they rely on relatives from both sides to provide a vital safety net.

A wife may divorce her husband, but there is no need to divorce his parents as well. Legislation now guarantees grandparents access, but until recently I met grandparents who had lost all contact with those they loved. And this was at its most malicious when an inadequate new partner had come on the scene. Often the grandparents' phone calls were obstructed, letters destroyed and birthday presents returned.

One grandmother told how, after the separation, she had cared for the children every day for three years. But when the new partner arrived all access was blocked. Now the only time she saw the children was a glimpse from a passing bus or looking longingly through the bars of the school fence.

With break-ups children need the security of grandparents. If relatives are prepared to keep out of the politics and give support, they should have the most open of access. An amicable settlement involves being amicable to all friends and relatives who genuinely wish to help.

Consistency and stability

After an upsetting event some parents turn their back on the past and restart with a completely new life. The very strong may succeed, but for most it is an act of destructive disruption.

When the adults in a child's life have lost the plot, the child maintains stability through consistent people and places. They do best when they still have their school, their friends, their extended family and the security of their own home.

Until the dust has settled, make no move or change that is not essential. Try to remain in the same district, at the same school and, if possible, in the same home. It is tempting to run away from unhappy memories but your home community provides the best base.

Starting a new relationship

After a split children can become extremely possessive of the parent who provides care. Often the sole parent and child develop an unusually close relationship, which will be fiercely guarded if someone tries to come between them. There is no trouble when Mum has a superficial friendship, but when a new companion competes for love and attention, children see this as a threat.

Younger children (under eight years) are generally reasonably accommodating. But older children are quite clear; they already have a dad and they don't need another. They also know they have been hurt once, and don't want a second dose. Teenagers are usually obtuse in the extreme.

Success comes with slow steps and gaining confidence over time. Initially it is best to interact mostly outside the family home. Don't force the new partner on the children and don't call them Dad. State that this friend is important to you and will be around quite often. When children are threatened they may protect their patch with confronting, limit-testing behaviour.

Don't rush to get married or create more children. Though second relationships may be more satisfying than the first, statistics suggest that over half will have broken up within five years. As for new babies, they never bring a bad relationship together; they just create a mix of loyalties that only the most together parents can sort out.

Step situations

Most of the fairy stories I learnt when I was young were about abusive step situations. But while Cinderella and Snow White may have lived happily ever after, it is not that easy for everyone. A recent study of Sydney street kids showed the majority came from an unhappy step situation.

Step relationships can work wonderfully well, especially for the under-eights. But teenagers can react very badly. The Brady Bunch had Alice, but you just have unsettled kids jockeying for power. As with any new relationship, it's important to move gently. It can take years to gain the trust of your partner's children.

When there are difficulties with discipline, the natural parent should be the main enforcer. Often older children defy, ignore or verbally abuse a new partner. While they are not the main disciplinarian, at a certain point, the partner must take a stand. Where that point is, is anyone's guess.

When children from two relationships come together it is rare to have harmony. During visits keep them entertained, don't expect miracles and be pleased when things go well. You may like the children's father or mother, but this does not mean the children like each other. Step situations, especially with older children, usually cause great stress. When in trouble be quick to seek professional help.

Split, sole and step: protecting the children

1. The main priority is always the emotional wellbeing of our children.
2. With unresolved disputes, try to avoid the legal adversarial system, as this is expensive and deepens the wounds. Where possible use the court counselling and mediation services, which aim at amicable agreement.
3. Never underestimate the detrimental effect of stress and hostility on children. Parents may feel angry, but that's their problem, not the child's.
4. You can't stop the break-up but you can ensure that it is as amicable as possible.
5. Children are unsettled by changes in housing, school, friends and the disruption of new partners.
6. Children need as little change as possible.
7. Children show their upset by clinging close, acting out or withdrawing.
8. Young children are open and intense in their reaction.

Their behaviour settles when the parents' behaviour settles.

9. Older children may carry a more chronic but less obvious wound.

10. Children need to be told what is happening in a way that is appropriate to their age.

11. Don't draw children into adult battles. They don't understand the rights and wrongs; all they know is that it hurts.

12. Children need to know they will have two parents and both will continue to care for them.

13. They should know where they will live, where their non-custodial parent will live, and when they will see each other.

14. Keep close to grandparents and any extended family who genuinely wish to support.

15. You may divorce your partner, but your children do not want to divorce their grandparents.

16. Access must be encouraged and made easy. It's going to happen whether the parents make it enjoyable or a time of tension.

17. Don't spy on or slander the other parent.

18. When a child is out on access, it is up to the accessing parent what they do and whom they do it with. You can't prevent your child being cared for by a new partner.

19. Most custodial parents get a raw deal. No one said this is fair but that's the way it is, whether we accept it or not.

20. Children often react badly to a new partner. They do not wish to share their mother and they have already had enough hurt to last a lifetime.

21. The over-eight-year-olds are usually most difficult.

22. New relationships are best started outside the home and approached gently.

23. Children may attention seek, become defiant and rebel against the new partner's discipline. Initially the natural

parent should be the main enforcer, though there should always be limits.

24. Blended families don't blend, they usually curdle. Don't be afraid to seek professional help when it's needed.

25. Children have more than enough love to share around. Never let a jealous partner obstruct the children's access to grandparents, father or friends.

26. When a new partner spirits the children interstate, ensure that their motive is genuine, not jealousy.

27. Be careful of rebound relationships. The statistics show sixty per cent of second marriages fail within five years.

28. Beware of new pregnancies. It takes a strong relationship to cope with these changed dynamics.

29. The best we can do for our children is to provide peace and stability in their living environment while maintaining access to those they love.

TWENTY-ONE

An A to Z of children's health

T his chapter covers A (abdominal pain) to W (worms). But before we hit A, let's address one of the questions that parents most commonly ask.

When to call for help?

In our teaching hospital we train bright young doctors to become specialists in children's medicine. To pass their exams they need an immense amount of fine-print knowledge, but to be a good paediatrician they must also have that intuition to know when a child is sick or not.

Parents and paediatricians recognise the danger signs in a child's eyes. When bright, interested and alert there is rarely a problem. When dull, distant and their mind is muddled, alarm bells ring. Other symptoms also cause great concern:

- headache with neck pain and stiffness (possible meningitis or encephalitis)

- persistent localised abdominal pain (possible appendicitis)

- cold, clammy skin (shock or serious illness)

- rapid shallow breathing in a sick-looking child (meningitis, diabetes or other serious condition)

- unrelenting vomiting (possible gut obstruction)

- rapid deterioration (meningococcal or other major illness)

- following a head injury, drowsiness, confusion or change in pupil size (concussion or brain bleed).

Any of these require urgent medical attention. If in doubt always play it safe and go quickly to your doctor or hospital.

The key points: dull distant eyes, rapid deterioration, confusion and/or disinterest, neck stiffness, extreme vomiting or persistent pain, and any occasion when a mother feels worried.

Contents

Abdominal pain
Adenoids
Appendicitis
Asthma
Bed wetting
Body piercing: infection
Bruises
Burns and scalds
Chicken pox
Colour blindness
Common cold
Convulsions, fits and seizures
Cuts and stitches
Dandruff
Deafness
Developmental delay
Dry skin

Ear infections
Eczema
Faints
Fever
Flat feet
Flatus
Flu, or influenza
Fluoride and teeth
Foreskin: how to take care of it
Freckles
Giardia
Glandular fever, or infective mononucleosis
Glue ear and grommets
Growing pains
Growth: too much or too little
Headaches
Hepatitis vaccination
Hernias
Hives, or urticaria
Immunisation
Itchy bottom
Left handedness
Measles
Meningococcal infection
Mumps
Nits
Nose bleeds
Nose block
Passive smoking
Rubella, or German measles
Snoring
Suntan and skin damage
Teeth: what to do if one is knocked out
Testes: undescended or retractile
Tonsillitis
Tonsillectomy
Tummy upsets
Warts

Whooping cough, or pertussis
Worms

Abdominal pain

This is one of the most common reasons for a parent to seek help from a paediatrician. Their healthy school child has vague abdominal pains that come and go. They start for no good reason and last between half an hour and six hours, after which the child returns to normal health. The pain may come back in a week, a month, or somewhere down the track.

Pain is usually situated just above and just below the umbilicus. It has none of the fever, urinary symptoms or localising features of kidney infections or acute appendicitis. Between times, the child is happy, healthy and unstressed.

There is much debate about the cause of these periodic pains. Most believe they are an abdominal equivalent of tension headache or migraine. Whatever the reason, it worries parents, and unfortunately we have little to offer as treatment. If abdominal pain has been an occasional problem over months or years, and no medical cause can be found, it's a case of making a minimum of fuss and possibly giving some paracetamol.

Adenoids

When your child says 'ahh', the tonsils are clearly seen on each side of the throat. The adenoids are similar to the tonsils, but you would need a little mirror to see them up the back of the nose. Both tonsils and adenoids have the purpose of fighting infection.

Adenoids live a quiet life, mostly remaining out of sight and causing no problem. The difficulty comes when they enlarge, which can affect the ears and the flow of air down from the nose.

The adenoids lie close to the tubes (the eustachian tubes) that equalise the pressure and allow drainage of the middle parts of our ear. If these become blocked, fluid collects, which can lead to hearing loss or repeated ear infections. When enlargement obstructs the nasal airway the child may breathe through their open mouth by day and snore by night. If the blockage persists the child may continue to breathe through their open mouth which can lead to an alteration of their bite.

Adenoidectomy is a simple operation, which can improve the drainage of the middle parts of the ears. It is usually performed at the same time as grommets (small tubes) are being inserted in the eardrums to release the chronic fluid collection of glue ear. Occasionally adenoids that obstruct the nasal airway are associated with sleep disturbance. Here a snoring child has restless, disturbed sleep leaving them sleep deprived and tired in the morning. Occasionally the child may briefly stop breathing in their sleep, which reduces oxygen levels at night. By day this can cause drowsiness or behaviour symptoms. In sleep apnoea, the operation of adenoidectomy will usually increase the flow of air through the nose. Children appear to show no adverse effects when we remove their adenoids.

Appendicitis

The appendix is a small, worm-like structure that sprouts from the lower part of the gut. Currently it has no known purpose, but presumably it was essential in the evolutionary days before man walked upright and ate today's refined foods.

This cul-de-sac of the bowel can become blocked and stagnate. If untreated it eventually bursts, releasing infected material into the abdominal cavity, which can cause life-threatening peritonitis.

The first symptom of appendicitis is a vague discomfort around the belly button that soon moves over the appendix (situated in the lower right part of the abdomen). The pain is sharp, causes difficulty standing straight and there may be fever and vomiting. When a patient has classic symptoms, appendicitis is easy to diagnose, but the picture can be much more confusing. Many who work in the emergency room eventually get caught out missing atypical appendicitis.

If appendicitis is suspected, call your family doctor or, if the situation seems quite certain, go straight to your local hospital. Surgical removal is a minor procedure and will be suggested if there are any reasonable grounds. A good surgeon will always play safe, which may result in removing some normal appendices. But this is preferable to risking the dangers of peritonitis.

Asthma

One in ten children has asthma. This is an allergy-related condition that causes spasm of the middle-sized airways in the lungs. The symptoms are shortness of breath and wheezing, especially when breathing out. Asthma is strongly hereditary, and many children who suffer from it have a mum or dad with the same allergy-asthma combination. Or, as a child, the parent may have suffered bouts of wheezy bronchitis and a telltale middle-of-the-night cough, but these were never recognised as asthma.

Most asthma is mild, occurring every few months in response to a respiratory infection, strenuous exercise or heavy doses of allergens (pollen or too many cats). These occasional bouts are treated with one of the safe, effective bronchodilator puffers (such as Ventolin (salbutamol)), which are given during the bad patch or prior to exercise.

Moderate and severe asthma used to cause immense trouble to children. When I was first a specialist paediatrician, some children spent half their year in hospital, while others missed months of school and were so breathless they never played sport. This has changed with the introduction of aggressive maintenance therapy. Now we do not wait for asthma to incapacitate; we keep it at bay with an everyday regime of inhaled steroids (preventers) and bronchodilators (relievers).

It is no longer acceptable for a child just to cope with their asthma – they must live life to the full. If this isn't happening, they should be in the care of a children's respiratory specialist. Allergy testing, air filters, avoiding milk and desensitisation are popular topics on the Internet, but they are not usually recommended by experts in asthma.

All chest specialists are united about the damage of side-stream cigarette smoke. It is hard to believe that, until relatively recent times, hospitals and ambulances had no restriction on smoking. In my days as a consultant paediatrician in Belfast, children were brought by ambulance to my clinic. The parents of one girl assured me she was well, yet at every review she was blue and in spasm. One day her mum innocently asked if the chain-smoking ambulance driver might be upsetting her asthma. Nowadays, to smoke in an ambulance would be viewed as an act of criminal negligence. But some parents still fill their children's home with the same pollution.

Bed wetting

At the age of five years, ten per cent of children will still wet the bed. Bed wetting (nocturnal enuresis) is due to a late maturation in normal bladder function. It is not in any way deliberate or of emotional origin.

Without treatment, the incidence will reduce every year, leaving approximately five per cent still wetting at the age of ten years. The majority of these children have never had a dry night (primary enuresis), though a few started with a period of full training, then relapsed (secondary enuresis).

There is debate regarding the difference between primary enuresis and secondary enuresis. In the past, we believed that those who slipped back had urinary infection or a major emotional upset, but experience shows this is rarely true. Nowadays we manage all children the same, whether a long-time wetter or one who has relapsed. The treatment of bed wetting involves the following:

Property protection

We don't want to upset the emotional sensitivity of our children, but parents must protect their property. This requires a waterproof mattress cover, a plentiful supply of bed linen and a smooth-running washing machine. Children attending school camps used to save their sleeping bags by spending the night in a large plastic garbage bag. Fortunately, drug treatment has removed the need for this assault on their dignity.

The 11pm lift

When a child is close to overcoming bed wetting they start to have a few dry nights. At this stage we can accelerate the process by lifting last thing at night. They go to sleep at 8pm, then at 11pm they are brought to the toilet. Some children stumble, half awake and happy to oblige; but a few are so stroppy that it's mission impossible.

Consider restricting fluid intake before bed

You don't need to be Einstein to realise that what goes in the top must eventually come out the bottom. For this reason it seems sensible to restrict fluid intake during the evening. However, despite the intellect of Einstein, there is no evidence that fluid restriction helps.

Alarms

The most effective treatment for bed wetting is a pad-and-bell alarm. A small sensor is attached to the pants or placed below the bottom sheet. When the flood arrives the sensor shorts out, sets off a buzzer and you have red alert. Often I am told, 'The alarm is no good. He doesn't wake,' but to be effective a mum or dad must struggle out, get John fully conscious and jointly remake the bed.

There are two essentials before starting this treatment: the child has to be motivated, and they must be completely awake during clean up. Alarms can be hired from children's hospitals, some community health centres and chemists. The top enuresis clinics will claim an eighty per cent success rate, achieved within two months. But there are some relapses, and the alarm should stay in place until the child has stayed dry every night for a reasonable period.

Drug treatment

The antidepressant drug imipramine has been used for thirty years in the treatment of enuresis. No one knows how it works but a dose at bedtime has a high chance of producing a dry bed. Unfortunately, wetting usually returns once the drug stops. I would have thought that any safe treatment that dramatically reduced enuresis was worthwhile, but for some reason this drug is rarely recommended by today's doctors.

However, a new preparation, desmopressin, is becoming much more popular. This is an antidiuretic hormone that acts through the pituitary gland in the brain and reduces the amount of urine released by the kidneys. It has a relatively short period of action so it is given last thing at night.

Initially desmopressin was used to provide temporary protection for sleepovers and camps. But there is now a body of research that shows good results with no side effects for periods of six or even twelve months. As with imipramine, those who have not resolved spontaneously in this time will relapse when the drug stops.

Desmopressin is currently given by a nasal spray but an oral preparation will soon be released. The dose needs to be adjusted to suit the individual child, so it must be trialed well before the child departs for camp. Most but not all children get a good response.

Despite the interest in drug treatment the alarm is still the first line of treatment, because, when it works, it provides a cure. Desmopressin is useful for sleepovers and for the every-night treatment of the older child.

There are still a few psychological dinosaurs who interpret bed wetting as a problem of emotion. But I learned at medical school that the brain is located a long way from the bladder. Emotional upset does not cause chronic enuresis but chronic enuresis can cause emotional upset.

Body piercing: infection

Recently when I took a long-haul bus trip, it seemed that I was the only adult without a stud, ring or piece of metal through some part of my body. I know I have old-fashioned ideas, but I don't understand body piercing.

Still, whether I like it or not, I see a number of boys and girls with one or more studs and earrings. As bits of metal are foreign to the body, it is common for irritation or infection to develop in the days after the piercing is done. It's a bit old-fashioned but you can clean around the stud with methylated spirits in the same way you dried the umbilical stump all those years ago. If a minor infection develops get an antibiotic cream or antibiotic tablets from your doctor. When in doubt, get rid of the metal and restart once the body has returned to normality.

Bruises

A bruise results from an injury that releases blood into the tissues. When a battered and bruised footy player struggles to the sideline, his trainer hands him the freezing sponge or magic ice pack. The cool temperature reduces the blood flow, which lessens the blackness and swelling.

In the past, people used a steak to reduce the black. Using meat in this way may help your butcher recover from their mad-cow losses, but twenty minutes of cool compress is a better treatment for a bruise.

Burns and scalds

Having lived through the hazardous preschool years, parents are hyper-alert to the dangers of burns and scalds. These can be painful, disfiguring and potentially life threatening. In the school years the main risk comes from stoves, ovens, kettles, fires, fireworks, methylated spirits, petrol and lighting barbecues.

Any significant burn, especially of the face or over a joint, must be brought to a doctor or hospital. The first-aid for burns and scalds is, where possible, to put the affected part under cold tap water for ten or more minutes, then decide whether there is need for medical help. Blisters should be left intact as they give some protection and allow healing underneath. For pain use paracetamol.

Chicken pox

Chicken pox is an extremely common viral illness that can cause an unsightly rash. It leaves most children looking worse than they feel. This highly infectious virus is picked up from a friend, then incubated for fourteen to sixteen days before the first signs of illness appear. Chicken pox starts with small red spots and a slight fever. The spots get larger, fill with fluid, and then form itchy scabs. Though your grandmother told you, 'If you scratch that spot it will leave a scar,' the marks of chicken pox usually heal completely.

Chicken pox can be a very mild illness, particularly when young. Sometimes you see a cluster of apparent flea bites, which would pass unnoticed except for the chicken pox contact two weeks before. When your child is covered in spots they are highly infective and should stay away from others. They will not be welcome at school until the last infective scab drops off. Calamine lotion is still the best treatment for itch.

Colour blindness

Most colour-blind children see plenty of colour; they just perceive things with a slight difference. It may affect their colour coordination when buying clothes, but most poor taste is a problem of dress sense, not colour blindness.

The main confusion comes with the colours red and green. At close quarters the colour-blind adult is quite clear when the traffic light signals stop or go, but a single light in the distance causes much more difficulty. This makes colour blindness a danger to loco drivers, sailors and pilots.

An eye specialist, optometrist or school nurse can quickly test for this weakness. There is no treatment and the only down side is the obstruction to careers that run on rails, the sea or high in the sky. About five per cent of boys and a lesser number of girls have this difficulty.

Common cold

Colds come from a virus that gets into the nose or throat and can irritate the chest. After recovering from a cold there is some immunity, but it gives limited protection against future infections.

Children are particularly susceptible to colds and 'flu viruses in their first year at school but this gradually gets better as resistance strengthens with age.

Colds are spread by droplet infection. We teach our children, 'Put your hand to your mouth when you cough.' Then we encourage politeness: 'Shake hands with the vicar.' Then in a moment of prayer his holiness pokes a nostril, and next week he splutters through the sermon.

Folklore suggests that Vitamin C prevents colds and 'flu but research evidence is not convincing. Medicines that dry the nose may help comfort but they don't speed recovery. Paracetamol is useful for aches and fever. A hot whisky does nothing for the child, but when taken by the parent it makes the child's symptoms seem less severe.

Convulsions, fits and seizures

When parents think of a convulsion, it is the generalised, tonic-clonic (grand mal) picture that comes to mind. The child suddenly loses consciousness, goes stiff, then jerks and convulses for some time. When they come out of the fit they are sleepy and confused and may have wet themselves.

This is a different picture from the simple faint. Here the child feels tingly headed, becomes unconscious, they are placed flat, the blood flows back to the brain, they pink up and come to. After this they may feel nausea but they don't wet themselves and are not confused or drowsy.

When a child has just one isolated convulsion, it may be a chance happening. When fitting is prolonged (over fifteen minutes) or repeated, it is of much more concern. The fever fits that were common in the toddler years are not seen at school age.

A major fit is a frightening experience for any parent to witness. Their child is out of contact and seems to be struggling to breathe. All we can do is place them on their side and position the neck in a way that helps breathing. Though terrifying for parents, our greatest concern is the fit that goes on and on (status epilepticus). If by ten minutes there is no end in sight, ring emergency and call an ambulance.

There are many other sorts of fit. One is the simple absence or petit mal seizure. This causes a brief switch off, the child stops, may blink their eyes, looks distant, then after five to thirty seconds they return to full awareness. There is no drowsiness or confusion but they are unaware of what happened in that time.

Teachers often send me a child who they believe has petit mal. Usually these are bored or attention deficit kids who prefer to look out the window rather than listen to their teacher.

If you have any concern about seizures, discuss this with your paediatrician. They will arrange a brain wave test (EEG) which usually, but not always, helps with diagnosis. A normal EEG does not totally exclude epilepsy, which prompted one cynic to write, 'The EEG is only reliable in diagnosing sleep and death, and there are easier ways to spot these.'

When anticonvulsant medication is prescribed it is usually continued for at least two years after the last episode. Children with reasonably controlled epilepsy lead normal lives, though they must avoid high climbing, bike riding on busy roads and swimming without supervision (as should any other school-age child). A good proportion of children grow out of their epileptic seizures before adulthood.

Cuts and stitches

Over the years the Greens' house has been like a field hospital for all the bumped, bruised and cut children in our neighbourhood. Often they come wondering if a cut needs stitches. The first step is to clean with cold tap water, then the decision to stitch depends on the length and depth of the cut and whether it closes or gapes.

Stitches have mostly been replaced by thin paper holding strips (steristrips). These pull the sides of the wound together and have greatly lessened the volume of tears in our emergency department. Nowadays we also use tissue glue for many wounds. The edges are pulled together and the glue is applied. This keeps the edges close until the wound heals, after which the glue rubs off.

With deeper cuts be careful that no important nerves or tendons have been damaged. If the wound is on the face or there is ever any doubt, discuss it with your doctor. Cuts should serve as a reminder to check that tetanus and all other immunisation is up to date.

Dandruff

Commercial television has greatly improved since they stopped showing adverts about dandruff. This may be riveting viewing for some, but it holds my interest like a feature on piles, athlete's foot or country music.

As long as humans are alive new skin keeps growing and the old stuff must drop off. Most of us shed the dead skin as specks of dust, but some release it as large white chunks – dandruff.

Treatment is through regular hair washing, preferably with a medicated shampoo like Nizoral. The chemist will recommend one, but the ultimate choice is based on results. Treatment does work: it may not happen overnight but it *will* happen.

Deafness

We know that a tiny infant will respond to the voice of their parents, but despite this only a few of our severely deaf children are picked up before the age of one year. This severe problem is due to nerve deafness where sound does not get from the ear to the brain. Deafness is often a genetic condition, where we see families with more than one child affected.

The deafness we diagnose later at school age is much less major and sometimes can be hard to pick. A few children have a hearing weakness with only one frequency, usually the high tones (high-tone deafness). This causes problems in the understanding of spoken speech, where a conversation sounds flat, like a radio with no treble and too much bass.

If you have the slightest concern about your child's hearing it is essential to get a high-quality test. In the big cities of Australia we usually recommend one of the children's hospitals or the Commonwealth-run Australian Hearing Services.

Fluid in the middle ear (glue ear) is by far the commonest cause of reduced hearing in the school-age child. The middle ear chamber, which usually resonates in air, becomes deadened with fluid. This reduces hearing by twenty to forty decibels (see this chapter, Glue ear and grommets, page 273).

Then, of course, there's selective deafness, when children switch off and leave parents looking like idiots. Scientists have now discovered a simple way to distinguish this annoying behaviour from true deafness. Parents should quietly whisper, 'Would you like Dad to book a trip to Disneyland?'

Developmental delay

This is a term used by paediatricians when worried about the developmental progress of a young child. Delay registers our concern but implies the probability of catch up. When delay continues over some years the name changes to the more permanent diagnosis of developmental or intellectual disability.

Delayed children do move ahead but all other children are also moving and the gap between them may remain unchanged. When I assess a child of three years and note the development of a two-year-old, this child is one year behind, but more importantly, this is two-thirds of their expected level. At six years of age the same child may show four-year skills. Certainly they have moved ahead, but the same two-thirds fraction remains, and the diagnosis is now borderline or mild intellectual disability.

Formal tests of intellect become much more reliable as we get closer to school entry. Results indicate advanced, normal or low average ability and borderline, mild, moderate or severe disability.

Between two per cent and three per cent of children and adults have some degree of developmental disability, of which the vast majority are borderline or mild. In most of this less severe group, no cause is ever found, with birth, family history, chromosomes and the most sophisticated scans and X-rays all normal. Even with all our advanced medical technology most parents in my care never discover the reason for their child's slowness.

Dry skin

Most little children have skin that is smooth as silk. But a few inherit a dry, rough exterior, which will always need extra care. This dryness is often associated with eczema. Dry skins are easily damaged by long, hot showers, the high alkaline content of normal soaps and an overdose of sunshine.

Keep showers cool, which usually keeps them short. Baths can be longer, provided you use a commercial bath oil. Move from soap to a sorbolene or other mild cleansing preparation. Buy a jumbo jar of a cheap brand of sorbolene with glycerine skin cream. If the surface breaks into itchy red areas, particularly behind the knee or front of the elbow, suspect eczema (see this chapter, Eczema, page 266).

Ear infections

The ear has three parts: the external ear, the middle ear and the inner ear. The external ear goes from outside to the ear drum. The middle ear is that air-filled cavity inside the eardrum. The inner ear transmits sound to the auditory nerve and also adjusts balance.

The air-filled middle ear equalises the pressure with the outside atmosphere through two tubes to the back of the nose (the eustachian tubes). These are the channels we clear, with a yawn or nose blow, as the plane descends. If the eustachian tubes get blocked, the middle ear becomes filled with fluid. The fluid in the middle ear may become infected (otitis media). If the fluid persists after the acute infection a condition called otitis media with effusion, or glue ear, may occur, interfering with hearing.

Outer ear infection (otitis externa) is an inflammation of the external ear canal. Otitis externa is a summer specialty for amphibious young Australians. As they dive, the canal fills with water, then they poke grot in the ear and then dive again. If the ear was kept dry there'd be no problem, but there'd also be no fun. Children can be taught to lie on a towel and drain one ear then the other after swimming.

Over-the-counter antiseptic drops help mild problems. Earplugs are useful but further prevent children from responding to our instructions, and the ear-plugged child can become intolerably noisy. If the canals are really sore a doctor will prescribe antibiotic drops or an antibiotic cortisone mix.

Middle-ear infection (otitis media) usually hits after a child has been stuffed up with a cold. The mix of blowing and sniffing with partially blocked tubes provides a fertile field for bacteria. The bacteria multiply in the confined space, drainage blocks and pressure increases to form an abscess. This can only resolve by natural immunity, antibiotics or release through a ruptured eardrum.

Otitis media can cause intense pain and some fever. When the doctor looks in the ear and sees a red, bulging drum, the diagnosis is made and antibiotics prescribed. When the ear is a reddish shade of pink the diagnosis is less clear.

Sometimes the middle ear fills with fluid but bacteria do not gain a firm foothold. This is glue ear, which knocks some decibels from the hearing and leaves the child open to recurrent ear infections (see this chapter, page 273).

Eczema

A child with eczema has dry, sensitive skin that can easily become red, itchy and weeping. Eczema often runs in families, and is closely associated with allergy and asthma. The rash can occur anywhere, but the main site in babies is the face, while in toddlers it is behind the knees and in the crease in front of the elbows. Children with eczema can be intensely irritated when they wear wool against the skin.

Treatment of eczema involves care for the dry skin with shorter showers, avoiding the usual commercial alkaline soaps and using moisturising creams, cotton underclothing and low-dose cortisone ointment. Eczema is generally at its worst in infants and toddlers. By school age the tendency is just to dry skin with the occasional flare up.

Faints

It is called 'the passing out parade': children stand still in the sun for school assembly and gaps begin to appear in the ranks. Faints are due to a temporary shortfall in the blood supply to the brain. This is associated with getting up to stand, hanging around in heat, an unpleasant experience, or being below par with some illness. With school children there is often a mix of heat, standing and an emotional overlay. On a school outing when one child keels over, others follow in quick succession.

Before falling, the child feels lightheaded and may be cold-sweaty and nauseated. Once they are down, the blood from the legs returns to the heart, which is quickly pumped to the brain. Getting flat or raising the legs is a matter of urgency.

A faint differs from an epileptic fit. It is short (under one minute) and there are precipitating factors. There is no convulsion, no incontinence, they respond to lying flat and their head becomes clear in a matter of minutes. Faints are quite common and generally benign. But if they are unexpected, repeated or unusual in any way, this needs to be looked into further.

Fever

When a child's temperature rises, this is a sign that things are running hot and out of balance. Fever tells us that our immune armies are rounding up some uninvited bug. The main invaders are the viruses that cause nose, chest, 'flu and gut illnesses, but any infection or imbalance can shift the body's thermostat.

Children and adults usually run at about 37 degrees Celsius (98.4 degrees Fahrenheit) and most fevers are 38.5 degrees Celsius (101 degrees Fahrenheit) to 39 degrees Celsius (102 degrees Fahrenheit), though I do occasionally see temperatures of 40 degrees Celsius (104 degrees Fahrenheit). You may hear parents claim figures of 42 degrees Celsius (107 degrees Fahrenheit), but this was either taken between sips of hot cocoa or they need a new thermometer.

The size of the fever is not proportional to the seriousness of the illness. A child with measles may have a higher temperature than one with deadly meningitis or peritonitis.

The most popular measure of temperature is a mother's hand on a flushed forehead. This is as reliable as a coin toss in the diagnosis of pregnancy. The face may be hot, but it doesn't reflect what's happening deep down in the corridors of power. Instead, fever should be measured by a thermometer placed beside or under the tongue.

When children are feverish, the main attention is to their comfort, fluid maintenance and to ensure we are not missing something serious. If they are happily snuggled under a rug by the television, let them have a little fluid to sip and leave them in peace. When I have the 'flu I don't want to be put in a tepid bath, sponged with cold water or left in front of a force-ten fan. If they are comfortable there is no need to give any medicine, but if necessary we can use paracetamol.

When I started paediatrics, any child with fever was prescribed aspirin. Then a pathologist who worked at our hospital, the Royal Alexandra Hospital for Children in Sydney, described a crisis condition that damaged the liver and brain (Reye syndrome, after Dr Douglas Reye). This was later linked to aspirin that had been given for fever. Though this syndrome is extremely rare and aspirin has only been barred in the under twos, it is now fashionable to avoid giving aspirin to any child under the age of sixteen years.

The key points for fever are: keep comfortable, maintain fluid intake, use paracetamol if needed, remember that fever can be a sign of something more serious, and that fever fits are unlikely after the age of four years.

Flat feet

About one in every twenty-five school children has feet that are flat. These are often inherited from a flat-footed mum or dad. As the child stands the inner side of their foot, which should rise as a definite arch, lies flat to the floor.

There are two views on the management of flat feet: those who insist on jacking up the arch with shoe supports and those who let nature take its course. Parents generally prefer to take some action, even if it is unhelpful, while I favour the no-support option.

If the feet are strong, move fully and the child walks with style, flat feet are of no consequence. If there is an unusual range of movement or foot pain, that is the time to take it further.

Flatus: generating gas that smells

When I was a very junior doctor I put in some hard labour working in a busy emergency department. In those days we alternated between an 'easy week' of eighty hours on duty and an impossible one with sixty hours work and sixty more on call. Life was not relaxing, especially as I was in Belfast, which was then gearing up to self-destruct.

But there were lighter moments, one coming with the visit of a large US warship. A fit young officer appeared. 'It's like this, Doc,' he said. 'My job is in a deep-water mini sub. Me and two others are down there for ten hours at a time.' He then got embarrassed and said, 'Doc, I have a problem with farting! People don't want to close the hatch with me inside.' I understood the dilemma, but I didn't have an answer.

Everyone, from the queen to her corgis, will pass wind. This escapes in small amounts and passes without comment. This gas is generated by benign bacteria that consume carbohydrate leftovers in the large gut. If the sugars and carbohydrates we eat are mostly digested, gas production is low, but sometimes output hits overload. The main offenders are cabbage, beans, broccoli and lentils.

As parents we can bring some relief by simple modifications to the diet. After this we must teach our children the adult art of silent release and implicating others.

Flu, or influenza

When adults have a runny nose and shiver, they often call this flu. But this is the common cold: true flu has fever, muscle pain, headache, sore throat, cough and major miseries. It lasts more than two days and knocks us flat.

Influenza is caused by a virus, and once we are infected, it provides short-term immunity. But when the virus returns it will probably be in a changed form and the previous year's infection gives partial or no protection. Sometimes we can go for years without flu, then suffer a devastating hit from some new strain.

A flu vaccine is available that is modified each year to reflect the change in virus. This provides about seventy per cent protection for that year, and some benefits for the next. Immunisation is not suggested for healthy children; it is only recommended for elderly or debilitated adults. Though I am not in either of these categories, I make sure I get my jab every year. Even if this gave a ten per cent chance of reducing the miseries of flu, it's worth it. With a seventy per cent reduction, it's a steal.

Treatment for flu consists of paracetamol, plenty of fluid and keeping comfortable. Following the virus of flu, bacterial invaders may get a foothold, causing respiratory, throat or ear infection. When flu hits a school it can decimate attendance. Children need to stay away for whatever time it takes to recover and feel strong enough to return.

Fluoride and teeth

I was brought up in a UK governed by post-war rationing. Sugar and sweets were a rare treat, I drank water, scrubbed my teeth and the result? A head full of fillings! But today most of the children I see have minimal or no decay. Many reach adulthood without experiencing the high-speed end of dentistry.

And why have things changed? Fluoride. It is clearly documented that adding fluoride to water has reduced enamel damage by fifty to seventy per cent. The addition of fluoride is supported by the World Health Organisation, as well as all the main paediatric policy bodies around the world.

Yet in this country fluoride is not universally added to our water. While around seventy-eight per cent of the population drink fluoridated water there still remains a large group who do not benefit from this important public health measure. This is prevented by the same freedom-of-choice argument that delayed the introduction of compulsory seat belts, motor cycle helmets and restrictions on cigarette smoking.

If you live under an administration unwilling to take a stand against the anti-fluoride activists, give drops or tablets each day. The most important time for fluoride protection is while teeth are developing – from toddlerhood to twenty. Brushing with a fluoride toothpaste twice a day is strongly recommended. For under eights use a toothpaste with a lower fluoride content; for over eights use a normal strength toothpaste.

Then, just as you thought it was safe to get back into the dentist's chair, they introduced fluoride paint. This is one of those rare taste sensations that adds extra strength to the surfaces at risk.

Foreskin: how to take care of it

I wonder if some of the enthusiasm for circumcision comes from parents who don't know what to do if this cover is left intact. Ten years ago, when I wrote my book *Babies*, I took a strong stand against circumcision. At the time, I caught a lot of flak for this attitude, but things have changed, and mercifully the demand for circumcision is now in steep decline. If I were to mutilate any other part of my newborn with no medical justification, I would be charged with child abuse and probably lose custody. And now, as I write, there are adults suing their doctors and parents for an operation that was done without any benefit or proper consent.

The foreskin is designed to protect the delicate parts of the penis and is also endowed with sexual sensitivity. The foreskin is still partly attached to its underlying tissues and is not ready to be withdrawn until two or three years of age. Approximately fifty per cent of one-year-olds, eighty per cent of two-year-olds and ninety per cent of three-year-olds can easily retract.

The hygienic care of the foreskin comes from routine washing at the earliest bath times. This starts with cleaning and when ready a gentle easing back of the skin. The aim is to get this established by five or six years, because after the age of eight years, doors get locked and personal affairs become more private. Some prudish people believe that so much focus on this part will lead to over interest and self-play. But I believe that this fascination will happen whether a child is taught hygiene or not. Children play with their private parts because it gives them pleasure.

There have been recent claims that circumcision reduces the risk of urinary infection, AIDS and various cancers. However, when these studies have been analysed more scientifically, the statistics are unimpressive. This country's top kidney specialists and paediatricians strongly discourage routine circumcision. If the foreskin does not retract easily by age four or despite adequate hygiene there are repeat infections, then discuss this with your doctor.

Freckles

These are part of that fair-skin, Irish-ancestry package that was never designed to be shown sunshine. Freckles are rare before the age of four years but after this those with the right skin type freckle quickly.

In the past freckles were seen as cute, but now they are recognised as a sign of sun damage to sensitive skin. Hats, shade and heavy-duty sun cream on every exit outdoors are the only way to protect skin from sun. The freckled adult is at greater risk of developing sun cancer than other fair-skinned individuals.

Giardia

This parasite hit the headlines when discovered in Sydney's water supply. Critics from other cities said they had no giardia, but most had never looked for it. At the time of writing it seems that the odd parasite in the water is not a major problem.

Giardia was well known to paediatricians long before this scare. The parasite is present in most countries, but while we are all exposed to the bug, only a few become sick.

Giardia inhabits the small gut where it has the potential to cause malabsorption, weight loss and diarrhoea. Over the years I have seen some very scrawny sick children with chronic giardia.

When Sydney's water was said to be impure, every ache, rash and pass of wind was blamed on giardia. But as the most reliable diagnostic test involves the collection of three fresh containers of faeces, few had their diagnosis confirmed.

Giardia is classified as a flagellate protozoan. As a flagellate it's not surprising that the usual treatment is the drug Flagyl (metronidazole).

Glandular fever, or infective mononucleosis

This is usually an illness of the adolescent and young adult, but sometimes it strikes school age children. Mononucleosis is suspected in the child with extreme tiredness, a low-grade fever and a throat infection that is slow to respond to treatment. The tonsils are large and of angry appearance, with neck and other glands enlarged.

As with many childhood illness, mononucleosis can be relatively mild or have a long, difficult course. It can be complicated by rashes, jaundice or even encephalitis. But not every throat infection is mononucleosis: the diagnosis can only be made by a positive blood test. As this is a virus it does not respond to antibiotics.

The drug ampicillin must be avoided in glandular fever, something I know to my personal cost. I once resuscitated a child critically ill with meningococcal infection. As this is such a dangerous bacteria I protected myself with the only antibiotic I had available – ampicillin. What I didn't know was that I was incubating glandular fever at the time. The rash was spectacular and the glandular fever not too pleasant.

Glue ear and grommets

Glue ear is a collection of gluey fluid in the middle ear. This air-filled chamber transmits clear, crisp sound from the eardrum to the hearing nerve. The middle ear is normally able to equalise air pressure and clear fluid through the narrow eustachian tubes that drain towards the back of the nose.

The cause of glue ear is uncertain but it may be the result of a low-grade infection and blockage of the eustachian tubes. It usually (but not always) affects both ears. Fluid in a drum is bound to reduce the transmission of sound (the Beatles would have been much quieter if Ringo's drums were full of glue).

Parents suspect glue ear when there is an even poorer response to requests than usual. The child's voice may be louder in the way we increase our volume when listening through a headset or talking over the sound of an engine. If the child does suffer from glue ear a diagnostic hearing test will show a twenty- to forty-decibel loss, and pressure studies will show little movement in the drum.

Glue ear can come and go, and for this reason it is usual to observe for a while before surgery. When the hearing loss is mild, some suggest a four- to six-week course of antibiotics in the hope of removing possible low-grade infection. There are also techniques to open the eustachian tubes, such as holding the nose while blowing up a balloon.

If the hearing loss is great or glue ear remains unresolved, treatment is through surgery. The child is anaesthetised and small ventilation tubes are placed in the eardrum (grommets). The fluid is cleared at the time of surgery and the tubes allow normal function to return. They stay in place for six months to two years and drop out when ready.

As grommets leave an opening to the outside world there must be care with diving and swimming. Parents can provide some sort of seal with earplugs, a nerd-like bathing cap or, in an emergency, blobs of Blue Tac.

Growing pains

This is yet another vague medical condition that we know exists but haven't a clue why it happens. Growing pains are certainly not caused by growth, which is as pain free as putting on weight or going grey.

The peak age for growing pains is eight to twelve years, and the main time is at night. The child wakes or can't get to sleep with discomfort or pain in the muscles and bones of their legs. Some associate these pains with exercise, while others believe they are part of the headache or abdominal pain response to tension. I wonder if this is a childhood variant of the restless legs syndrome of adults.

To diagnose growing pains we must first exclude a medical problem such as arthritis or injury. Growing pains have no known cause and no specific treatment. The best we can give is gentle massage to the legs, comfort to the child and possibly paracetamol.

Growth: too much or too little

The ultimate height of our children is usually predestined in their genes. Two basketball-playing giants should produce children who are taller than average. Two vertically challenged jockeys would expect smaller children with squeaky voices.

The pattern of growth is often a family affair. Girls with an early or late puberty are often like their mum. Skinny boys with a last-minute growth rush are often like their dad.

Height is also influenced by factors before birth. The baby who is full term (forty weeks' gestation) but starved in utero may be born small for dates and may stay small. We see this pattern with raised maternal blood pressure, placental problems and in some of our addict-created foster children.

The greatest concern for parents comes from growth that is too little, too early, too late or too much. When parents are worried we start by obtaining an accurate record of growth over a number of visits. We are not so interested in the centimetres on the day of the appointment but how this reading is keeping pace with normal patterns of growth.

Height and weight are plotted on standard growth charts (see Appendix I, page 293). The average child sits on the fiftieth percentile, which implies that half the population are taller and half are smaller. A small child might be on the tenth percentile, which shows that ten per cent are smaller and ninety per cent are taller. The tall child might measure on the ninetieth percentile, showing ten per cent are taller and ninety per cent are smaller.

A paediatrician would hope to see the short-statured child move along or rise above their initial percentile. They become concerned when an already-low reading descends to a lower percentile.

Parents should talk to their paediatrician if there is an unusually early start to puberty, if height lags significantly for age or if height greatly exceeds expectations.

Paediatricians who specialise in growth give their opinion based on family history, rate of growth and the X-ray appearance of the growing ends of the bones. Occasionally children are found to be deficient in growth hormone, which is needed for linear growth. When this deficiency is diagnosed in the middle school years, treatment with synthetic growth hormone is both safe and effective.

Headaches

Life is full of headaches. When the child looks pale, below par and holds their head, the parents think, 'It's tension, eye strain, she's tired, it's something she ate.' But headaches come and go, even in the most relaxed, sure-sighted, well-slept child.

Some children get a few headaches, while for others they are a regular occurrence. These are usually vague, not too severe and settle quickly. Though migraine is much more common in teens and adults, it can occur in young children. In its classic presentation, migraine starts with disturbed visual symptoms followed by a strong, one-sided pain associated with pallor and nausea. In the young school-age child there is often a mix of abdominal pain, pale appearance and a less clear-cut headache.

Migraine is managed with paracetamol and rest in a quiet, darkened room. Where headaches become frequent or severe, a consultation with a paediatrician or children's neurologist is advised. As heads and brains are so important, be quick to seek help if there are any symptoms that are unusual or rapidly deteriorating.

Hepatitis vaccination

Currently the two types of viral hepatitis that cause most concern are hepatitis A and hepatitis B. Hepatitis A infection comes through the faeces–oral route, usually from infected food. It causes an unpleasant illness but one that will usually resolve completely. There is a vaccine available for hepatitis A.

Hepatitis B comes from infected blood and intimate body fluids. It can leave sufferers infective for years and carries a high risk of long-term liver damage. This problem of ongoing infectivity and liver damage makes hepatitis B our main target for immunisation. The National Health and Medical Research Council of Australia now recommends hepatitis B immunisation for all infants and young adolescents.

Hepatitis A

In this country, with clean water, good sewage disposal and interest in food hygiene, the incidence of hepatitis A is low. Despite this, a recent outbreak caused great concern, when over 100 people were infected from sewage-polluted oysters.

In Australia, the main risk of contacting Hepatitis A is to overseas adventurers who travel to places with poor water and poor sewage and food standards. Also at risk are some health and child care workers who deal daily with youngsters who are unreliable in their toilet training.

There is a safe and effective immunisation against hepatitis A, but it is only recommended for certain travellers, as well as health, child care and residential care workers.

Hepatitis B

Though AIDS is the most highly publicised blood-borne and sexually transmitted disease, hepatitis B is many times more infective, much more common and can also be fatal.

The greatest risk of infection comes from blood contact. Hepatitis B is almost universal in needle-sharing drug addicts. But such is the degree of infectivity that it also poses a risk through sporting injuries and normal sexual activity.

There is a reliable immunisation, which until recently was reserved for high-risk groups such as migrants from high-incidence areas. The program was then extended with the recommendation of three doses to all adolescents, and more recently, our National Medical Research Council has recommended immunisation of all infants in Australia. The aim of vaccination is to lessen the reservoir of infectivity that is currently in this community. It is also to protect children from an unpleasant infectious illness, which can cause liver damage and death.

Hernias

Children have hernias not from lifting furniture, but due to a slight congenital weakness. A hernia is a small opening in an abdominal muscle that should have closed during the normal developmental process before birth. Parents become aware of the problem when a small bulge appears, usually in early infancy.

An inguinal hernia may show as a groin swelling that comes and goes. There is a danger that this knuckle of gut will get stuck, blocked and possibly go gangrenous. The defect that causes an inguinal hernia always needs surgical repair. As this is inevitable, the operation should be booked soon after diagnosis. If the groin swelling ever becomes hard, red and swollen, the hernia is now obstructed and has become a surgical emergency.

Many babies are born with a slight bulge beside their belly button (umbilical hernia). Most resolve in the first year while a few remain until four years or five years of age. As these rarely obstruct, they can be given plenty of time to resolve. But by school age their time is up.

Hives, or urticaria

When I was a child my mother blamed my itchy hives on eating strawberries, but I thought our dog had fleas. Hives or urticaria means an allergic skin rash. It varies from a few red spots to large, itchy islands. At its most extreme, urticaria can block respiration and endanger life.

The skin rash is a reaction to something we ingest, touch or that stings us. Often the offending agent is quite obvious, such as penicillin. When this is recognised it must be totally avoided.

Unfortunately, urticaria can be much more complicated, especially when it is caused by something your child ate. You can give your child a food on one occasion and there is no reaction, yet two weeks later it covers them in hives. This is due to the cumulative effect. A little of the offending chemical may be contained in one product, then more from another, until finally the body is tipped over the edge.

If your child's urticaria is caused by a sensitivity to salicylate, they may fall victim to this cumulative effect, because salicylate is present in many fruits like oranges, tomatoes and strawberries. So last week they had a heaped bowl of strawberries with no ill effects. But today, they drank a glass of orange juice, had a rich tomato-based pasta then followed it with a serve of strawberries. As the last berry is swallowed, urticaria is appearing before your eyes. Come to think of it, maybe my mother was right all along!

Treatment involves avoiding problem products, the use of antihistamine to ease symptoms and a trip to an allergist when it all gets too difficult.

Immunisation

My blood pressure rises when I hear media arguments against immunisation. Our National Health and Medical Research Council, along with every reputable scientific body in the civilised world, supports vaccination.

In my paediatric career I have seen a tragic collection of children who have suffered greatly or died through the irresponsibility of refusing to immunise. I have personally managed one child who died of whooping cough. I have watched copious children debilitated with the spasms, whoop and vomit of this preventable illness. I have seen two children die a slow death of brain degeneration from the measles complication of sub-acute sclerosing panencephalitis. I have managed countless children, extremely sick, with the cough, conjunctivitis and unbelievably high fever of measles. Even in the last decades of the twentieth century I have witnessed one adult die of tetanus, and a child die of diphtheria.

I accept that every action we take in life is a balance between risk and pay-off but with immunisation the equation is so steeply loaded against the anti-lobby, it's hard to know how they have such power.

Unfortunately, our media is more interested in controversy than accuracy. When challenged they tell me, 'It's only fair to give equal air time.' The reality is that for each anti-immunisation activist, there are 1000 highly qualified professionals who support vaccination. If equality entered the equation we should hear 1000 statements of support to each one of inaccuracy.

In medicine there must be a careful balance between risk and benefit. Open-heart surgery probably kills one in twenty patients. Refusing the chance of surgery assures the death of twenty out of twenty. Car seat belts save thousands of lives every year, yet it is possible they might occasionally slow a child's escape from a burning vehicle.

At this point my position must be crystal clear. The current immunisation schedules for Australian school children are set out in Appendix II, page 297.

Itchy bottom

Though bowel training is established at two and a half years, bottom wiping comes much, much later. At age five years there may be a small forest's worth of paper product in the bowl, but it doesn't guarantee hygiene. An itchy bottom is most commonly a poorly cleaned bottom.

It's not just undercleaning, but also overcleaning that can cause itch. Some children react to the usual alkaline pH of normal bath soaps or even residues of detergent in the underclothes. If in doubt use a product for sensitive skin (see this chapter, Dry skin, page 265) and make sure that clothes are well rinsed after washing them with detergent.

A classic but rare cause of itch is an infestation of worms. These wrigglers lie in the large bowel then crawl out at night to lay eggs around the bottom. This causes itching, which is diagnosed by examining what is happening by night and watching the toilet by day (see this chapter, Worms, page 292).

Left handedness

It is said that one in ten children are left handed. In the past the left hand was associated with a weakness in reading, spelling and learning but now the only proven problem is the mechanism of writing. English goes from left to right, making it mighty awkward for the left hander. Their work will be obstructed and smudged unless they write with a bizarre, hooked hand.

Hand dominance develops at about the age of two years and is firmly established by the age of four years. It is usual for the right-handed child to be strongly right. A number of lefties are less certain and able to put a bob both ways.

When there is weak or no dominance it's best to be right in a right-handed world. Thankfully, though, we have come a long way from my school days when you wrote with your right hand or 'God's representative' tried to change brain dominance with a ruler.

Measles

Measles causes a major illness with cough, conjunctivitis and extremely high fevers. It is one of the nastiest of the common childhood conditions and one that would not occur if the recommended vaccination schedules were more generally accepted.

Measles has a ten- to fifteen-day incubation period. The illness starts with a bad cold, cough, sore eyes and moderate fever. After about three days a red rash sweeps all over the body and the temperature soars to up to 40 degrees Celsius (104 degrees Fahrenheit). At this point most children are a picture of misery, with discoloured skin, conjunctivitis, a crusted nose and nasty cough. After this peak the rash and fever start to settle, leaving a weak, coughing child.

No child needs measles or its complications of bronchitis, pneumonia, ear infection, encephalitis and the slow degeneration of subacute sclerosing panencephalitis. In the years between 1978 and 1992, 164 Australians died of measles. Don't procrastinate – vaccinate.

Meningococcal infection

Meningococcus is one of the most feared infections of the moment. This has been increased by extensive media coverage. Out of the blue a child can embark on a devastating downhill course that may lead to death or disability. Despite this, it is one of the easiest bacteria to kill, responding to the most basic 1940s brand of penicillin.

The meningococcus bacterium is a relatively common fellow traveller in the community. Why it infects some people and misses the majority is unknown. It is an uncommon infection though cases have doubled in the past ten years. The bacterium enters the body, initially causing a mild illness with fever and often a fine rash. This moves on to septicaemia (blood infection) or meningitis (an infection of the tissue that covers the brain). Most children I have treated had both the septicaemia and meningitis. The presence of septicaemia is suspected in any extremely sick child with an almost-bruised-type skin rash that increases every minute. Meningitis is considered in the child with headache and a stiff neck.

A doctor can easily be caught out, seeing a vaguely sick child in the morning, giving reassurance, and sending them home. But some hours later the infection becomes all-consuming, with the child crashing onto the downhill course.

If any child looks sick and is dropping fast, this is the most urgent of urgent emergencies. The only way to prevent death and disability in meningococcus is a quick diagnosis, immediately followed by that first dose of life-saving antibiotic.

There are a number of different sorts of meningococcus. A vaccine effective against a dangerous strain (Serogroup C) will be included in the routine immunisation schedule in Australia from 2003. Meningococcal B vaccine is currently undergoing trials in New Zealand.

Mumps

You suspect mumps when your child has some fever and an obviously swollen face. Often mumps is so mild it is not suspected but in most it causes some fever and a characteristic swelling of one or both of the parotid salivary glands. These glands lie below and forward of the ears. The submandibular glands, under the jaw, may also be enlarged and tender to touch.

This virus has a variable incubation period, averaging out at about eighteen days. Mumps is infectious for two days before the swelling and until the glands return to normal.

Nursing a child with mumps has a strange effect on fathers. They cross their legs and maintain good distance, as they have heard the tales of swollen, sore testes that can occur in 20 per cent of adult males. Fortunately, mumps is not the most infectious of childhood illnesses and epidemics are much less common since the introduction of the measles, mumps and rubella vaccination.

Though mumps is not usually a serious illness, immunisation is recommended as it can occasionally cause deafness and more commonly a mild encephalitis (infection of the brain).

Nits

When two adults put their heads together they come up with a brilliant idea. But when kindergarten kids get together they catch nits. Nits are the tell-tale eggs of head lice. They show as hard, white flecks cemented to the hairs. Nits are an extremely common part of life for many children in the early school years.

The lice spread by direct contact or from shared hats and clothes. Head lice are probably more common than in the past due to our insistence on hats for sun protection. In the early school years hats may lie in heaps and many are tried before the child finds their own. Often the bug is not seen but an experienced infants teacher can spot a nit at twenty paces.

Once the diagnosis is made your meticulously cared-for child returns home like a leper, one hand clutching a note: 'Dear Mrs Smith, Your daughter has nits. Please treat before she can return to school.'

Treatment involves a special head lice overnight lotion and shampoo, which is readily available from every chemist. The rest is all those cliches of nitpicking with a fine-tooth comb.

Nose bleeds

Not all nose bleeds are the result of injury. Some children seem created with delicate nasal blood vessels that just bleed from time to time. For others, this is part of their allergic nose problem. Then there are bleeds that come as part of an upper respiratory viral illness.

Treatment involves a bit of boy scout first-aid. First have the head held still then, if needed, compress the soft part of the nose just below the bridge. Continue compression for ten minutes and see what happens. When bleeds keep recurring it's time for an appointment with an ear, nose and throat specialist. Any acute bleed that won't stop needs a trip to casualty.

Nose block

The nose is the first-line filter that screens air heading for the lungs. If allergens are about, it's the nose that sniffs them out. When one looks at the major problems listed in this book, a blocked nose seems pretty trivial. Yet nasal allergy is unpleasant for the child and sniffing is intensely irritating to the parents.

The allergy-troubled nose may run, but more often it is chronically blocked. The child breathes through their mouth, which affects their tone of voice, enjoyment of food and snore-free sleep. What's worse, an open mouth projects a vacant expression that makes the clever child look impaired.

The offending allergen can be demonstrated by pinprick skin testing. In my experience this usually shows that the child is allergic to most pollens, house dust and house dust mite. Desensitisation treatments are time consuming and reasonably unreliable. The preferred management of the allergic nose is the regular use of a cortisone-based nasal spray or antihistamines if symptoms are acute or severe.

Passive smoking

I recently spent some transit time in Bangkok airport. There the authorities forbid smoking in public areas, restricting the nicotine-starved traveller to a small, sealed-off room. Here they puff and pace like agitated goldfish in a glass bowl. Every so often a mask-wearing attendant mucks out the enclosure and quickly retreats. It may seem that I am an anti-smoking extremist. The truth is – I am!

I own a life insurance policy. As I am a non-smoker I pay a

premium that is reduced by fifty per cent. Now, I am no mathe-matical genius, but to my brain, this suggests that smoking can't be good for you.

A child spends the first eighteen years of their lives stuck in the atmosphere we provide. There is now a lot of evidence that it is not just those who smoke, but others who inhale their side-stream who are at risk. The list of dangers includes chest infections, cot death and asthma, to mention just a few.

If parents wish to reduce their life expectancy by fifty per cent, I suppose that's their business. All I ask is they don't damage their children's health in the side-stream.

Rubella, or German measles

Rubella is a mild childhood illness. It is very different from the high fevers and extreme sickness of measles. Many children and adults have such a low-grade infection they are unaware they have carried the virus and are now immune.

Rubella has a fourteen- to 21-day incubation period, which is followed by a slight fever and a faint pink rash. There is often a characteristic enlargement of the lymph nodes at the back of the neck (just above the hairline). For most children rubella is a vague unimpressive illness.

The main danger of rubella is its risk to a pregnant mum. When an unborn baby is infected, especially in the first three months, this can cause deafness, blindness, intellectual disability and major heart defects. In the first eight to ten weeks of gestation there is up to a ninety per cent risk of major foetal damage.

To protect the unborn babies of the future it is now recommended that all children receive rubella immunisation, through the triple vaccine (measles, mumps, rubella). This directly protects girls for their child-rearing years, and by immunising boys, we reduce the risk of the virus entering the community.

Women who are planning to become pregnant should have a blood test to check their rubella vaccine is still protecting them.

Snoring

It's not just Grandad who snores. The sleeping child can produce equally good vibrations. Snoring may be associated with the nasal airway obstruction of the common cold, allergy, enlarged adenoids or big tonsils. The nose blocks, the throat relaxes with sleep and the airflow resonates.

One much-promoted condition of the moment is sleep apnoea. Here a sleeping child has a marginal airflow, which reduces oxygen levels in the brain. They usually snore and the next day feel acutely under-slept. The effect of low oxygen can also cause problems with mental function and behaviour.

Occasional snoring is of no concern; just roll the child over to sleep on their side. When there is chronic snoring or any hint of sleep apnoea, discuss this with your family doctor, paediatrician or ear, nose and throat specialist.

Suntan and skin damage

It has been the dream of every Aussie adolescent to own a perfectly bronzed body. Now with ozone holes and increasing evidence of skin cancer, it's time for a rethink.

It may seem impossible to establish sun sense in children, but bigger battles have been won. When my bike-riding boys were at school only nerds and epileptics wore helmets. Attitudes were hard to shift, but a few years later, bike helmets are fully accepted.

The secret of sun protection is to start early. Protection is not a maybe – it is a must. Hats, shirts, avoiding peak hours and high-factor creams have to be an accepted part of everyday life.

If hats are to be worn they must appear 'cool' to the child. There is a difference between those favoured by a bald octogenarian and the hat of an iron-man or 'Bay Watch' babe. A pump pack of sun cream should be kept in a prominent place. Small containers that fit in pockets can be filled from this central vat. (In Sydney, the NSW Cancer Council sells top-value, easy-application pump packs.)

Once burnt, no expensive after-sun treatment can reverse the damage. The best we can do is keep the skin moist with an economy softener such as sorbolene with glycerine cream. After excessive sun exposure keep fluid levels high as this can cause dehydration and sunstroke.

Teeth: what to do if one is knocked out

Children should be encouraged to wear a properly fitting mouthguard for all stick-swinging and contact sports. Despite this advice, about one-quarter of all children will have tooth trauma before the age of fifteen. Many of these injuries will involve the permanent upper front teeth being completely knocked out. In the past, once dislodged, the permanent tooth was lost for life. Now dentists can save many of these permanent teeth if we follow a few simple rules.

Retrieve the tooth and, if dirty, rinse gently in milk, saline or the child's saliva **but do not scrub**. If possible put the tooth back in the socket and hold it in place. Otherwise preserve the tooth in a cup of milk (not water) and get to your dentist. They will reimplant and steady the tooth with a small splint. After about ten days the dentist will remove the splint but it will be six to twelve months before you know whether the reimplantation has been successful.

Testes: undescended or retractile

Ninety per cent of newborn males will have both testes present and easy to demonstrate. Most of the other ten per cent appear in the early months. But those not down by one year rarely make it without help. Surgery for undescended testes is now recommended at age two to three years.

Some school-age children have retractile testes, which are hard to locate on routine medical examination. If a tense child is met with a cold hand the testes may spring for cover, but an experienced doctor can easily demonstrate that these testes are present and correct.

If a testis is still undescended by school age and you have not already consulted a paediatric surgeon, this should be arranged now. An intact testis will function to some extent in any position but it works a lot better in those cooler climates of the lower latitudes.

Tonsillitis

The tonsils are two patches of lymph tissue situated on either side of the throat. These, along with the adenoids and other defences, act as the first line of protection against invading infections. When they are fighting some invader they may be enlarged and red with associated involvement of the lymph glands in the neck.

The tonsils are seen as two sentries guarding the entry to the lungs. But this exaggerates their true importance, as no one has shown any reduction in resistance following removal of tonsils and adenoids. Presumably these are one small part in a long line of defence.

Any cold or upper respiratory virus will cause some inflammation in the throat, which will generally leave it red. True tonsillitis specifically involves the tonsils, which will be swollen, red and flecked with infection. A generalised viral action requires no treatment. Tonsillitis is usually caused by a bacteria, and will be treated with an antibiotic.

Occasionally, glandular fever presents with a severe tonsillitis of viral origin. Though usually a problem of adolescence and young adults, it can occur at this school age (see this chapter, page 273).

Tonsillectomy

There was a time when it was said that any child old enough to open their mouth would lose their tonsils. Certainly this operation was overused, and its results were sometimes quite hazardous. This caused a major backlash, so most paediatricians then counselled against tonsillectomy. Around that time of overreaction I met many children who had been refused treatment but who had a dramatic turnaround in health, school attendance and quality of life after I referred them to a sensible surgeon.

At present, there is a more accepting attitude towards tonsillectomy, and if you feel that your child is disadvantaged by repeated genuine bouts of tonsillitis, insist on referral to an ear, nose and throat expert.

As a rule of thumb, tonsillectomy is considered if there are three or more infections each year for two or more years, or five infections in any one year. A wise surgeon interprets these with flexibility, taking into account the degree of the distress and the general health of the child.

Tonsillectomy is usually accompanied by the more minor procedure of adenoidectomy. The tonsil operation may be reasonably straightforward, but the post-operative care needs skilled nursing and good and regular pain relief. There is a small but real risk of life-threatening haemorrhage in the hours and days following surgery. For this reason most operations are now performed in hospitals experienced in the post-operative care of children.

Removal of tonsils and adenoids does not lessen a child's ability to fight off future viruses and bacteria.

Tummy upsets

A common problem for parents is the child who is off their food, feels sick, vomits or has diarrhoea. Parents usually blame this on 'a bad sausage' or 'an off prawn', but these are rarely the cause. Most upsets come from whatever virus is at large in the community. As viruses do not respond to antibiotics, we treat the symptoms, not the cause.

World-wide, more children die of dehydration due to gut problems than any other illness. In this country most upsets are relatively mild, but we must never lose sight of the danger of dehydration.

When a child is feeling sick, they don't need building up with solid food; they require clear fluid that stays put. With an uneasy gut, go for small sips, taken regularly. The contents of a sherry glass every fifteen minutes will achieve quite a load in a day.

Ten years ago we encouraged parents to rehydrate with flat lemonade. But today this is thought to be dangerous, and now we recommend one of the electrolyte solutions like Gastrolyte, which is sold by your chemist. If lemonade is used it must be diluted to one part lemonade with four parts of water.

It's not the number of vomits or toilet trips that indicate the severity of a tummy upset. What matters is the fluid balance in the body. If eyes are bright, skin is moist, mind is clear and urine is flowing, this would seem safe. Dull eyes, a distant brain, dry skin and little urine spells danger and the need for immediate hospital help.

The key points are: hydration with small frequent amounts of clear fluid, special electrolyte solutions or lemonade, but only if diluted; when becoming distant and dry, this is an emergency.

Warts

Warts are unsightly raised areas, and are mostly on the hands and sometimes the feet. They can be single, multiple or almost in a crop. They are caused by a virus, which is eventually defeated by the body's immune system.

Warts last for months or years but disappear quickly once immunity arrives. This has helped generations of gypsies and wart charmers who know that the virus is on a short-term lease. Warts are more unsightly than painful. Plantar warts appear on the sole of the foot and can be tender when walking.

The best treatment is to be patient until the arrival of immunity. If you can't wait, try a wart-shrinking paint or get a skin specialising doctor to freeze with liquid nitrogen. Freezing is painful and may require a number of applications.

Whooping cough, or pertussis

Whooping cough is a long, unpleasant respiratory illness. It is caused by a bacteria that is relatively unresponsive to antibiotics. There is a seven-day incubation period, then one or two weeks of vague upper respiratory illness, and after this comes the cough. This bursts through in characteristic spasms. The child coughs until totally breathless, then fights for air, which rushes in with an inspiratory whoop. Often the spasm ends in vomiting and the child is terrified of anything that may set off another cycle. The cough reduces and finally clears in four to twelve weeks.

Whooping cough is of greatest risk to infants who are too young to immunise, yet have little natural immunity. When epidemics hit, it is the young baby and unimmunised toddler who is at the highest risk of serious illness or death. Little children are much safer when the reservoir of wild infection in the community is reduced by general immunisation.

But with fewer children being immunised, school-age children and adults are currently contracting whooping cough. In the years 1993 to 1996 almost half of the cases of pertussis occurred in children over the age of nine and adults. There are some failures, but immunisation gives between eight-five to ninety-five per cent protection.

The whooping cough vaccine of the past was not without side effects. There were some relatively minor reactions but there was also concern over an extremely rare risk of acquired brain damage (encephalopathy). In the late 1970s this possibility was promoted in the media, with the result that immunisation rates dropped to under one-third. In the following epidemic that swept the UK over thirty children died from whooping cough. It is engraved on my memory: one child who could not be resuscitated was under my care.

The link between vaccine and encephalopathy is presumed but not proven. Research puts the risk at between zero and ten cases per million of those who are vaccinated. In an epidemic the risk of contacting pertussis is between seventy per cent and 100 per cent. Of these, the risk of encephalopathy caused by natural whooping cough is seven per 1000 cases. That is, 7000 per million may contract encephalopathy from whooping cough, while zero to ten per million may contract it from the vaccine. This puts the worst possible estimate of vaccine damage at one-thousandth of the risk of the natural disease.

But immunisation is not only about saving lives; it protects all those children from weeks of fighting for breath, choking and vomiting.

Worms

Australians have many preoccupations: beer, cricket, football and the treatment of worms. At this very moment, as I write, collections of men, women, children, cats and dogs are being lined up and purged against worms.

The most common villain is the threadworm, which lives in the lower end of the bowel and usually produces no problems other than the occasional itch. The female worm crawls out in the dead of night and lays eggs around the bottom. If observed at this time, little worms may be seen and all this wriggling causes itch. Children scratch, get eggs under their fingernails, and that's how reinfection occurs. Threadworm is not always easy to eradicate. The whole family needs an antiworm treatment, followed by special emphasis on well-washed hands and hygiene.

Infection with other worms is possible but unlikely. Worms do not cause tooth grinding or nightmares. The protozoan giardia is not a worm but can cause problems of diarrhoea and malabsorption (See this chapter, Giardia, page 272).

A P P E N D I X I

Height and weight charts showing normal growth

Boys' height chart

BOYS: 2 TO 18 YEARS HEIGHT PERCENTILE

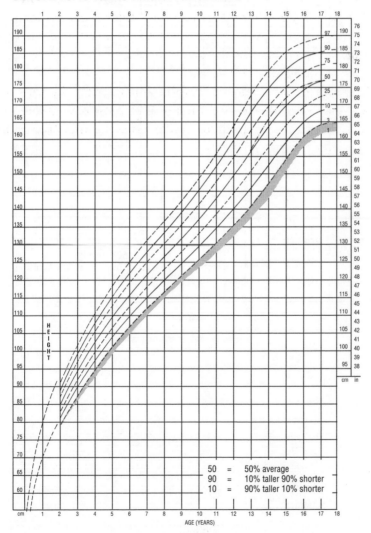

50 = 50% average
90 = 10% taller 90% shorter
10 = 90% taller 10% shorter

AGE (YEARS)

(Standards appropriate to Aust., UK & Nth America)

Boys' weight chart

BOYS: 2 TO 18 YEARS WEIGHT PERCENTILE

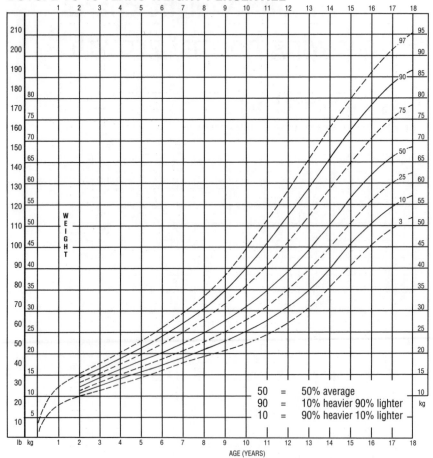

(Standards appropriate to Aust., UK & Nth America)

Girls' height chart

GIRLS: 2 TO 18 YEARS HEIGHT PERCENTILE

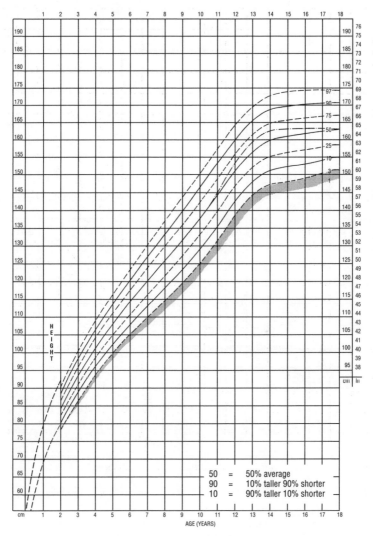

(Standards appropriate to Aust., UK & Nth America)

295

Girls' weight chart

GIRLS: 2 TO 18 YEARS WEIGHT PERCENTILE

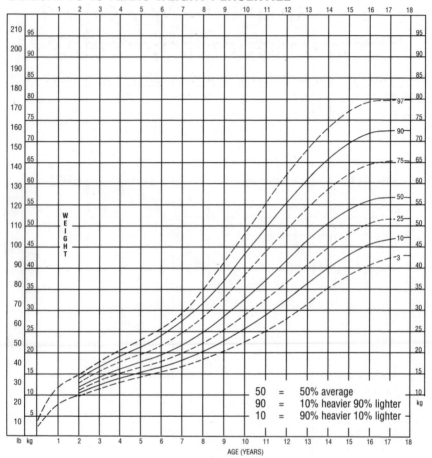

50	=	50% average
90	=	10% heavier 90% lighter
10	=	90% heavier 10% lighter

AGE (YEARS)

(Standards appropriate to Aust., UK & Nth America)

296

Australian and New Zealand immunisation schedules

The Australian Standard Vaccination Schedule* for 2000–2002 is:

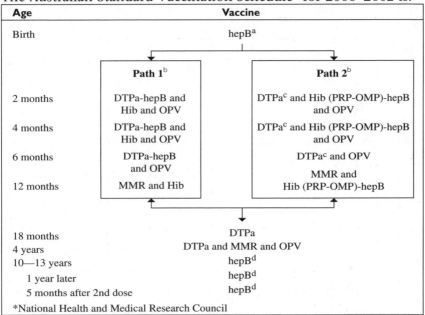

Age	Vaccine	
Birth	hepB[a]	
	Path 1[b]	**Path 2**[b]
2 months	DTPa-hepB and Hib and OPV	DTPa[c] and Hib (PRP-OMP)-hepB and OPV
4 months	DTPa-hepB and Hib and OPV	DTPa[c] and Hib (PRP-OMP)-hepB and OPV
6 months	DTPa-hepB and OPV	DTPa[c] and OPV
12 months	MMR and Hib	MMR and Hib (PRP-OMP)-hepB
18 months	DTPa	
4 years	DTPa and MMR and OPV	
10—13 years	hepB[d]	
1 year later	hepB[d]	
5 months after 2nd dose	hepB[d]	

*National Health and Medical Research Council

Disease	Vaccine	Available products
Hepatitis B	hep B	Engerix-B[TM] or H-B VAxll[TM]
Diphtheria, tetanus, pertussis	DTPa	Infanrix[TM] or Tripacel[TM]
Diphtheria, tetanus, pertussis, hepatitis B	DTPa-hep B	Infanrix-HepB[TM]
Haemophilus influenzae type B	Hib (PRP-OMP)	PedvaxHIB[TM]
Haemophilus influenzae type B, hepatitis B	Hib (PRP-OMP) -hep B	Comvax[TM]
Poliomyelitis	OPV	Polio Sabin[TM]
Measles, mumps, rubella	MMR	MMRII[¤] or Priorix[TM]

Notes

a Hepatitis B vaccine should be given to all infants at birth and should not be delayed beyond seven days after birth. Infants whose mothers are hepatitis B surface antigen positive (HBsAg+ve) should also be given hepatitis B immunoglobulin (HBIG) within twelve hours of birth

b When necessary the two paths may be interchanged with regard to their hepatitis B and hib components. For example, when a child moves interstate, she may change from one path to the other.

c Wherever possible the same brand of DTPa should be used at two, four and six months.

Immunisation schedule for Australian children 2000–2002

The Australian Standard Vaccination Schedule (8th edition) shown above is that recommended by the National Health and Medical Research Council (NHMRC). In drawing up its recommendations the NHMRC has sought to reduce the number of injections given at each immunisation session through the use of new combination vaccines, and to limit, as far as possible, the number of vaccine products that a practitioner would need to have available. For the immunisations at two, four, six and twelve months, two options for the use of combination vaccines which meet these criteria are recommended.

A vaccine effective against a dangerous strain of meningococcal disease (Serogroup C) will be included in the routine immunisation schedule in Australia from 2003.

For more information about immunisation phone the National Immunisation Infoline on 1800 671 811 or visit the Australian Department of Health and Ageing website at www.health.gov.au/pubhlth/immunise

Immunisation schedule for New Zealand children 2002

Immunisation is not compulsory in New Zealand, and there is no intention of making it so. Parents of children born from 1995 onwards are requested to show their child's immunisation certificate when starting at an early childhood education centre or primary school, but children can be enrolled whether or not they are vaccinated.

The oral polio vaccine (OPV) has been replaced by the injectable inactivated polio vaccine (IPV) and given as DTaP-IPV. Substituting IPV or OPV can be done at any stage of the immunisation schedule and children can be switched directly to DTaP-IPV.

At four years of age a fifth dose of DTaP wil now be given to reduce the risk of pertussis being spread through primary school aged children. A second dose of MMR vaccine will also be administered at this time.

Children aged 11 years will continue to receive the Td vaccine (tetanus-diptheria). For children who have not had four doses of polio vaccine a dose of IPV can be given.

Meningococcal B Vaccine is currently undergoing trials in New Zealand. These trials will be completed during 2003 and if the results are as expected the vaccine will be introduced in 2004. The introductory phase will involve a large-scale campaign, targeting infants, children and young adults, up to the age of 21 years. At this stage there has been no decision about how it will fit into the schedule. Interference trials need to be carried out to establish how best to do this. You can track progress by accessing the Ministry of Health's website at www.moh.govt.nz.

The New Zealand immunisation schedule from 1 February 2002 is:

Age	Immunisation given	
6 weeks	DTaP–IPV	Hib–Hepatitis B
3 months	DTaP–IPV	Hib–Hepatitis B
5 months	DTaP–IPV	Hepatitis B
15 months	DTaP/Hib	MMR
4 years	DTaP–IPV	MMR
11 years	Td	(IPV if < 4 doses)

Key
D: diphtheria, T: tetanus, aP: acellular pertussis, IPV: inactivated polio vaccine, Hib: Haemophilus influenzae type b, MMR: measles, mumps and rubella, Td: adult tetanus and diphtheria vaccine.

APPENDIX III

Permanent teeth: age of eruption

central incisors	lower	6th year
	upper	6th to 7th year
first molars		6th year
lateral incisors	lower	7th year
	upper	8th year
canines	lower	10th year
	upper	10th to 11th year
first pre-molars	lower	10th to 11th year
	upper	10th year
second pre-molars	lower	11th to 12th year
	upper	11th year
second molars	lower	11th to 12th year
	upper	12th year
third molars (wisdom teeth)		20th year

APPENDIX IV

Helping coordination*

C hildren with coordination difficulty will often have problems swinging a bat, throwing and catching balls, tying shoelaces, riding a bike, running with style and assembling things with their hands. When children see themselves as clumsy they can lose confidence in themselves, and when playing with other children they can be made to feel on the outer.

Parents can help to some extent, but no amount of practice will turn the poorly coordinated child into a top tennis player, footy legend or star of the ballet. To help, take the pressure off them and avoid competitive sports, unless they enjoy them. Here are a few simple suggestions that should be followed in a fun way:

Throwing and catching

Throwing can be practised by aiming at a large target such as a rubbish bin, then gradually decreasing the size to an empty milk carton. With catching, arms can't coordinate quickly enough to trap the ball. Practise with a large ball such as an inflatable beach ball, gradually working down until the child bounces, throws and catches a tennis ball with reasonable reliability.

Hand movements

Manipulation can be improved through simple activities such as paper weaving, threading paper clips and clay work. Construction sets should be encouraged, starting with large pieces and working towards those that are smaller. Simple craft suggestions, such as putting nails in a piece of wood and weaving string designs, help coordination. Have a desk set up with technicolour textas and reams of paper permanently on hand.

Bicycle riding

Some children find it hard to master a two-wheeler bike. They go quite well until the trainer wheels are removed, then after this it's hard work. Find a bit of open space where steering will be unimportant, and the surface not too tricky. After this there are no short cuts: it takes hours of parents running behind holding lightly to the saddle. If this gets too hard put the bike away for a few months and then try again.

Swimming

Some children find it easy to kick, easy to move their arms but extremely difficult to kick, move arms and breathe all at the same time. Be reassured that all these children will become proficient swimmers as long as we don't turn them off water along the way.

Swimming lessons that involve a lot of sitting around waiting to participate generally fail. A teacher who insists on perfect style rather than safe swimming may also be unsuccessful. When lessons are unsuccessful children do best splashing around the pool having fun with their mum and dad. This is better than a whole academy of swimming instructors.

* These ideas come from Neralie Cocks, Occupational Therapist, the Child Development Unit, Sydney.

Helping handwriting*

Proficient handwriting is not a skill that comes easily to some children, so be patient. Aim for legibility and content, not calligraphy. Spend short periods practising these ideas, and keep it positive and fun.

Check posture

Make sure the child is sitting in a chair that supports their back. The table must not be too high or too low, as this results in tense shoulders and slouched posture. Elbows should rest comfortably on the table and feet flat on the floor. It helps if the child leans slightly on the non-writing arm, which stabilises the paper and allows the writing arm to move freely across the page.

Check pencil grip

Some children develop a tense, awkward pencil hold that slows down written work and tires the fingers. A thicker pencil or special plastic grip can help reduce this tension.

Circular movements

Practise anticlockwise and clockwise circular scribble patterns across the page. Use a large sheet of unlined paper working from left to right then repeat using wide-spaced lines. Eventually introduce the lined paper that is used at school.

Individual letters

Start with letters formed in an anticlockwise finger movement: a, o, c, e, s, d, g, q, u. Then move on to the clockwise letters: r, n, m, h, k, b, p. Now string together a continuous row of n's and u's.

Curvy letters

Move on to letters with a curvy movement, such as v, w and y. As you go, check the sitting posture at the table and pencil grip. Praise and keep practising. If teachers are still concerned, ask an occupational therapist for help.

* These ideas come from Neralie Cocks, Occupational Therapist, The Child Development Unit, Sydney.

INDEX